LORDS OF
CREATION

LORDS OF CREATION

THE DEMENTED WORLD OF MEN IN POWER

To Sonitra

MARGARET COOK

Best Wishes

Margaret Cook

ROBSON
BOOKS

First published in Great Britain in 2002 by Robson Books, 64 Brewery Road, London, N7 9NT

A member of **Chrysalis** Books plc

British Library Cataloguing in Publication Data
A catalogue record for this title is available from the British Library.

ISBN 1 86105 522 8

Typeset by FiSH Books, London WC1
Printed by Mackays of Chatham, Chatham, Kent

Contents

Preamble		vii
CHAPTER 1	Too Big for his Boots	1
CHAPTER 2	The Origin of Supremacy	12
CHAPTER 3	The Phallic Pyramid	25
CHAPTER 4	The Learning Curve	38
CHAPTER 5	Swagger and Scrimmage	53
CHAPTER 6	The Classic Alpha Male	71
CHAPTER 7	The Military Celibate	97
CHAPTER 8	Create or Destroy	122
CHAPTER 9	Almost Homosexual	139
CHAPTER 10	Deference and the Disempowered	157
CHAPTER 11	The Amazons	181
CHAPTER 12	The Church Militant	206
CHAPTER 13	Birds of Ill Omen	236
CHAPTER 14	Of Blood and Brains	266
CHAPTER 15	Reverting to Seed	274
CHAPTER 16	The High Moral Ground	299
Bibliography		310
Index		317

Preamble

Big is most definitely not beautiful. It is mad to the point of lunacy; bad to the extent of depravity. It gorges insatiably on the fruits of the earth, expands without limits, proliferates without restraint, and destroys wantonly and mindlessly all within its compass. It invades like a tumor.

Yet humankind, with all its vaunted braininess, has not got beyond the hero-worship of Mr Big, actually enjoying deference, submission and blind obedience. Mr Big changes the rules, defies democracy, drives his stretch limo through human rights. Yet he stays and grows; and we bend the knee. Indeed, some of us beg to be allowed to do so. Like many malignancies, he issues orders that pervert the workings of other organs: he is especially prone to interfere with the proliferation of others, for self-replication is his unique privilege. He is on a course to perdition but, even as the doors of Gehenna are opened to receive him, he leaves behind a scorched earth liberally sown with the seeds of his kind.

CHAPTER 1

Too Big for his Boots

I am a revolutionary deep inside, the woman in me resenting any person who becomes disproportionately great. Women can be divided into two types: those who defer and those who deflate. The first will become traditional wives or mistresses, adoring and reverential; the second will attempt to become pattern modern wives, but are doomed to failure. The fate of the deflaters in the past has been sad indeed, for – besides being scorned or abandoned – they suffer at the hands of history just for trying to keep their husbands' egos down to a manageable size. Frances, wife of Lord Horatio Nelson, is generally described as inept, trivial, a drag on her husband's glorious heroism. Margaret Lloyd George is held up as an exemplary warning to political wives who do not dutifully trail after their husbands. Well, I sign up proudly with these ladies, while acknowledging some other trail-blazers of the cause of emancipation, because I at least was able to write my own bit of history.

Truth is not a difficult concept, nor even complicated, but it is often too painful to bear. This is because all living things learn very early the necessity for illusion and deception in order to survive, and humans are no different. The human problem, the distinction between us and other animals, is not a soul, but a massive brain. With this organ we have a capacity for understanding that far outstrips our power of handling it emotionally. Robert Burns was wrong when he wrote in his poem 'To a Louse' (1786):

O wad some Power the giftie gie us
To see oursels as ithers see us!

When I wrote frankly about my shattered, high-profile political marriage, breaking a few taboos, I was scarified by some sections of the press, but the public reaction polarised along gender lines, with mainly female support and male antipathy. Many droned on about revenge, though I was not conscious of that as a motive. I thought I had exorcised all my ghosts, yet the chains still rattled. I wrote of my former life:

> I am well out of it. Someone should be asking questions about whether the present system is the best way to obtain well-rounded, compassionate, balanced, soundly judging people of integrity to govern the country.
> But it won't be me. I've got other things to do.

I was deceiving myself it seems, because I have spent the last three years writing this book, asking precisely those questions and utterly absorbed in the ancient topic of gender contrast. There is almost no meeting of minds between men and women, until women get sucked into male catastrophes as innocent bystanders, or propelled into unknown territories of power as quasi-males. A man really does have more in common with a male ape than he does with females of his own species.

Women's emancipation is just one of many rumbling revolutions tending these days to buffer the effect of the strong on the weak. The ways of the world in the past have been strangely apt to magnify the disparities between individuals. One man is not essentially so very different from others, yet circumstances can conspire to augment that man's status, whether of wealth or power or influence, until his stature seems several thousand times greater than the average. The apparent difference is illusory. Examples of this overblown contrast crop up in several contexts. When I first saw the awesome display of terracotta warriors in the underground caverns of Xian in China, I was amazed by the sheer splendour of the uniform ranks with subtle facial differences – which made them eerily lifelike – and the craftsmanship and labour which had created them. But more impressive, and more disturbing, was the immense social gulf between the Emperor Qin Shi Huangdi, who was the subject (after death) of the model army's mythical defence, and the toiling 700,000 men, sentenced to hard labour and then death, who moulded the warriors along with their horses and chariots. Did he really believe he was intrinsically so much more important than those horny-handed masses? And could he live easily with his conscience as he accepted the fruits of their labours? And just as amazing, did the craftsmen believe in their own proportionate insignificance – supposing they had sufficient respite from work to ponder the matter at all? Even the most conservative modern mind could not justify such a disparity in status. But is there any sense in railing against inequality? It is ironic that the greatest social revolution of all time took place in China, where the rural landlords had their lands confiscated and distributed to the peasants in 1950–2, in an ideological attempt to attain a fairer distribution. This unique experiment in democracy was moving under the guidance of a leader who was to become as tyrannical, autocratic and inflated as any emperor in the country's history, Mao Zedong.

In other walks of life, to become ultra-big is to become less principled, less beautiful, less functional, less worthy, yet still the rewards seem to be compelling. Senior managers in business and industry who pay themselves giant salaries and bonuses are condemned as 'fat cats' but justify their personal rewards on the grounds of productivity – almost always measured in financial terms. No one measures or values to the same degree the productivity of learning, of teaching, of caring, of listening.

Economists portray income inequality with a powerful cartoon-like image called the Pen Parade. Imagine the workforce of the UK marching past in one hour with the height of the individual representing his/her income. To start, there is a long procession of miniature folk. The first person of average height and income does not appear until well after the half-hour. In the last quarter-hour the figures grow to seven feet tall, and, in the last minute, huge Goliaths, hundreds of times the size of a normal person, lumber past. Needless to say, the early diminutives are predominantly women and the later Titans are nearly all men.

A large percentage of the world's population is starving, yet still the would-be wealthy scramble for more money and goods. Daily we read in the newspapers of company mergers, of incredibly powerful media moguls, of pharmaceutical multinational monopolies, of supermarkets edging out corner shops, of brewery chains fostering clones of theme pubs to replace the honest, homely locals. The result: a huge profit for a tiny group of entrepreneurs who preen themselves on their leadership qualities, and a diminution of quality products for the customer, who shrugs, grumbles a bit and accepts his/her fate. The monster prize for one or two while the masses make do with mediocrity or deprivation is such a repeated theme that one might think it the natural order of things. In this country, the masses are even allowed to have a taste of the heady delights of exaggerated acquisition in the form of the national lottery. The chances of making a few million are remote indeed, yet the hope and the dreaming become addictive and maybe mollify or replace rebellious tendencies. For those who do win vast sums, the outcome seems to be turbulent and disruptive rather than joyous.

In those few societies in which the extremes of wealth are not too far apart, and people do not perceive themselves as significantly less well off than their neighbours, there is good evidence that the health, longevity and stability of the community is significantly better than in an unequal society. This would seem to be an attainable ideal – if it were not for the frailties of human nature.

Not one of us can handle power without being changed by it; changed progressively, adversely, even malignantly, and astonishingly uniformly. Undoubtedly, humans have evolved in circumstances that promote competitiveness, but not until the 20th century did we meet with situations of such unlimited potential. That century spawned an astonishing number of tyrannical megalomaniac leaders, and it is difficult to believe they are all isolated aberrations. I have a belief that they are examples of an extreme of characteristic, autocratic behaviour, released when a man, having been imbued with a sense of destiny, aims for the top, achieves it, and finds that there are no longer any checks or controls on his actions. Even those who begin political life with high principles and ideals seem to be deflected by power on to a pathway of self-admiration and vainglory that informs all their public actions. There are a number of other influences that distract a politician from his civic responsibilities, and turn his thoughts inwards. One is the interaction with the media and resulting fame. It used to be said that 'No publicity is bad publicity', though most people would not subscribe to that statement in these days of press intrusion. But pressmen know how to woo and flatter, and narcissistic people love to make the headlines and assume the whole world is fascinated by their achievements. Great orators are elated by their feeling of control over the assembled masses, and part of the fix is the praise and adulation that follows by word of mouth or print. The gratification is not only addictive but extremely damaging to close relationships.

Another distracting influence is that of competition, which may be directed against the opposition or against peers in the same party. Either way, the ego is challenged, and must rise to the occasion. To let another ambitious man gain a victory is unthinkable, especially in public debate. Too often we see important issues become subservient to personal vendettas, and the linking of a cause to a dynamic personality is by no means a guarantee of success. Perverse agendas creep in, and onlookers perceive that the politician's own self-projection is paramount.

Even a brief foray into the biographies of senior ministers and rulers of different countries and eras provides evidence of a number of common characteristics, many of which are disturbing to the idealist. But maybe that's not so surprising. Why should we assume that our legislators are endowed with goodness, wisdom, ability and sense of duty? But people do assume that – or at least they blind themselves with wishful thinking. This mutual deception that governing bodies and their followers throughout history have engaged in is another common theme, well worth exploring. It has been an issue ever since the time of Samuel, the Old Testament prophet, who tried to deflect the Israelites from their wish for a king, outlining with much insight the autocratic and grasping nature of the being to whom they would owe homage. He was right but unheeded, and it all ended in tears. No doubt the need of ordinary folk for a leader whom they can admire is an expression in adult life of the dependence of a child on a parent. If spin-doctors are highly motivated to present a charismatic figure with star quality to the people, the masses are in turn, pathetically eager to be mesmerised and to believe in his supremacy. Look at the hero-worship of the young, handsome Jack Kennedy, which has since been shown by gradual revelations to have been totally misplaced but still persists through myth and legend, and was much in evidence as recently as 1999 after the tragic death in an air crash of his lower-profile son, John Kennedy Junior. History suggests that on the whole the voters are rather bad at choosing a leader, if indeed they do so.

Powerful people in various walks of life are self-selecting. The masses do no more than defer and acknowledge. That being so, it is pertinent to ask whether the qualities of these self-promoting individuals are those that are desirable in a guardian to whom we are going to hand so much responsibility. The obvious fact that such ambitious people are nearly always men, as well as the extraordinary uniformity of behaviour patterns, give ample ground for the belief that they are responding to a primitive, atavistic urge. This urge is none other than that which drives males to compete against each other for sexual success. Many, though not all, high-flyers are highly sexed, and some of our prominent leaders of the 20th century have shown a pathological degree of indiscriminate lust.

One feature of prominent men that might appear to be beneficial and admirable is that of unflagging energy. As late as 1998, Donald Dewar declared he would run for a further term as first minister of the Scottish Parliament, although he would have been 65 at the next elections in four years' time – as it was, Donald died aged 63 in 2000. There are those who applaud an infusion of gravitas and experience in an era that worships and rewards youthful vigour, pointing out that someone as motivated as Donald was able to outrun and outlast the youthful members of his team by several leagues when on the campaign trail. But, though I share in the general respect and affection for our former first minister, his announcement about staying on rang an ominous bell, recalling many eminent men in the past who have clung to power like limpets, even when health and sanity were ebbing. The intense desire to hang on to top status is revealing, and in many instances undoubtedly has had more to do with self-perpetuation than an earnest desire to be of use.

When ailing and failing men, long past their sell-by date, hang in there like grim death, the outcome depends very largely on the immediate entourage. It is strange how frequently the close supporters react by concealing the leader's shortcomings, sometimes with extreme measures, and inevitably with pious rationalisation about stability and so on. Of course the supporters' survival and status is often closely linked with the leader's, though loyalty certainly plays a part. In this context it is noteworthy how ruthlessly Margaret Thatcher was dispatched by her supporters when it was clear her star was waning, and I wonder if loyalty and support of female leaders may be qualitatively different from that given to men.

Before exploring much further the characters of people in power, it is worth thinking about some of the perceptions of 'normal people', if I can use that term. There is no such person as the man on the Clapham omnibus, or Joe Public, but the minds of so many of us are incapable of grasping the diversity of people out there, in our town, country, world; of understanding the immense variability of experience, personality, thought, attitudes. Everyone's an individual – it's an amazing revelation that one may find difficulty in coping with, so it's common to categorise and compartmentalise people. It's an easy and a lazy habit to adopt. The innate selfishness of people is a barrier to understanding others, especially those in different walks of life. We never accord to another person the same degree of respect we accord ourselves; and we don't perceive the discrepancy. For instance, most of us will indulge in gossip, often spiced with malice, about close friends or relations, yet would be profoundly upset if we thought they did the same about us. Most of us don't need a lesson in spin from the likes of Peter Mandelson or Alastair Campbell to teach us to present our best faces to the world. We are constantly at pains to appear to best advantage and, if others are taken in, so do we also fool ourselves. Anyone who has been the subject of adverse publicity will know just how deeply unpleasant it is, and what a blow to self-confidence, to have those protective layers removed. It does not surprise me that some frail personalities have committed suicide under these circumstances, for a selective appreciation of ourselves is a method of surviving. If we had true insight into the opinions of the folk about us – or even their mere indifference – I don't doubt that many would be terminally depressed. So there's a take-home message for Robbie Burns.

A fair percentage of politicians, especially in the upper ranks, have narcissistic personalities to begin with, and so how much more extensive, lavish and vital are these metaphorical outer garments to people in the public eye? And when they see themselves courted and then quoted by the media, coaxed to appear on television, and invited as guest speakers to venues around the country, cossetted and cocooned in grace-and-favour houses, driven around in chauffeured cars and protected by bodyguards, how readily is that layer of false emperor's clothing going to become integral to the person it covers?

An ordinary person's impression of the world around them as gained from their life-experience is also distorted. I imagine a human at the centre of a bubble of circumstances, composed of the geographical and temporal limits of their being, full of memories, learning, people, activities, contacts, and enlarged from time to time by major events (like becoming a parent) or foreign travel, and perhaps enhanced marginally on a daily basis by messages from outside, like news from various media sources. Lifestyle will materially affect the contents of the bubble, but though it may shrink (for instance in old age), it can never grow beyond a definitive size or be enriched beyond a certain density. There is a surprising degree of consistency in the number of people in any one person's social acquaintance, as if we still behaved as members of a tribe of a given size. No person can do more than so many things in a day, or think more than a given number of useful thoughts in an hour. Those who become specialists in a field can usually embrace only one particular topic. If we occupy ourselves with one pursuit, we lose out on another. A person may be rich in social acquaintance but poor in time to spend in solitary musing. One may be widely travelled and so well-informed about many countries at a superficial level but about none in depth. One may be rich in work experience but poor in how to use leisure time; or may spend so much time holding centre-stage and discoursing fluently as to completely miss out on listening and receptivity. In the estimation of each person, those things one knows and understands are given a higher profile in our list of priorities than things that touch us more distantly. Selective bias begins at birth, with the nearest factors the most prone to impress. It's as well genetic influences are so strong or we would all be inconstant butterflies, wafted by every wind of chance. We assume folk we meet think like us, hold our set of reactions and values. There is a story about Mrs Thatcher that describes how once when visiting a girl's school she was asked to take a chemistry lesson. The subject being inorganic chemistry, she taught them about the reaction of sulphur with silver by referring to the effect of boiled eggs on their mothers' silver teaspoons. She was oblivious to the fact that this particular group had no experience of teaspoons made of anything other than base metal or plastic.

If those nearest to us are respectful and compliant, we assume everyone else in the world is so disposed. If those with whom we work are prone to praise and defer to us, it's to be expected that we will have the same effect on all others. If we are bad-tempered our perception is that we have a legitimate grievance; if we are successful, that we deserve it all; if we face disaster, that the world is treating us badly and owes us something better. Other people's extremes touch us much less closely. In short, we are supremely selfish, every last one of us. My nearest, closest and dearest has not always been able to fathom my obsessions, nor to engage me fully in his. Even at our best, in our care for our children, we are more strongly motivated towards our own than to someone else's. Yet few people, least of all politicians, realise just how narrow-minded and ill-informed they are as to how other people function.

Speaking as someone whose formal specialist training continued until the age of 31, I have often been amazed, and sceptical, at the way ministers swap portfolios and are expected to be instantly in command of their brief. Of course they can't do this, and have armies of advisers and civil servants to inform them, but the degree of understanding required for complex decision-making cannot all be present and digested within the mind of the key individual. It's part of the spin, I suppose, to appear omniscient, ultimately authoritative, better equipped than even professionals. And so a leader (like Tony Blair) will assume the populace to have a level of understanding and intelligence that is lower than his own. He talks down. He communicates with people in categories, Joe Soap, all the variability and diversity ironed out. He assumes without question that he is right, brooks no alternative, assumes he can change people by persuading, charming, convincing by argument. The reception he gets when speaking to selected crowds may convince him that this is so. He becomes paternalistic, doing things on our behalf, believing this is democracy. His attitude to the public is reductive, juvenile, demeaning. Complexities of human composition pass him by.

I imagine Emperor Qin Shi Huangdi thought of his workers as simple, ordinary, uniform folk, above all dispensable, and would have been unable to grasp the idea that some or many may have had skills and capabilities potentially vastly superior to his own. In previous cultures with a big social gulf, received wisdom has held that humble people are lowly in all repects, including morals, and exalted people are so because they merit their status. Whoever said the personal is not political did not have the remotest insight into human nature.

If we have little perception and understanding of even those close to us, and have enough trouble governing ourselves, who then should have the temerity to attempt to govern millions? But some aspire to do so, and it is precisely those people who project themselves as potential leaders who are least desirable in that role and who in power will develop and extend those adverse qualities which unfitted them for the job in the first place. The gender bias inevitably poses the question of whether women are radically different in a leadership position. Many top women seem to have come out from behind male relations, as if, having seen the faulty person fulfill that role, they realise they could do the job at least as well, if not better. Women are less driven by the destructive extremes of competitiveness, and may be more perceptive and altruistic in a position of authority. Is it possible that heads of government in an enlightened future could be exclusively women? I start with preconceived ideas, and would be disappointed if at least some of them were not changed as a result of this study. I shall explore the connection of behaviour patterns with inheritance, which raises uneasy responses from those who hate to think that our genes dictate our destiny. I'll question whether it might be right to alter our environment to enhance the possibility that, with the passage of time, a gentler, more peaceful set of genetic behaviour patterns will emerge. And whether our obsession with sex isn't related to the ever more confrontational style of politics, national and international, with which the world is stricken at the start of the 21st century.

Competitiveness is perhaps the most defining trait of the political animal. It is largely a feature of the climbing and waiting years, less in evidence, however, in the fully fledged ruler, in whom it lies dormant unless he is challenged by an aspiring rival. Competitiveness is innate in the psyche of those who are selected for a dominating career – it is instinctive. Acquired traits, on the other hand, are gained with experience in office, and belong to the realms of intellect and learning. These conflicting dictates between head and heart, intellect and instinct, nurture and nature, doing as I say not as I do, public and private, preach and practice, account for many of the otherwise inexplicable contradictions observed in public figures – indeed, in every one of us.

CHAPTER 2

The Origin of Supremacy

Analysing human behaviour seems to fascinate and repel in equal measures. We're not very good at being objective about ourselves, mainly because we are blindly obeying the rules while trying to find out what they are. Our immediate forebears are extinct, but studies of primitive peoples offer some clues as to basic patterns below the layers of sophistication. There may be very little time left to study our nearest living animal relatives, the chimpanzees, and other more distant ape cousins, before they are decimated by habitat destruction and local hunters (big-time and small-scale destroyers respectively, but both of the human breed). There has always been reluctance among humans to accept that we are essentially highly sophisticated, evolved animals. Much of the present-day antipathy to the emerging discipline of evolutionary psychology is the ancient need to feel superior to those around us, and to believe we have the right to direct and control them.

Another emotional hackle-raiser is the perennial argument of nature versus nurture. A great deal of professional and popular psychology even today assumes that environment has the greater influence over development. Courage is needed to accept the consequences of the converse. Humans in their arrogance like to believe they are in control, and believe their surroundings are more easily manipulated than their genes – though that's all changing.

One of the reasons why this debate creates such antagonism is because, carried to extremes, it has been metamorphosed into ideologies on the basis of which immense populations have been strait-jacketed, ruled without compassion, tortured and killed. Tragically, both ideological extremes, communism and fascism, favouring respectively environmentalism and genetic determinism, have both had terrible consequences, and an invading Martian would have some difficulty distinguishing beween the two. The best definition of the contrast between the regimes is that left-wingers use power to gain wealth, whereas right-wingers use wealth to achieve power. Which is one good reason for believing, as I do, that human behaviour is largely driven by determinants deep inside the individual. The theories, the -ologies and -isms, are used to justify, but do not intrinsically direct the actions.

Once, over a dinner among the chattering classes, I mentioned to my neighbour – who unbeknown to me was a sociologist – that I had recently encountered an identical-twin pair in my clinic whose details challenged a number of assumptions in my mind about the nature–nurture balance, tending to accord nature the greater influence. Abandoning all semblance of gentility, my companion went straight for the jugular, accusing me of postulating inferiority of non-white peoples and much else besides. Her olympic leap of logic left my mind reeling, as at the time I was unaware of the history of twin studies. In particular, I was unaware of how Joseph Mengele's evil experiments at Auschwitz had brought the topic into disrepute, forming as they did the basis for research into eugenics with the aim of perfecting an Aryan master race. Still less was I aware of the twin research at the Maxim Gorky Institute in Moscow in the 1930s, which was abruptly halted when the results began to indicate the importance of inheritance in character-moulding. This ran counter to Marxist theory of the *tabula rasa* or clear-slate status of humans who, it is postulated by that ideology, are shaped by their environments. This principle was the basis of communism as practised in the USSR and China. By contrast, scientific data suggesting the relative importance of inheritance over personal characteristics, especially intelligence and ability, have been quickly snapped up by those of a racialist or elitist bent to justify not only their beliefs but policies and ideologies based thereon. This work has been used to perpetuate racism in America, the British class system and the atrocities committed by Nazi Germany.

My dinner companion had much of this in mind when she made her totally unjustified attack on me. Unjustified, because, at the risk of sounding like a cliché, I would like to state that I have held egalitarian views for as long as I can remember. Yet our beliefs should not blind us to evidence, if we can view it in a detached manner. For there is a compelling body of evidence from twin studies, notably identical twins raised apart for all or most of their lives, that measurable aspects of intelligence, personality and behaviour are largely inherited. Even social attitudes such as political affiliation and religion have a strong genetic component. This conclusion is staunchly rejected by many, because of the implications for our individuality and the assertion of free will. However, gene-constellations (or units of inheritance) for behaviour create a tendency rather than an imposition. With sufficient motivation, behaviour can be changed, though it is an uphill struggle. We are all aware of the superhuman effort required to keep New Year resolutions, especially when they involve giving up things. Indeed, most personal experience will harbour small indications of how tenacious are habits that are primordial rather than acquired. In my clinic, trying to change patients' damaging, stress-related lifestyles, such as workaholism (especially where the reward is big money), or smoking, drinking and eating to excess, is rewarded with a low success rate; but occasionally a defining experience can galvanise the change. A heart attack, a death of a colleague, falling in love, for instance.

The huge intelligence we have, our powers of deduction and our personal experience, can be harnessed to withstand the dictates of our genes. Within these inner conflicts can be heard a cacophony of multiple voices from various stages of evolutionary development. I have often been aware of an approaching decision, the need to make a straight choice between a reasoned move and an instinctive one. I have determined on the cerebral route, only to find myself at the critical moment going the other way, almost as if an alien had taken over the controls. But I know that the decision-maker is not a stranger, but my deeper nature taking the driving seat. My first pregnancy came about in this way. So much for feminism. Children undoubtedly came before career at that juncture. I also observed, as do all mothers with whom I have discussed this, that my infants had well-defined characters from day one. How utterly terrifying if they had not, and were at the mercy of any passing influence. If I'd believed that, I would never have let anyone near them, never let them out in the hostile world.

My own revealing encounter with twins, which provided so much food for thought, started when a girl of 21 was referred with profound anaemia. This was due to a severe deficiency of the vitamin folic acid (producing what haematologists call a megaloblastic anaemia). On detailed investigation I finally concluded that she had no severe underlying disease, but that three factors had contributed to the deficiency. First, she admitted to a very poor diet, lacking in green vegetables in particular; second, she had been taking the combined contraceptive pill (which increases the need for folic acid); and third, in addition to her daytime job of clerical assistant in a legal firm, she had taken an evening job as bartender and had in consequence a rather high alcohol intake (which also increases the body's need for and usage of folic acid). All these factors appeared incontrovertibly 'environmental'.

Knowing that my patient had an identical twin, I suggested that she also should have a blood count checked. To my fascination, twin number two also had folic acid deficiency anaemia, although not to such a severe degree, and her lifestyle was exactly the same as her sister's. They were both saving up to get married, hence the pub job as well as identical day-work. The second twin's anaemia was ascribed to the same three factors, the exactly reproduced behavioural pattern, as her sister's. Both girls responded well to treatment and, as far as I could tell, to advice, and were married on the same day not long afterwards. After their respective weddings, I saw them in the clinic a few times until full recovery, when, though they both came from their separate establishments, they always arrived identically dressed. There was an uncanny, unscientific but very convincing impression that their mutual self-identification was too ingrained to have come about through mere social conditioning.

The nature–nurture conflict is not only simplistic but false because the two influences are intimately intertwined and interdependent. Several neat and illustrative examples of the interaction of genes and environment can be found in my own subject, haematology. Take for example sickle cell disease, an inherited condition affecting people of mainly West African origin. The full-blown condition is severe, with an abnormal form of haemoglobin in red cells, giving a tendency for those cells to adopt a sickle shape and occlude blood vessels, with consequent damage to vital organs and severe pain. Variable anaemia and jaundice are also features of the disease. Not long ago, few if any sufferers survived beyond their teens, and even fewer managed to have children. How then did the gene for sickle cell disease perpetuate itself? You would expect it to die out with the reproductive failure of those people affected by the condition.

Sickle cell disease occurs when the sickle cell gene is present in duplicate, one copy having been inherited from each parent. An individual who has only one copy of the gene forms a smaller quantity of sickle haemoglobin which does not normally precipitate the damaging shape-change of red cells. What it does, though, is to protect the cells from invasion by malarial parasites. Thus those carriers of sickle cell genes have a considerable selective advantage in areas of the world where malaria is rife. If ever we succeed in eradicating malaria, it is expected that the gene will eventually disappear. Because of the intimate relationship between a population and its environment, of which this simple example is but one of many, there is no validity in comparing racial characteristics. Increasingly, a race and a population are not the same thing, in our world of travel and mobility. Arguably they never were, as population shifts have occurred from time immemorial for more pragmatic reasons, such as simple survival. We only have to glance at human history in recorded time to recognise how adaptable humans are.

Much nonsense has been written about evolution, because people fail to understand it as a dynamic and adaptive, though almost unfathomably gradual, process. They (especially politicians who can only work with instant results) fail to understand that cause and effect take many generations. In a stable environment, such as the jungle, which shaped our far distant ancestors, random gene mutations are mostly unfavourable, but the few that enhance fitness to survive and reproduce are favoured and passed on. So, over generations, the species becomes ever better adapted to prevail. However, nothing is totally static. The genes held by the existing population are an elite selection and the bodies carrying them must compete against others of their own species for living space, food and sexual partners. Humans have compounded the problem by developing massive brains, enabling us to change the environment profoundly, instantly and unpredictably. Of course, we then make adaptations to suit the new milieu, but these are not evolved developments. Essentially, our most basic behaviour, which is always visible under the sophisticated veneer, is still comparable to that of our ancestors who dwelled on the earth even before *Homo sapiens* evolved.

Although humans are proud to the point of obsession of their most recent history, which has marked them as a separate species with superiority of brain and technical power over other living beings, we are also constantly tormented by the conflicting layers of development that peep through at times. The old Adam is still there, and many stages before him. It's a bit like someone who has left their rustic roots behind, who has become educated and cultivated, and who finds it painful to acknowledge his humble start in life. This elitist attitude is but one example of the dominance hierarchy that is so integral to social interactions and so clearly an inheritance from our animal origins – and it forms a central pillar of my argument. The ambivalence of the lords of the earth towards those they dominate shows up in the religious teachings of many centuries past, that animals were put on earth for man's use and pleasure; and that he is distinguished from them by his possession of an immortal soul. Yet exponents struggled to identify a point on the evolutionary progression from the Last Common Ancestor when that soul wafted into being. However, this issue has been solved by a pronouncement by Pope John Paul II to the Pontifical Academy of Sciences in October 1996, that God inserted the soul at some critical juncture of primate evolution. Matt Ridley, author of *Genome*, suggests wryly that, as chromosome 2 differs in humans from other apes in being a uniquely hybrid construction, formed by the fusion of two chromosomes that have remained separate in other apes, maybe the gene for the soul was created at the moment of fusion and is to be found in the middle of that sanctified chromosome.

The modern equivalent of the superstitious denial of our animal connection is pointed up in the horror shown by animal behaviourists over anthropomorphism, or the ascribing of human thought processes to animals. Jane Goodall, the distinguished ethnologist and conservationist renowned for her work with the chimpanzees of Gombe, describes feelingly the way she was frozen out by the scientific community when they heard her description of chimpanzee behaviour and adaptive intelligence, so uncannily like our own. Her study should not have surprised anyone as they are our nearest living relations and share over 98% of our genetic equipment. They are an offshoot from the same limb of apes as ourselves, though our common ancestor does not now exist as a separate entity.

Homo sapiens emerged as a distinct species a mere 125,000 years ago. Previous ancestral hominids had their origins in Africa and at some stage ventured from the dwindling forests into open country. Prior to that they occupied a similar habitat to chimpanzees, and one may presume that their lifestyles were similar. Working on that hypothesis, a look at chimps' daily lives is informative. Chimps are communal-living, intensely sociable animals with well-defined hierarchical structures. The social system and sexual strategy are intimately dependent on the food source. These animals are chiefly fruit-eaters and so their groups occupy and defend a large enough territory to feed the members of the group. They are also part-time hunters, and enjoy meat when they can get it.

Within the community of chimps there is always a supremely powerful male leader called an alpha male. To chimp-watchers it is often clear which young males have qualities that will enable them to get to the top. To come from a high-ranking family is undoubtedly an advantage. Males learn to put on a charging display, designed to impress and intimidate, consisting of sound and fury, hairy coats a-bristle, charging, stamping, thumping, shaking bushes, dragging loose undergrowth and chucking rocks, drumming on tree-trunks, all accompanied by a ferocious scowling face. Learning and perfecting this performance at a young age shows strong motivation, but also is highly risky because an older, stronger male can object to the challenge by a whipper-snapper and punish him accordingly. Sickness and injury can hinder or totally foil an aspiring social climber, and are ruthlessly exploited by observant, intelligent rivals. An ambitious youngster finds that making allies is vital in the struggle for power, not only to be able to stand against stronger individuals, but also to minimise rival factions. Coalitions can shift, as occasion requires, but becoming a disciple of the leader is a prudent move. Ultimately of course, he will have to be challenged in the final race to the top. Displays, to be psychologically successful, must create pandemonium among the onlookers, who start screaming, leaping to safety and running amok in general mayhem. Sometimes attacks and injury occur, but not always. Some individuals learn the particular manipulative advantage of cacophonic displays at dawn, while it is still dark and the community is befuddled with sleep. Lifelong loyalties and close family bonds are abandoned if necessary in the bid for the leadership, suggesting an all-replacing, single-minded motivating force.

Interestingly, an upwardly mobile male chimp must first work his way up the female hierarchy before he ventures to tackle the steeper and more perilous male one. Persistence in flamboyant displays, followed up with frank aggression where necessary, and demanding deferential gestures from other members of the group, are all essential for an individual to achieve and hold the top spot. During the reign of an indisputably controlling male, the community enjoys a peaceful life as contenders realise their time for challenge has not yet come. The alpha can maintain exclusive mating rights with any or all females if he wishes, and has first choice of feeding places. His mere presence is enough to quell the rest, who, if they are prepared to take the risk at all, must sneak their copulations in a secretive and furtive way. If, however, the alpha male has a lieutenant, this favoured one may share sexual and other privileges, as long as his attitude remains deferential and his loyalty unquestioned. The top chimp has hard work to maintain his position, requiring his constant presence in the troupe reinforced by displays as necessary, and regularly honing his theatrical capacity to intimidate would-be rivals. If individuals are not able to carry through a challenge, a group may gang up to topple a king, after which chaos may reign until the stepwise order is re-established.

A pair or group activity that is clearly very important in chimpanzee life is grooming, which takes place between pair-bonds, family members, allies of the same sex, parent and child, or even two individuals who have just had an altercation. In the last case, it happens when a clear outcome of dominance by one animal over another has been achieved, and he will accept the ministrations of the subordinate. This activity is one of the few that does not have an obvious counterpart in humans, and presumably it has been replaced by conversation.

Sexual strategies are various. The alpha male has access to whom he pleases, but group gropes also take place, with a female in oestrus surrounded by a crowd of eager males, who copulate with her in sequence. Tension runs high and can explode into fighting. A male sometimes lures a female away from the group, to elope with her to a quiet spot where he commandeers her for the few days in which she is sexually active. If a female is unwilling to follow she may be assaulted and badly wounded, but some females judge how much they can tease, and when it is prudent to give in. These honeymoons are called consortships by zoologists, and last only as long as the female is receptive. However, in this activity as in all other communal ones within his compass, the alpha male calls the shots, especially if he has thoroughly established his authority. Most of the impregnated females carry his offspring.

Male bonding in groups is important for patrolling and maintaining territorial boundaries, with threatening displays and exchanges of insults with other tribes as necessary. The same groups hunt for meat (smaller animals such as bush-pig and baby monkeys), after which the sharing of the spoils may occur with tension and aggression, or with favouring of friends and allies. Colonies can split, following which they treat each other with unmitigated hostility. Brutal and murderous attacks occur with a degree of ferocity reserved for strangers and for prey. In the aftermath of such a battle, the winning party shows wild, excited and triumphalist behaviour. Such engagements punctuate sustained hostilities, lasting months or years, to the extent that whole communities are exterminated.

Yet, for the most part, chimps lead lives that appear imbued with all the best of communal dwelling, with supportive and affectionate family groups, periods of childcare lasting for years, and with strong, lifelong parent–child and sibling bonding. They display much need for physical contact, for affection, for company, for play and frivolous fun. Infants show evidence of depression when they are weaned or displaced after some years by another child, and the loss of a mother can lead to profound misery, inanition and even death if no substitute is found. Even males show a capacity to care attentively for youngsters, and childless females adopt orphans. The presence of females, and the tactful use of grooming, can defuse moments of aggression. Female bonding is well defined in chimp society, centring on families and childcare. Female hierarchies, though explicit, are not so steep or maintained with such ferocity as male ones. There are clear variations in sexual attractiveness between females, though all are desirable when in season, and age is irrelevant.

The social life of our hominid ancestor was probably not dissimilar until he left the forest to become predominantly a ground-dwelling hunter, when it must have changed radically from the pattern of the forest-dweller. Hunting being then crucial to survival, male bonding and co-operation assumed much greater importance, and presumably modified the dominance hierarchy markedly, displacing competition as the most vital function. Because of the enormous distances a hunt could cover, territories came to be defined anew, with a vast stalking range and a smaller home base where the women and children remained. Caring and sharing with the weaker members had to take a higher priority, and so family units of a more durable nature came into being. Firmer pair-bonding and commitment were favoured by the lifestyle, as a result of which, sexual rivalries were reduced among the males, while females were more certain of constant male support, protection and food supply for themselves and their offspring. The pattern was set for marriage and fidelity – provided no other compelling changes in living standards took place.

A reasonably plausible postulate that humans are the most sex-obsessed animal alive is possibly explained by the permanent, or at least long-term, pair-bonding. The need to fall in love and become sexually imprinted, it is said, has led to the evolution of markedly attractive features, which are not seasonal, and which augment mutual sexual gratification. The possession of rounded breasts and of a capacity for reaching orgasm in the female, both of which are thought to be unique to humans, are examples; as also is the outsize human penis. Possibly our nearly hairless, sensitive skin is another. Copulation occurs without regard to fertility, and functions to boost the pair-bond as much as to reproduce. But modern humankind is very ambivalent about its explicit sexiness, and perhaps has to be, or we would never be out of bed. Sex signals are concealed by clothing and the sex act is carried out in privacy, usually under the bed-clothes. Fashions for the degree of cover-up vary with time and culture. In Victorian times, even piano-legs were clothed, and chicken-breasts were called 'white meat'. In the Edwardian era, bosoms were flaunted in décolletée evening dress, and bums augmented by bustles, but night attire was as prudently all-enclosing as a nun's habit. In modern times, we have become uninhibited and unzipped, seen in the portrayal of all aspects of sex in the media; and we are pruriently fascinated by other people's sex lives. We are perpetually anxious to assure ourselves that we are not missing out. Our obsessions are very much open to manipulation by advertisers.

To return to the hunting male in the savannah, he had by this time learned to use both weapons and tools. His increasing capacity to inflict mortal wounds on prey had, as with other hunting animals (though their arsenal takes the form of claws and canines), to be channelled into that activity, and not allowed to spill over into social engagements with his own kind. The mechanism of inhibition of violence to each other among some animals is very clear, with the adoption of submissive postures usually involving lowering of the body and the gaze. My cat, when I am cross with her, shows this very well. She sinks to the two-dimensional shape of a floor rug with ears flattened and eyes half-closed. Some animals, including chimps, adopt sexually receptive postures to turn away wrath. It is easy to understand how this habit of deferring to a mightier rival would enhance individual survival within a species. How humans perform this function is more complex, but the tendency to appease and to defer is strongly ingrained. It is potentially extremely dangerous because, although evolved to mitigate the rage of a blustering male in a community of twenty or thirty, its manifestation is nowadays a mass phenomenon towards a leader of millions. It is evident in the form of respect for authority and the establishment. It has been exploited to enable a tiny elite to govern a huge mass of people, usually to their detriment, as in British India and apartheid South Africa.

But though a legacy through millions of years of evolution, this deference appears to be changing, by an unknown mechanism. The change, if it continues, may be the saving grace of the world. Established attitudes, shaped usually by white male thinking, are being challenged by feminist philosophy, by the increasing tolerance towards homosexuals, by anti-racist laws, by a diminishing influence of established Churches in Western countries, and by a decreasing show of reverence generally towards people in power.

I need hardly point out the similarities between chimp behaviour as I've summarised it, and our own. I am of course wading into the highly contentious waters of evolutionary psychology, which besides capturing the public imagination have polarised views in the scientific world. Astonishingly, even that community, which should have objectivity written all over its epicardium, raises its collective hackles on issues concerned with personal identity. Evolutionary psychology is a young science which may yet transform, Mandela-like, from outcast to oracle. At present there is little known about links between psychological attributes and genes or chromosomes (other than an association between mental deficiency and too many X chromosomes; and between psychiatric illness/criminal behaviour and too many Y chromosomes). The evidence that there is such a linkage is indirect, as I've discussed earlier in this chapter.

Theories of evolution have occupied the combative tendency of the biological world ever since Darwin, but one of the most revolutionary shifts in thinking came in 1966, when a New York professor, George Williams, showed incontrovertibly that an individual creature would always act for the good of itself first and foremost, and would never sacrifice its own interests to the good of the species. It really is a harsh and cruel world. However, animals and humans can and do co-operate, when it is in their own interests, and most especially when close relatives are involved.

In his landmark book *The Selfish Gene*, Richard Dawkins uses anthropomorphic language to describe genes, the unit of natural selection (or a variable-sized portion of a chromosome). While reading his description of this 'selfish' scrap of molecular matter, for which he brought down from various quarters all kinds of moral judgements, I observed how very like a big-time political leader is the behaviour of a gene. It competes with its alleles (or alternatives) for survival, and aims at historical immortality. In order to maintain its influence it will collaborate with others of its kind, changing teams as necessary, but relying on alliances to express full potential. With other genes it creates an edifice (the body) which surrounds it protectively, and which functions by means of an executive (the brain), by which it can manipulate and control other bodies. The goal is self-perpetuation, and successful genes are risk-taking policy-makers, often survivors against the odds. Totally egocentric, they ruthlessly do down competitors so that their influence can spread around the world and precipitate unforeseen events. The fulfillment of their destiny owes nothing whatever to democracy or morality.

CHAPTER 3

The Phallic Pyramid

The hierarchical sex strategy of our ancient ancestors carried huge implications for the present-day world. Though we are talking of events that happened several million years ago, this is the merest eye-blink in evolutionary terms. It is one scenario for a chimp-thug to dominate a community of fifty individuals and for his propensities to prevail in the next generation. But hominids were destined to expand infinitely more successfully than chimpanzees, and in that era each generation was bred from the most effectively overpowering, brutish males.

Competitiveness is so fundamental to life as we know it that any vision of a completely egalitarian society is unrealisable. Even our genes compete with near rivals for success: for their own expression and the chance to be passed on to future generations. In primitive, pre-human societies, contests were simple enough and took place within small communities, between groups of limited numbers. In modern times we have come to populate the world in ever-increasingly crowded communities, but in the heart of every one of us there simmers an urge to better oneself, whoever else gets left behind. As a young man, Che Guevara did his pre-university, adventurous travelling around South America on a motor bike, pausing to wonder at the tenacity of the Spanish conquistadores, who endured the unendurable in order to fulfill 'man's undeniable desire to find a place where he can exercise absolute control'. He pondered on the philosophy of Julius Caesar, who opined it was better to be number one in a humble alpine village than number two in Rome. In the land of the Incas he observed not only how their militant power spread out geographically from their fortress of origin at Cuzco, but how they also desired their greatness to conquer time itself. To extend their glories to the past they created a religion and a priestly caste. To commandeer the future they created gold-adorned temples and wonders of architecture in inaccessible places. The problem with such aspirations is that evolution has not kitted us out with any limit to ambition. In times past, external factors have cut off the aspirant, who, in keeping with the characteristic riskiness of his habits, has often met a sudden and glutinous end, together with decimation of the people he led. In recent millennia, man's powerful brain has increasingly been able to save him from a violent death (though not necessarily to salvage his followers), and there are fewer restraints on unlimited power, once it is achieved.

Because of the sheer numbers of humans on the earth, competitiveness becomes ever more intense, greasy poles ever more slithery, mountain gradients ever more vertiginous. Man the inventor has found a way round even this dilemma. It takes the form of diversification of talent.

In the last chapter, from a work by Jane Goodall, I recounted how an ambitious young chimp learns to impress his peers by a charging display of great visual and aural impact, designed to make him look and sound bigger and fiercer than he really is. This is a vital technique to lever oneself up the social scale, but even in a small community it takes every ounce of bombast, courage, wit, deceptive powers, learning, wily cunning and ally-making, to achieve recognition as the alpha male and to maintain that desirable status. The effort to get there requires 100% of time and energy. In the wild, the rewards are, among others, an ability to mate freely and copiously, though it is certain that this is not the conscious motivating factor in the mind of the chimp as much as the driving force of his highly selected genes. The liberal capacity to reproduce his alpha-making genes ensures that an aggressive, ambitious character is reinforced in every generation by this particular social perk. Human ancestry, aeons ago, came under the same selection pressure, and one may perceive that the sexual monopoly of the top hominid ensured widespread dispersal of his personal features, to offspring of both sexes. Even though, in his evolved guise as *Homo sapiens*, man adopted a more co-operative and more monogamous lifestyle, his fierce, confrontational psyche was bound to direct his behaviour for almost unlimited time and generations to come.

And so it has proved. Hierarchies crop up like mini-mountains in every walk of life, each male trying to be the cockerel who crows over the rest on top of the midden. This happens most obviously in the workplace, where the hierarchy is formalised by graded seniority and managerial status. Where financial reward and future prospects are excellent but available to only a few, the fierce competition leads to a long-hours culture with total commitment, and a sacrificing of leisure time and family life. This, of course, works in the interests of the owners and share-holders. Because the employees are having their most basic instincts manipulated, they find it very difficult to break out of this stultifying engagement, and fear of losing status keeps them on board. Women tend to be less status-aware, and prefer leisure and freedom to monetary reward, which is in part an explanation of the 'glass-ceiling', which supposedly is the unseen barrier to women reaching top position.

Competition defines most sporting activities, with polarisation and passion sometimes amounting to disproportionate intensity, as we are only too aware. Awards and prizes abound in the arts world, less logically and sometimes even more controversially. League tables are applied indiscriminately to schools' and hospitals' performances. Everyone has to feel they can be the very best at something. Our increasing trend to sub-specialise within a subject means that fewer people know more and more about less and less. Within medicine, this means that a highly trained and skilled doctor may define the perimeter of his/her own responsibility, and within that boundary be undisputed top dog. But this pattern of knowledge, redounding to the expert's prestige, is not necessarily in the interests of the patients, who may suffer from Cinderella diseases that occupy no special interest.

Religious organisations are among the most steeply shaped autocracies. The pope holds sway over the worldwide Roman Catholic community and is accorded almost divine status; his words are said to be infallible, though history shows us otherwise. The

Church has been the last bastion of male dominance (apart from Edinburgh University Students' Union), which in the West is being invaded by women at a time when its influence is melting away. Rigid rank order and astonishing seniority-protectionism by inflexible discipline is characteristic of those other male refuges, the armed forces.

Geneticists have some difficulty in explaining satisfactorily why humans have developed such enormous brains and intelligence. But logically a species which had so successfully carved a niche in competition with other animals would come under great selection pressure with other members of its own numerous species. And so there would have to be a diversifying of talents, a form of specialisation. Clever people create their own intellectual hierarchy, with themselves sitting pretty at the top. Similar mechanisms favour other talents, artistic, literary, creative. If all else fails, you can prove yourself in the pub, downing more pints of beer and singing louder than anyone else, and thumping anyone who dares to challenge your supremacy.

Confrontation is the life-blood of party politics. Think of the steps an aspiring entrant has to take. He joins a party and establishes his credentials. He seeks and competes for nomination among his like-minded associates, and as a prospective candidate he fights those selected for other parties. This battling against other ideologies is seen as more morally plausible. But then as an elected MP he has to elbow those of his own persuasion aside as he seeks to grab the attention of the media and his own party leaders. Then in office he can be ferocious at the expense of the opposition and feel virtuous again. But climbing ever nearer the rarefied heights of senior ministerial posts, his opponents and enemies are his nearest colleagues once more. Excess baggage may need to be discarded in order to scale the peaks, and pathways taken that are not of his choosing. Once at the top the focus shifts again and the balancing act is achieved in part by verbal dexterity against his opposite number and in part by persuading those beneath him that he is too dangerous to topple. This is the perilous time. Looking abroad to maintain the intoxicating ego-trip, he is prey to the temptation to justify aggressive expansion in other countries.

It's easy to see why totalitarian regimes justify a one-party system: in order to avoid the time- and energy-wasting combativeness. But alas it does not do so. In the time of several Soviet Union leaders, factional fighting was intense and destructive, though of course it all took place at a lower level than the top man in the pyramid of power. This pattern is recognisable in European history also, in the reign of Charles I and other absolute monarchs.

Leaders of communities large and small achieve that position because they are good at competing and winning, in the arena and using the weapons of the era; and, having won, retaining. Arguably, the same people would arrive at the top regardless of the prevailing structures and ideologies of the time and place. Competitiveness in humans – and their near relations – is a strategy for survival, which is so powerful that, having it, some outlet must be found for it. Hence, the people propelled into high places may be well suited for heading a jungle-based community, with innate skills for commandeering all the privileges and exacting submission from society; but not necessarily suited for governing complex industrial countries with millions of people, multi-ethnic, multicultural; to say nothing of co-existing peacefully with other nations.

Perhaps the folk who have most successfully achieved sublimation of the male ambitious drive are mountaineers, who realise that once they reach the top there is nothing else to attain, so simply turn round and come down again.

The kernel of Darwin's theory of evolution, popularly known as 'survival of the fittest', was actually pushed one step further by him and by modern thinkers to 'reproduction of the fittest'. The antler-clashing and roaring and violent power-grabbing tactics in the wild are all about winning the right to beget lots of babies. This is the most cogent force in nature and there are many examples that show that the compulsion to breed takes priority over the instinct to survive. For instance, certain male spiders are regularly eaten by their mates after copulation, salmon starve when they breed, and with certain insects mating is the last activity before death. More-over, any species is equipped with an elaborate sensory network to enable each individual to pick out the partner with the best possible qualities for future survival and proliferation: health, nubility, fecundity, physical and mental fitness. This is called sexual selection, which everyone practises with greater or lesser success. The knee-jerk response is to say, 'That's the animal world, we're more sophisticated than that.' Well, we're not.

The power pyramid in the chimp world, and in others, is visibly rewarded by a monopoly of the harem. This is not by any means the obvious supreme prize in the higher echelons – or in any levels – of the power game in the human world. Many leaders give the impression that they are far too involved with mighty and weighty matters to give more than a passing thought to women and children, who may be put aside as a frivolous, time-wasting irrelevance or treated as objects of light relief for the odd leisure moment. But all is not what it seems.

Neo-Darwinism postulates that all individuals, including humans, behave as if directed by their genes in such a way as to maximise their chance of self-perpetuation. They have in particular evolved well-honed strategies to exploit positions of power to this most single and over-riding end. Whatever the present-day behaviour patterns may appear to be and however contradictory the outward manifestations are, man's ferociously competitive nature is due to the directives of sexual selection. We are by no means yet emancipated from our biological imperatives.

The evidence comes from various sources. At a simple anatomical level, the difference in size and muscle mass between a man and a woman is testament to at least a partial hierarchical harem system in the past. All animals that are locked into this sex strategy show a significant size difference, the most striking contrast being between male and female elephant seals. Closely linked is the male risk-taking and danger-seeking behaviour. These males must be equipped to face and prevail against each other to win breeding rights. As I postulated earlier, men have more in common with male chimps than they do with women of their own species. Men have always been required to win their feathers, favours, spurs, badges, medals, titles, by risking their necks (or their reputations) in some pugilistic arena, throwing caution to the wind, aiming for the *crème de la crème* among women.

Theories of why animals (and plants) require sex at all to reproduce are fascinating and not entirely resolved, but alas are not directly relevant here. Except for one bit of philosophy. It is an advantage to be adaptable in an uncertain and hostile world, for example to deal with attacking, wily parasites and devious invading organisms of all kinds. Asexual reproduction provides a series of predictable clones, but sexual propagation gives extremes, from best to worst and all stages in between. This pattern echoes the triumphs and disasters of vicarious dynastic ambition. Sex gives a distant chance that one of your offspring will be deviant enough to become a world leader; though he might equally well become the village idiot.

When prehistoric man emerged from the shrinking jungles of Africa (an exile analogous to the Garden of Eden) and had to face the perils of the open savannah, becoming a hunter in the process, his new lifestyle profoundly influenced his sexual behaviour, which changed (over generations) from harem to monogamy. With the advent of agriculture and farming some millions of years later, there arrived again an opportunity for a polygamous pattern of mating. In the West this is past history, but in some present-day tribal areas of Africa, in Namibia and Kenya for instance, where a simple farming life has been adopted, whenever one man gains an edge in productivity and thereby increases his wealth, his wives increase proportionately in number.

In history, whenever a single man has wielded immeasurable, despotic power, this has invariably been accompanied by acknowledged and stupendous sexual activity, most notably in the empires of Babylon, Egypt, India, China, Rome, the Aztecs and the Incas. For instance, the Chinese emperor Fe Ti had 10,000 females to choose from. Despotic rule implies the absolute and arbitrary control over life and death. Genghis Khan in the 12th century, founder of the Mongolian Empire by a process of unmatched conquest and pillage, equally unrivalled in his despotic ways, took for his own not only the riches of those he smashed, but their wives and daughters also.

The Inca kingdom affords a representative example of cascading sexual privilege. The king had the most concubines, 1,500, selected for their beauty at a young age – eight or less – to ensure their virginity. Lords of the kingdom had 700 women; principal persons had 50, chiefs 30, and so on down the rank order, the size of each harem being defined by law. The legal justification is significant: 'For their service and multiplying people in the kingdom.' The average guy in the street was fortunate indeed if he ever had an opportunity for sex at all. The penalties for violation by a lowly person were ferocious: death to him and all relatives, destruction of property and stock. Feminists may feel retrospective outrage, but it was men who had most to complain of.

In Imperial Rome, emperors were famed and glorified for sexual indulgence, right into old age: Julius Caesar, Augustus, Tiberius, Caligula (who regarded every ranking woman as his own, including his sisters), Claudius, Nero. At other levels of Roman society this pattern was echoed, for there is written evidence that slaves were used as concubines, with young, comely and virginal slaves commanding a high price. Male slaves were forcibly celibate. But illegitimate sons were sometimes freed and endowed generously enough to live well and even to become wealthy.

The Ottoman Empire, which was ruled for more than seven centuries by a dynasty known as the Osmanli, at its height extended from Central Europe to North Africa and from Persia to the Adriatic. As their military conquests extended their influence, so their grandeur increased along with the size of the imperial harem. Concubines in the harem were mostly Christians from conquered peoples, whereas wives were high-ranking Muslims whose marriage was a means for consolidating alliances. A sultan, such as Beyazit in the 15th century, might have several sons born to different mothers, whose status was thereby much augmented. In the time of Suleyman the Magnificent, sons of concubines were included in the imperial succession, whereby their mothers could achieve top status as 'principal and most beloved wife'. This upwardly mobile facility had dire consequences however, as it was commonplace for contenders to the throne to be murdered when one sultan died and was succeeded by his heir, who was usually the oldest remaining son. At a time when plague, fever and assassination were common hazards, child mortality was high and sultans tried to spawn as many sons as they could. Murat, who succeeded to the throne in 1574, had 24 sons and 32 daughters, all but two born in the last twelve years of his life, when he seems to have done little other than serve as the royal stud. As a result, there could be a veritable blood-bath of male siblings and near relatives when a new ruler was installed. This hideous practice was enshrined in law by the Ottoman code of fratricide to prevent wars of succession. When Murat died, nineteen young brothers, all under the age of twelve, were brought to embrace the new sultan, Mehmet, and were then strangled. Some of Murat's concubines were pregnant at his death, and their babies were drowned as soon as born. Then, to complete the clearing-out process, ten of Murat's wives and concubines who might have been still carrying his children were also drowned.

This practice has strong echoes of the habits of chimpanzees in the wild, who treat strange females on their territory with unmitigated, murderous ferocity, in order (it is supposed) to prevent progeny of other males becoming established in the community. In some primate groups, including baboons, up-and-coming males who achieve a successful take-over are liable to murder the infants of their predecessor.

The royal families of Europe have followed extravagant patterns of sexual licence and, although only the official queen produced legitimate heirs, it was accepted practice for the monarch to have a string of mistresses, official and unofficial. The resulting numerous royal bastards were treated with varying favour, depending largely on the mother's status. King Augustus II of Poland had 365 love-children, and, unable to keep track of them, made one of them his mistress. Hanoverian, Spanish and Bourbon kings and Romanov tsars were renowned for lusty appetites, their offspring becoming a hefty drain on the exchequer. Louis XIV of France and his son probably outdid the rest. Louis XV had, among others, Madame de Pompadour as official mistress, but also kept a private brothel called the Parc du Cerfs, which supplied him with girls of nine to eighteen years old. Their youth was supposed to be a guard against venereal disease. The numbers of girls passing through this enlightened establishment over 34 active years ran into thousands. No wonder he acquired the name Louis le Bien-Aimé. Secrecy over his activities means that the number of his natural children, quoted as twenty, is probably an underestimate; not even the girls knew who their privileged lover was. Tsar Peter the Great of Russia believed he had a patriotic obligation to father innumerable illegitimate children, and his unofficial harem was provided by the tsarina's ladies-in-waiting. On state travels abroad, one observer noted that about a quarter of the ladies had a child in tow and were prepared to acknowledge, 'The tsar did me the honour.' The Hanoverian George IV of Britain kept a lock of hair from each of his lovers, each stored in a labelled envelope. After his death, seven thousand such envelopes were discovered.

Until I happened to stumble on a scientific study equating human power with reproductive profligacy, I thought, as my reader is probably doing right now, that these examples were aberrations in a sea of contradictions. Such a study was conducted less than twenty years ago by Laura Betzig of Michigan University, who set out to test the postulate that men seek power not for its own sake but as a vehicle for sexual and reproductive success. Stated so baldly, it seems an improbable thesis. Her population samples numbered 104 and were picked by scientific principles to be unbiased and representative of human societies both geographically and temporally, as well as being politically free of colonial authority. They range from pre-Christian Israel, Babylon and Rome through 13th century Cambodia, Mexican Aztec and Peruvian Inca communities before the Spanish conquest in 1530, Mississippi in the early 1700s, 19th-century Fiji and Samoa, and assorted African communities in the last two hundred years.

Her results showed an almost mathematical correlation between the degrees of despotic power a man wielded and the number of women available to him for his delectation. In Dahomey in northeast Africa in 1880, the king held sway over thousands of women (essentially anyone who took his fancy), which meant that few of them ever had the chance to procreate. He was as monopolistic as business bosses are nowadays. Even in essentially monogamous societies such as ancient Babylon, it was the accepted custom that huge armies of slaves were kept solely for concubinage. The king named in the biblical 'Song of Songs' had sixty concubines and eighteen wives. The Inca kings kept houses of virgins in principal provinces to wait upon their needs as they travelled around the kingdom. In Ashanti on the Gold Coast of Africa at the end of the 19th century, numbers of wives reflecting a man's status varied from two to one thousand. In Azande (in the Sudan) the king had five hundred women whereas chiefs had a number ranging from thirty to one hundred. It was estimated that a quarter of adult men had no wife, and about half had only one; the rest had two or more.

In some communities such as Samoa, women were bartered by their families to kings and chiefs in exchange for goods, or presented as gifts in order to curry favour. For many people, emphasis on beauty as a signal to health and fecundity has been a prerequisite for admission to favour, with youth and virginity ensured by rounding up candidates as children. Members of harems, such as in the Ottoman Empire, were strictly guarded by eunuchs, by virtual imprisonment behind high walls, and by segregation, to ensure no inferior traits contaminated the imperial progeny. Various other cultural habits are geared towards perpetuating supposedly superior genes, for instance the practice of differential infanticide (differential with regard to gender as well as caste) in India. The Chinese emperors were taught how to conserve semen in order to cope with impregnating two women a day – a demanding duty for some. To select the most fertile women at any one time to keep company with their lord, careful menstrual records were kept. Wet-nurses were employed to enable the mothers to become fertile again as quickly as possible. All these practices are geared to population expansion by a stud, not mere sexual enjoyment of a potentate.

In medieval Christendom, prodigious informal sexual activity prevailed, but went into hiding presumably to enable the Church to continue pretending to uphold monogamy as the moral norm. A population census in the countryside showed a marked male surplus because so many women of lowly status were employed as serving wenches in castles and monasteries. In practice they served as a harem for the lords and abbots. In various societies the *droit de seigneur* has been exercised, the right of the local despot to spend the night with any new bride before she was taken by her husband, again ensuring the maximum dispersal of the lordly seed.

In anthropological language, rank is defined as an ability to displace other people over a conflict of interest. Betzig's studies showed the clearest correlation between a man's rank and the size of his female entourage. She showed that, in the most hierarchical societies, despotism and arbitrary rule were the norm, and concluded that power is invariably exploited and that self-interest is the ultimate motivator. People behave exactly as Darwinian theory predicts they will behave, and use power to gain reproductive rewards.

Unfortunately, the argument seems to fall apart in modern societies, seemingly parallel with industrialisation and increasing complexity. Certainly, it is not a pattern we readily recognise in Western 'civilisations' where democratic institutions are ever ready to replace a leader who gets too puffed up, or even if he simply takes a mistress. The competitiveness is still a prominent feature, but are sex and procreating potential still the rewards? Do Darwinian principles no longer apply? Are men losing their sex-drive? The worst that most seem to aspire to is serial monogamy and a furtive fancy woman. Has fear of the press and public humiliation driven all activity underground?

It's easy to miss the point – literally the pinnacle. Although most of our political leaders do seem to have enormous power, they really are limited at every turn by democratic institutions. Many spend their lives evading those restrictions, and it's no surprise that every oppositional advocate of freedom of information goes under wraps as soon as he steps into office. Another factor they must strive to control is access to money; and we become aware that power is more heavily concentrated in the hands of those giants of the Pen Parade than of politicians. No American president can arrive at that position without mortgaging his integrity irretrievably to big business concerns, after which he is a captive like a queen bee, a source of plenty over which he has very little control. This gives power to yet another group of people, the masters of spin. If he can't be a man of high principles, at least he can look like one. Opportunists leap for the band-wagon.

Population density may reach a critical level at which despotic power can no longer be wielded; or human society attain such complexity and sophistication that we are all totally interdependent. Everyone is a specialist and must have concessions and rewards. This echoes the change in social and sexual tactics that took place when our ancestors became hunters. Hierarchies are flattened but not obliterated. But man's power-lust is still in his genes and must have some expression. Are today's pyramids of authority made more dangerous because of frustration, lack of overt reward and the need for sublimation? Looking at our current leaders in the UK, it is difficult to believe that the uxorious family man, Tony Blair, or the flinty chancellor, Gordon Brown, are subliminally craving sexual adventure. No, indeed. But bewilderment as to where their drive originates perpetuates the mutual loathing, vicious in-fighting, and frenetic never-ceasing activity.

CHAPTER 4

The Learning Curve

Those who make it to the top appear to arrive there for one of two reasons. Some potential leaders seem to be marked out very early, destined to fulfill predictions about future greatness made by their family and friends. On the other hand, figureheads taken in the mass are so heterogeneous that it might be easy to believe their capacity to rise owed more to luck than to anything inherent. But by no stretch of the imagination could they ever be supposed to represent a cross-section of society, even in democratic countries. I believe that, as usual, both factors are at work and are mutually influential. Self-selection is an important factor, especially at times of stability, but in times of turbulence and conflict a much greater element of chance determines who first scrambles to the top of the detritus. Once in place, a converging of characteristics does take place, with accelerating alpha behaviour.

Hereditary monarchs and emperors have no choice about their accession, which is a fluke of birth, and many of them would have preferred – or so they say – to live out their lives in peaceful obscurity. Their early years are not of particular interest at this stage. The present chapter is concerned with the youth of those who pulled themselves up by any available handholds, when still wet behind the ears and brushing the eggshell off their backs. How much are they propelled by circumstances or fortune, idealogical motivation or egocentricity? Even among elected or semi-elected political leaders, though, families are highly influential. I assume an immense genetic input of course, but older generations already in business or politics can give their offspring a muscular boost up the greasy pole. Renowned dynasties that spring to mind are the family of Jawaharlal Nehru of India, the Kennedy mafia in the US, and the Chamberlains in the UK.

Objectivity about the formative years of the famous is scarcely possible. There will always be someone who claims in retrospect to have foretold a glorious career, and we can't know how many such predictions are made but go unfulfilled. Overmuch can be read into minor events of celebrities' histories which become encrusted with myth in the telling. Traumas and tribulations which are regular happenings in all lives become weighted with significance in theirs and have all kinds of fabulous outcomes attributed to them. How often do we read that Napoleon Bonaparte had to make himself mighty in order to overcome an inferiority complex induced by his small size? Thankfully, all men under five feet six inches do not behave like him.

My account of fledgling big shots is no more balanced than anyone else's, especially as biographical details are limited by faulty memories and biased agendas. My selection is non-random, my hypotheses unproven.

Intense ambition from an early age is a feature of some great men but by no means all. There is no way of knowing in any one case whether this was implanted by the suggestion of doting parents, or whether the parents simply reinforce an expression of early ambition. Bill Clinton so impressed his second grade teacher by his ability and enthusiasm that she told his mother Virginia, 'Some day he is going to be president.' His mother was blasé and admitted that she told him that every day. Later, a perspicacious friend was to comment that, though Bill always knew what he wanted to BE, he was far from clear about what he wanted to DO with that supreme role. In 1963, at the age of sixteen, Bill came face to face with John F Kennedy at the White House, only a few months before the assassination of the president. The photograph of their hand-shaking contact, with Bill's clean-cut, all-American look and worshipful gaze, is legendary. He used this highly defining moment to stake a claim on the god-like president, especially after his death, when

Bill's veneration assumed pathological intensity. 'Shake the hand that shook the hand of John F Kennedy' would become a rivetting introductory line.

At school, Bill was driven by the need for attention, to claim the spotlight, to win approval (often to a nauseating degree), and to excel at all things. He joined organisations seemingly for the express purpose of running for president of them. Occasionally, opponents would see the dark side of his ruthless determination to win. He accumulated medals and honours in the same way. At Georgetown University the pace of life became frantic, with the (self-imposed) need to collect acquaintances who might be useful, which he recorded on index cards with name and personal details, addresses and contact numbers: a network of future supporters. Maybe the same urgent need was the basis for his morbid fear of solitude. His campus activities and pursuit of class presidencies left little time for sleep, and he tried to make do with only five hours a night, especially as he knew this was a habit of great men including another of his idols, Martin Luther King.

Clinton's luminary Jack Kennedy in his youth was an almost complete contrast, a shy and bookish boy living in the shadow of his elder brother Joe, who was a replica of their tyrannical, all-controlling father. Jack's school-days were notable for his disorganisation and unruliness, by lack of direction and application. Though he was interested in a limited number of subjects, he had a short attention span and was readily bored. He was also gregarious and fun-loving. His father was highly instrumental in grabbing the presidency which he originally wanted for himself; but when he disqualified himself, the onus was placed on Joe Junior. Without his father's relentless ambition and the early death of Joe Junior in an aviation accident, JFK would never have made it on his own. He would never have got within shouting distance.

Oddly one gets the same impression of the young Tony Blair when reading his biography. He was so ordinary, so nondescript. Certainly his father had an expressed ambition to get into parliament as a Conservative, and was even said to have his sights set on the prime minister's place. When his aspirations were cut short by a stroke there is no evidence that Tony picked up the torch, or that his disabled father pushed him in this direction. It is possible though that his strings have been manipulated by another mentor, who imbued him with the necessary zeal. Of this, more in a later chapter.

William Gladstone, born into an affluent mercantile family in 1809, with a father who became an MP (though undistinguished), was a youth of boundless energy, both physical and mental. This drive was directed at first into reading and intellectual development at Eton and Oxford. The scope and extent of his reading, recorded in his diaries, is phenomenal and probably unequalled. He collected and stored information as avidly as we have seen Clinton collecting acquaintances, and he husbanded his time as carefully as his own father did his money. He was equally passionate about his Christianity, which permeated all his activities. Gladstone never did anything by halves, whether oration, travel, proposing marriage or conducting friendships, and his intensity at times verged on the maniacal. This could destabilise his judgment, with a tendency to obsessive fixation on the matter in hand to the exclusion of all else.

Sound judgment as a casualty of bottomless enthusiasm was also shown by Benjamin Disraeli in his early wrestlings with fate. He considered himself a youth of genius, misplaced and misunderstood, and indeed he had plenty of disadvantages to overcome. He was an outsider, a misfit, a victim of anti-Semitism, and hampered by a lack of classical education. He spent the first thirty years of his life trying to discover how to stand out from the crowd, which led him into a series of disastrous schemes, including wild financial speculation and the creation of a daily newspaper, both of which failed spectacularly and left him in appalling debt. His first novel, a reflection of contemporary society, saw him scarified mercilessly by the press. Everywhere around him in the *beau monde* he saw men achieving fame and fortune in an instant, and he wanted to do the same, by whatever means. When he eventually became an MP at the age of 33, his maiden speech, no doubt delivered with his usual flamboyancy, and on a controversial issue, was shouted down with howls of derision and mirth. The fact that he was not deterred but went on to become prime minister – in time – argues an unstoppable determination.

Characteristically, men of vaulting ambition are men in a tremendous hurry, often haunted by fear of an early death, before they have had time to achieve all the things their primeval instincts dictate. Winston Churchill on his 25th birthday, imprisoned and immobilised in South Africa as a spy during the Boer War, wrote, 'It is terrible to think of how little time remains.' The fear is realistic in such minds, for the reckless playing for high stakes invites catastrophes. Churchill was ambivalent: though he feared an early death, he wrote after being under fire, 'I do not believe the Gods would create so potent a being as myself for so prosaic an ending.' Horatio Nelson in his early twenties agonised over illnesses, fearing they might prevent him achieving the fame he sought. Oliver Cromwell was continually haunted by the fear that his time on earth would not allow him to complete his task as he saw it. Lenin had been told he would die young, and as a result put himself under relentless time pressure to pursue his brand of revolution. Napoleon Bonaparte, in his way as much a misfit as Disraeli, displayed an early taste for the military. When he entered the prestigious artillery corps in Paris, his social isolation and poverty (as well as the lack of imposed duties) led him to a self-imposed, workaholic lifestyle, spending all hours at his books, taking only one meal a day for economy's sake, and sleeping the bare minimum of hours. The Spartan habit was vindicated when he passed the two-stage commissioning exam in one sitting, an unusual feat attempted only by the most exceptionally gifted boys.

In times of turbulence and upheaval, ambitious drive may be thwarted and confounded at all turns, and is probably reinterpreted as sheer tenacity, though doubtless informed by opportunism. In 1920, Deng Xiaoping, then in his mid-teens, left his home in dislocated, war-torn China to join a work-study scheme in France, a project high on educational ideals but low on organisation and funding. When it failed, Deng, among others, was thrown back on his own resources in a foreign land, barely scraping an uncomfortable living. His experiences only made him tougher and more self-reliant, formulating ideals and joining the Communist Party, moving to the Soviet Union to study and thence back to China in a wave of young revolutionaries, travelling under conditions of unimaginable privation. Similarly, Mao Zedong was one of the legendary and mythical few to endure the appalling hardship and suffering of the Long March, emerging as a potential leader in the process.

Next to an iron will to succeed, a most important quality is charisma, that difficult-to-define magical attribute which few of either sex can resist. The whole Kennedy clan had it in cartloads, and so, manifestly (though it's lost on me), has Bill Clinton. What are the subtle messages that onlookers recognise? Some are obvious: a tall, imposing well-built figure, with handsome, regular, symmetrical features. A sense of self-confidence, ease and grace of movement, an impression of vibrant good health. Certainly an aura of controlled sexual potency, conveyed in body language, dress, facial expression, eye contact. Clinton's associates describe him as 'connecting' and liking to touch; when he shakes your hand, his other hand goes to your elbow or shoulder. Eye contact is hypnotisingly intense. It is all designed to make the recipient feel in unique rapport with him. It is identical to successful salesman technique: I can witness that drug company representatives do exactly the same.

The message must be received appropriately by both sexes. The voice is all-important. Leader figures even in embryonic form fill the room with their personalities and their talk; no matter if the content of the monologue is bland and banal. Shyness, reserve and self-doubt have no place in this make-up. It is axiomatic that, if your strength is to charm, your target must be susceptible to being wooed. Humans have extremely well-developed receptors for 'follower-ship' – a word first coined by Mrs Thatcher – which would-be charmers must locate and exploit to the uttermost. In their youth, many future leaders can be found heading small groups gathered for a variety of purposes. Vaclav Havel drew together a literary circle called the Thirty-Sixers, and his particular combination of personal attraction and diffidence saw him labelled 'a young sovereign'. More prosaically, Tony Blair's group activities were amateur stage-display of various sorts, in particular in a pop band, the Ugly Rumours. Disraeli was a wizard of wit and verbal elegance even at school, attracting a coterie of admiring scholars, and later on his enthusiasm and plausibility in his doomed business endeavours ensured a gullible few crashed with him. David Lloyd George led his school fellows in a show of disobedience at a public religious ritual, causing acute embarrassment to a devoted teacher, to whom he owed loyalty. A very attractive and popular person, with high spirits and a zest for living, he was accustomed to gaining approval of his actions even when he stepped out of line.

Yet charisma is hardly a core requirement since some successful aspirants have singularly lacked any claim to it. For instance, the continuing power to fascinate of Adolf Hitler is at least in part because he is so repellent. I imagine he functioned by mesmerising his listeners rather as a snake does with a sparrow. In his youth he was a loner, a failure, an indigent drifter, even a penniless dosser, totally lacking in appealing qualities. Richard Nixon also numbers among the unglamorous, described as unsexy by his fellow students. Prone to isolation and brooding, he had almost to dress himself in an interactive persona when it was needed. A journalist commented on how he would behave in social contacts like an automaton, or 'like a Barbie doll'. Napoleon Bonaparte and Horatio Nelson were diminutive men, neither well-favoured, and Napoleon was a morose lone-wolf in his youth. Slobodan Milosevic was described as notably lacking in physical grace, as being mundane, unoriginal, pedantic, self-effacing. Charisma is clearly not a *sine qua non*, and presumably other features can make up for the lack of it.

Coupled with personal attractiveness, perhaps an integral component of it, is sexual magnetism. Remembering Darwin's central thesis about the use of power for reproductive ends, it ought to be focal, and sometimes it obviously is. The modern public is selective in its attitude to overt sexual energy, and is certainly inconsistent. A man who is seen to dispense his sexual favours too freely is not one who will maintain his position on the pedestal. He will come crashing down, no longer viewed as a god. To maintain his mystique, his sensuality should be appreciated by individual members of his audience as their own private experience, potential energy, which female imagination can release and men can aspire to match. Women who discover the awful truth, that they are not themselves sole objects of worship, but mere facets to reflect masculine glory, can be severely and dangerously disillusioned, as happened with several lovers of Jack Kennedy and of Bill Clinton. Both of these men were obsessed with sex and women at an early age, and had multiple affairs, marked by a singular lack of commitment. Bill was repeatedly recorded as refusing to wear a condom in love-making. Both behaved as if determined to spread their genes around as widely as possible. The same propensities marked the ways of other Kennedy males, Vaclav Havel, Lloyd George, Disraeli; but again it is by no means a regular characteristic. Hitler's youth was remarkable for lack of interest in sex of any orientation, though it is said he acquired syphilis from a Jewish prostitute.

In spite of fanatical skirt-chasing, both Kennedy and Clinton were happiest and most at ease in the company of groups of men. Jack Kennedy in particular, as one lover described, always seemed to be surrounded by admiring men, avid for his friendship. They indulged in exciting, mysterious male-talk, during which women were side-lined, anonymous, unimportant. Yet the male adherents were mesmerised by his success with women. Even reporters seemed to want to be his friends, and their loyalty to him was assumed. This capacity for same-sex alliance-making, so crucial to the success of a rising politician, is very ancient behaviour. It dates back to the need for male bonding for purposes of defence, hunting and challenging a dominant figure. Clinton and Kennedy are incredibly accurately reproduced throw-backs to our pre-human, jungle ancestry. Feminists sometimes envy this capacity for male bonding, and believe women should try to interact in the same way; but it is an essentially utilitarian activity, however expressed in modern times, whether through old-boy networks, cricket clubs or the gang down at the pub. Or Clinton's remarkable collection of personal data, designed to make his acquaintance feel special, feel loved. This was pure deception, but it worked for him. Did he contravene the American equivalent of the Data Protection Act, I wonder?

Men on the make have a tendency to practise hero-worship themselves in the days of their novitiate, often with a fascination verging on the obsequious, and a habit of modelling their own behaviour on the figurehead. Sun Yat Sen's revolutionary activities awakened similar vibes in the mind of Mao Zedong. David Lloyd George fixed his sights on the star-qualities of Abraham Lincoln, a lawyer-cum-statesman; he was also fascinated by Napoleon. Napoleon himself favoured historical military figures such as Julius Caesar, but also took J J Rousseau as an intellectual mentor for his ideas on an ideal, equal society. Vladimir Lenin has much to answer for, having been held up as an icon to several generations of Soviet leaders, and responsible for a century of policies based on misconceived principles. Clinton worshipped JFK, of course. Tony Blair held up the Scottish philosopher J McMurray as his juvenile lodestar, with his take-home message of politics based on a community of individuals.

A recurrent and more prosaic theme in the development of famous men is a connection with the world of entertainment. Tony Blair's father was the illegitimate product of provincial show-people; John Major was a son of the circus; the mother of Lord Canning (prime minister in the 19th century) was an actress, a shaming disadvantage in that Victorian era; JFK's father's mistress (or one of them) was the movie goddess Gloria Swanson. The stage and screen have an irresistible allure for modern politicians, who naturally gravitate to the spotlight and admire anyone's ability to grab and handle universal attention. They are constantly available to view, and shrinking violets do not figure on the scene. Early histories show many politicians in school and amateur productions, usually quite successfully, which is a guarantor of delight in performing. Vaclav Havel's early career was in the theatre, writing his first play at 24, and risking his neck with satirical productions on the farcical contradictions of the communist totalitarian regime under which he lived. Many enjoyed early recognition in debate and oratory, logically enough; William Gladstone's genius in this regard was acknowledged at Eton and Oxford, where his reputation was immense long before he set foot in the House of Commons. Curiously, a number of political leaders have had a flirtation with the Church as a career, and though it is no surprise that people of a religious bent like Gladstone and Blair and even Robin Cook did so, Churchill's one-time thoughts of taking Holy Orders come as a surprise. Still more astounding is the fact that the arch-rogue, J

Edgar Hoover, chief of the Federal Bureau of Investigation in the US for fifty years, struggled like a demon against a perceived calling to enter the Church. But there is much theatricality in the Church, and a considerable amount of autonomous power to be wielded. Abraham Lincoln had it both ways: he liked to perform a skilled send-up of preachers for the entertainment of a circle of friends. The legal mind also takes naturally to politics, and examples are ten-a-penny: Lincoln, Attlee, Asquith, Blair, John Smith, Margaret Thatcher...

The level of intellectual ability and educational attainment of political leaders is diverse. In 19th-century UK, a classical education was deemed vital to a career in parliament, indeed an injudicious suggestion in the Commons that *The Times* was more useful reading for an aspiring man than a Latin primer was greeted with howls of derision. But other times and places do not have such rigid customs. Idi Amin of Uganda was of restricted intelligence, though streetwise, and, in the absence of any education to direct his career, drifted into the army – British, at that time. After independence he worked his way up to chief of staff and then took control of the country in an army-led coup. His lack of learning dogged him in his position of prominence, with insecurity and embarrassment accelerating his mounting paranoia, finally moving him to murder on a massive scale. Mao Zedong had memories of his youth as an assistant librarian – a humble low-paid job – in Beijing, when he was treated like a nobody, a country bumpkin of no means or importance. Later in life he affected to despise and distrust intellectuals, betraying them in his 'Hundred Flowers' campaign, labelling them rightists and uneducated bourgeois, sending them to the countryside to labour among the peasants. Mao, unlike many ambitious men, had not travelled in his youth, which undoubtedly helped to mould his xenophobia and Sinocentrism.

Mood swings are a common feature among men of drive, with the amplitude exaggerated or even caused by triumphs and disasters (leaving Kipling's sage, poetic advice unheeded). One might expect these oscillations in those whose turbulent nature made them social misfits, and indeed they are found in the early histories of Disraeli, Napoleon and Hitler. Disraeli spent much of his twenties, when he was submerged by failure and pursued relentlessly by creditors, in a state of morbid depression. Napoleon and Hitler, both dour loners, would break out into aggressive, violent diatribes in between spells of sullen withdrawal; these two had much in common. To Bill Clinton's few failures to win mini-presidencies at university he reacted with exaggerated grief and depression, a pattern that was repeated in spades when he lost the governership of Arkansas after only one term in office. This mood instability, verging on the pathological, is a pale preview of what happens later in life.

In pre-industrial times, and to a lesser extent since, men were accustomed to proving themselves in warfare or in hunting dangerous animals. Undoubtedly, over aeons of time these propensities were reinforced by natural selection because of the need to survive in a hostile environment. In a modern context, the most traditional way of all to win recognition is through military service and thence into politics, a path followed by Napoleon, Cromwell, Clive of India, Mao Zedong, John Kennedy and Churchill. Clinton on the other hand desired wholeheartedly to avoid the draft to Vietnam, and succeeded through influential string-pulling. Hitler welcomed the opportunity to fight in the First World War, falling on his knees with emotion (so he recorded in *Mein Kampf*) when called up. He is on record as previously avoiding the summons, though in peace-time. Those who achieve fame in the field have generally shown themselves unruly, undisciplined, even turbulent in formative years, with a particular propensity for risk-taking behaviour. In modern times this is often manifested as atrocious driving, with rule-breaking, reckless speed, tail-gating, and crazy overtaking (true of Clinton and Kennedy).

Winston Churchill was the prototype military-man-cum-politician, but he was in his most natural milieu when under arms. His early life, which reads like an issue of *Boy's Own* magazine, is a classic story of a primate learning how to display flamboyantly, present himself as a threat to the established order, challenge his immediate seniors, and single-mindedly fight his way to the top. His teenage years were marked by restlessness, a habit which has its roots in unlimited ambition more often than aimlessness. At 22 he was rebuked by his mother for drifting with no aim in life. With considerable difficulty he had been accepted for the Royal Military College, Sandhurst, then entered the Fourth Hussars, a cavalry regiment, as a second lieutenant. He loved danger and delighted to be in the thick of it, which propelled him into many risky situations, whether nearly drowning in Lake Lausanne or crashing through steeplechase fences on his horse. Born into class and privilege, he was able to dash around the world wherever trouble was brewing, looking for a chance to see action and hear shots fired. There was a double purpose in all this: first, in the excitement for its own sake, but more importantly his instinct told him that such adventures would equip him with fame and glory for a future political career, so he made himself known by headline-snatching and medal-winning, as well as by his own journalism.

At 20 he travelled to Cuba, where a rebellion was brewing. With gusto he joined the Spanish forces, being treated like royalty of course, but coming under frequent fire and pausing to ponder on the rights and wrongs of the dispute. A year later he begged his mother, Lady Randolph, to pull strings for him to be sent to South Africa, where there was a native uprising in Matabeleland. This time he was thwarted. He had foreseen such kudos for himself that he would be able to 'beat [his] sword into an iron despatch box'. Alas, he had to settle for India with his regiment and the path of duty. He agitated unsuccessfully to join Kitchener's army campaigning in Egypt, then panted after the war between Turkey and Greece, confessing he was indifferent as to which side to support. At last, in 1897, his regiment was sent to face rebels at the Afghan frontier, where he put himself in the front line in skirmishes, even when others were prudently taking cover, and frankly admitted he was playing to the galleries: his mother had persuaded the *Daily Telegraph* to publish his accounts of the war. Even at this young age his personal letters indicate a fixation that he was blessed in some way with special fortune, and marked by destiny, which may have been the reason why he took such risks in the firing line, admitting freely that he yearned for a reputation for grit and courage. He witnessed the savagery of the tribesmen in their treatment of captured enemies, and observed how the supposedly civilised British responded with almost equally barbarous reprisals, such as destroying water supplies and using the horribly shattering dum-dum bullet. While deprecating a descent into brutal practices, he had no compunction about labelling enemies with derogatory terms such as 'filthy' and 'odious', usually when justifying his primitive lust to kill.

Churchill had clear insight into his own ambition, and in a letter to his mother revealed, 'I do not care so much for the principles I advocate as for the impression which my words produce and the reputation they give me.' In this frank statement he admits how totally consuming is the fire of a man's desire for greatness – for its own sake. As with the genes, it has nothing to do with morality or philanthropy.

By dint of influence in high places, Churchill at last got himself attached to Kitchener's Expeditionary Force in Egypt, despite the fact that the general did not approve of his use of the army as a stepping stone to a career in public life. Churchill's account of the mighty Dervish army at Omdurman, viewed from the vulnerability of the tiny mounted reconnaissance patrol he was leading, conveys vividly the relish with which he pranced on his horse within range of the front ranks of combatants. It was here that he led his first cavalry charge, which nearly echoed the fate of the Light Brigade, as they faced rifle-fire rather than the expected spears. In the immediate aftermath, the leader and his men gave way to a wave of euphoria and animal spirits, looking for more action, before rapidly coming down to earth as they faced the obscene realities of blood and gore, disfigurement, death and ghastly destruction. The young officer was still sensitive enough to be appalled by the horrors of war and to retain a sense of honour, which condemned Kitchener's consenting to his men's acts of barbarity such as killing wounded Dervishes and vandalising the Mahdi's tomb and buried corpse.

Churchill's next serial adventure was in South Africa, as a special correspondent reporting on the Boer War. Attaching himself to an army captain on a reconnaissance trip by armoured train, he was soon in the heart of the action as their train was ambushed, derailed, then hammered by artillery fire. As always, Churchill rose to the occasion with a combination of heroic gallantry and automatic assumption of leadership, by supreme effort restoring the train and rescuing the wounded. By multiple miracles he escaped death but was taken prisoner by the Boers. The immediate indignities of his situation, which were not ameliorated by his credentials as a journalist, may have been a good trade-off for the headlines and front-page stories (reported worldwide) of his courage and daring at the derailment. But he could not bear to be idle, and so planned an escape with two others; by some mischance, Churchill alone got free. Without speaking Dutch and having no survival kit whatsoever, his chances of success were slim. By a stroke of fortune he fell into the hands of an English mine-owner, hiding deep in a rat-infested mine for days as a frantic search for him raged above ground. Eventually, concealed by bales of wool in a railway wagon, he escaped to Portuguese East Africa. These colourful exploits made him a hero both in South Africa and at home at a time of depressing British defeats. Pausing only to savour the heady delights of adulation in Durban, he dived again into the maelstrom of activity near the front line. This time he accepted a commission, so that he was a soldier as well as a journalist, and contrived to be at all the hot spots where decisive events were happening, such as the relief of Ladysmith and the advance to Pretoria.

Then, feeling he had won his spurs, and amazed at how his luck in self-preservation had held out for so long, he turned his sights to another arena: back home he became the prospective Conservative candidate for Oldham. He was still light-years away from the prime ministership, but in the ensuing years he was never far from the limelight, his fortunes rising and falling. Most men of ambition have only one chance to achieve the heights, but Churchill had several runs at it. Doubtless his rank in society, his wealth, courage, charisma, alliance-making skills and diversities of talent – of oratory, journalism and authorship – assisted him in this. But he seems to have been a lovable rogue too, with unusual honesty and insight.

I have said very little so far of ideology. Youth is a time of ideals, formulated in a situation analogous to opposition, when there is little or no chance to put them into practice. Undoubtedly they were there in all these examples, and most fervently held at times of chaos and disruption. Overwhelmingly though, in these lives there comes across a streamlined sense of self-propulsion, a pursuit of one's own agenda, a grim determination to dominate in some field, no matter who else gets left behind. These young sahibs wanted their own way and wanted to be highly visible when getting it. The boy Churchill's life, which I've quoted at length, is a particularly good example of this ingrained and over-riding egocentricity, which he frankly recognised and recorded. Morality and ideology are flimsy garments artistically draped to hide the nakedness of the winning streaker.

This self-absorption does not repel but rather the reverse: it attracts, which is a phenomenon in its own right. Thus dominance becomes self-perpetuating. It promotes some unattractive traits of course, including a common charge of extreme stinginess. Of both Jack Kennedy and Bill Clinton, the Duke and Duchess of Windsor and others, it was said that they never paid for anything if they could avoid it. Winston Churchill's exclusivity revealed itself in ugly, racist language, talking of the 'expulsion from Europe of the filthy Oriental', and in antagonism to women's emancipation, expostulating, as Hitler did, that a woman's place was to marry, give birth to children and to be represented only through her husband's opinions. Let this be the last word in this chapter; the emphasis has come round again to reproduction and exploitation of the weaker by the stronger.

CHAPTER 5

Swagger and Scrimmage

If you view history as the consequence of genetically programmed human behaviour, suddenly it takes on a completely different perspective. Earth-shattering events occur, not because of ideologies, principles, messages from God, mass movements or magnetic fields, but as the result of pretty conventional animal motivation. But men know that if they can obfuscate and convince the people that their aims are on a more elevated plane, devoid of self and replete with altruism, they are more likely to achieve their ends. Religion and morality are the most effective and clever means of disguising egotism.

Religion was used to convincing effect by Oliver Cromwell, as he clambered his way to power using the most ruthless methods, wholly contrary to his usual gentlemanly, affectionate and susceptible nature. He listened carefully to his atavistic promptings and misinterpreted them as the voice of God. He was deluded and truly believed himself the vehicle of God's will. His enemy Charles, no natural leader, having inherited his throne rather than seized it, was a typical weakling who resorted to control-freakery and arrogance. Out of tune with growing popular emancipation, he played into Cromwell's hands. Volumes have been written attempting to analyse the strands and sequences of the Civil War in Britain in the 17th century. Fascination is proportional to incomprehension. The event is encapsulated, simplified and most readily understood through the natures of the two chief protagonists.

Charles was something of an obsessional type, and stubborn, whose yearning for control was first practised on himself. Disciplined to the point of rigidity, he was instructed by his father's dictatorial precepts (rather than practice), ever aware of the disparity between expectation and reality. Having been a puny and delicate child, slow to achieve milestones and burdened with a stammer, he was not equipped for impressive centre-stage displays, apart from temper tantrums. His naturally reserved and undemonstrative nature, which made him awkward when interacting with individuals, was reinforced by the belief of innate superiority instilled into him every moment of his waking life. He clung to family members and needed to be loved, but was shy in making friends outside his circle of intimates, often preferring solitude to company. He was enduringly loyal to those in whom he placed his confidence, and showed an extreme of reverence for his royal parents and elder brother. His fervent desire to please his mentors may have been a protective device. He was also sexually inhibited. His father King James I, who was fond of disputacious discussion, pushed the ten-year-old Charles into a public debating contest with a group of royal chaplains on some religious topic. Oratory was perceived as a necessary princely acquirement. For a tongue-tied stripling this was an immense ordeal. Though he later spoke in the House of Lords, public speaking was never to his taste, and he even found it demeaning.

Enclosed and isolated in his structured world, Charles never developed any warmth for the people over whom his family ruled. When he became king he established a human shield around himself of like-minded councillors, and any outsiders would find this impenetrable to both persons and petitions. He was astoundingly lacking in tact, telling a challenging parliament in his arrogance that he did not threaten the House because he would scorn to threaten any but his equals. Such a remote person must have some outlet for his affections, which for Charles was his enthusiasm for the aesthetic, expressed in a passion for art and a preference for elaborate ritual in his devotional life. He would have been perfectly happy if destiny had left him alone as a wealthy, dilettante collector of paintings. As it was, he spent all available funds on this costly diversion while ignoring the more pressing dictates of his kingly debts and policies. This self-indulgence gave ever watchful opportunists a port of access to the king's inner circle of friends and influencers.

Charles' distorted perception of himself as the still point of the turning world is reminiscent of Machiavellian precepts, but his head-in-air notion of his royal station as ordained by God, *ergo* sacrosanct, would have caused that pragmatic theorist to despair. In Charles' era there occurred eruptions around the country which developed into metaphorical volcanoes, and which accorded men a foothold to clamber up and observe him perched on his lofty peak – and to ponder why this inaccessible, contemptuous, dandified weakling should occupy that desirable position rather than themselves. Among the volcanoes were the Church (or rather Churches), the army and parliament. Among the royal watchers was Oliver Cromwell.

Oliver, the gentlemanly squire, with a toehold in the world of influence, multi-connected, only became prominent as a result of his unexpected military capabilities and success as an army leader in the first Civil War (1642). If he had never had the opportunity to discover those skills, it is possible he would have lived out his life as a big fish in a small pond, a decent and forceful enough chap, though inclined to religiosity and unfulfilled yearnings for aims unspecified, which made him morose from time to time.

In his early parliamentary days, Oliver was no natural orator, though a sturdy self-belief gave his rustic tongue a 'strong and masculine eloquence'. He spoke with passion and vigour, verging on violence at times, capable of holding and moving the House; but it was a skill acquired by practice. When, however, he mustered a troop of horse in 1642 at the age of 43 to wage war for the first time in his life, he was quite suddenly in his element. Cavalry tactics at the time were slow-paced and ritualistic, an elaborate war-dance reminiscent of animals in the wild, posturing and measuring each other up before engaging. Cromwell dispensed with all this punctilio, leading his men in at the headlong charge, homing in to kill. He perceived the necessity of involving and motivating his troops, which he did by engaging their loyalty and working on their religious fervour. He also established other simple but brilliantly effective techniques, such as the discipline of gathering his forces together after a charge, to follow up and consolidate his attacks. There were no half-hearted measures for him. He was also the first to engineer a safe retreat when prudence demanded, an unknown military tactic at the time. His single-minded goal was to win the war decisively, unlike some of his allies, who more logically reasoned that war would not actually resolve the dispute with the king.

Cromwell's commitment, hook, line and sinker, to the war and its outcome is apparent from various emotional displays. The supply of money, such an enabling and motivating essential, caused him to write many letters and make much energetic pleading, resulting in even tears of frustration when it did not materialise. He poured in his own modest resources when he could. He adored his men and their horses, calling them 'my lovely company', revelling with them in bawdy jokes and roughneck repartee. On the eve of battle he could show uncontrolled excitement, with outbursts of hysterical laughter and euphoria: 'as another man is when he hath drunken a cup of wine too much'. This overdosing on adrenaline spread infectiously round the troops. The night before the Battle of Dunbar (1650) in the worst of Scottish east-coast weather, he rode among his men in his accustomed strange, elated, hyperactive mood, biting his lip till the blood ran, giving voice to his demonic laugh amid the earnest prayers of his wakeful soldiers.

Earlier in his careeer, as his successes in the field accumulated and his reputation grew, boosting his own confidence, he became progressively convinced that the hand of God was upon him, that he was fated to prosecute the fight as an instrument of the Lord's will. His triumphs he attributed to the approval of Providence. Thus do many people justify doing what their inner nature dictates, and for what their inherited skills befit them, truly unconscious of the false morality to which they are in thrall. What were the mighty motives that underlay such dedication? It is difficult to define them; indeed he couldn't do so himself. As a member of parliament under the leadership of Pym in the years leading up to the war, he had little depth of understanding or even much interest in the swirling debates and issues. He disliked autocracy as many profess to do when they are at the receiving end of it, distrusted the monarch Charles, and wished the voice of a strongly led but representative parliament to be paramount. He also desired the abolition of authoritarian bishops and a new freedom of conscience in devotional life. In a moment of clear-sightedness he responded to a challenger, 'I can tell you, sir, what I would not have, though I cannot what I would.'

The year 1643 saw the start of his meteoric rise, from captain of horse to most consistently successful parliamentary cavalry commander. His zeal and vigour in recruiting men and in moulding them into effective soldiers, at a time when most ordinary citizens were blissfully unaware or apathetic about the conflict, is in striking contrast to his wishy-washy professed motivation. Cromwell, at times eaten up by self-doubt, brooked no dissent on those occasions when he saw the way ahead, and in all his military life his decision-making was of this order. War was also a milieu in which he was supremely happy and fulfilled, not least because in war nothing succeeds like success. His victories made him popular with his soldiers and the people, and influential among the men of parliament.

Cromwell's fanatical mingling of religion and military fervour must have been terrifying to those of a moderate and peace-loving persuasion. He would tolerate no suggestion that their quarrel with the king could not be resolved by fighting. But he quite rightly doubted within himself that this might be true, and the rankling thought caused him depression and anxiety when away from the heat and success of battle. Nevertheless, at the end of a series of decisive victories in 1646, with the war temporarily at a stop, he was a figure of authority, his services recognised by financial reward and an access of veneration which never doubted that prevailing in battle would translate seamlessly into ability in governing.

But Cromwell was not yet well versed in politics. Moreover, the war had predictably resolved nothing; indeed it had polarised the people, who, wanting stability, peace and the old devils of state and Church, were more royalist than parliamentarian. In his own personal hiatus, Cromwell slid again into depression, disillusion and physical illness: a characteristic pattern. He hankered after pursuing his military career on the Continent, ostensibly in support of religious toleration for the German calvinists, but decided crucially to stay and pursue his novitiate in politics. In this, fate assisted him. With no strong hand at the helm of government, factions arose; the army refused to disband and began to threaten parliament with a long list of grievances. Charles, observing at a distance, felt his spirits rise as he perceived the descent of his enemies into infighting. But Cromwell's enormous prestige and influence with the army enabled him to act as mediator and defuse the crisis, adding to his credentials as budding statesman.

Charles stonewalled and refused to meet parliamentary demands, as threats of anarchy, revolution and bids for various forms of government by popular assent bubbled on. Cromwell's recurrent gloom deepened into despair, aggravated by the realisation that a growing faction distrusted him. He did not recognise his own powerful ambition, but others did. His well-known, mysterious statement that 'No-one rises so high as he who knows not whither he is going' was accurate. He did not recognise the primitive drives within him, and continued to act on them as divine inspiration.

In 1648, when war erupted a second time, Oliver resumed his arms, looking to God for guidance in prosecuting his holy war. It is agreed by those who understand such things that he had an astounding genius for these campaigns, and his sequence of victories ran on. He was still prey to mood swings and inner torment, wanting to believe that his successes were indeed marks of Providential approval, and maybe the promptings of his subtle ambition were already whispering that Charles as the source of all the disputation might be eliminated by a pact with the same high authority. The Rump Parliament in London came stepwise to the same conclusion, that Charles should be put on trial. But what then? And Oliver, who was by inclination pro-monarchy and no egalitarian, shifted his ground and, in spite of all the reasoned arguments against, fell in with those who planned the death sentence. This appalling step he rationalised by a piece of moral gymnastics, avowing that the stamp of God's approval made this traitorous act legitimate.

Oliver was a part of the tiny and wholly illegal court that tried the king as tyrant and traitor of his own people. The action stunned the common folk and repulsed the majority of those of influence, while

Europe looked on in horror. But the fanatical movers and shakers clutched at their usurped divine authority as well as their primitive urges and, most important, the army to reinforce their will. Cromwell's dismal mood dispersed and was replaced by one of elation, even intoxication, as he over-rode the waverers at the signing of the death warrant with a coarse mix of iron will and rough schoolboy humour.

Oliver was now part of a ruling oligarchy, the vestige of a parliament elected nine years previously, whose authority was only held by the backing of the army. The Council of State of which he was now president held a precarious existence, labelled a tyranny and so condemned at home and abroad, and with ferments of discontent in its military arm. The most immediate threats were Ireland and Scotland, where, it was believed, royalist supporters would muster forces to reimpose the monarchy in the shape of the young Prince Charles.

Revitalising his officers with a stirring speech, Oliver led a force to Ireland, charged with civic and military power to quell that country into subjugation. Conscious of the psychological impact of a show of grandeur, he left in a splendid parade of coaches, horses, uniforms and brash fanfare. Like the newly arrived alpha male in the wild, he had much strenuous business in rushing about noisily and visibly, displaying fiercely to intimidate challengers and rebels. The savagery with which he succeeded in Ireland reverberates down the centuries. His attack on Drogheda was ruthless, efficient and totally without mercy. No quarter was considered, with even churches being sacked and burned, escapees hunted down and slain in cold blood, every friar murdered and citizens mowed down in the orgy of killing. The Scottish author John Buchan describes Cromwell in his book *Oliver Cromwell* as 'rapt in a mood of blind animal ferocity'.

Part of his intention was to cow the rest of the country into swift submission to avert a prolonged campaign, so that he could dash off to defend his status in Scotland and elsewhere. As ever he ascribed his supremacy in Ireland to the Spirit of God, visiting judgement through his medium on miserable sinners. How else could he live with such a bestial manifestation of his prehistoric ancestry? For Oliver was not in his human self a cruel or a vicious man. There are

many instances of his gallantry and compassion, his strict control of
soldiers looting, his almost feminine softness to individuals in
sorrow and bereavement, and his tenderness to his own extended
family, to whom he was writing loving letters even as he prosecuted
his rape of Ireland.

Oliver consolidated his power-play by dispossessing many Irish
people of their lands and sending them into exile, while he headed
off to Scotland as commander-in-chief, with the same sense of
urgency and ever watching his back for signs of rebellion. He had
greater respect for the Scots, whose army was more of a match for
him, but at Dunbar, after much tactical skirmishing, his might
prevailed. Meanwhile, the young Charles had been crowned at
Scone, and this nucleus of royal support was the next threat to be
quashed. The ensuing cat-and-mouse chase down the length of
England to Worcester has been described as one of the most brilliant
pursuits in the history of British arms, and Oliver's organisation was
meticulous, fulfilling the definition of genius as an infinite capacity
for taking pains.

From being perilously isolated after the execution of the king,
Oliver Cromwell, the triumphant victor of Worcester, now was a
national hero to the fickle multitude, and was treated like a monarch.
In our habit of exalting and deferring to whatever is powerful and
victorious, we are at our least moral and most animal-like. Now,
approaching his zenith, Oliver dismounted from his war-charger and
climbed aboard his moral high-horse, as he looked around his
country devastated by years of war and its consequences, and sought
a way to govern it.

A re-assembling of parliamentary government in a republican
England might seem to be the logical step, but now Oliver began to
quarrel with the self-seeking and aggrandising propensities of many
members of the House and to suggest a supreme power to keep them
in check: 'Some authority and power so full and so high as to
restrain and keep things in better order.' At the time there were many
besides himself who saw him as destined for kingship. The common
people should have listened to the Earl of Montrose a few years
earlier: 'Do you not know, when the monarchical government is
shaken, the great ones strive for the garlands with YOUR blood and

YOUR fortune? Whereby you gain nothing . . . but shall purchase to yourselves vultures and tigers to reign over you.'

Cromwell's quarrel with parliamentary corruption overflowed in a furious speech of moral condemnation, which may have had more to do with an intercurrent threat to his position as Lord-General than an offended code of ethics. He dissolved parliament on the spot with a show of arms by a band of musketeers. He acted in the same despotic way as Kings James and Charles had done before him, and he was to do so again when the deliberations of parliament did not suit him. Under a new system of parliamentary franchise, Oliver as the supreme potantate became lord-protector – an interesting euphemism. This man of the people became ever more autocratic, as a law was passed rendering ill-speech of him a treasonable offence. Though he refused the title of king when it was pressed upon him, he had all the appurtenances of the royal state, the power, authority, prestige, riches, opulence and protection. He filled the new House of Lords with his cronies, supporters and family members.

Then, unaccountably and illogically, he set about extending England's influence overseas, at a time when the country was in chaos and social dislocation, with the discipline of a police state imposed and none of the comforts of prosperity restored. The spreading abroad of influence requires a heavy tax burden, which would have added to the oppression of his downtrodden people. But he thought of an expanding English influence (*Lebensraum*, it might be called), which would by proxy be all his own.

Lucky for him, he died before these inconsistencies could bring about his downfall.

In his climbing years, Cromwell had deplored the dictatorial nature of kingship and all its baggage, but as soon as he arrived at the summit, he perceived that order was more easily achieved under a single powerful influence. 'Remember that parliaments are altogether in my power for their calling, sitting and dissolution; therefore as I find the fruits of them good or evil, they are to continue or not to be.' This was actually said by Charles I, but it might have been said by Cromwell with equal veracity. Once in power, he replicated the age-old pattern. He became supreme statesman through his success as a fighting man, which sequence is recognisable throughout history, and in the present day happens uncomfortably often in the shape of military coups. Only comparatively recently, usually in periods of stability and order, have men become politicians without earning recognition through physical conflict. Let's look at some further examples of soldier-statesmen, practising their art of eye- and ear-catching displays.

Adolf Hitler's ego, being counterbalanced by no moderating influence, was the ultimate opportunist. From an early age he was fixated with a belief in his own destiny, and only needed to find a medium for fulfilling it. If he had only had genuine artistic genius, what a chunk of dreadful history the world might have been spared. Hitler possessed insight into his own capabilities at first, and likewise had a certain understanding of raw human nature. Just how he came by this knowledge is a mystery: it is an unusual acquisition for one so self-absorbed. He probably discovered as a young dropout the power of intimidation and fear as a result of his fierce rantings. His associates no doubt treated this morose and loud-mouthed eccentric with a measure of respect and placatory body-language, reinforcing his bully-boy traits. Although he evaded military service for years, he fought bravely at the front in the First World War, and was wounded, promoted and decorated. There is much evidence that he really felt glad and fulfilled to be in uniform, with enforced discipline and an aim in life, even seemingly content for the moment to allow the 'interest of one's ego . . . to be subordinated to the common interest'. A penchant for military paraphernalia stayed with him all his life, and underpinned his organisation of the Nazi Party. After the war, looking to maintain his new identity, he fell in with a group of agitators, recruited and quickly trained to counterbalance the communistic, anti-nationalistic propaganda being fed to the returning, disillusioned troops. He was a natural for the job. It was here he discovered his power of rhetoric, of compelling, rabble-rousing, street-corner oratory.

Within the embryonic Nazi Party, he practised his hell-fire brand of speaking. He drew a gang of thugs and bouncers around him to protect and intimidate, sometimes to actively threaten other political gatherings. This squad eventually became the notorious Sturm

Abteilung (SA). In the years of his struggle he spoke, night after night after night, in meetings large and small, in towns throughout the Reich. In this, his workaholic commitment is a pattern I readily recognise as an ex-political wife. His speeches were a two-way affair, judging responses, learning to manipulate his audience and secure their attention.

To these two formidable weapons of commanding speech and strong-arm intimidation, Hitler added a third: propaganda. He was fascinated by the ways by which one man could control a mass movement, observing in his idle years the management of huge demonstrations in Vienna and the tactics of Austrian Social Democrat leaders, also learning from enemy moral manipulation in the war. In *Mein Kampf* he declared, 'The art of leadership consists of consolidating the attention of the people against a single adversary and taking care that nothing will split up this attention.' The concept of an enemy being necessary for dictatorship is important for peace-lovers to note. In this ghastly book, the chapter on war propaganda is Hitler's analysis of how to mesmerise and lead by the nose the unthinking, uneducated masses by an appeal to the emotional side, a stirring up of moral hatred, and the implanting of a few memorable slogans. In putting this theory into practice, he succeeded; his assessment was correct.

When Hitler consistently failed to get a legitimate electoral majority in the Reich with his Nazi Party, the eleven or twelve million votes he commanded were nevertheless an essential support allowing no one faction to get a nose ahead of the rest. With the turbulent SA at his beck and call he was potentially a highly inflammatory opponent. Field Marshall Von Hindenberg, President of Germany and a tired old aristocratic soldier in his eighties, held emergency powers to govern. Surrounded by younger men who imposed their views, he was beset by factions, with scurrilous in-fighting, threats and blackmail, deals and backstabbing, men hovering like hyenas to advance themselves through the murk. Hindenberg believed that Hitler's might was more controllable on-side, and brought him into the coalition.

Thereafter, Hitler became chancellor, rode rough-shod over his opponents and began to look beyond Germany, to demand demolition of the Treaty of Versailles (which hamstrung Germany's power after the First World War) and to re-arm. The ominous pattern of radar blips was picked up by Churchill who had earned his not altogether unjustified reputation for bellicosity before the war at the Admiralty, observing the expansion of the German Navy. In 1934, Churchill was out of office, though in parliament. Courageously and persistently he warned of German military strength and expansionist intentions. He was a lone voice, often the target of organised hostility and mockery, as the government blindly pursued policies of disarmament, largely for reasons of economy, blithely ignoring the signs that were as much on display for them as for Churchill. The Oxford University Union mirrored the relaxed complacency of the times as the bright young things voted in a student debate that 'This House refuses in any circumstances to fight for King and Country'.

Churchill did in truth have an immoderate enthusiasm for guns and battleships. That seemed to come in his genes, but his brain and its ability to respond to experience made him by intellect a peace-monger. Prime Ministers Baldwin and later Chamberlain did not have the equivalent insight, and Churchill's vociferous views were ignored. To an accusation of anti-German obsession he said, 'British policy for four hundred years has been to oppose the strongest power in Europe by weaving together a combination of other countries strong enough to face the bully...It is thus through the centuries we have kept our liberties and maintained our power.' This glosses over British adventurism and other unspeakables of course. But his historical knowledge and understanding of alliances and posturing allowed him to read the situation accurately. It takes one alpha male to recognise another. His warnings about the unprepared state of the British armed forces held no weight with Chamberlain, who was a born appeaser and deferrer, ignorant of the ruthlessly tunnelled ambition of dictators such as Hitler and Mussolini.

When Chamberlain avowed that tension in Europe was easing, Hitler gave him the lie by seizing Austria, invading Czechoslovakia and stepping up the atrocities on the Jewish population. Hitler recognised even then that his true opponent in Britain was Churchill, whom he attacked in competitive mode: 'Mr Churchill may have an electorate of 15,000 or 20,000. I have one of 40,000,000.' This sounds immensely like playground discussions, everyone going one better, ending up in wildly exorbitant claims.

Churchill said publicly that Hitler did not need to fire a single shot to extend his power in the Danube basin in Poland, Romania, Bulgaria and Yugoslavia. He understood the power of fear to make whole countries helpless and deferential, just as it had rendered Chamberlain and his colleagues. Hitler rounded on Churchill repeatedly, sneering at his reference to anti-Nazi forces in Germany: 'I can assure this man, who seems to live on the moon, that there are no forces in Germany opposed to the Regime.' Indeed not: they had all been cowed. Churchill was at this time an MP with no official position, a lone voice crying in the wilderness, vilified by his colleagues, isolated in public opinion. Yet Hitler deemed it necessary to attack him. Hitler's finance minister imprudently mentioned to a visiting British general that Churchill was the only Englishman Hitler feared. But the fact that Churchill was kept out of office sent the message that Britain too was likely to prove supine.

With the invasion of Poland, Chamberlain's dithering had to stop. War was declared. Churchill had been right all along, and his stock rose in parliament and the country. He became First Lord of the Admiralty. With tempers roused, teeth and claws bared at the succession of calamities, parliament turned on Chamberlain in a devastating show of hostility. Members of all parties looked to the strong, big man in this terrible crisis, and Churchill at last became prime minister. One might fancy Hitler had predicted this sequence of events if we didn't know he was talking of himself in *Mein Kampf*:

> By virtue of a natural order, the strongest man is destined to fulfill the great mission; yet the realisation that this ONE is the exclusively elect usually comes to the others very late. On the contrary they ALL see themselves as Chosen and having equal rights for the solution of the task.

Historians are too enmeshed in the minutiae of their subject and its bottomless capacity for theorising and debating over brief episodes and ephemeral lives, its inevitable bias, to stand sufficiently far back to recognise how formulaic and quasi-cloned the behaviour of heroes really is. So many aspects of human sophistication enable us to obfuscate and screen the truth: the power of language to euphemise, the force of morality to mesmerise, the security of concrete walls behind which to conceal shameful practices. We live in a mysterious world similar to that of Orwell's *1984*, in which nothing is quite what it seems and history is constantly rewritten.

Any evolutionist will tell you that deception and misleading are capacities that are vital to the evolutionary history of all living things: plants and animals and unclassified beings. Whether we are talking of mimicry among insects as a protective device, the cuckoo's egg in an alien nest, or flamboyant features such as the peacock's tail to broadcast sexual fitness, these characteristics are unconscious. Richard Dawkins in *Climbing Mount Improbable* tells an amazing tale of mutually dependent figs and parasitic wasps that is riven with 'hard bargaining...trust and betrayal...temptation to defect policed by unconscious retaliation'. When deception has been such an integral part of development from time out of mind, it is no wonder that it continues to play a part in our behaviour patterns, patterns of such ancient, pre-human origin that it is doubtful whether we can escape them altogether.

Richard Nixon was an habitual liar, even while extolling the beauty of truth as he set out on his 1968 presidential contest. He had long since learned to hide his pugilistic tendencies under a semi-transparent veil of seeking national peace and security through a professed policy of 'taking the offensive in the ideological struggle'. There are many who know better now, and who certainly did so at the time of his death in 1994, yet all joined in the attempt to reinstate him as a great though flawed president, including the lasting memorial on his gravestone which reads: 'The greatest honour history can bestow is the title of peacemaker.' Peacemaker? This must be some new meaning of the word.

In 1972, as he faced the hope of a second term in office, his ruthless fight to remain at the top against his opponent Democrats is redolent of Machiavelli's Prince or any jungle-based conqueror. Nixon's self-love led him to record all his conversations in the Oval

Office of the White House, and they are ample evidence of the disparity between spin and substance. People who want to wield over-arching power, as we've seen, must identify an enemy – or enemies – presumably to polarise and focus the active support of allies. Nixon was a practised hater who saw enemies everywhere. On the 1968 campaign trail, human rights and democracy had fled before his strong-arm tactics. He wanted hecklers and protesters suppressed: 'Kick the weirdos and beardos on the college campuses.' He ordered his Secret Service men to act as aggressors, but they refused. So he got his aides to organise a posse of off-duty police and firemen to organise the rough stuff where needed. Here was a replica of Hitler and his embryonic Sturm Abteilung. In 1972, sinking to more blatant thuggery, Nixon's SA was composed of selected professional killers, instructed to kidnap, drug and contain anti-Republican demonstrators.

The best-remembered scandal of Nixon's time in office was the creation of 'enemy lists', which were a major preoccupation of himself and his aides. They included prominent people in politics, the media, business, industry and academia – all potentially capable of frustrating his plans or undermining his image. Indeed, anyone who had publicly slighted a friend or family member was registered, a target for revenge. One tactic was, by devious means, to launch a tax investigation to unearth any scandalous evasions. With the approaching 1972 presidential election, Nixon's venom was focused on his Democratic challengers, Edward Kennedy, Edmund Muskie, Hubert Humphrey and George McGovern, all of whom were pursued with predatory ferocity. Edward Kennedy's hopes had been crippled by the scandal of Chappaquidick in 1969, when he crashed his car off a bridge and left Mary Joe Kopechne in it to drown. But Nixon feared the charismatic Kennedys and, leaving nothing to chance, organised his own undercover investigation of the tragedy and its aftermath, hoping to stir up even more dirt on the senator. In particular they hoped to 'catch him in the sack with one of his babes'. Nixon, in his crazy arrogance and the privacy of his office, muttered for posterity into his tape-recorder, 'Catch this son of a bitch and ruin him for 76.'

The plan for Hubert Humphrey (who had run Nixon close

previously for vice-president) was to put a spy among his staff to undertake guerilla-style subversion; to foster rumours of financial misdeeds and to spawn accusations of war-mongering. Senator Edmund Muskie looked like the front-runner for the Democrats, and opinion polls showed him to be on Nixon's heels. He was a marked man. Unable to dig up personal odium, the Nixon team distributed scabrous false mailings, purporting to come from Muskie, which reflected badly on him. They also spread ugly rumours about his wife. Muskie was sufficiently traumatised to suffer an emotional breakdown in the middle of a speech, after which his image never recovered. Some say he had been fed a destabilising cocktail of LSD beforehand.

George Wallace, Governor of Alabama, was perceived as a threat on account of his standing in the 1968 election. If he could be made to lose the governorship, he would cease to be a candidate for the 1972 presidential race. Accordingly, funds were channelled by Nixon's collaborators to Wallace's opponents, and at the same time an in-depth tax investigation begun with rumours of corruption. Wallace survived the dirty tricks, remaining as governor and as challenger for the White House. But politics in the US are a high-risk sport, and he was shot by an unhinged protestor, not killed but permanently paralysed. Nixon put on an over-the-top act of public concern. Behind the scenes, however, his main agenda was to ensure there were no nasty rumours connecting his own campaign with the madman. Attack being the best form of defence, his team grabbed the initiative and spread implicatory stories about Senator McGovern, who by now was the only remaining viable opponent. In spite of Nixon's frantic machinations, there were those in the Washington press who speculated on his involvement in attempted murder, a suspicion shared by Wallace himself.

With Wallace now out of the running, Senator McGovern alone remained to take the full force of the savage squad. His committee offices situated in the Watergate complex were the object of the break-ins that were to prove Nixon's nemesis. Even now it is not quite clear what exactly they were after, but certainly it was information to damage the Democratic cause, whether on Cuba and Castro or sexual improprieties. Maybe they also wanted to retrieve damaging material on Nixon himself, his 'shit file'.

The Republican team resorted to illegal means to finance this campaign of violence, accepting vast contributions (which came in suitcase loads of cash) from foreign sources, including the Shah of Iran, President Marcos of the Philippines, and a fabulously wealthy Saudi businessman, Adnan Khashoggi. Threats were used to extort money from American business magnates who were told that nothing less than a million would do. Their livelihood was at stake. Bribes were gladly taken from those men who aspired to become ambassadors.

Getting drunk on his orgy of enemy-identification and hate, Nixon ordered ever mightier strikes against the Communist forces in Vietnam. Nor were these distant peoples the only object of his murderous intention. Long after the Watergate investigations had concluded, evidence would come to light that he and his aides discussed ways of murdering a journalist, Jock Anderson, who had repeatedly reported Nixon's scurrilous anti-democratic activities, bribery and corruption.

Finally, with his second-term presidency in the bag, Nixon celebrated by ordering an intensification of the war offensive in Vietnam, seeking through a blood-bath to smash and squelch his way out of the war. He announced to his family and close advisers that he did not care if he achieved a worldwide reputation for craziness: let them think he was mad, and fear him accordingly. Another of his first moves in his second term was to seek revenge on all who had opposed him. He commented that he now held 'awesome power with no discipline, that is, there won't be another election coming up to discipline us'. This is indeed a chilling thought, and one may speculate how Stalinesque Nixon might have become if it hadn't been for the American constitution and the bull-dog tenacity of the journalists who exposed him.

For the megalomania was now clearly evident. On Christmas Eve 1972, he recorded in his diary, 'It is God's great gift to me to have the opportunity to exert leadership not only for America but on the world scene.' This vision of sacred, personal destiny seems to be an illusion in the mind of every man who wields political power. Nixon also talked of altering the constitution to enable him to run for a third term, and of establishing a perpetual presidency with the power to pick his successor. He made plans for his family to stand for office in order to found a Kennedy-like dynasty.

In his moment of glory – his 'coronation' and landslide victory – he was not triumphant; he was morose and troubled. In this he behaved like the primitive animal who knows that at the top there are no friends, and you keep your position by fighting off all comers – until the time when someone is stronger than you. Every political career ends in failure and in an accumulation of enemies which must be terrible to contemplate.

CHAPTER 6

The Classic Alpha Male

The classic alpha male is defined (for my purpose) as one who follows Darwinian predictions, that he will use power to gain reproductive rewards. I've described in a previous chapter ('The Phallic Pyramid') how mighty overlords, emperors and chieftains in the past have done just that with an almost mathematical degree of accuracy. One huge puzzle to evolutionary philosophers is why they don't do so today – at least not so predictably. But look for despots, and there they are. Even in the mid-20th century, a king of Swaziland had 117 wives. Osama bin Laden's father, Mohammed, had 54 children, born to 11 mothers. As is usual in well-to-do Saudi families, he had three permanent wives and a fourth whom he would swap as often as he fancied. No ex-wives were ever put out, but continued to live with the hugely extended family, so he bypassed Islamic laws and had as many wives as he liked. Clearly the alpha male can still be found among suitable power bases.

A criticism directed at evolutionary psychology is that proponents treat sexual activity and reproduction as if they were the same thing. Clearly in humans they are not. Sex is for pleasure, for bonding, for release of tension, for power-play, sometimes for brutality – much less often consciously for procreation. Moreover, in recent times, humans have learned to control their reproductive potential by means of contraception, achieving the ultimate sophistication with the pill. It is vital to remember that all our archaic behaviour issues from a level much lower than our conscious minds. In previous generations – way back in time – our ancestors who practised sex most often, begat most progeny. The genetic mechanism directing such vigorous behaviour is still functioning today even though the multiplicity of sexual encounters may not perfectly match the number of offspring. This is even more true where the sexual engagement is not a standard heterosexual one. Evolution is not purposeful: it is blind. It is also thriftily adaptable.

Joseph Patrick Kennedy (the father of John F Kennedy) was in most respects the prototype alpha male, except that he failed in his bid for the supreme position, President of the United States of America. Yet his personal failure only served to sublimate his awesome energy into lining up his sons for the presidency, in the expectation that one or more would succeed. As the grandson of Irish immigrants, Joe was accustomed to the enforced clannishness of his people, who were given the cold-shoulder by mainstream, long-established, polite Boston society – a society that had provided three United States presidents. The excluded Irish responded by steeping themselves in small-time politics and commerce with the requisite degree of ruthlessness. They were selected survivors of the potato famine and the British system. The tenets of their Catholic religion made them prolific, and they multiplied. When Boston in 1887 elected its first Irish Catholic mayor, a foothold and a far-reaching influence were gained, which would not easily be released. Politics was no cleaner then than now, with sectarian interests paramount and votes on sale for jobs at all levels – survival and replication of the fittest in conditions as raw as the jungle. By the time Joe was born in 1885, into a relatively prosperous family, the Irish composed over a third of Boston's population, which is a Darwinian success story after only two generations in that environment. Joe's father Patrick had reached the top of his community, as a successful saloon-bar keeper, and was an elected member first to the House of Representatives, then to the Senate. He also ventured into the elitist banking world, till then the domain of the upper social strata, known as the Boston Brahmins. The ground was well-prepared for Joe.

Joe took to money-making like a duck to water, seeming to know by instinct that this was the irresistible currency of power, and that most things could be bought if the price was right. He did not shine at school, but needed no tutoring in methods of bartering, in favours and in kind, and in opportunism. His personal characteristics were of huge importance, most especially his reverberating voice and authoritative presence, which ensured that most conversations were conducted on his own terms. Photographs show a fixed smile, not extending to his speculative eyes. With his 'winner-takes-all' philosophy, he showed no mercy to an opponent, and no sense of fair shares all round. His risk-taking behaviour was as blatant as any ambitious male's, but channelled into a financial rather than a physical arena. He notoriously refused to volunteer for service in the First World War even when most of his peers had done so, and when in imminent danger of being drafted, pulled strings to land a job in ship-building and have himself excused. Yet he showed no compunction about borrowing massive sums of money to buy his first showy house and flashy car when already deeply in debt.

Joe would exploit any influence open to him, and commanded enough charm to woo and marry Rose Fitzgerald, the daughter of the Mayor of Boston, whose influence was crucial, although Joe liked to present himself as a self-made man. Much has been made of his election to president of the bank Columbia Trust at the tender age of 25, but he did so partly through his father's influence and partly through extensive inside knowledge, gained during his previous job as a bank examiner. His use of confidential information to further his own ends was a technique he would deploy throughout life, and on which much of his vast fortune was based. He and father-in-law Fitzgerald ran a collateral loan company – a pawn shop to lend money to the poor. Joe liked to cover his ruthlessness with a veneer of virtue, as image-conscious as any star of the TV era – as long as there was something more solid in it too. After the war, again with mayoral influence, Joe joined a stock brokerage company. He rapidly acquired the ability to milk investors by using sensitive information, and other unethical (now illegal) market-manipulatory techniques.

Characteristically restless, Joe would get bored with a job after a year or two and push on to the next moss-gathering challenge; but he was no aimless drifter. When Prohibition was enforced in 1919, an act that had seemed to threaten the liquor trade for some time, it offered a heaven-sent opportunity to join the band-wagon evading the law and make a staggering profit. He was associated with big-time crime syndicates, including that of Al Capone, in his smuggling, bribing and threatening activities, and linked with an underworld community which merged seemlessly with respectable society, since many police and politicians were ensnared by big payments to simply ignore what was happening. Making their own rules and keeping law-enforcers sweet, the bootleggers protected their own interests with hardmen and machine-guns. By his mid-thirties Joe had an estimated fortune of two million dollars (worth seven or eight times as much today), without visible source of income.

The glamour and profit-potential of Hollywood was the next attraction, as Joe bought his way into film-making companies including Pathé News, and set about improving their business methods. This entailed cutting everyone's salary but his own. Having kept up contact with a Boston legal patron, Guy Currier, Joe used confidential financial information from his office on stockholders in the film companies to enrich himself at their expense. Innocent, hardworking stockholders saw their lifesavings vanish while Joe's fortune continued its exponential rise. His net gains for this passing phase were said to be five million dollars, but Joe's requirements extended beyond wealth for its own sake. He had creative ambitions and wanted to make a movie with his mistress Gloria Swanson, but his taste and talent were execrable. Their affair fell apart in acrimony when she discovered he was swindling her even as he made love to her. Amazingly, Joe was able to get away with his manipulations of the stock market at the very moment federal investigators were frenetically studying the Wall Street crash; the rules for good financial behaviour had not yet been invented.

Having a fortune as big as any in the US, Joe now prepared to buy power with it, in Washington and in politics. He chose to back Franklin D Roosevelt, then governor of New York, as presidential candidate by donating vast sums of money to his campaign – a good investment for his own future aspirations, as he saw it. But Roosevelt was canny and knew of Joe's past. Doubtless he recognised the ambitious contender in future campaigns. Both men acted out a great show of back-slapping bonhomie while resolutely making maximal use of each other, yet expressing mutually low opinions in confidential ears. Joe to his chagrin was not given a cabinet post but was made chairman of a commission created to investigate financial irregularities in the stock market. In spite of the media storm this provoked, Roosevelt insisted in private that Joe's racketeering was the best qualification for exposing like practice. No doubt this was true, but Joe's committee investigated the small-time fraudsters and left alone his big-spending buddies, probably in exchange for favours. Indeed, Joe's obsequious support of Roosevelt in a book he ghost-wrote, *I'm for Roosevelt*, was a trade-in for deflecting an impending investigation over his own money matters. His camaraderie was reinforced by lavish gifts of whisky and exotica and by entrapping the unprincipled son, Jimmy Roosevelt, with an embarrassing degree of indebtedness. Joe also cosied up to Cardinal Pacelli, Vatican secretary of state, accurately identifying him as pope-elect.

For Franklin D Roosevelt, canny old dog that he was, Joe's presidential ambitions were limpidly transparent, and in an era when the president was not limited to two terms in office they were a genuine threat. Kennedy, bored with his commission, wanted the next step up, fancying the post of secretary to the treasury. He was offered ambassador to the Court of St James, England, which he accepted with alacrity. It is even possible that he paid Jimmy to put in a good word for him. Joe's perception, reinforced no doubt by accolades in the press, was that five ambassadors in the past had gone on to become presidents. Alas for Joe, the post for which he was neither qualified nor suited proved to be his downfall. With no sense of delicacy or diplomacy, he loudly pronounced his own self-orientated opinions as if they reflected establishment American views. He approved of Hitler's tactics; he denigrated democracy while accepting dictatorship as an alternative; he was loudly anti-Semitic. He referred to Roosevelt as 'son of a bitch' and predicted his imminent downfall. He engineered criminal fluctuations in the stock market from which he could benefit. Josiah Wedgewood, a Liberal MP, described him as 'a rich man, untrained in diplomacy, unlearned in history and politics, who is a great publicity seeker and ... ambitious to become the first Catholic president of the US'.

Joe's attitude of appeasement towards Hitler spilled over into forecasts of gloom and doom for Europe and Britain, and into personal panic at the time of Dunkirk and later when the Blitz began. He wanted out. He advocated standing aside while the war was fought out in Europe, then the US could ally itself and make trade links with the victor. Roosevelt held Kennedy at arm's length in England until he had secured his third election as president. Then Joe was recalled and shortly afterwards resigned his post. He would never again hold political office.

Joe liked the good life and used his fabulous wealth to enjoy it to the full. When required, especially early in life, he could be a disciplined workaholic. His boredom threshold was exceedingly low and his CV could read superficially like that of a rootless rolling stone, with few jobs lasting more than a year or two. What was the purpose of it all? He used his wealth and power for his own comforts, but most enthusiastically of all he used them to gain sexual privileges – reproductive opportunities in Darwinian-speak. Of course it was expected that his orthodox Catholic wife would bear him a large family, and she did: nine in all. But Joe's libido demanded more than this, and he was described as being as greedy a philanderer as a profiteer. He liked to have a regular mistress, but in addition looked upon any woman he met as a sexual opportunity, regardless of status or circumstance: wives and partners of friends, associates, even girlfriends of his sons – none were off-limits. He made use of chorus girls, models and prostitutes, and when his sons came of age he encouraged them to do the same. His aides would be expected to pimp for him.

Probably one of the attractions of the world of mob-owned nightclubs in Chicago that Joe frequented, was the ready access to bevies of lovely young women, and the same was true of Hollywood. Gloria Swanson became his mistress when she was at the height of her acting career. She set the standard for 20th-century film stars by having six husbands and countless lovers, so she was a good match for Joe. He wore her proudly like a trophy and became godfather to her adopted son, insisting that she call him Joseph Patrick.

Jimmy Roosevelt accepted supplies of chorus girls as well as money from Kennedy. A younger Roosevelt scion described Joe as prone to tell foul-mouthed stories in mixed company, ignoring blushes: an 'evil, disgusting man'. Some women he had pounced on viewed him the same way, calling him 'crass, unbridled, vulgar'. But plenty of young, well-endowed women were prepared to tolerate his uninhibited ways, and wherever he went he would be accompanied by at least two strikingly attractive girls, sometimes more, invariably young and voluptuous. He would introduce them as his nieces. One startling anecdote has him sitting in a classy restaurant between two beauties, eating his dinner with one hand and using the other to pleasure one of them under the table – to the offence of nearby diners. He was not asked to leave. He became more disinhibited with age. He would bring his paramours home for a meal, then indulge in noisy sex within earshot of the assembled company.

Sex could be used to gain power and control, as when staying as a guest of Lord Beaverbrook: he seduced a researcher, then bribed her with presents to give him a report of all that happened in those precincts. Joe's long-term secretary, Janet des Rosiers, was hired as a young innocent and soon became his mistress. She was given the soft-soap treatment, for she was to serve and support him in every way, remaining his worshipful Abigail for nine years. When she left he was approaching his dotage, and acquired another young lovely to dance attendance, though his needs by now were more those of a geriatric than a Don Juan.

If the ultimate reason for living is to procreate, and to propel your progeny into powerful positions where they can do the same, Joe Kennedy's life was undoubtedly a success story. His tribe included a president, three senators, an attorney general and three congress-men. But contrary to popular myth, no man is destined, that is marked by Providence, to achieve the glorious heights. To reach the top he must be single-mindedly selfish and ruthless in competing and winning by whatever means come to hand, illegal, unethical or otherwise, plus possess an ability for lying and cover-up. He will leave behind a disproportionate swathe of wreckage in his swaggering path. Joe was unquestionably a wrecker.

His activities in the money market before suitable controls were imposed, ruined countless people. He had no small hand in the events leading up to the Wall Street crash. The first act in his privileged, draft-escaping post at the Fore River shipyard was to precipitate a massive strike of ship-builders while his manager was absent on business: he cancelled a negotiated pay rise with predictable results among the five thousand workforce, and compounded his colossal left-footedness with threats of peremptory dismissal. Senior managers, politicians and Franklin Roosevelt himself, then secretary of the wartime navy, rushed in to smooth ruffled union leaders' feathers; Kennedy was demoted and shuffled out of the way, to concoct in idleness his own version of the story.

His wife had no option but to tolerate his philandering, and he controlled and directed his children like a dictator of dubious benevolence. In spite of frequent absences, he was a god-like figure in their lives, as he poured his ambitious philosophy into them. But they had to come up to the mark of his measuring, and one may wonder how much his domineering control contributed to the early deaths of no fewer than four of his children. The responsibility for permanently maiming a fifth was all his own.

Joe Junior's death in a suicidally gallant aviation mission during the Second World War has been attributed by some to his wish to live up to his father's exacting standards. Others see it as an endeavour to counterbalance by crazy courage his father's reputation for cowardice. Jack's presidency he owed not only to his father's money and networking, but his drive and determination too. His father's enemies were inherited by him, along with other material and genetic gifts, and his rashness. No doubt all these contributed to his destiny in Dallas. However, the most catastrophic effect of Joe's vicarious ambition was borne by his daughter Rosemary.

At a time when any form of mental illness was a source of shame and secrecy hedged about with ignorance, Joe responded with rejection rather than compassion when Rosemary developed behavioural problems. The details are shrouded in myth, but at least part of the problem was an inordinate sex-drive that caused her to behave violently, physically and verbally, if restrained, and to escape from her convent school to walk the streets at night seeking experience. She certainly did not fit in with Joe's notion of a super-family, excelling in all its parts; and she was banished from the Kennedy home in disgrace, to live with an aide and his wife. Joe's money could not overcome this problem, though he offered massive sums to hospital specialists to seek a solution. Finally, he persuaded a neurosurgeon to perform brain surgery – a lobotomy, which was semi-experimental treatment, supposed to have a calming effect. It succeeded in this but crippled her physically and mentally, to the extent of requiring permanent care. She was shuffled off to an institution and forgotten as far as possible: an embarrassment, a failure, a guilt-associated family skeleton. The other children were deeply troubled, and no doubt the worship-reverence-fear complex of feeling for their father took a significant right-shift.

It has been suggested that Jack Kennedy's fervent adherence to the concept of freedom stemmed from a reaction to his father's iron control. That may be so, but he did not rebel against his father's plans for his glorious career. In American elections, then as now, whether gubernatorial, congressional, senatorial or presidential, money was a factor central to outcome, and Joe splurged like his resources were bottomless, which they were, comparatively. Nor was the due democratic process given even a fleeting glance. Joe made a deal with Sam Giancana, the prominent Chicago criminal and murderer, to deliver mob-controlled union votes in Illinois and other states where the syndicate ruled. Details of the sums exchanged are unknown, but Giancana knew they had a hold on the future president. After the nip-and-tuck finish in the 1960 election, in which Kennedy beat Nixon by a few thousand votes, allegations of vote fraud against the Democrats were rife but ineffective. Kennedy's toe was in the door and judges deemed it prudent to find insufficient evidence to sustain the charges.

Long before Jack approached the presidential hurdle, his father's money, will and influence had backed him to the hilt. In his first foray into politics, Joe bribed the incumbent of an Irish-rich East Boston district congressional seat to stand aside for Jack. The sitting member, James Curley, was in dire trouble over an indictment for fraud at the time and found he could not refuse. Joe paid a janitor to enter the primary contest in order to split the opposition votes: his name (J Russo) was identical to the opponent's, thus ensuring maximal voter confusion. Joe's administrative wizardry held the team together at all points while Jack was the charming face of the campaign, wheeled out to smile, shake hands and give voice to the speeches written for him. Thus supported, eventually with three successful congressional elections under his belt, Jack was ready for the senate. He had long since discovered that his sex appeal was irresistible in one-to-one encounters, and now he used it to devastating effect to capture the mass female vote in Massachusetts. Meanwhile, Joe was busy trying to bribe the owner of the *Boston Post* to endorse his son. Later he would boast that for $75,000 he had got Jack's picture on the front cover of *Time* magazine.

Jack did as he was bid, ever in thrall to his powerful pa. He was not a natural speaker, indeed his early efforts were unimpressive, with a voice that was strained and high-pitched in its delivery of his handful of stock speeches. Even at his best he was regarded as a debater rather than an orator. He was not a mixer nor a natural politician, doing what he had to do and escaping at the first opportunity. It has been said of him that his political skills were as mediocre as those of his love-making: unwilling to engage in any depth, he would just get to the point as quickly as possible, then be on to the next thing. Giving generously of himself was something of which he was incapable in any context. Though always surrounded by a crowd of friends and attendants, this was always on his own terms. If the spotlight deviated elsewhere, boredom and indifference broke through.

Throughout his early life he had contended with physical illness of severity and mystery, which had kept him out of circulation for weeks and even brought him to death's door. Eventually diagnosed with Addison's disease, he looked thin and fragile when he should have radiated vibrant, virile health. He was not a workaholic, preferring a playboy lifestyle to the regular grind required by channelled ambition, nor was he a dogged fighter when the going got tough. His habits of irresponsibility bordered on the feckless, a family characteristic. He had minimal interst in local affairs, but world affairs aroused more enthusiasm, rising to passion on the impositions of the Soviet system and its iron control.

Altogether, Jack was not promising leader material, and it is a tribute to his father's energy and single-minded determination that he got where he did. The most important attribute that Jack possessed in super-abundance was his sex appeal. Even before stepping into the political arena he was aware of the power of his magnetism, but finding that it went up several notches on the scale when he became a public figure was a bonus. Without this supremely welcome reward for his labours, even his father's will might not have been enough to propel this dilettante into the prime position.

Ever since losing his virginity to a Harlem prostitute as a schoolboy, Jack found that his libido had led him into risky situations. At nineteen he was writing lurid accounts of cheap encounters in a Mexican whorehouse to his long-term friend Lem Billings. His letters of the time are replete with descriptions of one-night stands, fear of the clap and of unwanted pregnancies; indeed he was treated for gonorrhoea and non-specific urethritis as a Harvard student. He did not need to resort to the *demi-monde*, possessing the kind of animal sexiness that women die for, as he was soon to discover. Probably he inherited this particular trait from his maternal grandpa, Honey Fitz, renowned and nicknamed for his sugar-sweet charm and wit – and for his infidelities. But throughout his life, Jack had a taste for transient, anonymous sexual encounters, free of emotional baggage. The woman who many friends describe as the love of Jack's life, Inga Arvad, he obediently forsook at his father's insistence. Inga, a Danish journalist, a former beauty queen, had pre-war Nazi connections, which were far too dangerous to be linked with a potential politician in 1941. Like his father, Jack felt the irresistible pull of Hollywood, at its most enticing when following on the heels of some social or political success. Most notably he homed in on Los Angeles as a newly elected politician, seeking to 'knock a name'. He was obediently following the Darwinian power-for-sex rules. His name would be associated with a succession of film stars, including Jayne Mansfield, Grace Kelly, Janet Leigh, Rhonda Fleming and, most famously, Marilyn Monroe.

Given the profusion of his liaisons, and the fact that any one of them becoming public would have shot to pieces his political career, of which a cornerstone was this happily married man with beautiful wife and children, it is not difficult to believe that his most irresistible, primeval urge was to copulate. When he was engaged in the primary elections for president in 1960, he was introduced by

Frank Sinatra to Judith Campbell, a woman of unusual beauty. Known to Sinatra's Rat Pack, and in particular to the notorious gangster Sam Giancana, Judith became an innocent go-between, unwittingly carrying bribe money to the Chicago mob in exchange for organised votes. After Kennedy's elevation to the presidency, Judith was simultaneously his mistress and Giancana's, while her willing naivety was put to good use in the various plots and machinations to assassinate Fidel Castro. She continued her messenger role between the White House, Giancana, John Rosselli (another Chicago mobster) and associates, carrying vast sums of money and instructions. Equally reprehensible business was conducted via this channel between Kennedy and various businessmen seeking defence contracts. Who would suspect the president of the sort of shady deals his father had been famed for? The FBI and its Director, J Edgar Hoover, knew of Judith's links and her intimate relationships. Jack was therefore easy prey to blackmail, intimidation and manipulation both by professional criminals and by powerful men of the establishment. His power was no longer his own. He was constantly trading it in for sex.

Of course the White House establishment, and especially the security staff whose job it was to physically protect the president, knew of his sexual antics in undignified detail. Indeed they were expected to convey bevies of high-class prostitutes in and out of the backdoors, even to procure for him, to stand guard when he took his pleasure in impromptu fashion, and to liaise with the first lady's staff so that she never actually witnessed her husband's infidelity. His close aides confirmed that a good deal of time each day was occupied with his personal gratifying, and that it became a mounting obsession, which seriously distracted him from work and kept him unavailable for urgent decisions. He said when discussing the practicalities of setting up his harem, 'You know, I get a migraine headache if I don't get a strange piece of ass every day.' The White House swimming pool was the focus for his daily encounters, where there were skinny-dipping parties with assorted women, call-girls, rising starlets, air hostesses or willing White House staff. The security men were uncomfortable with the arrangements but had to look the other way, even when the president and his intimates made life impossible by flaunting security checks for strangers visiting the inner sanctum. Supervision was especially difficult when the partying took place outside Washington, at Bing Crosby's estate in Palm Springs, for example, where the animal shrieks and sounds of wild abandon would attract public notice. On official trips Jack's first concern was to disappear with a couple of ladies who were explained away to his hosts by shifty-eyed staff as 'secretaries'. Not surprisingly, the agents and military attendants were drawn into the drinking and debauching lifestyle, which became the prevailing preoccupation of the presidential entourage. The girls who had been brought in to service the president received 'counselling', on the way out; that is to say, they were threatened that careers or reputations and maybe other vitals were at risk if they talked. Of course there were unwanted pregnancies which were hushed up and disposed of by abortion.

Rumours of the luridly libidinous lifestyle would leak out at times, including a story that Jack had been married early on in his career – a mismatch that his father had quashed. There are also stories that discarded lovers tried to extort money by threatening exposure. Two of the high-class prostitutes featuring in the Profumo scandal in Britain had serviced Kennedy while working in New York. He narrowly escaped his own version of public exposure when a lover, Ellen Rometsch, an East German and one-time communist, was hastily hustled out of the country, deported to Germany on the grounds of being a spy – accompanied, it is said, by considerable hush-money raised by innocent campaign staff. To these and others caught up in the damage-limitation exercise to protect the presidential reputation there was devastating collateral trauma, including one suicide of a fervent follower tied up in monumental debt he could not explain.

Not satisfied with one-to-one encounters, Jack experimented with multiple sessions, *ménages à trois* or more, and liked to have framed photographs so that he could be a voyeur of his own bedroom romps. There are also allegations of homosexual engagements, particularly with his life-long friend Lem Billings, who worshipped Kennedy and claimed to have pleasured his hero when nothing better was on offer. Jack was fond of kinky sex, too, according to a New York party girl: a touch of bonding and sado-masochism for variety, as (this witness affirmed) many high-powered politicians enjoy.

Jack Kennedy's addiction to sex is readily labelled pathological by rational minds who do not expect democratically elected presidents in Western countries to behave like this. Distant potentates in fabulous, exotic, lawless empires, maybe. Or as Betzig's studies show, men with absolute power are accorded proportional sexual privileges by some unseen force of law; but an American president should have his hands tied by principles, constitutive restrictions, due legal process and all the paraphernalia of a fair and just society, as well as a lifetime's training in the service of the nation. Jack's deep-seated needs clearly acknowledged none of this.

There is good evidence that Bobby Kennedy, Jack's younger brother, who was on a rollercoaster ride aiming for the White House when his career was brought to a violent end, would have behaved in a similar way. As it was, his libido would have been astounding if it had not been eclipsed by that of his older brother. As a junior scion of a high-flying dynasty, Bobby's self-esteem in his youth was very low, and this is reflected in the late age at which he lost his virginity – 21 – and even then he did so by his father's decree at a friendly whorehouse. Later, Bobby followed worshipfully in Jack's footsteps, parasitising his power by intimate association as Jack had done with Joe. And, parallel to his increasing power, his sex-life became more intense, though never so frantic or so anonymous as Jack's. He also experimented with homosexual encounters, including sharing a soldier lover with Rudolf Nureyev. He had a reputation for blatant sadism. One informative tale about him relates to his law-enforcing days on the McCarthy Senate Investigation Committee in 1955 when his interrogation methods earned him the title of 'little fascist'. As a sideline he joined the Federal Bureau of Narcotics, described as a cross between the KGB, FBI and Gestapo: a drug-busting squad of intimidating thugs operating with illegal methods in New York, and an attached assortment of would-be cowboys and hangers-on of whom Bobby was one. Their ability to kick down doors and pin the terrified inhabitants to the wall at gun-point was usually asserted only over disempowered ethnic minorities. Drugs were seized – and usually kept – and there were other rewards too. The women of the household were forced into sex – intercourse or fellatio – either unwillingly or in exchange for their freedom. Bobby took his rewards in both kinds along with the rest. Only when he ran for the presidency in 1968 did his sexual appetite become really insatiable, and, unlike his brother's, his taste was for very young, immature schoolgirl types. After cavorting with three fifteen-year-olds – the best present he ever had, according to his procurer – he watched them having sex among themselves.

While Jack was working his way towards the presidency, Bobby as his lieutenant embraced his brother's ambition as avidly as if it was his own. His personal curriculum vitae was not impressive, though he was a law graduate. But there was much debate about which prestigious job he should be given as a reward, and much agonising about that of attorney general, tossing back and forth words like nepotism, youth and inexperience. Joe was determined Bobby should have this post. President Jack meekly tried to reason with his father but was shot down in flames: 'Bobby deserves to be attorney general and, by God, that is what he is going to be.' The president said, 'Yes, Sir!' And so it was.

The aging King Kong had conceded top place, but the new incumbent was his son, still imbued with habits of deference. Joe could wield power by proxy and line up his other progeny for the succession.

In the world of men, the close links between ambition and high-risk behaviour are incontrovertible. Whatever the patterns of inheritance are for human behaviour (still hotly disputed by scientists), the influence of gender must be profound. A genetic package delivered to a female will be expressed quite differently from the same package received by a male. Bobby Kennedy's eleven offspring hint at this truth most intriguingly. The males were chaotic, danger-seekers to the point of self-destruction. Wild and uncontrollable after Bobby's death, they sexually harassed their nannies and carers. David and Bobby Junior were drug addicts, and David, in spite of several attempts at drying out, died at 29 of an overdose of alcohol and a cocktail of drugs. Joe Junior, a characteristically reckless driver, echoing uncannily his Uncle Ted's notorious disaster, overturned a Jeep while heading for a ferry. One passenger was badly hurt and permanently crippled. Joe also drank heavily, abused his wife, and failed in his attempt at a political career. Michael Kennedy was an alcoholic whose marriage fell apart when he was accused of raping a fourteen-year-old girl. He died at 39 of a skiing accident, playing a high-risk, typically Kennedyesque game of ski-football. Other sons are described as loafers and ne'er-do-wells, living on the family name. By crystal-sharp contrast, Bobby's four daughters have been roundly successful, holding down between them legal posts, a lieutenant governorship, human-rights avocations, a United Nations post, a top-class film-making career, three of them being at the same time staunch wives and mothers.

Bill Clinton's Lothario lifestyle, though in many ways a carbon copy of his hero Jack Kennedy's, has shown subtle differences. He was equally indiscriminate and all-embracing in his choice of partners, happy to use courtesans and passing ships, yet Bill was a better actor and liked his women to swoon at his feet in the belief that they were the love of his life. It was part of his natural salesman technique, and in his student years, young women adored his 'puppy-like eagerness to please'.

Like the emperors of old he chose his empress for qualities of strength and resilience as well as others more personal and less definable; but this union made no difference to his limitless expectations. Indeed the risk of discovery by Hillary added to the zest of the relentless chase and conquer. She might fight his infidelities tooth and nail by deploying spies – first her own family, later paid detectives – but this deterred him not a whit. In 1972 on the Democratic Party campaign trail she was to discover Bill had thirty women receiving his favours: one for each county plus some extras.

As power and dominance added to the ambitious Bill's seductive aura, his licence took on a more sinister edge. He could turn nasty and forceful if the lady of the moment's willingness proved illusory as Christopher Anderson describes in horrifying detail in his book *Bill and Hilary*. Juanita Hall, an innocent volunteer in 1978, met Bill as he campaigned for the governorship of Arkansas. She thought his interest in her was on the level, but discovered her mistake when she received his unwelcome sexual attentions in her hotel room. Gennifer Flowers lay abed recovering from her abortion even as Bill announced his gubernatorial candidacy.

As governor of Arkansas, Bill's sexual exploits became more overt, and he seemed to believe the privileges of perfect freedom were his and would be universally though tacitly acknowledged. He held groping sessions in the back of his state limousine while his driver looked at the road ahead. His bodyguards were engaged to solicit women, make arrangements for trysts and stand guard during the brief coupling. Teenage students were easy prey, mesmerised into thinking they had captured the heart of a powerful man, whereas they were mere nibbles in an imperial feast. Bill stated that 'people go into politics because of their unsatisfied sexual desire'.

In his second term as governor, Bill's immoderate needs led him to use prostitutes. He had taken up jogging ostensibly to lose weight, and his path led him through the hookers' beat. He would stop, pull a girl behind a hedge, accept oral sex, then continue on his way. His official car would be instructed to pick up three girls and convey them to a holiday home of his mother's where he would hold court in a group grope, then dismiss them. According to Roger Morris in *Partners in Power*, Clinton would even let himself be serviced in the parking lot at his daughter Chelsea's school, unfazed by the audience of his security staff, and perhaps other onlookers.

It proved impossible to keep the lid on all the stories when Bill entered the presidential race. Most women denied the rumours for a multiplicity of reasons. There was undoubtedly intimidation used, much of it orchestrated by Hillary's legal mind. But some women really worshipped him. Susan McDougall of the Whitewater scandal, who was his one-time mistress, endured a prison sentence rather than split on him. One long-term girlfriend, Dolly Kyle Browning, was convinced she was the centre of his shifting world for many years, and was unfailingly loyal. Bill was bitterly resentful that the press were prepared to expose him, but the world had become less obsequious since the sixties. Damaged people began to talk. Even while wicked stories bubbled in the media, Bill continued to assert his *droit de seigneur* from the Oval Office of the White House. Hillary's network compiled dossiers on dangerous women in order to discredit them. She put about stories of a right-wing plot, but it was no use. The explosive material would not be doused, and the blue touch paper was lit in 1995 when Bill met Monica Lewinsky. Of all the steamy and undignified details that the world read, the story which captures Bill's essence is that of Monica kneeling to perform oral sex while he, accepting his pleasure from a lowly minion, talks power politics on the phone.

The reversion-to-seed, wild-type behaviour of Clinton and the Kennedys was not an aberration peculiar to larger-than-life Americans. Mao Zedong in the years of his power accorded himself similar privileges, and those years coincided with age and infirmity, not youth and vigour. In his earlier life he had a succession of four wives and had families with the last three. His fourth wife, Jang Qing, bored and irritated him so that they came to lead separate lives. She had to tolerate his hedonistic ways. Mao justified his licence by referring to the age-old Chinese tradition that sex with many very young women, preferably virgins, promotes health and male vigour. His immediate entourage accepted the still more ancient formula that Mao had power and could do as he liked. And Mao himself recognised the connection in his early twenties when he wrote that the implacable drive of great men was the same as 'the irresistible sexual desire for one's lover, a force that will not stop, that cannot be stopped' – a statement not too far removed from Bill Clinton's hypothesis about why men go into politics. Mao's promiscuity in the communist era took place at a time when the same behaviour by an ordinary citizen would earn a sentence in a corrective labour camp, and probable death. It is an echo of those far-off alpha male relatives who blatantly take their multiple privileges while seeking to obstruct all others from doing the same.

For the last twenty years of his life, Mao held court with his circle of young women who shared his oversized bed – singly or in groups of two, three, four or five – and his circle of equally young male bodyguards who orchestrated his every move and cocooned him from most outside contacts. Mao liked to hold parties behind the high walls of his official residence and in other privileged places, where he would genteelly waltz and chat with each of the young ladies provided for him. Dancing was another forbidden activity for the masses, particularly Western style, which was judged as being bourgeois and decadent. Periodically, Mao would disappear with a young lady in tow to enjoy her in private. He was unconcerned about maintaining secrecy about these goings-on, but his staff were obsessed about his privacy.

Most of the women, still in their teens, came from humble peasant backgrounds and were carefully vetted to ensure they held the correct attitude of worshipful adoration of the chairman. Few would last very long in his service. When he became bored with one, she would be married off advantageously. They were disposable, the supply unlimited. In the Great Hall of the People, the so-called Room 118 was decked out in imperial splendour for his seigneurial lifestyle.

Mao's doctor, Zhisui Li, records that Mao's insatiable appetite also extended to his young male attendants, who were expected to massage his body, including his groin, in preparation for sleep, and he would occasionally be seen drawing a young man into bed. Dr Li battled with Mao's venereal diseases throughout his years of attendance. But the great chairman was uncooperative unless he was actually suffering himself, and didn't care a fig about contact tracing among his consorts. He was sublimely careless about hygiene in general and refused to bath himself. 'I wash my prick in their cunts,' he announced.

No one can deny that there are considerable similarities between Mao's sex life in the years of his power and that of Jack and Joe Kennedy. How amazing that a Chinese communist leader of peasant origin should be so comparable to a US president and a prototype capitalist millionaire! There has to be some 'natural' (by that, I do not imply 'correct') process here. They are indeed following Darwin's – and Betzig's – universal formula of power and privilege.

One other small but intriguing analogy can be drawn between Jack Kennedy and Mao Zedong, and that is the way their lives came to centre on the swimming pools in their respective palaces. In Zhongnanhai within the Forbidden City, the pool was intended for all top-level leadership, but Mao's frequent use edged the others out. As animals do, he staked out his territory, and all his business was conducted at the poolside: eating, sleeping, even receiving foreign visitors, Kruschev included. In advanced age, when he was ill and could no longer swim, he still camped out there. In his extreme isolation, protected and cocooned in a watery environment, maybe he wished to return to the safety of the womb.

The behaviour of these men, truly imperial in the frequency of sexual congress, the anonymity, group orgies and non-specificity as to gender, is rare in a modern context. Many men do their best to come close, as my reader hardly needs to be reminded, in every sphere of life. Benito Mussolini was an alpha of a less spectacular order, but still a notorious libertine. He began with dancehall flirtations and before the age of sixteen had progressed to downmarket prostitutes from whom he acquired syphilis, a disease that dogged him throughout life. His lust was of the blanket variety, for almost any woman would do in the heat of the moment, plain or pretty, young or mature. He liked a spice of violence with his lust and would chuck a girl into a corner, then leap upon her with his boots on. The encounter was usually rough and primitive, accompanied by oaths, blasphemies and imprecations. He adopted a Hell's Angel image, of a rowdy and a jail-bird, a hooligan who carried a knife and was known to use it – and he once used it on a lover. As a youth he took particular delight in adultery, for the macho risk it posed and the histrionic scenes it provoked. Wanted by the police for desertion from the army, a revolutionary trouble-maker, he found refuge in Switzerland and the sympathetic arms of a number of Polish and Russian refugees.

He met his wife-to-be, Rachele, a peasant girl, when she was sixteen, and married her when she was carrying their second child. She was to bear him five. He had illegitimate children too, numbers unknown. Two long-term mistresses, Margherita Sarfatti and Claretta Petacci, kept his devotion but did not quench the indiscriminate lust. As head of government in Italy, Mussolini was quite capable of ditching his official programme or scheduled work at a moment's notice for a love-opportunity. Responsibilities came a long way behind his sexual imperative. He had a bachelor flat in Rome which functioned as a love-nest, where according to his personal attendant, Navarra, he entertained a woman every afternoon. Some might arrive in all innocence with a petition, but found themselves at the mercy of his sex-drive.

Among other national leaders, Vaclav Havel of the Czech Republic was a notorious carouser and skirt-chaser. The biographer John Keane recounts how Havel deceived his wife constantly while relying heavily on her for support, a habit that sat ill with his professed adherence to 'living in the truth'. Once when he faced arrest he was dragged out of bed from the arms of his mistress. On another occasion he was entertained with a strip dance by his lover and her daughter simultaneously. He was at his most libidinous after release from four years in jail.

Osama bin Laden has four wives and ten sons, plus an unknown number of daughters. As a student he was a hell-raiser, known for drunken merry-making and woman-chasing, even achieving notoriety as a sex pest. Saddam Hussein has extra-marital affairs, and a close loyal confidant to organise them. For reasons of public image he ensures they are a closely guarded secret, known only to his most immediate circle of courtiers. One mistress bore him a son and so he married her, again in secret as he already had a wife. The taking of a third wife coincided with a brief pause in his savagery. Though within Islamic law, his religion of Ba'athism does not allow multiple wives, still less illicit liaisons. His oldest son, Udai, groomed from an early age for high office, until crippled by an assassination attempt, was a notoriously aggressive libertine, liking to cruise the streets in his state car looking for women – any of whatever status that pleased him. Any that tried to refuse were beaten up. Udai had a friend who pimped for him, and regularly used prostitutes.

Moving back to the US and the time of power struggles between the Kennedy administration and the FBI over such issues as cash, communism, favours, sex and espionage, surveillance taps were put on the phone of the human rights leader Martin Luther King. These revealed a well-kept secret: the revered activist had a lusty appetite for illicit liaisons with women, including a glamorous school teacher called Phyllis Daitch. Drunken, high-spirited orgies went on behind locked hotel room doors, with multiple groups in bed together and irreverent, smutty jokes.

In the Soviet Union, the high command always behaved with

such obsessional secrecy that little is known of the personal lives of its members. Lavrenti Beria, Stalin's thoroughly nasty head of the secret service, was arrested and tried for assorted crimes under Kruschev. The fear he inspired even among the highest ranks was immeasurable, and all evidence was brought to bear to ensure his elimination, Soviet-style. The court heard in detail the sexual favours he had enjoyed with women procured by his bodyguard, including dozens of underage girls, all taken with a degree of force and humiliation. Women in high places were not spared, including the wife of a Hero of the Soviet Union.

Napoleon Bonaparte, like many military leaders, had an ambivalent attitude to women and probably much conflict between his conscious and subconscious sexual leanings. As consul in his mid-thirties, married to Josephine, he developed accelerating wanderlust, an insatiable appetite, which he slaked with a series of actresses, divorcees, ladies-in-waiting and adventuresses. As emperor he set the tone of immorality along with his nymphomaniac sister Pauline in the imperial court. It was rumoured he had affairs with this sister and with Josephine's niece Stephanie. He would peremptorily demand anonymous women to be procured for him in the aftermath of succesful battle. He was ever a misogynist, pulled against his will by lust and counteracting it with insults and boorish diatribes. Napoleon, like Mao Zedong and Jack Kennedy, also had a water fetish: he loved to languish endlessly in hot baths.

In 1756 in India, at a time when the British and other Western powers were making invasive inroads, there arose a leader in Bengal called Siraj-ud-Daula. Notable for seizing Calcutta from the British, and responsible for the infamous Black Hole, in which numbers of captives died horribly, his capacity for mindless cruelty was matched only by his sexual excesses. He simply helped himself to anyone of either sex who chanced to catch his eye, and often the encounter ended in some vicious act of humiliation for the victim. He had the usual court of sycophants who followed his example. Indian princes customarily had access to unlimited supplies of nubile women: slaves and artistes, women captured in battle or bought from compliant families. But Siraj-ud-Daula trampled over convention and protocol by capturing women of noble birth as they bathed in the Ganges, preferring sex accompanied by violence to the indolent harmony of the harem. Characteristically, after the Black Hole had yielded up its ghastly dead, survivors were subjected to sexual humiliation: two women were carted off to the harem and the men were paraded naked through the streets, and abused. A contemporary historian described Siraj as 'low-spirited and melancholy' on those few occasions when he had not indulged in his usual sexual depravities – an almost identical reaction to that of Jack Kennedy several centuries later and a few continents removed.

British colonial and parliamentary history is a rich source of anecdotes of exorbitant lechery. Settlers, soldiers, officials, traders, all found as they travelled that the restrictive laws surrounding sex in Britain were not applicable in foreign lands. Furthermore, with the power gradient amply favouring themselves, there were rich opportunities for the taking. They were not slow to do so. Sir David Ochterlony, Resident of Delhi in 1803–25, had thirteen Indian mistresses. Colonel James Skinner, in India at the turn of the 19th century – he of the famous crack regiment 'Skinner's Horse' – had a harem of fourteen wives and is said to have fathered eighty children. Various rulers, including Sir John Eardley Wilmot (Lieutenant Governor of Australia in 1843), Sir Charles Fitzroy (Governor of new South Wales in 1846) and Sir Henry Pottinger (Governor of the Cape Colony in 1847), gained public reputations for multiple love affairs causing scandal back home. Lord Clive of India had been a devotee of brothels in Covent Garden and was described as fornicating his way across India, though he was modest about it and expressed himself astonished at his own moderation. Richard Marquis Wellesley, older brother of the Duke of Wellington, had a mistress who bore him five children before he married her. He left her behind when he became Governor General of India in 1798, when he resorted to brothels and a series of mistresses, leading a life so profligate that he scandalised the duke his brother, who was himself no celibate. Charles and Vyner Brooke, two of the white rajas of Sarawak, both had white wives but preferred multiple local mistresses. Even early in the 20th century, British settlers, especially high-ranking officials in Africa and Asia, still took native concubines, and some had sizeable harems of local women, though missionaries would complain of the practice.

Of the 19th-century British prime ministers, Gladstone is apparently the only one who remained faithful to his wife; and he certainly had some highly idiosyncratic sexual sublimations. Lord Palmerston interspersed his work in the War and Foreign Offices with liaisons, as many as five per week, which he recorded in his diary in code. As described in Matthew Parris's book, *Great Parliamentary Scandals*, John Wilkes, a colourful figure of the 18th century, was a rebel, a hell-raiser and a folk hero, but his reputed ugliness did not prevent him from being a serial womaniser. He alleged that his repulsive face was counterbalanced by his ready wit. When told by Lord Sandwich that he would 'die either on the gallows or by the pox', he retorted: 'That must depend on whether I embrace your lordship's principles or your mistress.' Benjamin Disraeli, who may have been bisexual, had scandalised society by a number of publicly conducted affairs with older married women even before he scraped into parliament. He was treated for venereal disease in 1831 with a six-week course of mercury, on which occasion he received the following sympathy in a letter from a friend, James Clay: 'Between us we have contrived to stumble on all the thorns with which... Venus guards her roses; for while you were cursing the greater evils I contrived to secure the minor...' It seems likely Disraeli contracted syphilis, his friend gonorrhoea. Clay was notoriously promiscuous, and Disraeli enjoyed his company in the brothels of Malta, where he fled to escape his debtors.

Sir Charles Dilke, a prominent Liberal minister in the cabinet of the prudish premier Gladstone, cited in a sensational divorce case, was accused of multiple affairs with an assortment of respectable wives and mothers, and not-so-respectable servants. His career was ruined. David Lloyd George was cited in two divorce cases, but survived politically. His wife Margaret performed the 'fragrant' lady role in his defence, as Mary Archer so famously did for her errant husband more recently. Labelled 'the Goat', Lloyd George was known for bedding wives, noble ladies, secretaries and groupies from all quarters. He sanitised sex with an attitude similar to that of modern keep-fit enthusiasts, who work out in the gym as if their lives depended on it. His full-time mistress, Frances Stevenson, was the most famous secretary-cum-geisha who eventually married him after the death of his long-suffering (and much maligned) wife.

The reportage of the Profumo affair briefly opened to the public gaze the sexual indulgence of senior Conservative politicians, beginning with the naked romps around the swimming pool (that aphrodisiacal setting again) at Cliveden. But the establishment closed ranks and protected their own, while Christine Keeler and Stephen Ward became the scapegoats, lightning conductors for public outrage. Edward Heath lost two ministers whose patronage of a high-class prostitute service became too public for comfort. Lord Lambton, one of the casualties, was mystified: 'Don't all men go to whores?' And after Earl Jellicoe's resignation, still bewildered, he remarked, '. . . It will soon be clear that Heath is the only member of the government who doesn't do it.'

Other names slip off the tongue easily: Alan Clark, whose exhibitionist playing of the upper-class goat became his watermark, as if he had invented sex, plus the likes of Nicky Fairbairn, Steven Norris, Jonathan Aitken and David Mellor. Besides them, the press fingered a whole host of MPs who could attain no more than the wife-and-one-mistress. In John Major's time, the media made mincemeat of anyone who traded on the wholesome, moral, family-man image. The falsity of this stance has recently been shown in all its duplicity by the revelations about Major's affair, before his prime ministerial years, with flamboyant MP on the make, Edwina Currie. The hypocrisy is no longer acceptable to an empowered electorate who expect increasingly that democracy will mean shared power and accountability. Which is why the age-old, flamboyant manifestation of leader-privilege is no longer acceptable.

Alpha males are not confined to politics and statecraft, of course. For example, authors are not perceived as being particularly powerful but do seem to have a colourful reputation for sexual freedom. Their influence must be estimated within their own special world. Indeed, H G Wells' string of mistresses were mostly authors themselves, including Rebecca West and Elizabeth von Arnim, all exotic and outstanding in their own right. The South African heart surgeon

Christiaan Barnard died in 2001, and his obituaries reminded me what a textbook example of the classic alpha he was. His one and only claim to fame, namely his ground-breaking first human-to-human heart transplant in 1967 'bought him all the power and the openings he desired'. No matter that the patient survived only eighteen days and that the required immune-modulatory techniques were not sufficiently developed, so that he was accused by purists of unethical experimentation: rival surgeons around the world leapt aboard and tried to outdo each other for several months, until the uniformly disastrous results forced a halt. But by that time the magic of instant stardom had done its work. Barnard had become a legend, a media figure, revelling in interviews, cameras and press frenzy, travelling the world in a blaze of publicity, meeting with the glamorous and the famous. He could elicit particular hero-worship from caring women, because he could pose as a saviour, a saint in a surgical gown. In no time he had a string of beautiful names linked with his, including Princess Grace of Monaco, Sophia Loren and Princess Diana. He had affairs with Gina Lollobrigida and Françoise Hardy as well as with a queue of lesser lights. He described women as falling over themselves to get at him, and no nurse was immune to, or safe from, his charm. Once he had sex with three women in six hours. He married and divorced three times; the last two wives were in their teens, he being more than twice their age. His second wife left him because he was getting older, a demoralising event which brought on a confidence crisis. This educated specialist succumbed to superstition, receiving rejuvenating treatment at a Swiss clinic, the active ingredient of which was foetal material from lambs. His third wife divorced him because of his liaisons with even younger women (she was 42 years his junior).

Professor Barnard had no doubt where his priorities lay and his lifestyle proved it. He would rather have women than the Nobel Prize, he said. He had six children, of whom four survive, the last having been fathered when he was 73.

The next chapter describes men of a different type, altogether darker, more violent, more puzzling, who appear, like the robots of science fiction, to be sufficiently empowered to defy the rules of their creators.

CHAPTER 7

The Military Celibate

Military fanaticism, the recognised enemy of full heterosexuality
— Rodney Collins

Unteachable from infancy to tomb – there is the first and main
characteristic of mankind

— Winston Churchill

Modern *Homo sapiens* is at his most intellectually uneasy when forced
to face his own aggressive potential. Let me not mince words: his killer
instinct. It does not require more than a passing acquaintance with
history to appreciate that conflicts readily degenerate into fisticuffs and
thence to wholesale slaughter, given half a chance. Yet penetrate back
in time beyond the era of record-keeping, and you might think our
early ancestors were sociable, neighbourly, rational beings with no hint
of violence in their make-up, according to much science writing. The
noble savage is as mythical as Piltdown Man.

Recent palaeontological work has shown the existence of other
human species in the past, all of whom were extinct by 30,000 years
ago, after which *Homo sapiens* ruled the roost. There is evidence that
we coexisted with other humans for a time, certainly Neanderthals
and maybe others. Until recently, science writers shied away from
any suggestion that this may have been an early example of ethnic
cleansing. The Neanderthals (*Homo neanderthalensis*), however,
could be offloaded with all the worst of human attributes, with dense,
vulgar brutality, because they were a race apart – a sub-human

species. This idea has even passed into popular speech. Yet few people discuss how this 'thug' was beaten at his own brutish games by the intellectual, artistic, domestically virtuous *Homo sapiens*.

Our capacity for self-glorification is limitless and prevents a rational interpretation of pre-history. In recorded (modern human) time, there are examples aplenty of invasions of one country by aliens from another, in which the indigenous population has been decimated. Information about how that happened is usually scanty and historical accounts brush past the embarrassment or try to find alternative explanations and moral justifications. The Spanish conquistadores decimated empires in South America. When they invaded Cuba, the Indian population fell like nine-pins. Contemporary wisdom insists that they mostly died from imported diseases such as measles, or mass suicide because they could not cope with enforced labour. Being treated as dispensable, they were soon wiped out, after which the Spaniards imported African captives to work as slaves.

The West was won in the US by systematic obliteration of the Native Americans. In Arizona and other western states, the memory of Indian art and culture is nowadays romantically and ruthlessly exploited by commercial outlets. Tierra del Fuego, unlike its name a land of inhospitably cold and harsh climate, was home to four tribes of Indians living in a primitive Stone Age setting when first sighted in the 19th century by European travellers who attempted to sail round the southernmost tip of South America. The tribes' turbulent interactions with well-intentioned but seriously ignorant Victorian missionaries is a tragi-comedy of mutual exploitation and incomprehension. Later in the century as prospecting miners moved in looking for gold, the Indians were shot on sight. The Indians acquired guns from trading settlers and wanton murder was unleashed between their tribes, ever mutually hostile and now terminally so. Sheep farmers moved in next and commandeered the land, elbowing the Indians off traditional nomadic routes. Food chains disrupted, they died of starvation and imported infections as well as violence. The remainder, seen as vermin, were systematically hunted down with a fee paid for every one killed. In 1850 there were roughly 7–9,000 Fuegian Indians of all tribes. By 1947 there were fewer than 150 in total. Today there are probably none.

The story of the displacement of native Tasmanians by white settlers from 1800 onwards is a similar tale of *Lebensraum*, ethnic cleansing and genocide. Women and children were enslaved, used as labourers and consorts. The men were usually shot. When they put up some resistance, the governor commissioned mounted police to hunt and kill the remainder. The new pursuit became big business and 'black-catching' became a leisure-time sporting opportunity. Finally, the remaining few hundreds were resettled on Flinders Island, where they died off under the harsh and inappropriate regime inflicted on them. On mainland Australia a similar final solution could not be accomplished, although it was attempted.

On the Spanish island of Gran Canaria, in a national park not far from Puerto Rico, set off the road to the magnificent volcanic mountains, you can find a reproduction of the aboriginal life of the island. The site is called Mundo Aborigen. Until the 1500s a relatively undeveloped people of large muscular build, physical strength and flaxen hair lived in stone-built shelters, pursuing their agricultural activities. They had a socially integrated but hierarchical lifestyle and seem to have been an evolutionary backwater, though clearly well adapted to their environment. But they were not, alas, adapted to withstand invading Spanish forces, and they too were ruthlessly eliminated.

Jared Diamond, author of *The Rise and Fall of the Third Chimpanzee*, listed genocides that have happened worldwide from 1492 onwards. There are 26 examples from the 20th century alone. One may sophisticate about the precise definition of genocide, but one may not escape the conclusion that humans in groups frequently show lethal hostility to other groups who are different, not 'one of us'. It is in our make-up. That is not to say it is justified or even natural. 'Motives' for these murderous assaults, whether they stem from conflicts of interest or are simply a stronger group displacing a weaker one, are secondary to the inherited behaviour pattern. When the 'motives' are ideological or, more confusingly, psychological, the reasoning can only be incomprehensible to an onlooker.

In northern Spain, near Burgos, is a deep, vertical shaft called La Sima de los Huesos (The Pit of Bones), at the bottom of which, the remains of 32 humans (thought to be *Homo erectus*) have been found, dating back 300,000 years. They were almost all teenagers, and seem to have been interred at more or less the same time. Among the suggestions for the calamity that caused the deaths of a closely related group of young people, many of whom show evidence of previous injury, is the idea that they had been fighting, maybe trying to defend their patch against a group of invaders. Tossing enemies, alive or dead, down a well-shaft – an oubliette in medieval terminology – was practised by our more immediate ancestors: a well-preserved example is found in Barclay Castle near Bristol. It does appear that violence towards rival groups or outsiders has marked hominid interaction since the beginning of time.

Although armies are composed of young, lusty men who traditionally make liberal use of brothels, and take their reward by the rape of conquests, modern military leaders do not behave like the satyrs of the last chapter. There is danger in generalising about sexual habits because so much happens in secret. But a large retinue of underlings around a great man usually ensures there is not much about him that doesn't leak out into the history books.

Adolf Hitler married his loyal admirer Eva Braun, whom he had treated with as much callous contempt as any woman close to him including his mother, only to make a suicide pact with her when his Reich lay in ruins about him. He was never in any doubt about the role of women, as docile producers of loyal soldiers for Germany, as compliant helpmeets for their menfolk, but never under any circumstances as holders of authority or as men's intellectual equals. In spite of all the unsubstantiated stories that are recounted about his genital deficiencies and his lack of potency, there is no doubt at all about his predominant heterosexual orientation. At sixteen he fell in love with a blonde girl called Stephanie, whom he worshipped from afar. He fantasised about her and dramatised his love-lorn role. What sixteen-year-old does not? This is no bizarre, obsessive trait; this is normal behaviour. With his friend Kubizek in Vienna, at nineteen he found release by talking about women and love, but remained alone either through shyness or lack of success. But later, in the days of his growing fame and eccentric, hypnotic reputation, though not yet among the ruling class, women responded more warmly to him. His gifts as an impassioned speaker had brought him to the notice of some wealthy society ladies (Frauen Bechstein, Hofmann and Wagner), who lionised him and tolerated his cranky behaviour as that of a budding genius. He would play the gallant charmer to his hostesses, with bouquets of flowers and elaborate Austrian courtesy. With his histrionic, almost palpable power, he mesmerised women, and revelled in doing so. In 1921 a small rebellious group within his embryonic Nazi Party, trying to undermine his authority, referred to his 'excessive intercourse with ladies to whom he describes himself as the King of Munich', and the cost of such goings-on. His confidence and its contrast with his former shyness towards the fair sex must have grown particularly as a result of his speeches, when the adulation and hysteria were identical to that accorded to pop stars in more recent times.

Hitler used this power over women en masse as a reason for not marrying in the days of his rise. In a social setting he loved to have beautiful women around him, seeking his favour and generally making a fuss of him. Albert Speers spoke of his rather gauche attempts at decorous gentility when in female company, and his 'shy eagerness to do nothing wrong'. This is rather like the description of Bill Clinton's 'puppy-like eagerness to please'. Yet how vast a difference between the two. Clinton slept with loads of women, yet there is speculation as to whether Hitler had intercourse with even one. Nobody knows for sure about his intimate sex life. There is no good evidence for the venereal disease he was supposed to have had, and the conjecture that his health problems and his late personality can be ascribed to syphilis are to be discounted. Hitler's capacity for sexual intercourse has been debated, and a close friend, Putzi Hansfstaengl, considered he was impotent, while Putzi's wife called him a neuter. Relationships with girls were plentiful, but intimacy? Possibly not. Hitler was much too busy at his favourite pastime, talking endlessly, holding forth in café society with a meek little woman in tow. But among political aspirants this is not unusual.

Hitler had two or three long-term relationships, and I believe this would have been impossible if he had not had some form of sexual congress. It may not have been strictly 'normal', but it would have had to satisfy his physical needs as well as more influential mental ones. Hitler's ego was vast and he would not have tolerated a feather-brained chit seeing him fail time and again. One of these nymphettes was Geli Raubal, the daughter of Hitler's widowed half-sister Angela, whom he had invited to be his housekeeper in 1925 on the Obersalzburg. Geli was attractive and, at seventeen, twenty years his junior. The extreme youth of consorts of important men is a regular theme going back into recorded time and implies nothing specific about Hitler. He fell deeply in love with her, indeed called her his life's one great love. He installed her in a room in his Munich home (as well as at Obersalzburg), and took pride in having her with him. He was at the beginning of his steep political rise and she no doubt enjoyed the reflected glory. He seems to have had much happiness in the six years they spent together, possibly the nearest he ever came to domestic contentment.

The rumours of Hitler's sexual deviancy have become accepted lore, but the origins of those stories must be questioned. False stories don't usually grow legs as long and run as far as these, but one must maintain a degree of scepticism, especially as the sources of those allegations had reason to be antagonistic. The photo-journalist Nachum Tim Gidal, who recorded Hitler's career in the 1920s for the *Munich Illustrated News*, said, 'Everyone in Munich knew that Hitler was some sort of sexual pervert.' And Hermann Rauchning, mayor of the free city of Danzig, who met Hitler on many occasions before he became an influential figure, talked of the 'reeking miasma of furtive unnatural sexuality that fills and fouls the whole atmosphere around him like an evil emanation'. In this there is much subjectivity, and since then reams of lines have been penned linking his sexual and socio-political perversions.

Otto Strasser, a journalist, and with his brother Gregor one of the early members of the Nazi Party, was at first a close associate of Hitler but later became a sworn enemy. He has talked of Hitler's deviancy with Geli Raubal in frank detail: that he achieved arousal by inspecting the girl's genitalia at close range as she squatted naked over him, then demanding that she urinate on him in order to reach climax. Raubal confessed to Otto that she found it disgusting. Hitler allegedly combined his fixaton and artistic talent to make drawings of Geli's intimate parts in full anatomical detail.

At a time when any sexual practice that deviated from the missionary method was regarded as wicked and depraved, one may imagine the effect of such demands on a bewitched and confused girl in her early twenties. Rumours abound about her infidelities, with love affairs, engagements and even pregnancy by other men, including Hitler's chauffeur. They cannot all be true. There is no doubt there were rows between them as to whether or not she should go to Vienna to have her voice trained, one of which stormy scenes occurred on Friday 18 September 1931, the day before she was found dead in her bedroom in Hitler's house, shot through the chest by Hitler's Mauser. Reputable biographies repeat the official verdict: suicide. But from what little one knows of Geli, on purely behavioural grounds, I doubt that. Her mother and her sister doubted it too. What would be more in keeping with Hitler's narcissistic, ego-inflated, masterman response than to kill (or have killed more likely) the thing he loved when she planned to desert him, perhaps for someone else? Such a wound his pride would never tolerate. His whole-hearted grief, his refusal to take meat or alcohol for the rest of his life, is wholly in keeping with her death at his instigation.

Hitler had an earlier romance with a sixteen-year-old called Mimi Reiter, whose account of his hoydenish and uncouth wooing of her, and his actual seduction, was free of any mention of perversion. Of his twelve-year relationship with Eva Braun, remakarbly little is known. She was 21 at the start, blonde, blue-eyed and vacuous, and is said to have made all the running. She was kept behind the scenes, and certainly in the war years his energies were channelled elsewhere. However, she lived with him, was his leisure-time companion whenever he had any, and was sufficiently submissive for him to unwind with her and ultimately to repay her loyalty.

If Hitler appears to defy Darwinian predictions that men use power to gain reproductive rewards, he is not alone in that respect. He is a prototype for the despot that I've called (with some poetic licence) the military celibate, a tyrant who owes much of his behaviour pattern to the ancient alpha male (other than the muted libido), but whose powers of destruction are infinitely more global and destructive. Of others who fit this pattern, more later. There was, however, an outlet with Hitler, a form of sublimation or compensation for his lack of attempt or desire to reproduce himself: his plans to propagate an idealised (in his view) Aryan, Germanic, blond, blue-eyed, healthy, sporty, militaristic master-race, free of all 'tainted blood' or 'inferior genes'. In *Mein Kampf* he wrote: 'A State which in this age of racial poisoning dedicates itself to the care of its best racial elements must some day become lord of the earth.'

He adopted an ill-educated form of Darwinism to justify his own penchant for a military lifestyle and his ambition to prevail over all around him. He believed struggle and warfare to be the natural order of the world (as Mao Zedong believed in perpetual revolution), and fitted his other beliefs round that central one, including his theories about eugenics and developing a master-race. He personalised 'Nature' and endowed her with his own will and intentions. 'Aryan' is a term originally defined by language, but several 19th-century writers had distorted its meaning to a specific race of superior qualities, conveniently Caucasian, and Hitler adopted those views, explicitly excluding people of Jewish origin. He had never travelled beyond Austria and Germany, other than during his war service in Flanders. His education was abysmal, yet he declared with the authority of the bar-room loud-mouth that all the best of art, culture, science and technology stemmed from Europe. The Aryan was destined from pre-history for supremacy, he wrote. Therefore, he justified the use of 'lower human types' as slaves and even as beasts of burden, but never, never as suitable mates for his alleged upper order. His notion of racial 'purity' became racial 'hygiene'. In the same way, the term 'ethnic cleansing' was coined elsewhere in Europe later in the century. In *Mein Kampf* Hitler proposed that German states should determine who procreated and with whom, while those regarded as degenerate should be forced into sterility.

Eight years later he began to put these ideas into practice. After he became chancellor he elevated the position of women in Nazi Gremany to a highly privileged one – provided they were suitable wives and mothers. Excluded from the professions and from positions of power, they were encouraged to come out of the workforce altogether to give place to men at a time of high unemployment. In 1933, newly married couples received a state loan of which the debt was cancelled after the fourth child. Mothers of four or more children were honoured with a medal and venerated, almost sanctified. Increasing the birth rate was deemed a priority for the chosen ones. To hasten the process, mass weddings were held in which forty or fifty couples could be signed up for procreation. Elite bridal schools were established for those women ambitious to win approval and gain a diploma as 'Master Housewife'. They learned all the domestic skills and virtues, notably how to provide a haven for their goose-stepping husbands. But marriage was only for the racially pure, the Aryan.

Women were indoctrinated with Hitler's unfounded genetic theory and required to show racial and medical purity before permission was granted to wed. For a prospective spouse of the elite SS, approved genealogy going back to great-great-grandparents was required. Contraception was forbidden and for abortion (if discovered) the punishment was death.

The other side of this ill-minted coin was that eugenics committees decreed who was not worthy: not only Jews, Slavs and Gypsies but those with mental and 'heritable' disabilities, so-called 'asocials'. Decisions were arbitrary. Such persons faced compulsory sterilisation.

Hitler became a pope-like figure, denying himself the privilege of progeny but acting the mystical father to his flock, regulating their behaviour so as to maximise reproduction. His selective breeding machine also has echoes of ancient Chinese emperors, except that they accorded the privilege to themselves alone. This difference in power behaviour is of immense significance. The modern tyrant has evolved through generations of pugilistic ancestors who could only conquer by the co-operation of their troops, to which end the sexual opportunities were bound to be shared. This theme will be expanded in the next chapter.

Of Hitler's fixation with all things military, his incredible successes and devastating defeats as commander-in-chief of the armed forces in war, others have written more fluently than I can. Preserved images of him are mostly in uniform. Acting out his belief in the inevitability of war, he is responsible for the mega-millions dead in the Second World War, including an estimated 4 to 4.5 million Jews. One million German women were left as widows.

Even before he dragged the world into his vortex he was busy practising systematic murder. His euthanasia programme in 1939, to dispose of 'defectives' – their disabilities erroneously labelled as inherited – probably led to 100,000 deaths before being stopped by the public outcry. And before that his taste for blood was gratified by street violence between the Brownshirts he led and the Communists in the early 1930s; and by legalised terror when he came to power, directed against all opposition groups, leaders of every faction who had opposed him or against whom he and his followers held a grudge.

Hitler, who to most minds is the epitome of evil, has defied explanation among the cleverest academic minds and the most profound thinkers. One crucial fact about him, amid the reams of theories, has been overlooked; or at least its significance has. This man with his merciless vendetta against miscegenation was himself misbegotten. His mother Klara was a serving maid in the house of Alois Hitler, her uncle. Alois himself was born out of wedlock and there is some doubt about the identity of his father, but the likelihood is that it was Johann Georg Hitler (Hiedler), whom his mother eventually married, or his wealthier brother Hohann Nepomuk, who brought Alois up. Either way, Alois was too closely related to Klara for the local bishop to allow the wedding, which eventually went ahead only after papal dispensation.

Now the reason why close kin are discouraged from breeding is that every last one of us carries recessive traits, which, if present in our genetic blueprint in double dosage (that is, received from both parents), programme damaging and undesirable characteristics. Closely related people have more likelihood of carrying identical recessive traits. Remember the example of sickle cell disease in Chapter 2. The single dose is beneficial; double dose is disastrous. Which aspects of Hitler – specifically which aspects of his behaviour – can be attributed to his consanguineous parents is a matter of pure speculation. Much of his behaviour is not unique, and is shared by 20th-century tyrants. Heaven forfend that one should call anything about it 'normal'. Many of the stereotyped features of these despots are behaviour buttons that are activated by a critical acquisition of power (or perception of power), and maybe these traits lie dormant in every man living, and in the genetic make-up of every woman. Few people have the mental strength to accept this view. Hitler does stand out among other arch-fiends in his capacity to hate so thoroughly and fixedly, but this is just a difference of degree. He did not hate Jewish people for any specific reason, conscious or subliminal; he simply inherited the capacity to hate, and he found an object for that malevolence in the Jews. Just because they were there, distrusted and vilified in Viennese society, where Hitler had prowled in his idle youth. Moreover, the popular perception in Vienna and elsewhere in Europe was that Jews were at the heart of the 'November criminals' who had supposedly stabbed Germany in the back at the end of the First World War and who were also in people's minds linked with the shady Bolsheviks. In *Mein Kampf*, Hitler proposed leading the people by provoking their hate against an enemy – any enemy – and fixing it there unswervingly. This is, alas, the likeliest explanation for the Holocaust I have read. Had there been other ethnic-minority populations on which this violent prejudice could fixate, they would have been the targets for the Final Solution. It is another example of the them-and-us syndrome. In a different historical setting, Hitler could easily have been 'merely' a Thomas Hamilton, wreaking his hatred on the children of Dunblane.

Hitler's ability to define his *Weltanschauung* at a young age, write it all down when he was at the bottom of the pile – a prisoner, a rebel with his power base scattered – and then go on to carry it out so literally, argues a deviant mind-set. But, to my mind, Hitler's most defining feature is the total absence of any moral dimension. Authorities have argued over whether he thought he was a criminal; Trevor-Roper stated that Hitler was convinced of his own rectitude. We moderns have so much morality ingrained in our behaviour that we have difficulty getting inside a mind devoid of all such shades. To Hitler the grabbing of power, the exploiting of weakness (especially courtesy), deceiving, manipulating, concealing, lying, blackmailing, threatening, intimidating, destroying, murdering, were what one did. To succeed was to be right. He was not in the least concerned about his own reputation. And though other despots sink to this lower common denominator gradually as they rise to power, Hitler was there already, even as a drop-out in his late teens.

There are plenty of examples of the military celibate in recent history. Most of the handfuls of names who have been instigators of wholesale slaughter can be fitted into this category. The combination of a taste for warfare with narcissism and an alpha-like craving for absolute power is especially ominous. Those alpha traits were dispersed so widely during the aeons of their monopolies that power freaks will keep on appearing for centuries to come.

Joseph Stalin was in my reckoning a shade more evil even than Hitler. If Hitler was devoid of morality or compassion, Stalin had no vestige of loyalty or fellow-feeling even for those around him: they were dispensible on the flimsiest pretext. In his later life, he seemed to need no emotional prop. In his mind he endowed all his associates with the same treachery as himself. When reading his biographies I experienced an almost unbearable depression, something I'd never felt before. A Western observer who visited the USSR commented on the unnerving and palpable fear of his entourage, for whom his vicinity was a minefield peppered with grenades. No wonder that Stalin suffered an extreme of paranoia: with no friends, his only safeguard was to hedge himself about with terror and thraldom. Whether we like to admit it or not, it worked for him. He didn't, in spite of unspeakable and uncountable crimes against humanity, come to a sticky end. He died of a stroke, in his bed, with an army of physicians trying to save him (and incidentally their own skins).

Nikolai Bukharin, an acolyte of both Lenin and Stalin who was ultimately arrested, tried and shot, may have anticipated his own downfall when he was prompted to speak frankly about Stalin on a visit to an exile in Paris. He said that Stalin above all needed to convince everyone, himself included, that he was the biggest, the greatest:

If someone can speak better than he can...write better than he writes...that person is doomed, as he won't let him remain alive, because that man is a constant reminder to him that he is not the first, the very best.

So, no honourable measuring of tooth, claw or antler in the jungle clearing for Stalin. Stack the odds on your side and obliterate the opposition till everyone around is more mediocre than you are. And what a job of work he had. Fear, force and subjugation were his weapons. He identified enemies everywhere – potential rather than real, names fed to him by his secret police – then ordered arrests, mass deportations, sham trials and executions. Any group labelled 'class enemy' or 'anti-revolutionary' was doomed.

In the 1920s he dealt with his political rivals for the leadership. By a clever process of shifting alliances, reading signs inexplicable to female minds, in the small group of momentarily equipoised leaders, he turned on and demoted Trotsky. Then he beavered away till the rest were undermined. It is a process familiar to politician-watchers today, except that Stalin's victories were ruthlessly followed up unto death. In 1924 in the top cadre, the Politburo, the seven men elected as full members were Zinoviev, Kamenev, Stalin, Trotsky, Bukharin, Rykov and Tomsky. The other six were eventually to die at Stalin's behest. In 1927 he created a law that legitimised the assassination of anyone he regarded as a threat to the regime. Soviet citizens who fled the country, immediately became candidates for summary execution. In the early 1930s, he waged civil war against the peasants, whom he saw as backward rustics opposing the utopia of communism. When landlords had been dispossessed of their lands, the peasants naturally expected to benefit. But this was not the idea in the minds of the urban rulers who only nominally believed in dictatorship of the proletariat. Stalin conjured up the notion of an exploiting rich peasant class – the kulaks – which he determined to eliminate. Indeed all his policy could be simplified to this principle: fixate upon your enemy and destroy him. The collectivisation of agriculture with deportation of kulaks, requisitioning of grain and formation of factory farms led to famine, revolts, much untold misery and the deaths of 9.5 million people. Anyone who even questioned Stalin's interpretation of Marxism–Leninism was given the catch-all label 'enemy of the people' and faced ostracism, nearly always dying soon afterwards by some means.

Suspicions were harboured against non-Russian republicans within the USSR; Georgians and Ukrainians, for instance, and anyone who showed more fervour for his own ethnic group than the Union, was courting annihilation. People who had known Stalin in his youth, particularly relations of both his wives, found themselves facing execution on some pretext or other. In 1937 he claimed that remnants of the former exploiting classes, ex-capitalists and officers, would become increasingly embittered and dangerous. They were to be pursued. More millions died. A massive 'cleansing' of the army began, with the arrest of 43,000 senior personnel, of whom 15,000 would be shot. Of the 85 members of the Military Army Council, 68 were shot. He had devastated the senior ranks in the run-up to world war, which he might have noticed had he looked out at world affairs instead of his own back.

During the war itself, Stalin brooked no argument from his military leaders and, when his own tactics proved disastrous, scapegoated them by charges of treason followed by torture and death. He cascaded down his method of mass terror to prevent wavering in the troops. He made himself a marshal and a generalissimo, and accepted accolades of 'the greatest military leader of all time'. During the war, 26.5 million Soviets died, half of them civilians. Then those returning from occupied territories were objects of his paranoia, earning deportation and twenty years' hard labour, in effect a death sentence. He backed Kim Il Sung in the Korean War and with Mao Zedong contemplated provoking an East–West third world war. By 1952, his imagination still providing hallucinatory enemies, Stalin attacked Jewish groups and leading physicians. Not long afterwards he required medical attention on his death bed, when his doctors were threatened with dire consequences if he did not survive. But fear was not omnipotent after all, and he expired despite their collective efforts.

For Stalin, as a biological being, what was the driving force behind the relentless pursuit of total power? Was it a mindless obsession? A genetic irrelevance? He sought few sexual indulgences. He married at 27, but his wife died the following year of typhus, leaving a baby son. In 1913 he fathered an illegitimate child with a peasant woman. At 40 he married again, Nadezhda Alliluyeva, who was 22 years younger than he. She bore him a son and a daughter and was a traditional wife, providing the infrastructure of a life of passionate politics untainted by any other vice or pleasure. Not even the accumulation of possessions nor external symbols of power did he seem to need, certainly not women or dalliance. Nadezhda died violently of gun-shot wounds, allegedly after a humiliating public quarrel with Stalin, following hearing that he had a woman with him in his dacha. Echoes of Geli Raubal perhaps? After her death, he was supplied with a succession of pretty housekeepers for his basic necessities. A low-key sex life indeed.

The United States Constitution (22nd Amendment) prevented the emergence of a Stalinesque figure in the shape of Richard Nixon. When he won a second term in office he actively explored the chance of changing the goal posts to give himself a third term. Had he achieved that he would, like Stalin, have been stopped only by death itself.

In the years before his target of gaining the presidency in 1968, public feeling against the Vietnam War ran high, and though it was Nixon's instinct to oppose with all American might the blustering communist regime in North Vietnam, and he was even willing to deploy nuclear weapons, he vacillated on spoken policy. He fingered public opinion, seeking out the most popular line to take to win the election. President Johnson, meanwhile, actively arranging peace talks in the pre-election run and halting the bombing with that in mind, looked set to engineer a beginning to the end of the war. The Democratic candidate's popularity vote rose accordingly. But President Thieu of South Vietnam, already fearing for his downfall if the US withdrew, was got at by Nixon and persuaded to back off from the talks. Nixon cynically tried to spoil the drive for peace in order to tip the election stakes in his favour. He remained opaque on specifics but posed as a man of peace while holding the paradoxical view, as many have before and since, that he could bomb a country into submission and peace on his own terms. It took the next four years of bloody slaughter to convince him he was wrong, in which time nearly 21,000 more Americans died, nearly 110,000 South Vietnamese soldiers, almost 500,000 communist opponents, and an unknown, exorbitant number of innocent bystanders. Neutral Cambodia was drawn in by Nixon's first saturation bombing campaign around

Vietnam's borders, which by an ignition effect led to the loss of 2,000,000 more lives, and which was a fiercely guarded secret since it was totally illegal. Nixon liked to project to his foreign enemies the image of a slightly unhinged aggressor with his finger hovering over the nuclear button: a modern equivalent of animal-posturing. In private his language on Vietnam was hawkish: 'We'll bomb the bastards off the earth', 'We've got to have more of this. Assassinations. Killings', 'The bastards have never been bombed like they're going to be bombed this time'. After his second election to the presidency in 1972 he wanted to be rid of the troublesome war and ordered round-the-clock bombardment, bludgeoning a way out of the mess that he could call an honourable victory.

Nixon was unmoved by atrocities committed by American soldiers, including the wanton massacre of old men, women and children at My Lai. In his attempts at various stages of his career to topple left-wing regimes such as those of Castro in Cuba and Allende in Chile, he was at ease with the notion of assassination of national leaders. He was convinced that communists orchestrated the staunch, youthful protests against his wartime policy, besieged as he was at such times in the White House by the 'liberal bastards'. On one occasion he had ordered 300 soldiers armed with machine-guns to be on stand-by in the basement in case things got out of hand. He was prepared for his own massacre of youthful protesters, Tiananmen Square style.

Richard Nixon was as emotionally constipated as a man can be. He hated physical expression of love, which equated with his terror of appearing weak. He was a man's man par excellence. As a high-school lad he professed to hate girls, and contemporaries say he was never comfortable among women. Reluctant to begin dating when everyone else was doing so, at sixteen he got his first girlfriend, Ola. Once the relationship was established he began humiliating her, going home from parties with someone else, two-timing her, spending the evening ignoring her and chatting in an all-male group. It was the same pattern he would adopt with his wife Pat at a later date, only more so. Even at that age he was described as 'a man of no warmth with a nasty temper'.

Nixon remained a virgin until his marriage at 27, and even after that initiation continued to be shy and afraid of women. He was never suspected of philandering. Though he would indulge in coarse obscenities and leering innuendo in all-male company, his discomfort on sex translated into misogyny and insults towards women. His psychotherapist described him as a blushing, stammering schoolboy whenever sexual topics were approached.

To onlookers, Nixon's treatment of his wife Pat was cold and functional. He used her ruthlessly to promote the stable, family-man image (they had two daughters), accepting her manifold sacrifices as his due, but off-stage he would pointedly ignore her, reject her affection, stalk through doors in front of her as if she were his minion. During stressful campaigns he would treat her with wounding contempt, even swearing at her in front of the staff: 'Keep your fucking mouth shut.' In private she would feel the brunt of his vile temper, which was worsened by his driving himself beyond the limits. There seems little doubt that he physically abused her in his vicious loss of control, punching and beating her to the extent of her needing hospital care, especially after he had been drinking. This was probably in part a result of anger transference because of intermittent impotence, which his psychotherapist obliquely confirmed, and to which Nixon's pressurised lifestyle and alcohol excess would make him especially prone.

By his staff Nixon was perceived as sexless and there were jokes exchanged to that effect. One of his aides labelled him 'the Mad Monk'. Democrats were never able to ferret out bedroom stories about him, though they tried. In spite of his strait-laced image, more women voted for Nixon in 1960 than for J F Kennedy.

Nixon was capable of loving and of maintaining long-term mutual relationships – with men. There is no evidence whatever that he was actively homosexual, though he may have been covertly so. His longest-serving colleague was Murray Chotiner, his press adviser, whose motto was 'Politics is war', and who had known links to crime. The equivalent to Nixon of Blair's Alastair Campbell, Chotiner was at Nixon's elbow in all his election campaigns, justifying any means to the end of winning. Nixon's other shadow was his lifelong close friend Bebe Rebozo, his Peter Mandelson, a wheeler-dealer and a go-between, ever on a remarkably intimate footing with Nixon, who called Bebe his 'alter ego'. Bebe was seriously wealthy, a bank-owner, who worshipped and adored Nixon, and they indulged in mutual money-grubbing. Bebe was his sole companion on holidays, on sponsored travel, on rest-cures and, at times of profound depression following episodes of defeat, occupying the place that Pat should have held. The number of times they were seen alone together roused wagging tongues to gossip, especially as Rebozo's colourful reputation establishes him as bisexual. They were even seen holding hands under a table in a restaurant. But the prevailing opinion seems to be that the relationship was that of 'arrested adolescents', limited to gawping and sniggering at topless women on beaches and exchanging bawdy jokes.

Amazing to relate, Nixon was a charmed admirer of the young Jack Kennedy in their early years in Congress, when they discovered much in common. As Nixon embarked on an official trip to Paris, Jack handed him a list of young, compliant women and their phone numbers, but Nixon was too embarrassed to take it. In 1954 when JFK was seriously ill and had been given the last rites, Nixon dissolved into tears, sobbing to his bodyguard, 'That poor young man is going to die. Poor brave Jack is going to die. Oh God, don't let him die.' Close friends confirmed Nixon's warm feelings, varying from liking to admiring to loving.

Other modern leaders who qualify as military celibates (or mad monks) are Winston Churchill, Augusto Pinochet, Slobodan Milosevic and Vladimir Lenin. Going further back, Oliver Cromwell is a classic example, as is Horatio Nelson, and so, oddly, is Napoleon Bonaparte, at least in the early phase of his life – he can be regarded as a hybrid, oscillating between this identity and that of classic alpha male. The same is true of Mao Zedong.

Throughout his life, Winston Churchill experienced the extremes of ambivalence in his fascination with warfare and all things military – indeed his 'genius for war' as one cabinet colleague remarked – and his perception at a different level of the devastation and obscenities resulting from it. This violent contradiction and his awareness of it contributed to his depressions, his 'black dog'. He was widely read on the subject of war, loved to visit historical battlefields, and knew in fine detail the interactions of famous engagements. He would regale dinner guests with an analysis of, say, the Battle of Jutland, with cigar smoke and goblets as props, vocal rat-a-tat noises, and extreme boyish enthusiasm. At the outbreak of the First World War he wrote to Clemmie, his wife, about how 'geared up and happy' he was, yet he admitted his 'hideous fascination' was horrible, an affront to morality. Asquith, the prime minister, wrote of his bellicosity, that 'Winston has got on all his warpaint'. Yet even two or three years earlier Churchill had predicted that, if two modern, scientifically developed nations came to blows, 'they will be heartily sick of it before they come to the end of it'. During the war, after visiting the front line, he begged Asquith to relieve him of his political post and give him some military command; military glory had more compelling appeal. Caught off-guard in a moment of euphoria by Margot Asquith, he enthused of history in the making, future fame and 'this glorious, delicious war'. Later, after the Gallipoli fiasco and his part in it, removed from government office, he felt released from care and thoroughly content to take his place in the trenches.

No wonder then that he earned a reputation as a warmonger, which was reinforced when he persistently opposed the disarmament trends in the thirties, with blunt truths about the menace of Hitler and his sinister colleagues. Churchill's role as a wartime prime minister was identified with defeating Hitler and winning the war, and his countrymen were content to allow him his dictatorship for the duration, but no longer. Churchill's most delectable moments were when Britain stood alone before the US entered the war, after which major decisions were taken in cahoots with Roosevelt and Stalin. A German newspaper in the 1950s, the *Deutsche Zukunft*, recorded that he had 'driven out the devil Hitler with the aid of Beelzebub, Stalin', which was incontrovertibly true.

With his pugilistic powers fading in later life, Churchill rationalised his obsession by becoming a proponent for peace. He cited the existence of the hydrogen bomb as a compelling reason for world disarmament. Although he considered the essence of man's history as warfare, he did not believe conflict to be inevitable – and certainly not 'right' – as Hitler did. But he thought that men would always need constraint, suggesting that the Almighty should create English Channels round every country and scupper at base anything attempting to fly.

Churchill had a wife and six children, but though he wrote devoted and affectionate letters to Clementine, he spent much time apart from her. Lord Moran, his doctor, admitted that Churchill never referred to women in conversation; he was just not interested in them. Indeed he intimidated most of them into deferential silence in his presence, unless they were supremely self-confident like Lady Diana Cooper, or shared an interest with him, such as painting. Moran talked of the 'formidable ramparts of indifference' he presented to females. There were traces of misogyny, and he bitterly opposed women getting the vote. Yet he loved the company of men, and made close, affectionate alliances with them, usually for specific purposes, such as with Roosevelt for instance. During the Second World War his emotional attachment to Roosevelt was a cause of concern to colleagues at home, especially Anthony Eden. Desmond Morton of the Secret Intelligence Service, a long-term friend, described Winston's dependence on the President as an 'enthusiasm and affection that was almost homosexual in its entirety'. There is some evidence that Morton himself was speaking out of pique and jealousy at having been displaced from a confidential and dependent friendship with Churchill.

Churchill took strong likes and antipathies, and his judgement of a man was invariably influenced by personal factors. His friends, writes Moran, were all men of violent thought: Lloyd George, Mountbatten, Max Beaverbrook and others of that ilk. Not a man to engage easily on a personal level, he would nevertheless be attracted and engaged by masculine beauty and charm. He inspired affection in his turn. Top-ranking naval and army officers agreed: 'You cannot help loving that man.'

Reaching back in time to find an ancestor common to both Augusto Pinochet and Slobodan Milosevic might require an extension lead measuring many millennia; yet the two could be blood brothers.

Both seem to have been dull, grey, pedestrian, dutiful subordinates in their early years, neither destined for fame and glory. Both were influenced by extremely strong wives, and in Pinochet's case, a feisty mother too. Ideology for one was communism; for the other Roman Catholicism and anti-communism. But, in each case, the ideology was but a vehicle to power, while the wives were more staunchly orthodox. Both wives indulged in ostentatious consumerism and luxurious indulgence; but Mira Milosevic is seen as an evil Lady Macbeth or Red Queen, a power behind the throne with blood on her own hands. Pinochet, the uxorious family man, produced five children with his wife Lucia. By 1999 his own dynasty included 25 grandchildren and four great-grandchildren. The Catholic attitude to birth control assists dynastic ambition. Milosevic only ever had one girlfriend, Mira. They met in their teens and became totally inseparable, married and had two children.

Pinochet, a man of mediocre intellect, had wanted nothing better than to become a soldier, though struggled to make the grade as an army cadet. A boring and rather prudish obsessional, possessed of little charm, he wormed and engineered his way to commander-in-chief of the army of Chile in 1973. He had a defining moment, a transubstantiation, when he took part in the bloody coup to depose Marxist President Allende. The day before, in the midst of his daughter's birthday party, while surrounded by the squeals and high jinks of the innocents, he plotted and doubted with his brother fighting men. On the day of the coup he arrived late at the rendezvous having gone to see his sleeping grandchildren, for a possible farewell. But it all worked out for him, and he came to dominate the military junta as supreme chief with unlimited powers. He ruled by fear and repression, assassination and torture (including hideous methods of sexual torture). Chile became isolated on the international scene, and in response, Pinochet fostered a home-grown arms industry, linked to the narcotics trade, all of which helped to feed his coffers. Connecting with other military dictatorships in South America, Pinochet's State Police ran an organisation of terror against communists and radicals, ultimately responsible for tens of thousands of deaths and permanent maimings.

Milosevic, by contrast reversing the more customary order, progressed from politician to warrior. He also had his meeting with destiny, his metamorphosis, which would propel him from mediocrity to mastery. He had risen in the Serbian communist establishment, and in the wake of his mentor Ivan Stambolic, who loved him as a brother and did not perceive him as anything other than a loyal lieutenant. Milosevic was not a front-line man, neither an orator nor a headline-grabber. He lived modestly and seemed to harbour no high ambition. In this low-key capacity he was sent to conciliate rebellious Serbs in Kosovo in 1987. Faced for the first time by an angry crowd, he abandoned his set soft-soap speech and became subsumed by their prevailing angry mood. Probably his instinct was to mollify by appearing to agree with them. He was so successful that the crowd fell in love with him, applauding their new instant hero. And he, after one shot of mass adulation, was addicted for life: a Jehovah junkie. He began a vendetta against Stambolic, which caused his friend's downfall and his own advancement. The genie released from the bottle waged war, fomented vicious ethnic cleansing, wreaked personal revenge by assassination, and committed whatever atrocities were needed to maintain himself in power for thirteen years.

Who would have thought that Oliver Cromwell and Vladimir Lenin had much in common? They were both regicides for a start, and justified that act with a welter of incoherent, populist, reforming theories, which after seizing power thay shaped to their own ends. Lenin formulated his theories as an armchair intellectual in exile, a theoretical revolutionary who hated the tsar with more venom even than Cromwell hated Charles I. Lenin's brother Sasha had been hanged for anti-tsarist plotting, but Lenin himself was propelled not by revenge but by the same genetic behaviour pattern. Cromwell's early politics were a confused mixture of pro-parliamentary, pro-royalist crusading fudge. Both considered themselves men of destiny, sent to overthrow the ruling order, but Lenin was too arrogant to acknowledge a higher authority as Cromwell did with his fixation with God. Cromwell, the supremely gifted, self-taught militarist, was in his element on the field of battle, where he bared fangs, claws and all his armamentarium. Lenin never killed a man in his life, and had no experience direct or indirect of warfare, though he was much given to hunting wild animals. But he unleashed the dogs of war following the October 1917 Revolution with uncontrolled malevolence and minimal discrimination.

Throughout most of his life, Lenin's pugilistic vocabulary of struggle and conflict referred to the virtual warfare between his Bolsheviks and other left-wing factions. Unlike Cromwell, his youthful character in the days of his obscurity showed alarmingly vicious streaks, unmoved as he was by human suffering on a massive scale in wartime and famine, and even coldly accepting these things as a necessary fall-out on the road to revolution. In the early abortive attempts at revolution in 1905 he took an appalling delight in bloodthirsty and sadistic plans, though it was never he who did the dirty work. After 1917 his orgy of revenge in the name of class struggle became so extreme that it seemed he was hell-bent on destroying not only the Romanovs and the aristocracy, but all the bourgeoisie: the landlords, the rich and privileged, bankers, merchants, civil servants, professionals, priests. In the Civil War, his violence knew no moderation. His Red Army had to win, no matter what the cost. Like Hitler he demanded the impossible from his generals, wanted instant success, brooked no failures, no backsliding. His relish for the kill rolled ever closer to those he purported to champion; the ordinary people of Russia. Peasants who horded grain were to be poison-gassed and bombed. Industrial strikers and nationalist rebels of Georgia, Armenia and Azerbaijan were dealt with ruthlessly by the secret police, the Cheka. A naval garrison that rose in revolt at the oppressive rule was quashed ferociously. Even those accused of minor fraud or profiteering were to be shot. This supposed left-wing extremist had much of the hang-'em-and-flog-'em philosophy about him that we associate with a fascist mentality.

The Red Army emerged relatively victorious from the Russian Civil War, which gave more impetus to Lenin's desire to extend revolution to Europe and beyond. He enthused about 'seizing capitalism by the throat' and set his sights on Poland. He alone was eager for more bloodshed, oblivious to universal war-weariness and lack of sufficient preparedness of the army for more combat. His iron will mowed down his colleagues' objections. Even while his regiments were doing their stuff by advancing into Poland, Lenin advocated subversive, guerilla-type murderous assaults on the class enemies in that country, slavering for the way to be cleared for his dominance to extend, with all elements of society cowed before him in terror. One may well see him as the spiritual father of Stalin in his promiscuous death-dealing.

Lenin was never a lady's man, his passion being channelled into his revolutionary zeal. He married Nadezhda Konstantinovna, who slaved for him and his ideals as women often do; and also had a long-term though intermittent French mistress, Inessa Armand. There were no known children. Throughout his life Lenin relied heavily on support from a family of women consisting of wife, mistress, mother and two sisters, who supported him loyally and unstintingly even unto death. Obsessional emotional intensity was reserved for his male relationships, for his rivalries with Kautsky, Trotsky and Stalin, and likewise for his idolisation of Marx and Plekhanov (a left-wing political theorist). His adulation of both these philosophers was of an intensity equivalent to a love affair, with sexual echoes, as he and his wife recognised. Plekhanov used the analogy of marriage to describe their relationship, which was to fall apart in a bitter 'divorce' when there came to be an ideological difference between them. Lenin was severely disillusioned and distraught at being humiliated by someone whom he – HE – had treated with such meekness and veneration. He determined to imprison his emotions in the future and let them reflect upon himself.

Oliver Cromwell's intimate life was exemplary, after he had sown a few wild oats in his youth. He was the adored youngest son of a large family of which he was the only male to survive, and spent his formative years as the focus of attention of a worshipful mother and six older sisters. His wife Elizabeth was a traditional, self-sacrificing, fecund handmaiden with inner reserves, who ordered his domestic life with unfailing serenity and provided him with six children. He undoubtedly enjoyed the company of pretty women and liked to play the gallant charmer. Rumours of a couple of mistresses circulated when he was lord-protector, but with no more evidence than contemporary gossip to substantiate them.

*

Here are numerous examples of the modern, sexually ascetic leader, and yet more spring readily to mind. There is no strict division into either this type or the orgiastic one of the last chapter; indeed it is clear that a man may show features of both types at different times of life, or under varying circumstances. With any individual, one may discern a predominant behaviour pattern of one type, but with echoes and shades of the other.

Yet the conundrum that requires an answer is, why have modern despots divorced themselves from the behavioural drive to reproduce? In an era when, for reasons yet to be explored, tyrants have been able to flaunt unparalleled power over the lives of millions, without themselves having to face the business end of guns and missiles, so they seem to have stronger emotional bonds with other men and perfunctory, merely functional interest in women. Even as Darwin propounded his prediction that individuals have evolved to strive to maximise their own reproduction, at that very moment humans were giving him the lie, setting out to refute that axiom. And I will give an answer to that riddle as I progress.

CHAPTER 8

Create or Destroy

Bill Clinton's sex drive might suggest that he had descended directly from ape-like stock without any intermediary stages, whereas Adolf Hitler's was so unproductively restrained as to suggest he was a genetic aberration, a mutant destined to end in a cul-de-sac. The whole Kennedy tribe copulated feverishly, yet their kamikaze lifestyle almost seems to have counterbalanced the reproductive advantage. What are powerful men up to these days in the reproductive stakes? The Kennedy family give an anecdotal hint of at least some of the things that have been happening in recent aeons. Where stakes become ever higher and out of reach, risk-taking must become equally extreme. A point may be reached where the chances of an individual going into self-destruct are much higher than the chances of him begetting offspring. Alternatively, if a man aspires to collective risk-taking, gets himself to the top of a small group of pugilistic males, makes allies with mutual loyalty to self-protect, then he is afforded some security. The more he is established as the leader of that small group, the greater is his protection. Then his task is to increase the size, power and loyalty of his clique and quell any opposition by fear or decimation or whatever means come to hand. In the jungle, the alpha male of various primate species has two broad tactics: one is to mate as frequently and as effectively as possible, while the second is to destroy other males' offspring, prevent them mating at all, even slaughtering them before they can do so. In pre-industrial humankind, the first ploy seems to have been slavishly followed.

But maybe in modern times, with so dense a population, and with such a predominance of alpha genes scattered around that population, it has become more efficient to emphasize the destructive side of the equation. Remember that it has always been part of a despot's power – part of his definition – to kill off his subjects arbitrarily. In modern times a powerful leader can mangle whole continents at the press of a button. The risk to him is not negligible, but he is not in the front line.

The 'reproductive strategy' of the Kennedy family, of Bill Clinton, of Mao Zedong and other classic alphas could with the required technology and patience be traced all the way back to the Last Common Ancestor we shared with chimpanzees about six million years ago. My inverted commas imply that the avid sexual activity is driven by motives well below conscious level. This behaviour has been seen in the chiefs of despotic societies in recent millennia, according to Betzig's study, in a predictable power/harem-size equation. Though uncommon nowadays, we still see hints of it, and I would predict that this behaviour module is present in most if not all men, ready to kick in if the moment is right. In our crowded world the chances of the right moment arriving are vanishingly small. The newer strategy replacing the older one is likewise of ancient lineage. It came about like this.

Approximately seven million years ago, with the dwindling of the forests in Africa, our ancestors found their comfortable lifestyle challenged. Gathering of edible plants, chimpanzee-style, became less predictable. It seems that, like modern chimps, they had indulged in some hunting of small forest creatures, so the capability of adaptation was already present as plant food sources became progressively scarce. It is not difficult to imagine that hunting would, over time, become more important to the daily diet, and that tightly knit family-social groups of hominids would become increasingly aggressive towards other foreign groups who threatened their patch or collided with their hunting party on the now more open scrubland. Alliance groups would tend to increase as the dangers loomed larger. Here are the roots of xenophobia and of the need to expand the group's territory. And here within this interdependent society began the evolution of co-operation, of mutual rewards for allies and exclusion of free-loaders, of the need for imprinting faces and friendly acts on a long-term memory, to register favours given and received. These characteristics are still part of our human make-up, and the punishment of the vulnerable in our society, the single parent and the pensioner, the chronically sick and the elderly by the establishment (of whatever political persuasion) dates from this primordial need for collective survival, to offload perceived freeloaders. We are not generous at heart; we do not give free lunches. In mutual back-scratching lies the seeds of trade also, though that came later.

The impact of the change from gathering to hunting lifestyle impinged most fundamentally on family relationships and on sexual strategies. By the time the earliest humans evolved (*Homo erectus* in Africa about 1.6 million years ago), whose diet was thoroughly meat-orientated, a man was obliged to co-operate with his mates in a democratic way, and range far from home to achieve success at this dicey occupation. The preoccupation with sex and leap-frogging the hierarchy had had to be drastically rethought. Lifestyle strategy was to be turned upside down according to the dictates of material need at least twice in the ensuing millennia. The females of the pack were excluded from hunting by the need to care for the young. Undoubtedly other reasons played a part too, for their smaller size, less muscular build and relative lack of warlike aggression would be ill-adapted to the pursuit-and-kill. Here began the divergent patterns of gender roles that feminists today work so hard to banish – logically enough, for they evolved to fit us for a lifestyle several millennia old. Men hunted and women gathered. Men left the home-base in groups; women stayed and occupied themselves with domestic activities. Men spent longer and longer hours with the macho group, and home-life became a pause, a rest, a pit-stop between the pulses of rash, dangerous living. When they returned from several days of exhausting activity, perhaps with rich rewards, or maybe with none, perhaps with injury, they expected to be welcomed with every comfort and the assured arms of a waiting woman, a Stone Age geisha. There would be little energy left for any nonsense about harems and, in any case, every hunting man deserved his just recompense. Pair-bonding became the fundamental sexual strategy, though not the exclusive one. Males wreaked their risk-taking propensities against prey or against foreigners rather than against each other, for no longer could one Mr Big seize the monopoly. A woman would try to corner and keep the most successful hunting man she could. For many millennia these hunting packs must have been nomadic, for they spread from Africa into Europe and Asia; but, as in modern Mongolia, the wandering would have been punctuated by episodes of settlement.

By 100,000 years ago, the first social groups of modern humans were composed of 150 individuals. The society changed very little. Old folk died and young ones were born; everyone knew everyone else, and strangers were hostiles by definition and considered threats. This lack of anonymity in the group would have assisted in a rough and ready system of justice. Rather like an Agatha Christie whodunnit, with an enclosed and limited set of people of known character, culprits would have been readily identified. By this time it is believed that language had developed. It is debatable which facet of survival value drove this acquisition but, once in place, many benefits would ensue: better co-operation with hunting and gathering, sharing of acquired wisdom between siblings and down the generations, gossip, alliance-making, exchanging of reciprocal favours, the establishment of reputation. As language became more sophisticated, it acquired another potential use: that of dominance. A man who talks loudly and without cessation in a commanding voice can dispense with the flamboyant display of the chimpanzee. This behaviour has a reciprocal effect in onlookers, that of deference. Women especially would meekly sit and listen while other males, depending on status, got irritated and tried to interrupt and steal the floor. We've progressed now to modern boardrooms, and to the House of Commons. The importance of speech as a dominating strategy has been neglected. It has been a crucial tool among men of power to gain and keep ascendancy.

The nomadic troupe of 150 or so would have suffered a degree of internal conflict at times, over such issues as cheating or sexual rivalry, and if groups got too large would split up, with family bands moving off to begin a separate society. This process would aid the amazing worldwide dispersal of humans that took place over the last hundred millennia. The diaspora effect of quarrels and disputes on such bands is evident in social studies on more modern African tribes. Replacing competition by co-operation does not eliminate conflict, it seems.

The advent of agriculture some 10,000 years ago brought its own socio-sexual revolution. The control of food sources by crop-growing and the domestication of farm animals meant that individuals could accumulate wealth and thus the capacity to buy the favours and labour of other men. There was again an imbalance in commodity and privilege availability, and in power (I recall when domestic deep freezes became available in the mid-20th century, a parallel event took place in microcosm. The landed gentry, when they had a day's shooting, could now stuff the massive surplus of pheasants into a freezer chest for their future consumption. Previously they had shared the perishable game with underlings, employees and friends). In the embryonic days of farming, as a man grew richer with more fields, more oxen, greater skill with husbandry, so he gained more political clout and took on proportionately more wives. There is ample evidence in Betzig's study that men have followed this rule as if they had been instructed and indoctrinated, until the last few hundred years.

With increasing population density, flowering of knowledge and technology, proliferation of desirable goods and skills, sociologists argue that society comes to behave as an organism itself, with specialised parts, all of which are mutually interdependent. This certainly happens in certain insect groups such as ants, wasps, bees and hornets. Here even the sexes become ultra-specialised and all co-operate in turning a queen into a machine for reproduction on behalf of the whole colony. The theory that individuals can merge to become part of a larger being is not at all in the realms of science fiction. The arrangement of our body cells is organised on similar principles to social insects, and evolutionary theory holds that 600 million years ago our ancestors' cells were free-living entities who merged for more efficient preservation and propagation. So it is not unreasonable to detect a trend that pushes our society towards true integration. We should welcome it. It may be salutary to know that certain cells in our bodies are programmed to die when their duty is done; if they do not but attempt to endure and become immortal, madly proliferating all the while, they can turn into monstrously destructive, all-consuming clonal cancers. What an accurate analogy this is for despots and tyrants! In a more enlightened age I hope we will control such phenomena before they acquire those illusory intimations of immortality, as the immune system does in the body in most instances.

In human post-industrial societies, specialisation in skills of all kinds, trade, crafts, science, technology, teaching, physicking, have made single members and groups indispensable, and accordingly the trend has been towards increasing democratisation. So it has been also with sexual privileges, and so yet again there is a return to hunter-style monogamy (with maybe a little furtive cheating). It is clear that humans are highly adaptable and have sexual behaviour modules in their brains to suit every circumstance. The switch from one style to another can occur within one personal lifetime. Matt Ridley describes a tribe of salmon-fishing Indians of the Pacific who clicked over from polygamy to monogamy and back according to the balance of the prevailing hunter-gatherer economy.

Napoleon Bonaparte showed the same flexibility. In his soldier-boyhood he was sexually repressed, a prude and a misogynist who hated female intellectuals and thought women were simply vehicles for breeding. Though he held in distaste adultery and over-indulgence, he was oddly tolerant of Josephine's multiple infidelities. Beset by guilt and alternate fascination and repulsion by sex, he was accused of a youthful homosexual relationship. Before battle, fantasising perhaps that his male parts were weapons, he habitually masturbated. Yet in his rising power he had serial mistresses and sometimes prodigiously lecherous orgies, especially after fighting. He divorced Josephine because of her barrenness and remarried to produce a legitimate heir.

Although both types of socio-sexual lifestyle are associated with intermittent violence, it does emerge that by far the more frequent, more wholesale and more integral mayhem comes with the hunter-type package. This is what one might expect, and the contrast between the two contemporaneous dictators, Hitler and Mussolini, prototypes respectively for the monogamous hunter and the

polygamous alpha, illustrates the point with crystal clarity.
Mussolini, although an apostle of violence, was anti-military in his
youth. His attitudes were shaped to suit the moment and, although
he headed the Fascists and adopted military-style marching and
swaggering, he never made military expansion and investment his
raison d'être, as Hitler did. In 1937, already anxious about German
hawkishness, Mussolini travelled to Munich as Hitler's guest. He
was treated to an immaculately choreographed display of
officialdom in impeccable uniform, driven along streets lined with
pallisades of soldiers standing rigidly to attention, backed by crowds
of cheering, animated admirers. He was then taken on an inspection
tour of factories stuffed with hardware, cannons, guns and tanks,
and watched a display of military manoeuvres. Mussolini was
dumbfounded at Germany's invincibility, jealous, impressed and
drawn along in Hitler's wake in spite of himself. To Hitler he was
first an admired dictator-icon, later a brother-in-arms, then a junior
partner whom he could snub and treat with contempt. Mussolini
swithered between extremes of indecision before committing
himself to war on Germany's side. At the historic meeting in the
Brenner Pass in March 1940, Mussolini was stunned into silence by
Hitler's onslaught of hysterical rhetoric. All he could do in his
stupefaction was agree to join the Axis. Events spiralled out of his
control thereafter; he was always to play second fiddle to the man
he could not match in single-minded enemy fixation. Mussolini as
commander-in-chief of the Italian army never approached nearer
than 500 miles of the front line; he was a nominal soldier-chief and
his heart was not in it. Rather his heart was in bed with a woman;
and his self-love was more concerned about his manicure, his
creature comforts, his safety and his image. At last, deposed and
arrested, then rescued by the Germans, he became a puppet ruler.
His ignominious fate was sealed.

By contrast, Hitler's obsession with hate, kill and expand never
wavered until he was trapped like a rat in the bunker in Berlin.

Whether the genetic apparatus for coupling and for fighting are
parcelled up together or whether they are closely linked but separable
is an open question. Desmond Morris describes two reasons for

fighting: hierarchical and territorial. Hierarchy is the domain of the classic alpha male whereas territory is the stamping ground of the military man. Humans in their infinite complexity have both types of aggression triggers to contend with, plus at least two more. First, each family has its own patch within the group territory, and that too must be defended against intrusion. Primitive man would include his chattels and his wife in this mini-territory. Second, in an overcrowded society, simply being so densely packed creates its own tensions and outbreaks of bickering and fighting. Related to the last is the ready perception of wealth and privilege differentials, engendering jealousy, anger, protests, rebellion, inner-city violence and mass revolution. This may well be an inevitable part of the path to co-operation and unification but alas the turbulence is only too likely to throw up yet another malignant leader.

Let us return to the hunting hominid. With a brain size that was showing rapid enlargement under some evolutionary directive even as he developed his hunter lifestyle, at some point he learned to use and fashion tools, then weapons. Weapons for hunting would enlarge his scope for bigger and swifter prey as killing at a distance became possible and survival of himself more probable. Thus armed, encounters at the margins of the territory with 'foreign' groups of other humans would become more lethal. War evolved. In Tierra del Fuego the four tribes of Indians living there two hundred years ago in a primitive state were mutually hostile and given to intermittent fighting. When trading white settlers moved in, making guns (and alcohol) available, mindless violence between tribes escalated horribly – serving, of course, the incomers' purpose, the ultimate decimation of the Indians.

Post-industrial man has moved on a great distance since these days, for no longer is a man's power potential a function of his size and muscular strength. Nelson, Napoleon, Stalin, Mussolini, Churchill and Franco were undersized men. Wealth is vital, and the upwardly mobile man will generally find a way to pad his pockets in transit, by fair or foul means. Other vital attributes are cunning, political skills and above all an ability to stitch up alliances with loyal supporters. The connecting threads are never so tight that they can't be snipped, to fashion new coteries shaped for the present needs. 'Old clothes' can be discarded and condemned to the rubbish-bin at a moment's notice.

The male alliance-making formula I've outlined was tailormade by Hitler, by Stalin, by Lenin, by Francisco Franco. This particular skill can be traced back to our ape-like ancestors and beyond, but became most crucial to survival in the hunter-specialist era. Vladimir Lenin was brilliantly endowed with tactics of this sort. He had a passion for hunting hare, rabbit and fox with a double-barrelled rifle when he was exiled in Siberia in his twenties, and pursued this sport later in life whenever he could. He was also a keen fisherman. But this was the nearest he ever got to direct physical aggression. His chilling, innate hawkishness was channelled into his plans, theories, manipulations and eventually decrees, and effected through his Bolshevik followers. Cross-currents of revolutionary fervour were rife in the Russian Empire at the time, and it was not difficult for Lenin's magnetism to draw to himself those of similar Marxist convictions. His personal prudence was evident after his brother's execution for plotting against the tsar: 'We shall not take that road.' Martyrdom did not bring sufficient immortality. So he reined in his rashness and let others take the risks. His visceral hatred of the tsar matched his brother Sasha's, but a single magnificent sacrifice, a *grande geste* to oblivion, did not suit the size of his ego. He expected security and protection as the Bolshevik leader, and comfort too. After his exile in Siberia, he was a marked man in Russia and found it more congenial to live abroad, keeping a distance between himself and the authorities, always arguing that, whoever else needed to be sacrificed, he must be kept safe. He settled in Switzerland, where he avoided pressure to return even for the insurrection of 1905. He bided his time, travelling around Europe to meetings and speaking engagements with other political exiles, keeping up his reputation and dominance until the moment was right. He lived in modest comfort on inherited money, which may have blunted his power-hunger for a time as he lost himself in faction-fighting, rhetoric and theory instead of keeping his eye on the big scene. He was living his easy retired life in Zurich, well away from the hazards of the European war, when the Revolution in Russia blew up in February

1917. He made his way hotfoot back to Petrograd to consolidate the leadership of the Bolsheviks, elude the hand of the provisional government, and ultimately to challenge it. The hunter with his pack stalked his prey for years and, at the critical moment, pounced and showed no clemency.

Francisco Franco, self-appointed dictator of Spain from 1939 to 1975, was like Pinochet a man of very average intellect and no personal charisma, and as with Milosevic he could not have been predicted as a mighty and enduring despot. He was small, effeminate and insignificant, yet, like Oliver Cromwell, discovered when he joined the military that he had a particular gift for warfare. And like Churchill he took a delight in displays of bravado in risky situations, 'seeking the bubble reputation even in the cannon's mouth'. In this he succeeded, earning respect and loyalty, getting himself noticed and becoming a general at 33 years old. In the 1936 uprising his genius for war rapidly established him as head of the nationalist military and state faction. With echoes of Lenin, he was coldly ruthless and devoid of compassion, though prone to tear-jerking sentiment. With none of Lenin's intellectuality, Franco had no ideology yet firmly believed he had a God-given mission to wipe out communism, and was utterly convinced that he did this out of self-denying love for his people. In this he was a paler version of Hitler and his hatred of Jewry. Franco was sexually prudish – like Napoleon – and beset by rumours of impotence, in sharp contrast to his father and two brothers who were renowned as Kennedy-style libertines. When Franco was in Africa with the Spanish army his colleagues observed that he never dallied with women, and speculated about homosexuality. There was no proof, but hints such as narcissism and a liking for smartly turned-out men were observed. In fact he was repeatedly distracted from the arms of his fiancée to join the commanding ranks of the Spanish Foreign Legion and leapt at the chance. The appeal of war drowned any emotional ties. He proclaimed that his soldierly duties would 'take precedence over any feelings, even those with roots deep in the soul'. The marriage seemed a cold affair from the start, enduring as a formality and producing only one child, a daughter.

Like Lenin, Franco had a fixation with hunting, fishing and

shooting, and interspersed his soldierly forays with depredations on wild animals, often at times of worry and anxiety about his own authority. He formed intensely close bonds with men, including a lifelong one with his near relation Pacón, and with fellow soldiers. This mediocre man had a genius for playing men and factions off against each other so that he emerged from virtual fights unscathed and in charge, just as he did in pitched battles. His own inadequacies of character and person, which he understood at a sub-cerebral level, served him well in this process, giving him an insight into how other bottomlessly greedy men would behave, setting them to neutralise each other, then stepping into the vacuum. Franco's supreme confidence in his right to rule seemed to derive directly from his fighting prowess, and he had withering contempt for civilian politicians. His biography reads as one long obsession with butchery, from the colonial campaign in Morocco onwards. He used military terror tactics with wholesale civilian slaughter of his *own* country-men, starting with the supression of miners' strikes in Asturias in 1934. He needed to imbue himself with an enemy fixation, which now became bolsheviks and anarchists, upon whom to release his death-dealing; and so he joined the uprising in 1936, which gave him multifold opportunities for his favourite sport, the man-hunt.

To the philanthropic mind it is incomprehensible that a man can talk emotionally about his '*patria*' and yet visit bloody, unrelenting genocide on his own people. Franco found it necessary to keep reminding himself that he was not waging war on his country but liberating it from Marxism at whatever the cost – even if it should mean annihilating half of the population. So hell-bent on his objective was he that Moorish troops and Italian and German air power were engaged in his pursuit of 'reds' and 'military rebels'. Like their big brothers the Nazis, the Franco nationalists used the language of racial purification to justify auto-genocide. As each town fell to his horde of thugs and mercenaries, the inhabitants – peasants and workers all – were rounded up and massacred, machine-gunned where they stood. Presenting a mirror-image of Lenin and the bourgeoisie, Franco seemed intent on annihilating the working class. Commentators at the time observed his tactics made no sense in military terms, fixating as they did on flushing out tiny pockets of resistance. He was driven to found a regime in which he would be safe from challenge, to which end he pursued Stalinesque methods, increasing rather than diminishing his personal paranoia in the process.

Even after the war was over, execution of the humble undesirables continued, with witch hunts and purges launched, Stalin-style. The international press were fed brutish far-right theories of destruction and regeneration being intimately linked. One of Franco's liaison kites spoke of death to one-third of the Spanish male population, looking back longingly to the Middle Ages when plague and pestilence kept down the plebeian masses. Meanwhile, Franco's distrust and fear of women was taken up by his courtiers. They would have no truck with equality of the sexes. Moreover, women were always either saints or whores and would be treated as such. They were stripped of all rights and subjected to their husbands' control in all things. While rape was considered justifiable male behaviour in a military context, blatant sexuality went underground. Franco's prudery became *de rigueur*. He even described his devoted followers as 'half monk, half soldier' (reminiscent of Hitler's nickname, the Monk, by his fellow soldiers in the First World War, and Nixon's label, 'the Mad Monk', by his underlings).

An ardent follower of Mussolini and Hitler, Franco copied their methods, including the use of film for propaganda. Mostly films of the time glorify the soldier-hero, idolising the virtues of independent macho nobility, debasing women to a contemptibly lowly status. As one critic pointed out, the latent suppressed homosexuality of the Caudillo and his entourage was glaringly obvious.

My series of soldier-monks – or military celibates – which is by no means comprehensive, began with Hitler and ended with Franco. The last is perhaps the most perfect example, but they show an astonishing degree of commonality. I've juxtaposed Lenin and Franco in this chapter to emphasize the similarities of these two men in power; two chillingly twin-identical vehicles of misanthropic mass murder, whose motive at base was quite simply a gut hatred and fear of a class of people to which they did not belong. Though they came from completely different social backgrounds, with nationalities sharing little or no recent cultural and historical identity, and though their leanings were disparate – Lenin the bookish, arrogant intellectual live-wire, Franco the inhibited, lonely, unappealing runt – and, most important, though their ideologies were at opposite ends of the political spectrum, yet when possessed of unfettered power they pursued identical aims of mass extinction. So do they all. There is a behaviour module locked away in human minds, a Pandora's box, evolved long before the technology of the 20th century could render it so obscene, for which the master key has been used increasingly often in our time. As I write, this very week, Slobodan Milosevic is being charged with war crimes at the United Nations Tribunal in The Hague, the first time in history that a state leader has faced his accusers. Augusto Pinochet's prosecution in his own country was facilitated by Spain and Britain, and sovereign immunity will no longer enable a man to sit with his little band of courtiers, smug and safe above international law. Hopefully humanity can learn in future to neutralise these horrors before they develop into wholesale malignancies.

While endeavouring to understand these hunters of men in the context of evolution and 'normal' behaviour, one observes that their comportment does show striking contrasts with pack-hunting animals in two particulars: the extent and wantonness of their destructive drive, and the fact that there is a leader at all. Successful pack hunters, of which the African wild dog is top of the league with a 90% strike–kill rate, do not mangle everything in sight. Even if it were possible, they would simply suffer more injury and waste valuable energy. Nor when you observe their mesmerising co-operation, is there a leader who imposes his will on the rest. Co-operation on a level playing field is the strategy. During the long-distance chase the animal heading the pack is exchanged, sharing the strain of being the trail-blazer. Considerable altruism is evident (selfish altruism of course!), with organising care for the young during the hunt and sharing of the spoils with vulnerable members including hunters who have serious injury. No doubt there is some sort of flattened hierarchy but it is not much in evidence to watchers, and decisions seem to be reached seamlessly, without internecine squabbles. Perhaps the absence of complex language is an advantage to this sort of efficiency. The !Kung San bushmen of the

Kalahari Desert fully comprehend the importance of not competing with one another, leading as it would to over-exploitation of the food supply, so hunting skills are not vaunted. These people are noted for their modesty, vital when they may be relying on someone else's generosity the next time. In this particular they are one step ahead in evolutionary wisdom. The !Kung San do fight each other, however, sometimes to the death, and adultery is the commonest single cause.

Looking at the far-reaching depredations of modern man-hunters, so utterly and mystifyingly pointless, it seems to me that two behaviour patterns have become entangled with mega-volcanic consequences. Evolution is not a benign and intellectual Mother Nature who intends and directs with foresight. Her very randomness can lead to some nightmare results. Perhaps the most crucial event in our evolutionary history was the switch from predominantly gatherer to hunter lifestyle. The residual, intensely monopolistic competitive traits still form much of our make-up alongside the selected hunter-style endowment. The men of Chapters 6 and 7 seem to be constructed with facets of the prototype of each module, with modified sex drive. Their emotional proclivities, in so far as they have any, for they are a cold and inhuman bunch, are reserved for other men. Why this should be is the subject of the next chapter.

Yet before we pursue history as made by the leaders, in the context of the conflict between creating and destroying – love and hate – we should cast an eye on the contrasting behaviour of those who are led: the cannon fodder, the disciplined and unified organism, the military. Articulate soldiers who have faced an enemy in mortal combat in those most ferocious blood baths of the 20th century have been aware of the link between creating life and destroying it. The fathomless sex drive of soldiers on active duty is notorious throughout history and in all cultures, with barrack-room talk, macho ribaldry, obsession with women, seeking out sexual opportunities with local talent or with prostitutes, and orgies of rape of enemy women in the aftermath of conquest. In all this there is a significant expression of misogyny, yet women almost universally thrill to a man in uniform, and most especially teenage girls. Brothels mushroom wherever an army is based, despite vigorous attempts to prevent sexual licence. The authorities in the Second World War, bombarded by moralising pressure groups, sought to control the appetites of the rank and file by preaching continence and plugging the horrors of venereal disease, but all to no avail. Men ordered into battle knew they faced death at every second, which was, incredibly, a powerful aphrodisiac. Evolution of necessity created fighting men, but she was canny enough to instill a desire to spill the seed on the fruitful earth before the charge into chaos. The highest death rates in the Second World War were suffered by the Allied Bomber crews (20% on each mission), and their sexual freedom at this time of living with imminent death went into orbit, as the gobsmacked letter-censor discovered. Venereal disease, which habitually explodes to epidemic proportions during wartime, and which is always blamed onesidedly on women, was used as a marker for prostitution. Accordingly, in the capture of Naples in 1943 by British and American troops, it was estimated that virtually all the female population of all classes, from the nobility downwards, were on the game to make ends meet at this time of starvation; the same applied to Sicily. Attempts by politicians to close or outlaw bordellos in various countries has simply led to street-walking and unofficial soliciting, and unchecked VD spreading more gleefully. Such evidence as exists shows that the vast majority of American GIs succumbed to peer-group pressure and enjoyed womankind wherever they could, regardless of who waited for them back home. Though there were romances, much of the sex was a means of urgent gratification, anonymous, cold-blooded, crude and primeval, sometimes cruel and sadisitic. Soldiers equated sexual aggressiveness with formidable fighting skill, and identified their weapons with their virile parts. Yet many GIs did not consider they had been unfaithful to wives and sweethearts. It was as if they had two mental modules for the two totally separate worlds.

Waiting with their heads down during the frenzy of artillery bombardment to go into an offensive, many men have experienced sexual hallucinations, often violent, explicit and obscene, provoking arousal to the point of ejaculation. Others clung together in a brief ecstasy of anonymous sexual exchange. The conditioning and the close calls with death induced a callous indifference to violence, and this readily extended to their next encounters with women. Such men felt in those moments of disorientated madness that they understood rape thoroughly.

In the aftermath of hostilities, many found themselves capable of this ultimate confusion of love and degradation. Hitler's army marching eastwards were instructed to hold aloof from unworthy Slav and Russian women, but they had intercourse with them nevertheless and with bestial savagery. When the tide turned, the incoming Red Army in turn raped an estimated 1.4 million German women (18% of the female population), 100,000 in Berlin alone, and even children were at the mercy of gang rape with drunken violence and at gun-point. British and American troops were no different: during the liberation of France in 1944 many French women and girls suffered the same treatment, defiled as often as not in front of their families, and lucky to escape without serious injury or even death. Some women submitted, resigned to suffering; others committed suicide.

In Britain, illegitimate birth rates doubled in the six years of the Second World War, and tripled in 1945. Among the more than five million infants born between 1939 and 1945, one-third were illegitimate, and this occurred across all social classes. Backstreet abortions and concealed infidelities by married women mean that these are serious underestimates of the explosion of spontaneous and random couplings that took place, as if to compensate at all costs for the equally random loss of life. In Germany in 1945, one-fifth of births were illegitimate, mostly fathered by Allied servicemen. Both German and British women were fascinated by black American soldiers, finding them exotic as well as more courteous than their brashly confident, white brothers-in-arms. It is said that 1,500 mixed-race babies were born in Britain in those years. In the Reichsprotektorat of Czechoslovakia under Nazi rule, the birth rate rose from 15 per 1,000 in 1938 to 16.7 in 1940, to 20.7 in 1943. Though 135,000 Czechs died from persecution, death camps and anti-semitic murders, births in those years exceeded deaths and the population rose by about 236,000.

It seems that, whatever madness consumes a psychotic leader, the followers behave blindly, robotically, atavistically, to counter-balance demolition with renewal. The phoenix phenomenon flourished, uninfluenced and undirected by Hitler's notions of racial purity, Himmler's *Lebensborn* stud farms, Eisenhower's non-fraternisation policy, or the Archbishop of Canterbury's crusade of moral reconstruction. The impulse to reproduce is as uncontrollable as war itself.

CHAPTER 9

Almost Homosexual

The recurrrent theme of sexual ambivalence in the lives of military-monk leaders will not have escaped the reader. All of them have been overtly heterosexual men, married with numbers of children varying from none to six or more. Yet with all of them the family unit was only a part of the supporting apparatus of a life spent most intensely when living on the edge, engaged with other men in fluid exchanges of confrontation and alliances – military or political – with the emotions engaged to such an extent that, for many of them, onlookers have speculated about homosexuality. This was true of Napoleon, Tsar Alexander, Cecil Rhodes, Lord Horatio Kitchener, Lord Baden Powell, Lenin, Hitler and Goebbels, Hitler and Mussolini, Churchill and Roosevelt; of Franco, Field Marshall Montgomery, Brezhnev and Chernenko, and Richard Nixon. Even some of the prototype alphas such as Jack Kennedy were naturally gifted with male-bonding skills, as was observed enviously by one of his mistresses, who felt marginalised when he was surrounded by the admiring wannabes, talking their incomprehensible male language. And Jack experimented overtly with homosexual acts, as did Bobby his brother, and Mao Zedong, and Benjamin Disraeli.

To evolutionists, homosexuality is an unexplained mystery. When all genetic selection and drive is based on reproduction, one would expect non-productive homosexual beings to crash out of existence, but fortunately they don't. Perchance the proclivities of the pack leaders may help to explain the paradox.

The parallels between the lifestyle of military leaders and that ascribed to primitive hominids is astonishingly close. Consider Franco, for whom his fiancée's charms were no match for the appeal of war in Africa. Once he had secured a mate, his interest in her was purely functional, and for most of his life he would desert her for the battlefields – at first literal ones, later political arenas. Hitler's domestic life with Eva Braun, especially during the war years, consisted of brief and infrequent pauses for recuperation from an exhausted extremis. The same pattern of life was followed by Napoleon, Cromwell, Churchill, Lord Nelson and Lord Clive of India. The war diaries of Field Marshall Lord Alanbrooke describe in somewhat tedious detail his interlocutions and interactions with warrior and political leaders of the time, interspersed with a repetitive and trite 'came to spend the day in paradise with you [his wife Benita] and those two beloved wee ones'. It is oddly unpassionate, this dutiful little formula. Strikingly, in all the 700-plus pages of this tome, which is pictorially graphic about the complex character of Churchill and his physical and mental decline in the war years, besides depictions of other historic figures, the reader gets not a jot, not an iota of insight into Benita's personality and ways; and hardly any more into the children's.

Modern women will recognise the same pattern among sport-loving men, particularly adherents of a team game such as football. Their menfolk go off to either play or watch the game in packs with much camaraderie either way. The forlorn female's plea, 'Do you love football more than me?', is even used in TV adverts. Plenty of women and family groups watch matches of course, but female bands of, say, schoolgirls would be more fanatical about an individual sport like tennis where they can fantasize about the men (who behave like alpha males) and identify with the women stars.

Male alliance-making skills are apparent in many walks of life: the boardroom, the committee meeting, the cabal gathering in dingy corners at the back of pubs, the old school network, Freemasonry, the House of Commons. Corporate life in large businesses is geared to male-bonding behaviour, each contender holding the floor in oral combat in interminable meetings, working hours at least as long as anyone else, showing over-riding loyalty to the firm, even attending social gatherings after the official end of the working day. Women feel like aliens in this world and mostly get squeezed out – willingly or otherwise.

Male bonding has been so essential to survival in the past that it is no wonder there is so much of it still around. Of huge importance is the fact that this skill in a primitive context will tend to prompt collective survival and thereby influence that of the individual. It is clearly not incompatible with hierarchical patterns of interplay, because our most successful menfolk with supreme facility use the one to promote the other. It seems probable that male homosexuality, so common in our culture, has come about as a result of this male–male networking in situations where group co-operation is vital for group survival, such as in wartime. Inevitably, it will be most apparent where all-male society is unleavened by women: in public schools, the armed forces, the Church – even in political circles, according to Matthew Parris. Various reports from Kinsey (1948) onwards have identified a figure of 2–5% of the US population who are exclusively homosexual. But studies of part-time same-sex behaviour among males in different countries tend to yield much higher figures, with around 50% having had homosexual activity before puberty and around 15% showing a degree of consistent bisexuality.

The nearness of sexual love to social bonding is not novel or surprising. It is not just in humans that sexual activity serves more than reproductive function, for in our near relations the bonobos (or pygmy chimps), sexual activity is used even more creatively than in ourselves. That's one in the eye for homophobes who quote animal behaviour as a standard for what is natural or normal. Indeed homosexual acts have been observed in a wide variety of animals, wild and domestic. In bonobo society, sex is an unselfconscious free-for-all, used for all sorts of social situations in many positions and in any combination of age and gender, even to showing affection for infants in arms. Low-ranking bonobo females offer genital contact to senior, secure females to achieve protection and acceptance within the group. Male bonobos are relatively non-aggressive and confrontations between them are resolved by conciliatory gestures, including one animal mounting another or by back-to-back scrotal rubbing. Interestingly, these resolutions appear to emphasize equal status between the males, not a dominance–deference stance as with ordinary chimps. In such intensely sociable, group-dwelling creatures, some form of mutually mollifying mechanism would be absolutely vital to de-escalate trouble and strife. The same is true of human male groups, though with our passionately confrontational natures such a mechanism is even more crucial to prevent spreading mayhem. Male-to-male bonding, spilling over at times into homosexual exchanges, has undoubtedly served that function.

In other animals who practise homosexual contact, it has been used for many different purposes: dominance, learning or practising sexual activity, appeasing, affection, aggression, showing off, pleasure or even celebration at finding a food source. The more one studies evolution and behaviour in both animals and humans, the more one realises that certain patterns have evolved for very definite reasons, or rather causes (for evolution has no foresight or intention), prevailing over vast periods of time and composed of challenging elements in the physical environment and in the social context. Homosexuality and even other minority sexual patterns begin to be understood. In the sexual hotbed of the bonobos one may see the origins of all sorts of sexual practices.

There are enough properly conducted twin studies to demonstrate that sexual orientation is in great measure – perhaps 50% – heritable. As a persistent feature of our development, clearly it has conveyed an evolutionary advantage, and presumably still does. What determines orientation, what exactly is inherited, and what is the nature of the advantage to the individual's reproductive potential?

Male to female orientation seems to depend on critical events in utero, when certain brain nuclei found in the most primitive parts of the infant's brain are exposed to a testosterone burst. This happens early in pregnancy – the third to the fourth month – and is a separate process from other aspects of masculinisation. If the early burst does not occur, it is said, homosexuality results. A second testosterone peak later in pregnancy, by contrast, influences the perception of dominance/subordination. It appears that the two behaviours are under separate (temporal) hormonal control, and can be disconnected. This is hugely important as an individual man may have predominant homosexual feelings, yet endeavour to compete with straight men at their own game.

The genome is currently a fashionable topic and scientists are exercised in searching for the putative 'gay gene.' Recently a popular candidate was a site on the X chromosome, of which males carry only one. The gene would presumably influence the early hormone burst in the womb, and would act differently in the female, who carries two X chromosomes. If the gene in the female could be shown to enhance female fertility in some way, this would, the theory goes, account for the persistence of homosexuality. I find this unconvincing. If fertility is to be manipulated at all in such a way as to account for the enormous frequency of homosexuality that exists, it could only be achieved by the modulation of male fertility, which has vastly more capacity to be increased than women's. Just think of the contrast in the following. The largest number of offspring attributed to a man was 888; for a woman the record stands at 69 (a Russian who specialised in multiple births). The woman's achievement is more startling than the man's, in terms of investment and endurance, and very few women ever have had as many children as even twenty.

Another attractive theory – because it seems to fit the facts as we see them – is a Mendelian model, almost certainly an over-simplification because it is most unlikely there is only one 'gay gene', and more likely there is a cluster of mutually modifying, antagonistic, hierarchical, amplifying ones to produce the spectrum of patterns that exist. This theory hypothesizes that exclusive homosexuality is the ' double dose' (homozygous) expression of an inherited trait whereas bisexuality is the 'single dose' (hetero-zygous) outcome. This is exactly comparable to the sickle cell example quoted in Chapter 2. The rough estimates of homo- and bisexuality in the population of 5% and 15+% respectively would be supportive evidence. To hold water, the thesis must postulate a survival/reproductive advantage for the bisexual as an individual as well as part of a collective organism. If the bisexual can be attributed with a reproductive advantage, then none need be postulated for the pure homosexual. The evidence for this premise is staring us in the face.

It is relevant to recollect patterns of behaviour before the advent of AIDS caused drastic modifications. Matt Ridley points out the awesome feats of sexual prowess and staying power achieved in the San Francisco bath-houses before safe-sex became a buzz word, where it was usual for a gay man to have had at least a hundred lovers, and 25% had had more than one thousand. Sexual novelty has always been an accepted part of the gay scene, and gay pubs are gathering places for those who look for one-off, anonymous fun. There are other locations too: public toilets and Clapham Common. The blatant libido and naked promiscuity is reminiscent of ultra-powerful emperors of the past, and undoubtedly is simply uninhibited male behaviour. When female sex is offered by prostitutes on the same terms, heterosexual men leap at the chance: witness the sex-tourism industry of Cambodia and other Southeast Asian countries. In this respect, male gays are thoroughly liberated (it is noteworthy, in passing, that lesbians are the opposite, tending to be constant to one long-term partner with little risk of infidelity – more traditionally female even than straight females).

This freewheeling behaviour seems to be characteristic of bisexuals as well as exclusive homosexuals, and what is more probable than that the free-love habits extend also to their heterosexual life? For if it does – and remember we are talking of trends and generalities, not rigid rules (which are unknown in nature) – this would amply explain a generative edge, with the numerical extras being illegitimate offspring.

Anecdote is not proof, but may at least show that my argument is not far-fetched. In his book *Empire and Sexuality*, Robert Hyam describes the high level of sexual activity of the British army in the days of imperial dominance, as it stretched around the globe. He describes the daily fare of one particular officer, identified as 'GR', who left detailed diaries. At his public school he had had regular ejaculatory sex with other boys. Then as a teenager he visited prostitutes and acquired primary syphilis. At 22 he had his first non-commercial sex with a female. In the army he was solicited by a fellow officer and learned that this was common practice. Travelling with the army to South Africa and India he resorted to brothels at every opportunity – and these were frequent. Women were compliant and did what they were told (or paid for), including attendance at dinner table, to be handed round the guests after port and coffee. He endured unrequited love for a younger male colleague. On home leave he took care to travel by the eastern ports to visit the renowned houses of sin. He married a white European lady in India but, when she returned home, took his delights with alternately officers and casual female acquaintances. Back home in Britain he eased himself into bed with compliant married women. A natural confessor with no neurosis about guilt, this man listed his preferences for partners: first, a beloved lady of his own class; next a casual female friend, then prostitutes of any race or colour (though Japanese were undoubtedly the best), then men, boys and animals, then melons and finally masturbation. The degree of bisexual promiscuity in this army man is only known because he chose to write about it. If he is representative of bisexuals, then we need hardly wonder at the potential of the bisexual for handing on his genes.

One other fascinating and consistent observation should be mentioned in connection with the genetics of homosexuality: that of birth order. The chance of a man being gay is greater if he has one or more older brothers by the same mother. This has been ingeniously explained by a part-immune, part-inherited effect, analogous to a rhesus-negative mother forming antibodies to her rhesus-positive baby in the womb. These antibodies, the theory holds, are directed against sites on the Y chromosome, which are concerned with hormonal bursts and masculinising the infant brain in the womb. This theory is not incompatible with the other one described, but much more remains to be clarified. It is certain that novelty-seeking genes also exist, and owners of these are more likely to indulge in Kennedy-style experimentations in their sex-lives.

Within the armed forces, such evidence as exists suggests that homosexual behaviour is commoner in the ranks than in civilian life. Some might attribute this to 'deprivation homosexuality' owing to the lack of women especially in wartime. But the establishment is hardly permissive, though may find it prudent to turn a blind eye, certainly in the navy. Churchill said of naval tradition, in his salty style, that it was all 'rum, sodomy and the lash'. A British army study of those charged with sexual offences concluded that many military homosexuals were anxious to dominate and lead, to gain respect and admiration, to prove their masculinity in feats of derring-do on the battlefield. This is a carbon copy of Franco's behaviour. The same over-compensatory behaviour has been seen in heavily decorated, Battle of Britain gay fighter pilots.

Some long-serving army commanders have had enough insight to be tolerant; indeed not a few connived at situations because they were themselves gay. In India, especially among Sikh regiments, homosexual practice is apparently common and unremarked. One brigadier in the Second World War, angrily dismissing a case of sexual misdemeanour, which he felt should have been quashed sooner, spluttered that in India at reveille, 'every man came tumbling out of someone else's bunk'. In the Pacific theatre in the same war, highly erotic male-to-male exchanges were widespread and remarkably inventive. If the official policy of discharge in the US and British armies had been stringently followed, most insightful seniors realised that the ranks would be literally decimated.

There was considerable embarrassment at how to deal with heroic and first-rate fighters caught in flagrante, and often they had to be swept away, out of sight, under the label of psychiatrically ill. There was evidence of mental breakdown, however, when stable male-to-male relationships broke up, or one partner was killed, suggesting that same-sex bonding is a vital coping mechanism under wartime (and maybe other) conditions. Some of the moving descriptions of such relationships, formed under hell-fire, show a depth of devotion and passion that many women, dismissed disdainfully as 'the wife', would die for.

In the past, where societies have had a stronger military tradition, homosexual bonding has been actively encouraged: in the Spartan buddy system for instance, in which men rejoiced in fighting alongside their male lovers, and likewise in the Thebes Sacred Legion. The global wars of the 20th century violently shook up perceptions of sexuality, which insight was not lost even in the inevitable post-war counterreaction supporting 'family values'.

Before my researches had led me to these illuminations, I had wondered why gay men succeed so often in getting to the top of a hierarchy, to become a leader of men, if we are to believe that achievement is fundamentally grounded in male-to-male clashing for access to females. Certainly, plenty of homosexual men have held kingly positions: the mad King Ludwig of Bavaria, Frederick the Great, James VI/I of Scotland/England, for instance; and Gore Vidal maintains that, of the first twelve Roman emperors, only one was exclusively heterosexual. Military leaders whom history accords a homosexual aura are numerous: Lawrence of Arabia, General George Gordon, Richard the Lionheart and Alexander the Great, in addition to my own collection. It may well be that these men have an evolutionary advantage when it comes to the male bonding necessary during wartime.

The naive perception that great men conform to socially accepted norms is favoured by obsessional establishment secrecy. Sir Roger Casement, a pillar of rectitude in the British Consular Service, knighted for his crusade against vicious slavery practice in Africa and Brazil, then hanged for high treason for Irish patriot activities, was clearly a man not averse to taking risks. He had a sexual career equally colourful and eventful, which he recorded in 'black diaries', which were suppressed until 1959. In his lifetime, his high moral standing before the world for work in the public good was constantly jeapordised by his insatiable need for young men, yet this diplomat skilfully covered his tracks. His achievements in exposing abuse of power in rubber companies for both physical and sexual exploitation ran parallel to his own use of his position for sexual opportunities. This double life was practised in cities where his sensitive antennae enabled him to home in on the rent-boy network. Ironically the stress of this Jekyll and Hyde existence led to a bipolar disorder in later life, that of manic-depressive psychosis. Yet he should still be revered for the good he did for the oppressed jungle rubber workers, in which his knowledge – in the earthiest, biblical sense – gave him insight and motivation.

General Sir Eyre Coote, MP and then Lieutenant General of Jamaica at the turn of the 18th century, visited a boys' school regularly with apparent benign intentions, until he was caught in flagrante in a sado-masochist session with six teenage boys. The overwhelming catastrophe of facing opprobrium when the public became aware of such an ambiguous existence was too much for him and many like him, so suicide was a frequent outcome, as with Sir Lewis Harcourt (MP and one-time colonial secretary), Sir Hector Macdonald (commander-in-chief, Ceylon) and Viscount Drumlanrig (private secretary to Lord Rosebery, quondam foreign secretary and prime minister with whom it is alleged Drumlanrig was romantically linked). According to Matthew Parris, a disproportionate number of British MPs are gay. Homosexuals are clearly not deterred from the antler-clashing competitiveness on account of their orientation, as women are. But that's not surprising, particularly given the new insights into hormone bursts.

Among homosexual parliamentarians who have achieved greatness is Francis Bacon, a man of towering ability as judge, lawyer, philosopher, royal adviser, sometime chancellor, writer and historian. He was renowned for philandering especially with his male servants, but he lived up to Enoch Powell's aphorism a few centuries later that all political careers end in failure. He was disgraced, driven from office, imprisoned and fined – ostensibly for well-founded corruption charges. Benjamin Disraeli, one of the 19th century's multiple prime ministers, caused scandal by dalliances with married women, but there were many rumours about him practising bisexuality too. His career was brilliantly successful in wordly terms but he glumly observed that by the time he had arrived he was too old to enjoy it.

The rise of Jeremy Thorpe, scion of a political (Tory) dynasty, one-time President of the Oxford Union, famous for his debating skills, to well-connected, charismatic MP began in 1959. He seemed unstoppable when he became a privy councillor, then leader of the Liberal Party in 1967; after which he married and produced a son. In parallel he was struggling with an importunate and unstable Norman Scott, allegedly a lover from 1961 onwards. Scott had become a harbinger of ruin, an incubus. With hideously embarrassing revelations, Thorpe resigned the leadership, but worse was to come. Charged with conspiracy to murder Scott, he lost his North Devon seat and, though he was acquitted, retired into obscurity.

Risk-taking in the pursuit of love is every bit as much a defining feature of homosexual drive as of the hetero equivalent it seems. What stands out from these anecdotes is that career-failure is a gamble worth taking. Sex is the ultimate ambition. Very Darwinian. In a minority group that has been the target for so much discrimination, the capacity for rash behaviour is enormous. In Matthew Parris's book *Great Parliamentary Scandals* are numerous anecdotes of men who risked carefully built, respectable reputations for a sex-life that was at the time perceived by the public as scandalous. Tom Driberg, MP for 34 years, an addicted pursuer of anonymous sex, believed that the wholly heterosexual male did not exist, and seemingly set out to prove it. Astoundingly, for he was repeatedly caught in flagrante, and once even charged with indecent assault, the press was muffled. It is thought that he had a hold over many influential people, who kept the covers firmly battened down lest they themselves should be implicated. It is alleged, if not confirmed, that he had an encounter with both Nye Bevan and Jim Callaghan. Ian Harvey, minister in the Macmillan government, prudently married for form's sake, and in 1958 lived conveniently near Hyde Park, where he repeatedly solicited members of the Household Cavalry. He knew the risks he took: loss of office and a possible five years in prison if caught. Yet though he struggled to resist his impulses, he could not, and at last suffered the feared exposure.

Another minister, Sir Ian Horobin, a highly regarded air force war hero, a survivor of Japanese prison camps, sublimated his interest in young men by acts of charity in London's East End. His altruism also gave him access to many young 'sweethearts', one of whom shopped him. Harvey Proctor in 1986 was also exposed by a boyfriend after a lover's quarrel, when stories of spanking and rent boys hit the tabloid headlines. He had other enemies it seems, who leaked stories to the press. Jerry Hayes, married with a family, was betrayed by his under-age gay lover as an act of revenge after being spurned. David Ashby was brought down by his wife's allegations of homosexual acts; he ruined himself by catastrophic attempts to sue the press. Alan Amos, who had a reputation for being the epitome of civic virtue, was arrested on Hampstead

Heath in 1992. He denied homosexual leanings, becoming the recipient of much moral mud-slinging on the crest of John Major's 'Back to Basics' campaign, and his career fizzled out in days. Some men when charged with homosexual acts have persuaded their wives to vouch for their heterosexuality, as if the one precluded the other. In the nineties public attitudes changed, and MPs now find it wiser to be open about themselves, as Michael Portillo was. But until the age of consent was reduced in 1992, the favoured youth of gay lovers could be a stumbling block, as Michael Brown discovered, even when his homosexual nature was known and accepted. Soliciting, or being solicited, can still put careers at risk, such as that of Ron Davies in the Blair government, who resigned from his post as Welsh secretary after an episode on Clapham Common.

Church leaders, like those of the armed forces, officially disapprove of homosexuality, and since their purpose in life is to preach goodness and adherence to certain moral standards, hypocrisy in their personal lives can precede a tremendous downfall. Taking a high moral stand gives a man enormous power, and in this profession as in any other, men have been quick to use that power for personal gratification. It is possible that the world of religious fervour embraces more than its expected share of gay men, just like the army and parliament, especially where priests are expected to be celibate as in the Roman Catholic Church. Periodically, the press declares open season on Church dignitaries as it does on politicians, doctors and other supposedly responsible orders. Again with the research mole Matthew Parris as my authority, I can assert that Churchmen are as sexually obsessed as anyone else, and somewhat ambivalent about orientation. Or maybe just multi-potent.

Among British aristocracy in centuries past, it was customary for younger sons to go into the Church. Not infrequently, since some other occupations were more prestigious, the selected divine would be the youngest of several sons. It is an interesting thought, in the light of recent researches into the origins of homosexuality quoted earlier in this chapter of the association between birth order and gayness, that these younger sons were highly selected for a much increased chance of being gay. One such scion was the Anglican Bishop of Clogher, Percy Jocelyn, in the early 1800s, who had noble and highly placed connections. He was the third of four sons, never married, and pursued an uninterrupted path to greatness, not deterred by his shocking indolence, but aided by influence rather than merit. Accused of seducing a coachman, Jocelyn denied the charge and saw the underling flogged almost to death, knowing that the allegation was true. Not influenced by his near escape, for in England sodomy still invited a death penalty, he seduced a soldier in the back room of a London pub, and was caught in the act. The preferred disparity in rank or class in these encounters is characteristic, and suggests that powerful men always like to feel more powerful than their lovers. Jocelyn was allowed to escape justice by Church and government, perhaps because the then foreign secretary, Lord Castlereagh, was fighting a homosexual scandal at the time, and maybe being blackmailed. Castlereagh also is said to have compromised himself with a soldier, and he committed suicide. Bishop Jocelyn escaped incognito but spent the rest of his life tasting the gall of shame, degradation and obscurity. Maybe it would have been better to be hung by the neck as was a similar Protestant bishop of the 17th century, John Atherton of Waterford and Lismore, who engaged in anal intercourse with an inferior. A married man with children and a reputation for philandering, he made enemies through being overbearing, greedy and self-promoting.

Missionary bishops with vocations overseas could be drawn into the sexual freedom that prevailed away from the puritanical home-base in the days of Empire. For being too fond of the boys of Northern Melanesia whom they were supposed to train in the paths of righteousness, in the nineteenth century Wilton and Molyneux, both Anglican Bishops, were forced to resign. Twells, Bishop in the Orange Free State, simply abandoned his see and fled when about to be charged with sodomy.

Modern bishops with gay pasts may expect different treatment. In 1994, the Bishop-elect of Durham was outed by the *News of the World*, who ran a story of him and a farmer being charged 25 years previously for an act of gross indecency to which he had pleaded guilty. The church knew about the conviction. The Bishop elect, now married with three adult children, provoked the increasingly confident and visible gay rights movement by condemning the notion of gay priests. Peter Tatchell's OutRage! lobby group then ran a campaign to force certain Church leaders to acknowledge their gay orientation. They revealed the names of ten Anglican bishops they believed to be homosexual. One such, the late retired Bishop of Stockwood, was defiant. He said, 'Tell them I've had a lot of women too.'

There have certainly been occasions when the carers of high-flying homosexuals have crashed more spectacularly than others. Ernst Röhm, head of Hitler's paramilitary force, the SA, took particular risks when he chummily called his leader 'Adolf' rather than 'Mein Führer'. He was higher up the social scale than Hitler, officer class indeed, and in the semi-anarchy of Gemany at the end of the First World War was transformed into a natural mercenary, able to use the rules as well as break them. Recognising the zealot in Hitler, he facilitated his access to funds, well-to-do connections and military personnel. Hitler owed him much, which as he rose to power made Röhm highly vulnerable. The pathway to Hitler's takeover demanded regularising of the SA and an increased veneer of respectability. Not sufficiently ruthless, the homosexual Röhm lacked the instinct to use his forces to menace and protect himself. He was shot on Hitler's orders, an expendable embarrassment. By contrast, an alpha male would have known in his innermost soul that loyalty is an ephemeral virtue even among brothers and buddies, and recognised that the moment had come to stand and challenge.

Peter Mandelson's career hit the wall in spectacular fashion, and to make no mistake he even did it twice. In his early life he could easily slip into any gathering of upwardly mobile young men on the lower slopes of greatness. Intellectual ability, leadership potential, a love of the limelight, undistractable drive were his hallmarks, and his way was paved by belonging to a Labour dynasty (Herbert Morrison was his grandfather). Schoolfriends recall him announcing repeatedly his intention to be prime minister (Oxford friends say it was foreign secretary); likewise they remember with awe his encyclopaedic

Above: Vladimir Lenin, whose iconic hold over radicals worldwide endured for nearly one hundred years. (HULTON | ARCHIVE)

Below: Adolf Hitler, the most bizarre and contradictory tyrant of the 20th century. (HULTON | ARCHIVE)

Above: Francisco Franco was prepared to dispose of half of his country's male population to eradicate communism. (HULTON | ARCHIVE)

Below: Benito Mussolini. Distracted by his love-life, he was no match for Hitler. (New York Times/Archive Photos)

Above: Winston Churchill combined the extremes of self-propagating egotism and awesome heroism. (HULTON | ARCHIVE)

Below: Aneurin Bevan, author of the most humane experiment in philanthropy the world has ever seen: the British National Health Service. (HULTON | ARCHIVE)

Left: Joseph Stalin played upon his rough, tough peasant image to disguise a tsar among tyrants.
(HULTON | ARCHIVE)

Below: Mao Zedong honoured in Moscow. He rarely left China, and even more rarely donned Western dress.
(Archive Photos)

Right: John F Kennedy, supreme risk-taker in a notoriously reckless dynasty. (HULTON|ARCHIVE)

Above: Fidel Castro's speeches lasted as long as seven hours. (HULTON|ARCHIVE)

Right: Margaret Thatcher and her steely, messianic stare.
(HULTON | ARCHIVE)

Above: Margaret Thatcher mangages to talk down even Mikhail Gorbachev. Alan Clark looks on.
(HULTON | ARCHIVE)

Left: Indira Gandhi. In power she was no longer a shrinking violet.
(Herbie Knott/Rex Features)

Left: Bill Clinton, the Super-Salesman.
(WIN/Rex Features)

Below: Hillary Clinton has an air of regal authority.
(Diana Walker/Timepix)

Above: For all his clean-cut, clerical looks, Tony Blair has no charisma.
(Julian Simmonds/Rex Features)

Left: Second in the Bush dynasty, George W – the accidental president.
(Ron Sachs/Rex Features)

knowledge of the House of Commons and its sitting members. He was enormously endowed with charm, a feature that seemed intrinsic, not just the turn-on, turn-off variety, as I can testify personally. A litmus test of its genuineness was the rapport he always had with children. As scholar and student he took himself seriously, being a ring-leader, a director of events, a visionary with an aura of power, as if destined to rule. Characteristically he hero-worshipped a leading politician; uncharacteristically that leader was female, Shirley Williams. He never made his mark as an orator. His voice does not project and his power to please flourishes in small seminars rather than plenary sessions, like a chamber group rather than a symphony orchestra. He passed through an idealistic phase, flirting with communism and taking a year out to do voluntary work in Tanzania, at which time he insightfully observed that life held stronger attractions for him than the class-struggle.

Mandelson's power in the political scene was achieved by an unorthodox route, and I believe this was connected with the strengths and weaknesses of his sexual orientation. Because he is gay he has not been able to fight the way up the pecking order in a conventional manner, which requires skills in both alliance-making and in macho posturing. He is well-endowed with the first, and used his contacts to get as near as possible to the throne without actually usurping it. Unfortunately, vicarious power-wielding has not been enough for his hungry ambition, particularly in its potential for self-aggrandisement.

His particular talents lie overwhelmingly in being the power behind the throne, probably a result of his electric mix of feminine intuition and male ambition. He has found himself cast in this unusual role twice, the first time with Neil Kinnock, the second with Tony Blair. The supportive role to Kinnock as shadow leader gave him only a fraction of the power he was to wield as prime minister's confidant, but at the time (as early as 1986) he was regarded with suspicion by those who stood at various levels in the standard hierarchy. Tony Benn observed that Mandelson was a threatening figure because of the speed with which he began to exert influence on Kinnock; and Roy Hattersley remarked on his 'maniacally ruthless loyalty to his chosen champion.'

It was while reading Mandelson's biography that I first received an inkling of the link between homosexuality and male–male bonding, though it seems now so obvious. I have postulated that same-sex bonding is a peculiarly male knack, which is considerably enhanced in the bisexual, yet seen at its acme of perfection in the pure homosexual, for example, Mandelson. His loyalty was uninfluenced by the orientation of the person he worked for, but whoever earned his loyalty had a formidably devoted lieutenant. His relationship with Kinnock reads like a relationship formed under Blitz conditions, with all the instant warmth that entails. He spoke enthusiastically, even passionately, about the leader (who called him 'kid'), nursing him through stultifying depressions after election failures, offering to iron his shirts at moments of domestic crisis, signing exhortatory letters 'Love, Peter'. Kinnock, a private and defensive man, who could be elusive with his colleagues, was always accessible to Mandelson, which naturally irked the colleagues considerably. Rivals rationalised their antipathy by accusing him of putting leader before party, of not being a team player, but in truth, no man is. Mandelson as Kinnock's mouthpiece was singled out as the authoritarian voice by the press, that Greek chorus stalker of the power-base. From spokesperson to freelance, on-the-hoof policy-maker was an easy step, and Mandelson was considered to be promoting his own policy agenda. He would also take the flak from both sides, a defuser of attacks on the leader, a blame-repository, a court-jester. Kinnock called him a true friend and was outraged with feelings of desertion when Mandelson took himself off to stand as candidate for Hartlepool.

Mandelson was playing political fast-and-loose even before this event, for, fearing that the future did not lie with Kinnock, he had been nurturing the two bright young stars Blair and Brown. He gave them a master-class induction course in media management. In the outback during John Smith's leadership, Mandelson went into a huddle with these two, spending endless time on the phone with each, every day: a 'love triangle' as it was described. At first he had seemed to favour Brown as a challenger to Smith – to whom Mandelson could not relate – and, after Smith's death, undergoing the much-discussed change of mind to support Tony Blair. Whether this was opportunism in the face of forces he could not control, or a perception that he would be able to exercise more influence over the lightweight, inexperienced one, is unknown. Certainly he and Blair together seemed like soul-mates, whereas he never adequately assessed Brown's measure.

With Blair as leader and looking increasingly like a destined prime minister, Mandelson's allegiance was his to command. 'I only exist to serve,' Mandelson liked to say, earnestly believing it. His shadowy control of, and family intimacy with, the kingpin is oddly reminiscent of Joe Kennedy, a man who, recognising the obstacles to holding the reins in person, positioned himself to pull the strings of the figurehead. But Mandelson's charm, his capacity to awe and attract, were used too liberally. People he dropped felt almost like discarded lovers and metamorphosed into enemies; most notably Brown.

Both Blair and Mandelson are mesmerised, hypnotised even, by wealth and by rich, glamorous, influential people. It is expected that prime ministers will walk among their ranks on equal terms. Politics is all about the exchange rate between money and power. Roy Jenkins observed the three heavyweight prime ministers of the last two centuries – Disraeli, Gladstone and Churchill – all accepted favours of a spectacular order quite openly and complacently. Tony Blair accepted a million pounds from Bernie Ecclestone for the Labour Party in January 1977; only ten months later a Labour minister was lobbying for exemption from the ban on tobacco advertising for Ecclestone's Formula One racing. Whether or not the two were connected was hotly debated. In the US no one gets to run for president without the exchange of an incredible number of dollars, to then find as Clinton did that your every altruistic intention is scuppered by some vested interest.

Beside all these enormities, Mandelson's two peccadilloes, a highly impolitic personal loan, and involvement in the Hinduja money-for-passports affair, do not seem terminally seismic on the Richter scale of political sins. Ah, but he was not the leader; he was merely the leader's shadow, who made the mistake of substituting the leader for his own power-base. When he began to wield a leader's privilege of being above and beyond accountability, his enemies closed in and cut him down to size.

*

Homosexuality is a Western concept of recent times, with attitudes conditioned by its past classification as a crime, an illness, as being possessed by demons, or as a minority trait requiring liberation. Probably most men are facultatively bisexual, but societal disapproval forces this facet of behaviour underground, especially in Britain. In many cultures it has been an accepted norm, especially in the Orient, notably Japan, where dislike of anal intercourse is considered effeminate. Taoism authorises boys of fourteen to have two ejaculations per day. Buddhist monks in some places openly practise anal intercourse. In some New Guinea tribes, bisexuality is institutionalised, with men and boys living communally together, and the men keeping a separate family home for women, infants and young girls. In South African mining communities, boys brought in to do 'women's work' would often serve as the equivalent of female sexual partners as well. The arrangements were called 'mine marriages'. As the boys grew older they could take boy-wives of their own and achieve status. The 'wives' benefited from security. Eventually the young men went back to their own community, to a traditional marriage, after earning enough money. In Buganda in Africa at the end of the 19th century, King Mwanga had a conventional harem and one of 500 pageboys, selected from the best families in the country.

Highly emotionally charged British disapproval of homosexuality may stem from Victorian times when leaders became fearful that sexual licence would cause social chaos and the decline of British imperial power. They may have understood mistily that sexual energy, conserved and channelled, can achieve great things. The Nazis perceived something similar. But it led to a restrictive code, with guilt, repression and misinformation leading to depression and eccentric practices such as Gladstone's self-flagellation; to say nothing of risk-taking and self-destruction.

Part of Western disapproval may stem from the tendency of empowered people to prevent others having sex at all, or at least attempt to regulate their sex-lives. This is another trait of the alpha male that I will discuss at more length in the next chapter.

CHAPTER 10

Deference and the
Disempowered

For a man to be extravagantly elevated, there must be a distortion not only of his own perception of himself, but that of the common herd also. Of what is a system of deference composed? Fear undoubtedly plays a part. Interwoven in this, as in all archaic forms of behaviour, is a sexual theme, the asymmetry between the male exploiter and the female appeaser, who need not be biologically female. In the face of a huge power gradient with little prospect of change, deference also contains an injection of apathy, maybe relieved by furtive, rebellious black humour and satire. Yet another element is the wish of most people to feel safe and secure, to relinquish responsibility to a father-figure, all good, omnipotent, who will act invariably for one's protection and benefit. This dangerous delusion is particularly to be found among women, who are as a result open to the worst of abuse. It is of course a recollection of the security of childhood, when we were on the receiving end of love at its most altruistic, from parent to child, a state that maybe we all aspire to replicate throughout life.

Submissive behaviour in herd animals, shown by a lower- to a higher-caste creature, has been exploited by humans, who direct that deference towards themselves, thereby domesticating these animals. Solitary animals, with few exceptions – cats for instance – cannot be domesticated. All humans perceive animals as belonging to a lower order than themselves, which is reflected in the use of animal names as abusive labels: pig, bitch, louse, rat, swine, worm, slug, snake, viper, reptile. Jared Diamond (in *The Rise and Fall of the Third*

Chimpanzee) observes the almost invariable 'hierarchy of scorn', which cascades down from literate, technologically advanced peoples , to herders, to farmers, to nomadic hunter-gatherers, in that order. Where genocide is practised, the victims are presented as savage creatures, barely human. By contrast, there is an uncritical faculty in our brains which whitewashes powerful people and assumes they have great virtues to match their great status.

In our intensely sociable human way of life, every person belongs to a number of societies: our families, immediate and extended; our neighbourhoods; our peer groups at school or work; our friends in leisure interests and sporting activities, political or charitable groups. In every one of these areas there is a hierarchy of sorts or set of subtle power games in play. It is impossible to avoid them all, or elide the allotting and receiving of a specific place or role. Some are more formalised than others, such as club committees. A superficial study of any one of these will convince how insecure we are with the concepts of equality and democracy. People who dislike being typecast and strait-jacketed to the extent of removing themselves from company altogether, risk becoming loners and eccentrics, mistrusted, rejected, tormented, excluded.

In my minority role as a hospital consultant – only 15% are women – inevitably I have found some male trainees who have difficulty in relating to a senior female. A few play one-upmanship, trying to find areas where I show technical or academic weakness. One uncommon ploy is to treat me with undue deference, leaping to the feet when I enter the room and other rather unnerving ways of emphasising the difference in rank. In these colleagues there is an equivalent tendency to be just a little patronising to those they perceive as being lower on the ladder than themselves, including patients.

Once, as a lowly medical student, I hovered at the periphery of the entourage of an eminent orthopaedic professor doing his ward round. The number of the attendants reflected the eminence of the grandee, who stood at the bedside, delivering words of wisdom to the silent listeners. To emphasize his points he slapped his hand down on the protective cage over the patient's leg. On each thump the patient's face contorted with agony, yet no one interfered or spoke up. The senior registrar tried to steady the cage. I was no more courageous than the rest. The professor's prestige and ego were more influential than the patient's suffering.

As an observer at the edge of the Labour Party power-pack during the making of several leaders, I was struck by the instant changes that took place on these occasions; not only in the leader himself, but in the attitudes of the entourage, as if a deity had suddenly been revealed. My ex-husband Robin Cook, for all his faults, had an impressive track record on the left of the party, with radical support of minority groups and human rights, and an in-depth understanding of problems in housing and health. As a renowned unilateralist and peacemonger, one of the best brains and most brilliant speakers in the House of Commons, he was altogether a politician of depth and distinction. Yet to the *nouveau arrivé*, the vapid, shallow, opportunistic Tony Blair, his meakness and subservience would have done justice to the chorus line of the *Mikado*. I found it chilling, revealing as it did a press-button response to the exigencies of ambition-on-hold. It underlined the flexibility of respect according to circumstance, and my researches have certainly confirmed that those men with the most urgently ambitious drives hold correspondingly huge reverence for heroes past and present. And this makes sense in terms of the tools and techniques needed to stay near the source of power until an opening presents itself.

There is no better examplar of these principles of transition from kow-tow and cringe to kingly contempt than the history of the Soviet Union in the 20th century. No slogan has ever had greater capacity to obfuscate than the 'dictatorship of the proletariat'. Lenin was the first self-appointed voice of that dictatorship, on which the proletariat was never consulted through any democratic means. Not one of the seven leaders of the USSR was elected. The old, imperial social order was decapitated, turned upside down, and a new imperial social series of protected, privileged tsars imposed; to whom the people humbly submitted, as they always had.

Trotsky observed that, in 1917, power was lying on the streets of Petrograd, anyone's for the taking. It was seized by the most avaricious man, Lenin. It took the best part of a century for the lies and the secrecy to be revealed, yet Lenin is still an ideological god to millions, the star they steer by; this man who in the Civil War alone was the cause of 13 million lives lost in his own country. He promised utopia to the downtrodden in the shape of peace and prosperity, food, work, freedom, all basic needs, and power to the people. I am sure he believed in this idyll himself, but his indomitable will planned to hand out these good things only to people who did not oppose him, people who were totally subservient. Yet the empty doctrine was snapped up by China, North Korea, Cuba, Yugoslavia; was imposed on Eastern Europe; and inflamed segments of the population in Spain, France and Germany. Do people feverishly reverence freedom so fervently because they know how readily they are induced to part with it? That capacity in our brains to back down before a stronger-minded person is something we are aware of and scared of in our inner selves. Lenin certainly did have a super energetic power, fanatical belief in himself and capacity to ride roughshod over those around him. In these circumstances, mortals with less certainty give way, then blindly follow. They think they are pursuing an ideal, an earthly god, but it is simply a mighty, mindless gorilla.

After seizing power, Lenin metamorphosed into the cold, amoral pragmatist who totally disempowered the people he purported to serve. From then on he was a deity, regarded by all as infallible. He reinforced this subservience by a system of universal control with rewards for spies and severe punishment for errancy so that sickening fear guaranteed obedience. Lenin's time in power was short – a mere six years after the October Revolution to his death in 1924 – yet the myth of genius lived on. After he died, research was begun on his brain at a newly created institute, which began by examining 30,000 slices of his cerebrum, the idea being to discover the secret of his genius (those who were thus inspired had probably never done post-mortems before: one pickled brain looks very much like another). His collected works were printed in their millions, in five editions over the following decades, yet his philosophy was sterile and acknowledged no other great Russian thinkers apart from himself. Leninism substituted for religion right up to the time of Mikhail Gorbachev, his name being immortalised in monuments, institutions, buildings, prizes, honours and awards.

One of the few who, living at a distance, had not been hypnotised, was the emigré writer Ivan Bunin. He bitterly mourned the destruction of the culture and religion of Russia, the good things caught up in the mayhem as innocent bystanders. In 1924 he spoke out about 'Fratricide...the mocking slogan of liberty, fraternity, equality...the global villain, the congenital moral imbecile, Lenin.'

Lenin's mantle passed to Stalin, not without considerable manoeuvering on his part and a terminal breach with Lenin, from which he was saved by one of a series of strokes that rendered the leader speechless, in the nick of time. Stalin occupied, as it were, the god-space where Lenin had stood, and directed the people to worship at the shrine. Trained for ten years in theology, he discovered anew the capacity of a religious leader to govern the lives of the masses by a few punchy, inviolable principles, and to threaten with hell-fire those who strayed: like Hitler he was a pope figure. Totally cowed, the people of the Soviet Union endured deprivation of a degree incomprehensible to free peoples, while the Bolshevik leaders had, even under Lenin, learned how to accord themselves luxuries and protected privilege.

Rigged elections were held in 1937, and no one was under any illusions about Stalin's total control over the results. On this occasion he made a highly theatrical speech at the Bolshoi Theatre, emphasising the freedom and democracy of their system, and repeated this message often enough for it to sink in. His picked and packed audience of yes men applauded roundly. He then recommended the electors to Lenin as their spiritual leader, with emphasis on the name, Lenin, Lenin, linked to each supposed virtue. The message was hammered home. Blind obedience. The truth is what I say it is. Revere me as Lenin's mouthpiece. And don't step out of line.

Nobody did; nobody dared. But some subversive thinking went on and surfaced at times in sacrilegious political jokes. People needed some outlet for natural rashness. The writer Dmitri Volkogonov described how easy it was to live a life when others made the decisions and fed you incontrovertible truths. He awoke by degrees to the century-long thraldom, and regarded the awakening as his life's achievement.

Stalin had little natural charisma, and the technique of terror that he inherited from Lenin was his favourite weapon, the obverse of his own mega-paranoia. He reinforced this oppression by bloody purges until the visceral fear of those around him filled the room. His huge portrait lowered over the workers in every street, over every workplace, an intimidating Big Brother – a technique usual in totalitarian regimes. Whether it is effective, or the dictator simply wills it to be, is not known.

At only one point in his long, ghastly career was Stalin himself vulnerable, himself paralysed by fear, and that was in June 1941 when German troops began their offensive against the USSR, ignoring their non-aggression pact, and taking Stalin completely by surprise. He had discounted uncongenial information and the messengers had funked pressing the point. Stalin went to pieces, vanishing into his dacha for three days, and behaving like a cornered animal when his colleagues came to consult. He expected arrest; if only one of them had seized the day. But they treated him with the usual respect and he was given time to pull himself together. He scapegoated the military leaders, and dozens of generals were arrested and shot. In spite of this and other strategic catastrophes, the Party Journal, *Bolshevik*, lauded and applauded Stalin as a military genius unequalled in history.

By default – for Stalin neither appointed nor groomed a successor, thinking as all dictators do that he was beyond the laws of nature and would not die – the mantle fell to Kruschev. His qualities were those of a nimble, wily survivor, well trained in acquiescence and subordination – an affable, uneducated peasant. Most of the contestants feared a takeover from Beria, Stalin's evil head of NKVD (spying and state security organ), who was a threat to everyone's safety (an earlier incarnation of J Edgar Hoover). Once Kruschev had his knees under the desk he began a demolishing of his revered predecessor in a manner that was to become sequentially routine. He and others attacked the iconic worship of Stalin and his autonomous control. No matter that Kruschev had grovelled with the best of them as an underling. In three short speeches in the election process of 1937 he had used the terms 'genius', 'great leader' and 'great creator' 54 times, no less, and called for more ardent love of Stalin. But after Beria had been disposed of and everyone was able to breathe more freely, it was no longer politically correct to honour Stalin's memory. The process of de-deferring was delicate because Kruschev himself had been so intimately involved in the repressions. He would not have survived otherwise. The difficulty was resolved by referring back to the still more sanctified image of Lenin, whose ideals were now presented as a contrast to the lawless hegemony of the Stalin years. Symbolically, Stalingrad was re-renamed Volgograd.

Kruschev was energetic, innovative and prepared to learn. But in no time he had his own circle of idolators, for he was highly susceptible to flattery. Channelled into the only ways he knew, those of an autocracy, and surrounded by a protective cocoon of fawners, he came to believe in his own infallibility. He lectured and pontificated, speaking at length and brooking no interruption. Even when receiving an Italian Communist delegation he subjected them to a six-and-a-half-hour monologue that substituted for discussion. Thus his mind funnelled into a channel so narrow that, without benefit of any grounding in education, he could make himself ridiculous, as in his eight-page letter to President Kennedy at the time of the Cuban missile crisis. Yet no one dared advise or gainsay him. Indeed it was he who devised the plan to send missiles to Cuba, an order that every member of the Presidium dutifully signed. Kruschev's backing down over this issue was the beginning of the disaffection with him, and of his downfall.

Leonid Brezhnev took part in the coup that toppled Kruschev, and not only was he reluctant but absolutely terrified, fearing instant annihilation for such sacrilege. Steeped in subservience to Stalin, he was himself a nonentity, uncultured and uneducated, of plastic principles, and as party leader and general secretary he was progressively self-obsessed. But the party apparatus was now so well established that the leader could, if he chose, or if his capacity failed him, become a figurehead manipulated by the climbers around him. Brezhnev was indolent by nature, and his preserved doodlings, of unbelievable trivia, personal and barely literate, betray a mind that was incapable of penetrating much beyond his own vanity. That particular quality had much to feed on, being the object of the statutory oleaginous adulation, and himself as excited as a child with

the numerous prizes, medals, honours, orders, trophies and titles –
hero, marshal, supreme commander – heaped on him, earnestly
believing he had earned them. Those of his colleagues with hawkish
tendencies exploited this exaggerated vanity to their own ends, while
jokes flourished about the foppish leader. They had plenty of
opportunities for quiet mockery, for Brezhnev loved to make
speeches and appear on television, even though he was no gifted
orator. He was beset by age and infirmity and, like Mrs Thatcher in
her later years, his undistinguished diction was hindered by poorly
fitting dentures.

With easing of tensions, corruption flourished at every level in the
USSR, including the very highest, where Brezhnev's puppet status
was well established. At the time of the Prague Spring in
Czechoslovakia in 1968, signalling that country's yearning for self-
determination, he was led by the nose by combative men of the
Politburo into the crushing military invasion that followed. Face to
face with Dubcek, the Czech leader, Brezhnev behaved like a heart-
broken parent berating an insubordinate son who owed him
unquestioning obedience. The tongue-lashing, threats and
dominance rhetoric of the delegation rained down on the Czech
leader for hours, while the troops with their iron-ware stood to arms
throughout the country. The fragile buds of dissent were squashed
beneath the hobnailed boots.

Brezhnev the figurehead was a dove in disguise and as such did not
suffer the paranoia and resulting isolation that Stalin had. Lonely at
the top, Brezhnev needed a favourite, and found a soul-mate in
Chernenko. They had met when Brezhnev as Governor of Moldavia
was much higher in rank than Chernenko, who was well versed in the
arts of fawning flunkeydom. They kept in touch, with Chernenko
sending letters and cards of servile congratulations on every suitable
occasion. When Brezhnev was established in Moscow he had
Chernenko transferred, and sponsored his promotion up the tree.
Finally as head of state, Brezhnev could make his worshipful servant
his chief of staff, a source of great comfort to one and of future
prospects to the other. Chernenko became a vital prop, secretary,
valet, confidential companion; for all we know, knight of the
bedchamber. Recognised as Brezhnev's indispensible aide,

Chernenko now came in for his own share of respectful treatment. Perceiving what worked, Chernenko's toadying and grovelling became more blatant, and in public more cringingly embarrassing, yet Brezhnev lapped it up. The assembled audience was obliged to follow the lead with thunderous applause. Brezhnev really believed the adoration was genuine, and letters from him to Kostya (Chernenko) were brimful with mawkish affection, concluding, 'I embrace you and kiss you . . . '

Brezhnev, like Lenin, was a keen hunter and his subordinates were obliged to accept his invitations to go out in the country with him, whether they would or no. Chernenko did not enjoy the sport but never refused, even when his crippling asthma was at its worst. He aspired to the leadership at the death of his patron, but was overtaken by Andropov, who had the backing of the army and the KGB. Chernenko the proto-opportunist, a Jonathan to Brezhnev's David, dropped all mention of his patron, the fount of his political existence, once the leader was dead: by now this was established Bolshevik tradition. Brezhnev the embarrassment, after a few token mourning gestures, could now be revisited and blamed as the author of the regime's failings, dismembered and consigned to oblivion. It is noteworthy that this comparatively gentle man who inspired no fear sank without trace while the memories of the feared ones, Lenin and Stalin, endured.

The succession had passed to Yuri Andropov even before the people knew Brezhnev had died; such contempt for the masses is almost unparalleled. Andropov was a KGB man who believed firmly that the populace should be forced into happiness in spite of itself, and expanded the pernicious system of millions of small-time, paid, incognito spies to maintain the baseline of fear, apathy and paralysis of resistance. He believed he could control thought, mood and opinion, and he certainly suppressed the outward expression of those things. How unsurprising that he had to battle against stagnation and lack of motivation in all areas, despite his lectures about hard work and discipline, his campaigns against absenteeism and slackness in the workforce, corruption and nepotism in the officials. Even rhetoric about the threat of imperialism, focussing the people's mind on the enemy, failed to light up any nationalistic fervour. Nuclear parity with the US had been achieved at the cost of 70% of the state budget being spent on military demands, but the deprived, poverty-stricken masses had no fight left in them.

In 1983, a South Korean jumbo jet carrying 269 passengers was shot down in Soviet airspace, apparently being mistaken for an American military carrier. American spy-planes had not infrequently been brought down in such circumstances. The Politburo met, realising the catastrophic error, which was stirring up worldwide revulsion and condemnation. The records of the discussion of that meeeting are available, and demonstrate the priority of extricating the leadership's credibility, with no concern or regrets in the least for the loss of life or the crass error that caused it. But why should they show compassion for foreign civilians, men, women and children, when they had so little for their own? Accidents were happening in nuclear installations long before Chernobyl, and the amorphous masses were deprived of any powers of legitimate protest, or of demanding accountability, by the simple device of hushing up all such events.

After Andropov's death, Chernenko, the third of the trio of sick, elderly leaders, more or less fell into place as the natural successor by virtue of his prestige gained under Brezhnev. Supremely unqualified for a heroic role, his life history had to be extensively rewritten in order to give lustre to his undistinguished past. At 72, crippled with asthma, he spent most of his limited strength initialling papers while leaving the major decisions to others in the Politburo. He liked the pomp and circumstance of trips abroad and receiving foreign statesmen, but such meetings were excruciatingly rigid because of his puppet status, trying to read out his prepared text between puffs on his inhaler. The love of public appearances and speechifying never left him, painful though it was to him and all who watched. His competitive receptors were constantly prompted by the sight of the fit and active Mikhail Gorbachev, beavering away while he lay seedy and immobile, and whom he overwhelmed with mundane tasks to keep him dutiful and humble as long as possible. There was no disguising even from the cowed public that their leader was a figure of ridicule and shame, a true reflection of their downtrodden national pride. One journalist dared to write that Chernenko would be forgotten before the candles went out on his coffin.

Mikhail Gorbachev, who was fated to spearhead change, was not a rebel but an orthodox Leninist. Ensuring his name was the first proposed in the Central Committee Plenum after Chernenko's death meant that no one dared oppose him, and each of the members in turn praised him more extravagantly than the last. He had many usual alpha traits such as vanity and egomania. He was a speaker, not a listener, a lover of adulation and display, had frequent recourse to foul-mouthed language, and was duplicitous in political relationships. Yet he began to dismantle some of the nonsensical ritualistic leader-worship, opening himself to bringers of liberal ideas. Like the rest he condemned the ostentation of his predecessors, but he struggled to free himself from the same honey-trap. Perhaps no one in the West can guage the effort this required, to emancipate himself from the myths and measures of the past. Most crucially his policy of glasnost – opening – meant that the people had access to information hitherto kept out of reach. Education is enabling; knowledge is power. His tentative moves acquired their own momentum. The people of the Soviet bloc were not after all terminally trampled, and the world watched in wonder as Stalin's empire collapsed. Hundreds of thousands of people left the Communist Party, no longer fearing recrimination. In Czechoslovakia the long-suppressed re-awakening took place in the form of a 'Velvet Revolution', projecting Vaclav Havel the convicted rebel into leader position. In other satellite states, similar changes took place. Gorbachev quietly and unostentatiously dismantled the accepted aim of global war, especially after Chernobyl. There was personal danger in removing his own iconic status, as Machiavelli's most able pupil Stalin would have told him; danger in loosening restrictions on shameful and long-guarded secrets; danger in sharing his own omnipotence. His fate advanced in the shape of Boris Yeltsin, a long-distance traveller towards democratisation, who dared to criticise the enthroned general secretary in a Politburo meeting. Gorbachev's alpha instincts came to the fore and a terminal rivalry began, which Yeltsin as people's advocate, younger and with more to gain, was bound to win.

Tyranny is a two-way affair, needing one person to practise it and other persons to defer to it. The equipment for either part is inherent within us all, every man and every woman, requiring only the right circumstances to press the switch and turn it on. Hitler's Reich could not happen here, they say. Oh but it certainly could. It is chilling to bear in mind that it was not just police and army thugs who committed the atrocities in that regime. Most of the German psychiatric profession were engaged in the new thinking on 'defectives' and a large section of the medical profession twisted their ethics to cope with 'mercy killing'. Recognising the truth about our potential for evil might go a long way towards controlling it. The campaign against terrorism being waged by Tony Blair and George Bush as I write is naive in the extreme. They need to direct their efforts inwards, and recognise that to eliminate evil would mean exterminating all members of the human species.

Psychological experiments have put a scientific gloss on what many of us already know: that we have a capacity for blind obedience of varying degree. This is well recognised in the armed forces, who depend on it in action, and who spend much time and training in peacetime to refine and hone it. The experiments have shown that few people will disobey an instruction given in an authoritarian tone by a person in uniform. Some unsophisticated people do not even need this trigger. I have employed childminders who would instantly obey a stranger who came to the door claiming, 'Mrs Cook owes me money and you've got to pay.' When this happened I had to assert my authority sufficiently to ensure they never did so again!

White coats also carry an aura of hegemony. During experiments on learning and memory with volunteers, based on 'punishment' by electric shocks for wrong answers, psychologists found to their horror that two-thirds of the volunteers would unquestioningly be prepared to escalate the shocks to lethal levels if told to do so by the experimenter. Our capacity for following the herd is deeply ingrained. This offers enormous potential to those individuals who by virtue of inheritance or circumstance, or a mixture of both, have seriously shifted dominance–deference ratios.

One other exploitable and embedded tendency is group identification; it is so important to belong. Our own social and ethnic groups we readily recognise and identify with, and it is very easy to be persuaded that ours is superior to the rest. Simple experiments with children and students in mock situations have degenerated rapidly into 'us and them' confrontations of such violence that they have had to be stopped. Most of us, if asked to predict how we would behave, in a given situation, outline how we would like to behave; and have minimal insight into what our first-line automatic reactions would actually be.

It has often been a source of historical comment that people do not always flee from organised tyranny. In fact, they do so wherever an escape route is available. Remember the Jewish diaspora, the exodus from Ireland at the time of the potato famine, the present-day waves of asylum seekers. But escape routes may be hazardous or impassable, and perhaps non-resistance born of apathy and depression is a last-ditch defence strategy. Those who witnessed the massed Jews being herded into the gas-chambers commented on how almost willingly they trudged to their fate. Journalists observing mass executions during the Spanish Civil War by Francoists, described how the prisoners watched, terrified, as machine-guns were set up. They were not shackled or tied up, but no one attempted to flee or charge their oppressors with teeth bared and hands clawed. It is clear that there are inherited sets of powerful aggression-inhibitors at work, and though we should be very glad of them in some situations, they do not always serve the individual well.

Army leaders recognise a significant proportion, about one-third, of their men will not fire when ordered to do so. Hence the hours spent square-bashing and being trained to obey automatically; similarly the rigid and ferocious discipline reinforced by a steep hierarchy in which you pass on the humiliating aggro inflicted on you from the man above to the next below in line. Those who adapt well to this lifestyle welcome the elimination of the destabilising randomness of liberal human relationships, and on gaining power assert their rigidity on all their subordinates. Pinochet and Franco both fit this descrption to a T. Both showed the complementary sides of the coin of subservient deference and sadistic tyranny. The essential Pinochet, the dull, inhibited, prudish, teetotal plodder, a model of soldierly obedience and conformity, could have been Franco's *doppelgänger* as well as that of Milosevic. When the moment came for them to show their primitive colours and to metamorphose into usurping fiends, each man trembled on the brink. Pinochet agonised in the midst of his daughter's birthday party, and brooded at his grandchildren's bedside before finally sealing his Mephistophelean pact.

Franco likewise was terrified of failure and disaster. Believing that military authority should supercede the civilian equivalent, he nevertheless possessed supersensitive antennae to detect the prevailing direction of political winds in pre-Civil War Spain, and an aptitude to be on hand near the current ephemeral power, just long enough and no more. But even he sailed near disaster in the brittle situation before the Second Republic, failing to foresee the withdrawal of King Alphonso XIII of whom he was a favourite. He displayed the ardent need for a father figure to approve and reward him while simultaneously doing all he could to reach that exalted position himself. To that end he had to swallow his royalist pride during the Second Republic by swearing allegiance to the regime, which he justified by moral flim-flam. All the authorities Franco revered were being demolished: the Church, the monarchy, the aristocracy, the military, even the hegemony of husband over wife. Yet he bit his lip and stayed outwardly loyal, swithering when enticed to join right-wing monarchist or military rebellions, and managing to distance himself from those coups destined to end in failure. Indeed, Franco's vicious and bloodly suppression of the miners' rebellion in Asturias had given him such prestige among the generals that no takeover would be accepted without his explicit involvement. With the narrow election of the Popular Front in 1936, opinions polarised tempestuously. Revolutionary rhetoric in the mouths of the usually downtrodden peasantry prompted a convergence of the senior military, and yet still Franco hesitated. His supremacy he owed to the government. By rebelling he would cast it all to the winds and have to work his way up again, even if the rebellion was successful. He had enormous reluctance to divorce himself and his interests from the establishment and President Azaña. He was even mockingly called 'Miss Canary Islands 1936' and 'the traffic light of military politics'. Meanwhile, Franco, ever a hare-runner and hound-chaser, repeatedly reassured the prime minister of his loyalties. He was finally pushed into a decision to join the rebels by another spate of assassination and reprisal; and visibly losing confidence, aged ten years overnight. Yet amid the battle-cries of the uprising, all his pugilism and military dominance came flooding back, expressed in a tirade against self-seekers, deceivers, toadies and destroyers. Thus he projected his own patterns of behaviour on all those he branded as enemies.

The psychology of deference is thoroughly understood by tyrants, who seem to need no teaching or experience in how to exploit it. Hitler, writing not long after his dropout years, spelled out in *Mein Kampf* that the belief in one's superiority must be inculcated from early childhood, after which it will never be demolished. For the fostering of this self-confidence he later intitiated the Hitler Youth Movement, from which he envisaged his future military elite would evolve. He had also worked out how to engage the minds of the masses, by an appeal to emotion and instinct rather than intellect and reasoning. He had perceived in himself a stirring response to impassioned rhetoric and massed military marches, from which he dreamed up his own Nazi displays of martial music, stark red-and-black colouring, the ancient talismanic swastika paraded as insignia, serried repeated banners, gleaming metalware, rhythm, stamping, saluting, a sense of disciplined aggression – enthralling if you are on their side but menacing if you are not. He believed that most people are lazy and indolent, in which, like Franco, he was projecting his own propensities onto the masses. Hitler was driven only by matters affecting his power, prestige and personal ambition; in other ways he was bone idle. His reasoning was erroneous, though the effect was the same. The people follow a show of potency-with-violence because their jungle ancestry has left them programmed to do so, when the right button is pressed.

Nor was this display an idle threat, as the German people knew throughout the 1930s. Aside from the street violence, which was visible to everyone, Hitler's message was delivered through his amazing oratory. Nowadays, watching this unappealing Chaplin-esque figure transported with rage, spitting, snarling, angrily gesticulating, it is past understanding how he held hundreds of thousands in the palm of his hand at the famed rallies. Yet this uniquely self-obsessed man found common cause with the public because his atavistic drive was, under their courteous shell, no different from theirs. The substance of his rhetoric was right-wing orthodoxy, but his tapping into prejudices, half-suppressed and shameful, was liberating. All this, inspired conviction, a hint of destiny, a malevolence for a common enemy, came from the bottom of his black heart, and they received it ecstatically.

Much has been written about Hitler's hypnotic powers, his penetrating eyes and bizarre fits of hysteria, as if he was some kind of shaman working black arts on the unwilling populace. No one wants to believe that this reviled creature was a version of themselves, a human, a close relative. It is a source of infinite shame that an evil man of essentially inferior parts should use ordinary human skills to gain such ascendancy. But instead of the stacks of volumes written about him, we should be writing about ourselves.

Hitler was arguably mad, certainly psychiatrically unbalanced, incapable of foresight except in terms of his own desires. He is not the first madman whom people have followed blindly to their perdition. King Ludwig of Bavaria, whose mind was adrift in a whirl of manic-depression, paranoia and delusions of grandeur, was not altogether dissimilar. Those courtiers surviving his paranoid purges were the usual cynical self-seekers, who willingly assisted him in his crazy schemes of monumental folly. In fact, when a man has been set on a pedestal and duly exalted above the common herd, by whatever means, few people have the courage to bring him down, and those that do are often themselves tyrants in the making.

Saul, the first king of Israel in 200 BC, sponsored by the mystic holyman Samuel who wanted to wield power through him, suffered from delusional melancholia. But the population, manipulated to fixate on someone who stood out from the crowd, took his visions as a sign that he was their God-substitute. Saul's psychosis deteriorated with age, to the cost of his subjects.

In 19th-century China, near Canton, within a well-to-do family a son was born called Hung Siu-Tshuen. The times were turbulent with ethnic conflict and Western aggression and invasion. Hung looked at first like a promising scion, but began to fail academically and to show unmistakable signs of a paranoid and hallucinatory disorder, probably schizophrenia. Part of the symptom complex was a delusion of greatness and a messianic calling to save the peasantry from the ruling Manchu caste, and he was sufficiently self-convinced and plausible to gain a large following. He called himself Jesus' younger brother. In schizophrenia, part of the brain functions very normally while others are quite out of the loop. Like many skilled religious rabble-rousers, Hung led his troops to astonishing military victories at first, but inconsistency and loss of touch with reality doomed his cause. He was defeated and killed himself with poison, betraying all those who pinned their colours to his mast.

Self-selecting leaders with unswerving self-belief and a soupçon of charisma, barely distinguishable from the insane, can hardly fail, one might think, so ready are the silent majority to follow blindly like the Gadarene swine.

The power of speech is crucial for dominance, and again it is very wonderful that ordinary people, whether singly or in crowds, submit to having their ears battered for so many hours together. In Western politics the capacity for oratory has always been critical to success. William Gladstone was the most celebrated parliamentary speaker of the 19th century, whose capacity to gain and keep men's ears was apparent by the enthusiasm with which the chamber filled when he was scheduled to speak. Even at midnight after a long weary day, men would halt in their tracks when he stood up. In that more patient age they would listen to a peroration of at least two hours, and his budget speeches were four hours or even longer. The content, as we know from Hansard, was detailed, accurate and well researched, but could have been condensed into one quarter of the volume. Why was he allowed such prodigality? Even more amazingly, at 28, when he was but a whipper-snapper in terms of parliamentary significance, he made a two-hour speech on an obscure topic for which he received plaudits rather than scorn.

But debates were expected to be lengthy, and when over extraordinarily trivial subjects such as the Don Pacifico debate of 1850, in which Lord Palmerston (foreign secretary) made several speeches of four-plus hours, and Gladstone answered in three, the whole debate lasting for four nights, the topic did not matter a jot.

Gladstone was consolidating his reputation. His most renowned foe was Benjamin Disraeli, with whom he had famously hostile verbal collisions. The similarity to animals posturing, engaging and fighting is manifest, and there is no doubt the House of Commons, then as now, was a bear-pit in which to aim for power and ascendancy, and only secondarily an institution concerned with running the country. Men recognise the form without being told, and revere the great man as Gladstone was revered over 62 years. They acknowledge that his potency was all in the delivery, his towering presence, informed eloquence, use of the actor's gesture and occupation of the moral high ground, richness of language, theatricality tempered by both authority and humour. He was a master of measured oratory but even more of the impassioned, extempore response. Mostly his style with its godly gravitas overwhelmed Disraeli's flamboyant cleverness, but that nimble wordsmith's sardonic sallies could sometimes make Gladstone look pompous and sanctimonious. When Disraeli was prime minister in 1868, Gladstone made a point of breezing in and speaking on any and every subject, as if off-the-cuff; measuring his mettle in public and challenging the incumbent. When in a fix in controversial debates, under duress, he would experience an injection of strength as if from an external force, sustaining his might – as fighting animals do. In 1898 when he was taking a turn as prime minister, he was challenged by a peevish, jealous Chamberlain: 'Never since the time of Herod has there been such slavish adulation.' But the House was in thrall to its leader, and Chamberlain was demolished with shouts of 'Judas', and a descent into physical scrapping by forty members on the floor in a furious rough-house; how reminiscent of the gang-brawls of chimpanzees. How readily the all-night sittings of the House of Commons are understood in terms of the ancient drive to confront and to seize power. In the 1886 parliament, every night dragged on until 5 a.m., with some men taking a perverse delight in drawing out the proceedings. At the end of the night men flaunted their slept-in, crumpled clothing and stubbly chins like insignia. The elderly, sick and weak were given no redress, and probably some lives were shortened by the strain of the interminable hours.

Gladstone was the first parliamentarian to go out into the sticks and speak to the people en masse. Maybe he foresaw a major power-shift in the future. He was received with astonishing enthusiasm, drawing crowds of thousands even in rural outposts such as West Calder, and 20,000 in the Waverley Market in his Midlothian campaign. He recorded in his diary that he was 'hooked on crowd adulation'. More remarkable was that they were hooked on him. Why are we so mesmerised by the big man strutting his stuff? The capacity lies within ourselves, deeply ingrained, and biographical authors are also under the spell, half in love with the subject, and reinforcing the dependence on every possible occasion.

Great speakers recognise the sexual content of their relationship with their audiences. Hitler admitted he wooed the crowds like a woman. Aneurin Bevan, the greatest debater of his time, analysed his art in terms of courtship, using terms like 'establish an ascendancy', 'aspire to intimacy', 'belonging' and 'warmth and sympathy'. His speeches were all passion and impetuous persuasion. Listeners beware: you had better read these speeches rather than hear them if you want to judge with your brain rather than with your heart.

Leaders likewise dominate by perorations in small gatherings and in intimate conversations, and give no quarter to anyone. As a parliamentary wife I endured dinners of unspeakable boredom when some arrogant wannabe got his talking boots on. Hitler's 'table-talk' has become famous because it was recorded for posterity. On the Obersalzburg, over a leisurely paced afternoon dinner, he would talk in an endless boring monologue that nobody dared interrupt. Then after a forest walk he would repeat the process in a forest teahouse. It was a stultifying, appalling waste of time for the courtiers. In the war years, over tea and cakes after midnight, he relaxed with his entourage, who received, hour after hour, night after night, his banal and ill-informed opinions about every topic under the sun, focussing mostly on his own world and his aims for the future. His magic in this setting must have evaporated long before dawn. But this behaviour was far from unique, and was shared with Churchill for instance, though he had infinitely greater powers to entertain. It was a measure of Churchill's egocentricity (as it was of Hitler's) that during the Second World War he would keep his high-ranking attendants (political and military) round the dinner table, listening to his monologue until one or two in the morning. Of course he talked of war, but it was self-indulgent and reminiscent rather than constructive. According to Lord Moran (Churchill's doctor), he liked to bat while others fielded in the conversation – if you could call it that. Max Beaverbrook, a man of similar habits, had to play second fiddle when at the prime minister's table, fretting at the tedium and waste of hours. Lord Moran once, recognising how soporific everyone was, essayed an intelligent interjection and was shot down in flames. Anyone trying to slip away early caused dangerous offence, and was likely to be peremptorily and royally recalled. Gladstone could behave the same way, holding the conversation for an entire dinner party, as described in awed tones by the young Lloyd George in 1892.

Stalin also, having no close friends, enjoyed his only relaxation around the dinner table with his inner cabinet and occasional visitor, passing many hours of the night feasting on words as well as lavish victuals. Stalin was too wily and devious to commandeer the talk exclusively, dominating with his ears and eyes as well as his voice, but setting the tone of the debate and discussion. He followed a pattern set by Peter the Great, whose domestic policy was decided over similar orgies of excess. Stalin ruled by fear and no one dared disagree with him. When tired of politics he would amuse himself by getting someone drunk and watching him make a fool of himself. Multiple toasts with the obligation to down-in-one meant that only Stalin could control his intake. His peasant humour was ever crude and earthy.

Speech-making may be the new, subtle, hypnotic sexual dominance, but the ancient method still abounds in our society. Power-wielding takes place in other micro-climates, tucked away in nooks and corners, by-ways and backwaters, just as long as there is a power gradient. At the bottom end of the social scale, unseen in its obscurity, Darwinian rules are also obeyed in ways that at least offer an explanation for the otherwise incomprehensible. In the past decade, which has seen major inquiries launched into the abuse of children in care in Cleveland, Leicestershire and North Wales, no one can be left unaware of how commonplace is the sexual exploitation of undefended children in residential homes, and even in more favoured settings. For years the attempts to complain by these bottom-of-the-heap youngsters were ignored or punished by the establishment. Once people began to listen, the extent of the abuse became horrifyingly apparent. In January 2001 the *Independent* newspaper conducted a nationwide survey, showing that nearly 100 mega-scale inquiries, involving 2,500 children in around 500 homes, were under way throughout England, Wales and Northern Ireland. With police forces conducting investigations under a cloak of secrecy, this would appear to be a conservative estimate. In Scotland, similar investigations in Edinburgh and Fife have led to heavy sentences for carers for gross sexual abuse of youngsters in their charge. In the United States, the Catholic Church is undergoing a cleansing of its own Augean stables for toleration of priestly pederasty.

The wretched story was depicted in a fictionalised TV drama, *Care* by Kieran Prendiville, based on the Welsh inquiry. These perpetually excluded had a life that was the polar opposite of that prescribed by Hitler for his anointed Aryan youth. Having been so firmly fixed under the heel of society, they could never ever recover. In all the multiple tales of grief there are factors in common. These children were sometimes difficult, disturbed, uncontrolled, prone to petty criminality; others had suffered social dislocation, trying to cope in broken or violent, doped or drunken homes. Residential homes are not top of the list for government funding; the pay for workers is mediocre, with little capacity for cross-supervision. Anyone sufficiently committed and keen would be left in total charge, doing a service to society one might think. Without doubt many do just that. But in this underprivileged, underfunded, obscure corner, there is the capacity to exploit a power gradient for sexual relief in just the same way that kings, emperors and presidents do at the other end of the scale. All too commonly that opportunity is seized.

Some carers have manipulated cunningly with intimidation and fear, or bribery, presents, music lessons, trips to the seaside, caravan weekends, swimming lessons. Others practised divide and rule, fostering quarrels between the children so that they did not make common cause. In *Care* we see a warden of hearty do-goodery, befriending the children; a man relied on, respected in the community, with a long history of service. A bedrock figure, with allies in the establishment. Who would believe a disturbed and troubled child with fantastic stories of sexual engagement? They were dismissed as fevered imaginings in an ungrateful ne'er-do-well. Guilt and worthlessness and total disempowerment occupy the child's mind like squatters and are all but impossible to evict. I can't put it any better than Polly Toynbee: 'Where human beings are utterly powerless there is a high probability that they will be abused in almost every way.' The figures tell their own tale: one in six girls leave 'care' either pregnant or already burdened with a child. One in three people in prison come from 'care'.

Children who end up in homes run by religious orders may fare even worse, under the thumb of guardians of rigid views and sexual confusion. Their complaints against supposedly celibate, holy men are even less likely to be believed. Moreover the children in this setting are regarded as intrinsically bad, objects for punishment, repositories of sin. One horrifying tale reported a priest abusing boys as young as six through decades, and allowing nuns to chastise the babies for complaining. Punishment verging on torture seems a particular risk in this setting; the children were to have the Devil whipped or beaten, bullied or even electrocuted out of them. No wonder they did not complain of the sex. In a hostile world it was just another trouble to be endured.

You do not have to be poor or dispossessed to be vulnerable, for sex–power games abound in expensive, prestigious schools for the wealthy. At Charterhouse in 1817, Thackeray remembered the first command he received from a senior boy: 'Frig me!' At Harrow School in 1858, a pupil, John Symonds, discovered a friend of his was engaged in a love affair with the hugely respected headmaster, the Reverend Dr Charles Vaughan. His mingled reaction of passionate fury, disgust, fascination and jealousy revealed to Symonds the nature of his own homosexuality. He reported the headmaster, opening the way to his resignation. For Vaughan it was the end of an expected high-flying career in the Church. Yet it is worth noting that Vaughan was an inspired, affectionate, devoted and caring teacher, possibly (dare I say it?) all the better for his visceral love of his pupils. No doubt Symonds, his nemesis, was strongly motivated by envy and desire. This ambivalence, this recognition of the pleasures of sex even at a young age, causes the confusion, guilt and self-blame among the youngsters, and keeps them silent. They need to be protected from themselves as well as their overlords. Symonds' reaction is strikingly similar to that of Don Boyd, drawn into a love relationship with his French teacher at the elitist Loretto School in Musselburgh, almost exactly one hundred years later. This charismatic teacher was adored by his pupils, who enjoyed his raffish innuendo and aspired to be one of his special friends. Don Boyd described how, when the moment arrived, he wanted sex with his teacher more than anything else in the world. The comedian Billy Connolly who was abused by his own father, has also admitted that the victim is engaged and inculpated because he joins in the pleasure.

Paedophilia raises unprecedented levels of fury and violent outrage, some of which may be prompted by a deeply shameful empathy. But to most people, the sexual abuse of the vulnerable elderly, disabled and even demented, in their supposedly safe nursing homes, is incomprehensible. Yet it happens. Those whose relatives have been traumatised in expensive, well-kept homes have tried to raise ginger groups, working against the usual wall of government apathy.

These situations demonstrate that, where there is a power gradient, the uppermost will be tempted to seek or extort sexual favours. There are other examples. Wherever slavery has existed, in the 1800s, for instance, on tea and sugar plantations in Assam and Ceylon, in Fiji, Trinidad, South America, South Africa, British men of every rank exploited the slaves for sexual release. Indeed it was usual to begin one's sex life with such an encounter. Men could not be accused of raping their own property. But this is not just past history. The sale of children as prostitutes by parents in desperate poverty still happens. They come from Africa, Asia, Latin America, Eastern Europe, to Frankfurt, Bonn, Paris, Amsterdam, Berlin – and recently to London. Helplessly dislocated, with no legal identity, numbed by drugs, they have no choice but to submit to cruel exploitation. Endemic child prostitution occurs also, as on the streets of Glasgow: schoolgirls in socks and clumpy shoes sell sex for a fiver, often propelled by heroin-addicted mothers. Victorian prostitution involved many juveniles, with some London brothels specialising in girls under thirteen. European and Oriental houses of ill-repute of the time specialised in boy brothels, so the child-sex trade is not a new phenomenon. Prisoners of repressive regimes such as Japan in the Second World War, Chile in the Pinochet era, and more recently of Turkey, suffer vicious methods of sexual torture under interrogation, and protracted sentences for daring to speak out about such crimes.

Even within the nuclear family there are thousands of violent episodes, including rape, daily in the UK; besides evidence of undercover incest which more and more people are finding the freedom to vocalise. But incest has been around since the beginning of time, and again is not new. We are only just recognising that it ever happened.

Readers may well recoil in disgust from this catalogue of repulsive truths. I emphasize these distasteful and sometimes bizarre examples to stress how much deviant sexual behaviour occurs on a power gradient. Darwin was right in this; but wrong in defining the rewards as reproductive. This is not reasoned or cerebral behaviour. Men seek sexual favours, pleasures, release. They perhaps justify the moment because the pleasure is mutual. It feels right, therefore it is right. Their lives may be otherwise exemplary in terms of duty, rectitude, commitment, kindness – though not always. There is a terrible conflict with which men of all persuasions wrestle, between visceral and intellectual perceptions of how a man should behave.

Women do not have these conflicts, or at least not to the same degree. Our sexual lives do not generally prompt us to lie and cheat, to compete and dominate, to shout others down, to find an enemy and take arms against him – do they? Women should make better leaders, motivated to promote health and welfare of their subjects. In tandem with their relatively peaceable natures, women do not prostrate themselves before heroes, or make sycophantic worship at the altars of power. They are at once more level-headed, rational and pro-democratic. Aren't they?

CHAPTER 11

The Amazons

Almost unbreachable bastions of male dominance are the military, the Church and politics. Men also have a greater claim on death and disease, with a higher mortality rate than women (in the UK for all 15 leading causes of death) and a life expectancy that is seven years shorter than women's. Other areas where they steal a march are in alcohol and drug abuse, road-traffic accidents, murder, violent crime, depression, suicide and domestic assault.

While feminists have a tailormade case that women are superior beings, this concept has not gained general acceptance. Not only Hitler and Mao Zedong but also Charles de Gaulle believed that war and the use of force were integral to life. Progressing his visceral argument in easy stages from historical to inevitable to glorious, de Gaulle elevated the profession of arms to the highest ideal, with cant about self-sacrifice for the community, the age-old hypocrisy: *'Dulce et decorum est pro patria mori.'* You would have thought that the obscenities of the First World War would have done away with all that. Yet at the time of writing, men are still kindling, fanning and propagating some thirty wars around the globe, the things they are best at. While history is largely determined by conflict, women will ever be portrayed as inferior.

Women do not readily choose to be warriors, preferring to resolve conflicts using their skills of mediation and pacification. It is not surprising that there have been so few female leaders in history; perhaps more astonishing is that there have been any at all, given the usual entry ports of arms or politics. An anthology called *Women*

Rulers throughout the Ages by Guida M Jackson scrapes together a mere 500 names, including some more mythical than real. Whereas, for men, the leader opportunities throughout the shifting nation states of the world since recorded time began have been as numerous as the grains of sand on the seashore. If I were then able to sketch female cartoon characters corresponding to the alpha male and the military celibate, this work would begin to look contrived. Some patterns and generalities do emerge though.

Some of the best-known lady-leaders, perhaps most, have come from a dynasty. They step out from behind a mighty man, father, husband or son, who as often as not has been deposed or assassinated. It is as if, knowing the figurehead in an intimate family setting, and deeply imprinted by love and loyalty, they are at the same time less fazed by his superiority. The deference factor works in their favour too, with the perception of the people that some families have what it takes. Sirimavo Bandaranaike, Prime Minister of Sri Lanka, came to power in 1960 after her husband, prime minister and leader of the nationalist–socialist coalition, was assassinated. She had no previous experience and was expected to follow his socialist policies. She held the high office twice, and her daughter, Chandrika, also became prime minister. Chandrika qualified in the same way, actually witnessing both her father and her film-star husband being killed by fanatics.

Benazir Bhutto was raised in a family that moved with the elite of Pakistan. Her father Ali was leader of Pakistan for eight years until he was deposed, tried by a kangaroo court and murdered in a military coup by General Zia in 1979. Ali Bhutto became a martyr while his wife and daughter, in prison and then in exile, were identified as the focus of national hopes of liberation. Benazir was able to return to her country, whose people received her ecstatically. When Zia died in a plane explosion, she won an election to become Prime Minister of Pakistan. She was not the first woman to rule an Islamic state, but is the most celebrated. Like Bandaranaike, she was defeated yet returned to office a second time.

Corazon Aquino of the Philippines had a remarkable similar background, born to wealth and educated with the cream of society. A mother of five, she was happy to do the little woman bit for her politician husband Benigno, who opposed Ferdinand Marcos, a tyrant hanging onto power by the usual means of martial law and selective murder. Benigno Aquino was jailed, exiled and assassinated. Corazon was fired to join the dissidents, oppose Marcos and eventually get herself elected president.

In the case of Indira Gandhi, her father was India's first prime minister, Jawaharlal Nehru, who had led the movement for Independence from the British Raj. Indira's upbringing in her aristocratic family was steeped in the non-cooperation movement, and as her parents were deeply involved – and in and out of jail – her formative years were anything but conventional. Indira had travelled widely in her youth and everywhere was treated as a celebrity for belonging to a notorious freedom-fighting family. But she was ambivalent about her own place, though she immersed herself in a variety of political activities, nearly all in a subsidiary or background role. Her attempts at public speaking trembled on the brink of disastrous. In her elitist schools and at Oxford University she behaved like a shrinking violet, undistinguished in academic and social scenes. During Nehru's prime ministership she continued as the multi-purpose supportive woman/secretary/hostess/factotum, since her mother had died. She did the same for her husband Feroze.

Nehru relied heavily on Indira, as men do, but treated her as a subordinate and did not see her as his successor. He may have rationalised this as being due to his egalitarian principles, which were incompatible with there being a Nehru dynasty. Indira had become Congress president, but refused a second term and declined the leadership when it was first offered. The unseen, blushing-flower syndrome again. But in Shastri's cabinet she still carried the aura, the popularity, even the majesty of Nehru's daughter, and when the incumbent died after two years, she finally accepted the leadership.

Begum Khaleda Zia of Bangladesh had no elitist or political connections, but by an arranged marriage became a middle-class army wife. Her husband rose to major-general, took part in a military coup and emerged at the top of the heap, becoming head of state in 1977. Although she showed no interest in politics, when her husband was killed after five years during a military coup by another army general (Ershad), she became head of her husband's

Nationalist Party, waging fierce opposition against Ershad until she achieved power in 1991.

The first Bangladeshi leader, Sheikh Mujibur Rahman, had come to power on the back of democratic principles but rapidly forsook these for progressive absolute dictatorship laced with flagrant nepotism. When the tanks arrived to surround his house he was mown down by gunfire with his three sons, two sons' wives, brother, wife and two servants. They missed only his 28-year-old daughter, Sheikh Hasina, who was away from home – it was a significant omission, for she became Prime Minister of Bangladesh 21 years later.

Revered and democratic principles regularly go to the wall when there is no check on the fiercely selfish, atavistic ones. However hard we try to shed our royal families, they keep sneaking back again by some mystical pact between the conqueror and the conquered. Certainly, the womenfolk of great men are primed to act as magnificent she-bears when disaster strikes their lords. Our own national icon Boudicca was a typical example. She was of royal descent, and married King Prasutagus who ruled the Iceni tribe in the east of England, while acknowledging Roman rule. When the king died, the Romans arrogantly moved in and deposed Boudicca, inflicting chaos, looting, raping her daughters, flogging her in public and finally setting up their own governor. Her organised retaliation when it came was terminally ferocious, as if anticipating the escalating retribution that would cut short her bloody triumphs. The Iceni took no prisoners during their sacking of towns and camps, dealing death to soldiers and civilians alike, high and low indiscriminately, with every bestiality, barbarity and improvised humiliation they could devise. Seventy thousand Romans perished, it is said, with three major towns demolished, and all hamlets in between. But British warfare with its overtones of paganism, Celtic myth, ritual sacrifice and tribal theatre was no match for the professional Roman variety, which was ruthlessly businesslike. Boudicca's ranks received their comeuppance and, when it came, it matched theirs in every bloody way. It is believed she poisoned herself rather than face the Roman reckoning.

An exactly parallel tale of breaking-faith, avenge and revenge occured in 19th-century India with the British as the wicked suzerain and the Rani of Jhansi, Lakshmi Bai, as the valiant subordinate. Did any Britons of the time recognise this reincarnation of their own ancient goddess? The Rani's husband ruled his princely state independently but with mutual co-operation with the British Raj. On the death of the rajah the Governor General of India, Dalhousie, mowed down the planned succession of the rajah's adopted son with his wife as regent, and high-handedly annexed the state. Dalhousie was a narrow-minded, arrogant ass who hated India, and out of whose fathomless turpitude such devastating decisions would be sandwiched in, no doubt, between coffee and tiffin.

Three years later, the Indian Mutiny errupted. Jhansi was not immediately involved in the rebellion, and a small group of British women and children took refuge in one of its forts. But the rampaging sepoys reached this haven which, under siege, could not hold out for long. After surrender and apparent assurance of a safe passage, the defenceless civilians were attacked and murdered.

Meanwhile the British had had their hands full, and for a few months the rani governed her own province, very effectively by all accounts. In these troubled times, it was not surprising that she practised the martial arts, including riding a horse while brandishing a sword in each hand, her reins clamped between her teeth. Prudently she tried to make common cause with the British overlords, to regularise her rulership; but she had been identified with the revolutionaries, the disobedient and ungrateful wretches. Though Queen Victoria, Empress of India-to-be, sitting on her throne back in England, might deprecate any retribution, the army of reprisal was out for Lakshmi Bai. Besieged in her city with a huge army of volunteers, she held out nobly, in the thick of the action, and inspiring all her defenders to do or die. Only when the siege was broken did she escape on horseback. The city was razed to the ground in an orgy of vengeance as terrible as any inflicted on either side by the other, with indiscriminate violence meted out to soldier and civilian alike. Lakshmi Bai was killed in later action, and so moved into perpetual memory, praised for her martial courage and love of her own country; honoured by both sides for these same qualities; and deemed the most dangerous of all the rebel leaders.

Weak-limbed and self-effacing women can take arms with the best of them, it seems, when the stimulus is sufficiently strong. For women the spark that ignites is an attack on their most precious concerns, child, husband or home-base. It is a defensive response, not a voluntary entry into the lists. Yet once in warrior mode, there are no limits to the grisly and ugly deeds that women can perpetrate. An identified enemy can expect no mercy. Similarly, disaster to a woman can switch on the dormant political mode, even in those who have previously shown no affinity whatever with the feint and thrust, debate and harangue, double-dealing and deception, which are the daily fare of macho politics.

A recent example of what Antonia Fraser calls the 'Appendage Syndrome', that is, a woman-satellite deriving power from close male kin, and one with a curiously modern twist, is Hillary Clinton. In this instance, the impetus was her own husband, who first gave her the springboard by making her First Lady of the USA, then the kick-start by humiliating her through the shambles of his much publicised sex life. Hillary is now a vocal and feisty senator, and will no doubt, unless stopped by ripples from the continuing Whitewater corruption allegations, make a bid for the presidency.

Women rulers endowed with beauty and sex appeal, naturally aware of the power these gifts give them, are likely to use them for maximal advantage; but they must beware how much they impart to predatory men if they are to remain in charge. Cleopatra VII, Queen of Egypt in the first century BC, that icon of seductive mystique, managed the ruling Roman lords in a way that Boudicca and Lakshmi Bai might have either disparaged or admired. She took them to bed and had children by them. When she first appealed to Julius Caesar in the renowned rolled-up-carpet episode, Cleopatra had been deprived of her throne. Once Caesar's cunning gonads had been engaged in her favour, and had given her a son, Cleopatra's restoration to the throne was easy, enabling her to get rid of inconvenient brothers and sisters, and rule jointly with her son under Roman suzerainty.

When Julius Caesar was assassinated and the Roman Empire was divided, Mark Anthony pursued Cleopatra for a day of reckoning. From Tarsus in the eastern Mediterranean he summoned her to answer charges, but she did not bend her beautiful neck so humbly. Arriving by boat with pomp and panoply, she caused such a stir that Mark Anthony forgot himself and allowed her to graciously receive him aboard as an honoured guest. Thus started a twelve-year relationship with three children resulting, and a considerable extension of Cleopatra's sphere of influence, as, between them and their children, their rule extended far into Asia Minor. When at length the might and fury of Octavian's troops were visited on them, they enacted a *Romeo and Juliet*-type tragedy, and though Cleopatra tried to get out of trouble by turning her charms on Octavian, he was not susceptible; or she was no longer bewitching. At 39, her potent sexual powers were at an end. Life without them was worth nothing. Her death by the bite of an asp clutched to her bosom was symbolic, not of the sun-god, but of the phallic power she had harnessed while her nubility lasted.

The beauty and charm of a royal consort can eclipse those of the Prince himself, as did Diana, Princess of Wales, causing much jealousy among those of the true blue-blooded line. When such gifts are combined with strength of character and determination, as with Queen Louise of Prussia in Napoleonic times, they can threaten to turn the events of history. Louise's chief claim to fame was her famous physical perfection, which ensured she was selected from among numerous minor, hopeful German princesses, to marry Prince Frederick William of Prussia. She performed her duties in due order, producing nine children in fourteen years, and adorning the Prussian court with her statuesque figure and her smiles. Her irresistible charms bewitched, among others, Tsar Alexander of Russia, with whom it was rumoured she was having an affair, which was probably an untruth. Her husband was not very admirable, being slow, indecisive and very uncouth.

Meanwhile, Napoleon was on the rampage in Europe. King Frederick was supine, hating war and not wanting to face the aggressor. The combined enthusiasm of Louise and the tsar prodded him into a Russian–Prussian pact, and Napoleon's success at Austerlitz finally convinced him that arms and not negotiations were required. Napoleon was in no doubt that Louise was the inspired and metaphorical leader of the army, prompting a series of sexist remarks; for Louise, probably using the strongest language she knew, had vowed to 'Beat the Monster down'.

So followed Napoleon's inevitable triumph at Jena-Auerstadt, which wiped out the army of Prussia and tore apart its empire. Arriving at the palace in Weimar he amused himself by riffling through Louise's pretty feminine knick-knacks, and adopting the age-old stance of blaming the woman for all the death and destruction. The rulers of Russia and Prussia being thoroughly humiliated by defeat, and forced to negotiate with Napoleon such fragments as could be saved from the wreckage, Frederick William was prompted to ask the enchantress his wife to try her powers of fascination on Napoleon, Cleopatra-style. All Europe, it seems, awaited this meeting between the irresistible object and the all-consuming force. Talleyrand, Napoleon's foreign minister, was nervous. Others wondered if Beauty would fall in love with the Beast. Bets were taken. Probably all the publicity worked in Louise's disfavour, though she did her duty as always and pleaded for a softening of the swingeing terms imposed. Napoleon, aware that his reputation was on the line, deftly side-stepped and put her down by demeaning compliments. She returned to the attack again and again, begging for mercy, but he would have none of it. He was in military-celibate/misogynist mode.

All women, even feminists, will sympathize with Louise. To me, one of the most poignant things about her was her sturdy attempt to make sense of history. She had always tried to rectify her minimalist education even in the days of her queenly stability, before the monster appeared. After her passionate but disastrous inspiring of the military resistance, her attempts to read the heavy tomes of war literature became more fervent. 'I am so stupid and I hate the stupidity... What does hierarchy mean?' Her bewilderment encapsulates that of women everywhere who try to enter a man's world without the least understanding of a man's psychology. Queen Louise became an icon, revered as a guardian angel by the remnants of the Prussian army; as someone who only showed her claws to defend her patch; as one of the few who achieve immortality through gentleness.

Many prominent women in history have been labelled 'honorary men', but strictly the name should only be awarded to those very few women who have made it without any prior male influence. Two such examples are Golda Meir and Margaret Thatcher. Golda Meir, who, under David Ben Gurion was called the 'only man in the cabinet', is all the more remarkable for being Premier of Israel in the years 1969 to 1974, well before the feminist revolution. Her family were Russian emigrés escaping persecution in Russia for a working-class life in the United States. After marriage she emigrated to Palestine with her husband for kibbutz life, then two children and making ends meet as a laundry woman. Her life became subsumed in the Zionist movement, unlike her husband, from whom she parted. Deeply involved in the Independence process for Israel, she served on Israel's first governing body for 25 years variously as ambassador to the Soviet Union, minister of labour, secretary general of the Labour Party, minister for foreign affairs and finally prime minister for five years. In an emphatically male world, her passionate defence of her humble home patch ('the one place in the Middle East where there is no oil') was her defining feature. She could match any man with her oratory, which raised fifty million dollars in the United States for the embryonic State of Israel in 1949. She was not mealy mouthed about her intentions, did not talk of peace when she meant war. We will fight, she said, and meant it. Yet her strength derived from the most admired qualities of both sexes, as her political adviser Simcha Dinitz observed: female intuition, insight, sensitivity and compassion, with male strength, determination, practicality and purposefulness. Her motherly and grandmotherly air gave her iconic status among the soldiery, who loved her as Louise of Bavaria had been loved.

The mechanism of Golda Meir's election to prime minister was not dissimilar to Mrs Thatcher's. Both slipped in between embattled rival male claims and after a demise – real or political. Mrs Thatcher's election to the leadership of the Tory Party was astonishing and unpredicted, the first intimation of genius in a career that had been successful in a fairly humdrum way. One definition of genius is an infinite capacity for taking pains; and perhaps for giving them, in her case, for relentlessness was a quality she owned and used freely, especially in debate. It was a formidable attribute, and one she often deployed to mow down the opposition through playing on their boredom, apathy, intimidation or lack of conviction. This coupled with her absence of imagination, both derived from her narrow-minded, prudent father, informed her political persona. She could never entertain any other way than her own. The tediously tenacious schoolgirl debater translated into the harridan who hectored President Jimmy Carter for the space of 45 minutes with no concession to chivalry. Her fixed aims at any point in life were as unrelenting as those of Lenin.

The young Margaret Roberts was a conformist, never a rebel, studiously following the path of duty and self-denial in a life bereft of risk or indulgence – not a promising background for a male-style leader. But she had solid respectable virtues, the stuff of which head girls are made. She achieved that position at school, and later at Oxford became president of the University Conservative Association, thus behaving like a watered-down Bill Clinton. The years of deference to her father Alderman Roberts were translated into hero-worship of Keith Joseph. Later as leader of the opposition she sat at the feet of Indira Gandhi and begged to know how she did it. Idolomania is a good bedding for the growth of heroic status. Yet she only recognised hierarchy on the slopes of her own chosen pinnacle, and treated the civil servants of Whitehall with consistent contempt. This was characteristic of her tunnel vision. She could only learn from her own experience, whether through fury followed by unremitting hostility at the Labour Group in Grantham for sacking her father as an alderman, or propagating her personal take on child education when she was education secretary. But the Whitehall mandarins act as a necessary buffer to soften or direct the short-termism of political enthusiasm, a role that the rising, egocentred Thatcher could only view as obstructionism.

She had an immense capacity for unremitting hard work and became known as a forensic speaker, through detailed preparation rather than brilliant, compelling oratory. Her voice was a disadvantage. Women's voices did not evolve to project and direct, and hers was brassily strident rather like Boudicca's was reputed to be. She showed an ability to dispense with loyalties to people and principles when her own career demanded it, thus earning her spurs as a politician. All the seeds were there, in embryonic form, waiting for her to find the right pasture.

Her prejudices towards groups of people she never knew or understood was one fertile area that worked in her favour. Her insular upbringing in Grantham, from which she scarcely moved till her student days, chimed with her tribal instincts and those of her party. Ethnic minorities, union activists, welfare dependants, the poor, underprivileged, elderly and disabled would never gain her sympathy. She liked the hard-working and the successful because that was what she was. If others were different, that was a source of blame and shame. This ignoble instinct was one shared by a great many people in the country, perhaps the majority. When she gave voice to those politically incorrect notions, many voters would support her in relief and gladness, for the identical reason that people had followed Hitler in the 1930s. Her swash-buckling speech in 1976 about the Soviet Union's aim for world-dominance was an expression of the same instinct, and earned her the sobriquet of 'Iron Lady'. Her steam-rollering self-belief stood in place of social confidence, as when dealing with the likes of the supremely top-drawer Valery Giscard d'Estaing. Yet another example of her tribal insularity was her implacable stance on the EEC and Britain's budgetary contribution; and again the people loved her for it. She must have realised early that with three weapons she could go on and on: bravery, brashness and an appeal to narrow self-interest. Top male jungle savages have been doing the same for aeons. The cock-sure certitude, which she probably did not always feel, but had to display as an alpha animal does, ensured that her listening capacity, probably never very sensitive, shut down completely. On her trips abroad – an almost brand-new experience even as leader – her receptors were blocked to new cultures, new ideas. She really was cast in steel, hardly human any longer.

She coined the term 'One of Us" and stamped her image on it for ever. Never worried about dissembling over her persona or giving offence by her abrasiveness, she totally lacked the male instinct for glad-handing and alliance-making. Those officials who did not belong to her immediate circle of advisers were treated with intimidating hostility at first encounter: an initiation rite or ceremonial blooding in which they might or might not become imprinted and accepted. There was a pressing need for enemies, and in this she was undoubtedly masculine; people like Galtieri of Argentina, Arthur Scargill and Jacques Delors fulfilled that role. In tandem was her missionary zeal, and her self-view as the embodiment of goodness and rectitude, while all around were people who were bad or faulty, who must be lectured into the paths of docility and rightness. There are uncanny echoes of Stalin in the way cohorts of ministers were despatched when they went off-message one way or another: Lord Carrington, Francis Pym, Michael Heseltine, Leon Brittan, Geoffrey Howe, Nigel Lawson. Surrounded by scorched earth, she would pluck people out of obscurity to fill the void, if they were reverential and obedient like John Major, who had as narrow an early life as she. Unlike Stalin she could not arrange for the physical elimination of her discard pile, so the number of her enemies grew and came back to haunt her. The old lags looked for revenge while the younger generation wanted their ambition to have a chance to flower without being terminally handbagged.

In the end her primitive clannishness was her undoing. Ever like a fish out of water in the Commonwealth, Mrs Thatcher's pathological hostility towards Europe culminated in her almost hysterical speech in the Commons, rejecting the single currency. Geoffrey Howe, already humiliated by his summary ejection from the foreign secretary post, now resigned from the Cabinet with a devastating accusation of autocracy verging on tyranny. Such events led inexorably to her downfall. In truth she had always rejected consensus government. She was a heartfelt hierarchy freak, and in this she was truly an honorary man.

As many leaders do once they are ensconced in state, Margaret Thatcher had her own piece of belligerence: the Falklands War. Though many of us recall with revulsion her triumphal display as Victrix, and the authority it gave her, the diplomatic failure that preceded it was so reprehensible that it ought to have brought her to her knees. But by that time she was a thorough-going politician whose every action would be prioritised according to how it affected her hold on power.

It seems clear that male characteristics are lying dormant in women and can be activated when they find themselves in positions of dominance. Mrs Thatcher was not unique in that respect. Women are behindhand in achieving the single-minded ferocity and unprovoked aggression that mark a Napoleon or a Hitler, certainly, but a handful of the 'gentle' sex have been able to discard all vestiges of womanly compassion and reserve. Among these stands Queen Jinga of Angola, who led her warriors against the invading Portuguese, traders whose incursions were not made with territorial intent but to capture humans for their lucrative and expanding slave trade. Women warriors are not unusual in African tradition, and usually augment their authority by adopting a priestess-sorceress mantle. Jinga came to power in the 17th century after her brother and nephew died suddenly; by her hand it is said, for her way to the throne was now unimpeded. One unconfirmed story says she ate the nephew's heart. Amid the ensuing tribal skirmishes, Jinga took over a neighbouring tribe, the Jagas, adopting some of their customs such as cannibalism, human sacrifice and infanticide. Accurate descriptions of her in ritualistic mode portray a Kali-like figure, ferocious and terrifying, girt about with animal skins and an armoury of assorted weapons, leaping like a demon and beating a cacophony on two iron bells. Having made an impact with this thoroughly animal display she would gruesomely thrust a feather through her bored nose, before beheading her first victim and gorging herself on his blood.

Jinga's territorial expansion at the point of her primitive weapons is unusual in a female ruler, but one could argue that it evolved from a defensive position. Her name could almost have given rise to the term jingoism. She behaved like an alpha male in other ways, keeping fifty or sixty young men for her sexual convenience. They were allowed wives without restriction, but all infants from those unions were destroyed by her order. Some stories describe her preferring her young men dressed in female garb. Highly skilled at gaining the respect and fear of her own and conquered tribes, she used her family female network for support and intelligence in a wholly masculine manner. The most famous story of her innate imperiousness was when she attended the Portuguese governor to negotiate early in her queenly career. He sat resplendent on his throne while she was expected to stand like an inferior. Jinga summoned a slave to crouch down and form a seat for her convenience and dignity. After the interview the slave was executed on the spot, having served his purpose – a piece of flamboyant one-upmanship that would be hard to cap.

As in African and Celtic heritage, so also in pre-Islamic Arabia there exists a tradition of queens-regnant who draped themselves with an aura of the supernatural and equated themselves with previous revered icons. Queen Zenobia of Palmyra in Syria in Roman times was one such, who claimed connections with Cleopatra and the semi-legendary Semiramis of Assyria (who dated back a further thousand years). Zenobia's beauty gave her a key to fortune in the form of marriage to King Odainat, after which her latent masculinity became her dominant feature. The couple were addicted to hunting, spending whole days in the pursuit of dangerous big game, oblivious to the perils and discomfort. Such activities translated easily into the prosecution of war, in which Zenobia also rode beside her husband. She is reputed to have had an authoritative male voice and to have loved a drink with the lads, though ever able to remain in control. She chose eunuchs to attend her rather than females. Most strangely, she is only supposed to have slept with her husband for the specific purpose of conceiving a child; otherwise she held aloof. There were at least three sons, maybe more. Zenobia's ways translate rather neatly into the female equivalent of the military celibate.

Then Zenobia's husband, and his heir – not Zenobia's child, but one of a previous marriage – met their ends in mysterious circumstances, maybe with her connivance. Zenobia as regent on behalf of her own son was liberated. Not content to remain prudently as a vassal of Rome as her pygmy husband had done, she embarked on a conquering and expanding spree, into Egypt, Syria and Asia Minor. At the time, the Roman overlords had their energies engaged with the troublesome Gothic fringe in Europe. Zenobia declared her empire independent of Rome, striking coins with her own and her son's images, glorying in her control of trade centres and routes vital to Roman economy. She ruled magisterially in an opulent court, marked by richness of intellect as well as material splendour, and learning on the hoof, as it were, the value of diplomatic relations. But not with Rome. Inevitably the time came when the seasoned campaigners returned to put her in her place. Zenobia's commanders had not learned the crucial art of controlling the headstrong cavalry charge, just as she had not learned to rein in her unquenchable ambition, and so she met her nemesis.

But Zenobia, strong as she was, in ruin and humiliation switched back to fragile feminine mode. She did not proudly die by her own hand like Boudicca, or seduce her conqueror like Cleopatra. She shuffled off the blame for the rebellion onto her advisers as best she could, not showing overmuch loyalty in the process, and undermined Emperor Aurelian's victories by presenting herself as weak and helpless. She ended her days as a Roman senator's wife, incredible and unheroic though it may seem, and apparently quite content in her reincarnation.

Queen Tamara of Georgia in the 12th century pursued a policy of military expansion for twenty years of her rein, and like Zenobia's, her skills had been learned in the hunting field. Arguably she needed to attack in order to keep her turbulent kingdom under control. She used every self-image to inspire her soldiers: the saintly figurehead, the honorary soldier, the cunning strategist, the royal speech-maker on the eve of battle. Under her rule the Georgian Empire was at its most expansive and, when briefly relieved of her fighting duties, Tamara was known as a benevolent ruler. Her name, as with many female rulers, is surrounded by myth and folklore, which in her case shows the extremes of contradiction over her sexual life. Some stories portray indiscriminate lust, with death the fate of each lover after a night of passion; others make her out to be prudish and austere (necessary perhaps as she was to be canonised). Both her son Georgi and her daughter Rusudani who ruled after her had a more firmly established reputation for wanton lustiness.

Histories of licentiousness in men are taken for granted; in women, especially ruling-class women, they can be exaggerated or distorted. Misogyny takes over, for such excesses are seen as unnatural, and perhaps neither gender knows how to cope with them. Catherine the Great of Russia has a scurrilous reputation for profligacy in her love life, yet she had only twelve lovers in all, and in a reasonably orderly sequence after her husband Tsar Peter. Her enjoyment of sex and her assertion that she would not live for one hour without love are perfectly understandable to modern women. She would undoubtedly have liked the stability and comfort of marriage during her 34-year reign, yet realised as forcibly as Elizabeth I of England had done, that a woman autocrat cannot keep her dominance and marry; she must choose one or the other. Both of these staunch ladies chose power. It was an easier choice for Catherine perhaps, who had an heir by her first lover, Saltykov; but Elizabeth was torn and tormented throughout her lengthy reign, and was probably quite as passionate as Catherine, if supernaturally restrained. That they could both make such a choice over all that is supposed to be most fundamental and defining for a woman, is testimony to the compelling lure of untrammelled power.

Much of the scandalous nature of Catherine's love life came from its perpetuation into her ripe old age while her lovers were ever splendidly youthful exemplars of masculine military perfection. King Frederick of Prussia might observe, 'It is a terrible thing when the prick and the cunt decide the interests of Europe.' It may be terrible but it is the usual thing. Men only deplore sexual monopolies when the female is in charge. If you compare Catherine's serial monogamy with the love life of a Clinton or a Mao Zedong, there is not much in it to raise an eyebrow. She was essentially a woman wanting an enduring relationship. Myths about suspended stallions can be discounted as barrack-room humour.

Throughout her life, Catherine was to suffer the inner conflict resulting from her two irreconcilable drives. Trying to fit her man of the moment into her life, she would lavish honours, titles, lands and riches upon him. Macho ambition would be fed in abundance, but could not be satisfied, unless by marriage or a coup. One of her lovers, Gregory Orlov, the *crème de la crème* in the guards regiment, who had helped to mastermind the deposing and death of her feeble and immature husband, was undoubtedly considered as a consort. She had a son by him who could not be laughed off as a product of her impotent husband (who was now dead), and the boy was spirited away into obscurity. Catherine owed her throne to

Orlov and his network. Soundings were made as to his acceptability as the tsarina's spouse, and uncovered such a can of worms that she backed off, aghast. Later she suppressed much of the inflammatory material. There was subterranean hatred and rumbling of plots to commit wholesale murder against the Orlov clan if the marriage proceeded. The outcome would have been similar to the disastrous fate of husbands two and three of Mary Queen of Scots, and Catherine herself would have been seriously threatened by the ensuing turbulence. She never overtly considered marriage again, though historians do wonder if she secretly wedded the strongest man in her life, Lieutenant General Gregory Potemkin.

Profound depression is a usual consequence of irreconcilable conflict between two powerful drives, and Catherine suffered from it increasingly as age advanced. The same phenomenon probably besets other lady rulers. Photographs and portraits of Queen Victoria and our present monarch Queen Elizabeth II convey a mood of unremitting gloom. Elizabeth I also suffered increasingly severe attacks of melancholy after the menopause. Loneliness and isolation played their part in Catherine's periods of gloom, which were more pronounced during the sway of a less authoritative lover such as Vasil-chikov. Undoubtedly, she wanted a dominant man but refused absolutely to be dominated. Potemkin was the nearest to her ideal man and in her correspondence she calls him 'husband', 'spouse' and 'master', counterbalancing these with animal endearments such as 'peacock', 'tiger' and 'doggie'. Letters to the next swain, Zavadovskii, are embarrassing in their over-effusiveness and excess of feeling verging on the self-abasing. There followed a series of short-lasting lovers, then Lanskoi (another guards officer), who at 23 was 27 years her junior. His sudden death – possibly from diphtheria – plunged Catherine into one of the most serious and protracted depressions of her life, with translation of her grief into physical illness. The low moods were to become an annual event, worsened by her own aging and deaths of those she had loved; or sometimes when a lover became cold and distant, as they did. One may speculate that many, in spite of the lavish rewards of wealth, status and honours, found their position impossible. Overwhelmed by an aging, bossy, jealous and hugely obese mistress, it is no wonder they became hypochondriacal and tempestuous. In the dying throes of a relationship it was often she who clung and suffered. Yet Catherine was not vindictive, and most of her past lovers retained the spoils of their success. In this she bound them to her by loyalty and perhaps the hope of more good things – a technique perfected by Elizabeth I in her day, in her management of Robert Dudley and others.

Elizabeth's love life reads very like Catherine's minus the physical fulfillment. Robert Dudley, Earl of Leicester, ruled the roost in the earlier years, but she adored being wooed by numbers of dashing young courtiers whom she would admit to her inner circle and allow remarkable liberties. In her nubile and fertile years, her marriagability gave her enormous value in the royal European markets. Unfortunately, as she perceived only too clearly, her personal power would evaporate as soon as the vows were made, and like Catherine she clung to her divine supremacy before all else. All her royal swains were given her loving devotion until the time came to commit, when they were rejected. Her home-grown suitors (Hatton, Raleigh, Essex, Blount) jockeyed for her attention and her favours with much rivalry and hostility between themselves. They were expected to reinforce the myth of her eternal beauty and youthfulness by flattery and adoration, while she, with minimal insight in this particular, would even at sixty wear her necklines daringly low, and bolster her fading femininity with a sumptuous wardrobe, cascades of jewels, hours spent making up to disguise the ravages of age.

As with Catherine's lovers, Elizabeth's had much to tolerate, but in spite of her royal pride she was not hard to manipulate. Her capacity for magnanimity and forgiveness was proved again and again by them, but one darling of her older years went too far – Robert Devereux, Earl of Essex. He captured Elizabeth's heart when he was 33 years her junior, aged 21. There was nothing complex about Essex, for his parts could be drawn from any of the men I have discussed in this book. Manly and attractive, aristocratic and ambitious, he imperiously expected to possess himself of all the good things in life, including women. Sexual magnetism he had aplenty and Elizabeth was as susceptible as the rest. He charmed her and used her to forward his unlimited goals, measuring his power with her and no doubt hoping she would succumb to him altogether. Like an encroaching and challenging male, eyeing the reigning alpha in decline, Essex would defy and quarrel with her, so that the court trembled at his insouciance. He unwisely provoked her jealousy by having multiple affairs and even by marrying in secret, and also by making himself popular with the common people, something she regarded as her own exclusive right. He did not intend to rely on her for ever. Elizabeth was not blind to his go-getter qualities and wrecker potential, and adroitly kept him out of politics, though he was knighted and given lucrative offices.

As men do, Essex yearned to prove himself in military forays, and this was to lead to his undoing, since in the guise of a warrior he thought he could altogether cast off her authority. In the various skirmishes with the Spanish, he repeatedly thumbed his nose at her instructions, earning her formidable wrath, but was ever able to charm and flatter her into forgiveness. In their disputes over the conduct of wars, the gender roles are clearly delineated: she went to war of necessity, for the defence of the realm; he sought risk, excitement and greater glory, with no thought for the consequences, and certainly none for the expense of which she was ever conscious. In one electric exchange between them, Essex turned his back contemptuously. She referred him to the devil and slapped his face, whereupon he drew his sword, spitting words of affront. Before the situation could escalate, they were separated. The court held its breath, expecting Essex would be arrested and sent to the Tower, but no. His fate was deferred.

His day of reckoning came in the shape of the rebel Irish Earl of Tyrone, with whom he longed to measure swords. He browbeat Elizabeth into sending him with a huge army to Ireland while many at court began to think she feared him as much as she loved him. The expedition was a disaster as Essex, unshackled, lost touch with reality. So anxious was he to engage with any rebel band, he bungled his main objective of confronting Tyrone. Men and money were sacrificed. Elizabeth began to doubt his motives and his loyalty, rightly, for there were no military victories but scurrilous attempts at deals and a truce. He returned to confront her but there was no glory this time, and no way to expiate her magnificent royal fury. Though he had been imprisoned and disgraced, his meteoric career might still have been salvaged, for he had much popular support and Elizabeth eventually freed him; but her generosity and trust were no longer his to command. Feeling his power slipping, Essex's latent misogyny towards his uncontrollable royal mistress erupted in a manic rage in which he swung wildly between extremes of fury and gloom, giving vent to unforgivable insults and tipping over the edge towards madness. He cobbled together a rebellion, which failed. No longer in any doubt about his treachery, Elizabeth condemned to death her lover, her rival, the infernal genie she had created who was poised to destroy her if she stayed her hand any longer.

Catherine and Elizabeth had other features in common, notably their instinctive hatred of war. One of the most practical reasons was the crippling cost, besides more humanitarian considerations. Catherine's detractors portray her as a tyrant, an autocrat with a masculine lust for expansion, an anachronism in an age of incipient revolution and enlightenment. It is true she deposed the rightful ruler and probably permitted his murder. She formalised her position in the political belief that an extensive and varied empire was best ruled by a single sovereign who has only the good of her subjects at heart – an impossible task to which all absolute rulers must perforce subscribe. But one of her first acts in power was to withdraw Russia from a pointless war with Denmark and an unpopular alliance with Prussia. Her empire expanded under her 34-year rule to encompass an area twice the size of Europe, with significant extension into Poland and the Crimea. Yet she was cautious rather than rampantly acquisitive, with more concern to consolidate boundaries and establish peace for her people than to pursue unlimited glory. Elizabeth's philosophy was similar. In both cases the national finances had a chance to improve and to benefit the population, with a greater focus on domestic policy. Yet an absolute monarch must always look to her back and Catherine was supremely vigilant to detect any threat of a coup against herself. During her reign an ex-tsar, Ivan VI, was kept imprisoned, but remained a potential focus for king-makers and rebels. At her behest, he was murdered promptly when the inevitable attempt to free him was made. Both Catherine and Elizabeth were sensitive on the question of succession. Catherine's relationship with her son and heir Peter was highly ambivalent, and she did her best to undermine his power-base. Likewise, Elizabeth flew into one of her stupendous rages whenever the topic was raised, and refused to name her successor, ever aware of the uncontrollable lust that anticipation provokes, and the risk consequent to her own person. Both ladies were convinced that they ruled by divine right.

There have been other women who, without any ambivalence, thoroughly earned their evil reputations. The reputedly most bloodthirsty queen in all history, Fredegund of Neustria (part of present-day Belgium) who ruled in the 6th century, was so addicted to power that she murdered by various means and agents anyone who stood in her way. Most incredibly, these slaughters included some of her own children, of whom she had at least six. However, her last son she preserved when her husband King Chilperic died, because he was her vehicle of power, to rule as regent on his behalf. Another lady ruler with the same grimly extreme determination was Wu Hou of China at the turn of the 8th century. Many of her closest kin, including sons, sister, niece, grandchildren, besides other numerous more distant challengers, met a grisly end at her hand, until she had cleared her path, Stalin-like, to rule supreme. There is a contradiction here to Darwinian theory about the motivation behind power-wielding. These ladies, along with many male counterparts, seem to rate power as the supreme aim, and not even offspring are allowed to stand in the way. Maybe they think, as Catherine Sforza did in 15th-century Italy, that they always have the wherewithal to make more heirs if and when necessary.

So the relationship that women rulers have with their sons is complex. Elizabeth's foolish infatuation with Essex and her total lack of wisdom in indulging him, suggest that he was more of a substitute son than a lover. Two other powerful ladies who have taken leave of their prudence with regard to their sons are Indira Gandhi and Margaret Thatcher. In both cases the sons adopted the worst aspects of stereotypic power behaviour under cover of the maternal umbrella, in a manner very similar to that of Essex. Mark Thatcher's business activities have never fully come to the light of day. He made a fortune of millions of dollars as a Texas-based businessman, and many allegations surfaced in the press which raised questions as to his business dealings. It seems probable that he used his mother's name and status to boost his own reputation as a middle man, in which capacity he was involved in selling British arms to Saudi Arabia in a mega-sized deal.

If Elizabeth I at length put her incubus to death, and Margaret Thatcher, while making inept excuses for hers, at least had the grace to claim in private to be heart-broken, Indira Gandhi allowed hers to negate all the egalitarian principles she and her antecedents had stood for. Her younger son, Sanjay Gandhi, was well along the road to becoming one of the worst despotic and egotistical tyrants of the 20th century, when he was fortuitously killed in 1980 during a show-off display of aerobatics in his new two-seater plane.

Indira's prime ministerial status achieved in 1966 was as accidental as it could have been, and even after years in the shadow of Nehru and Mahatma Gandhi and their heroic associates, she was terrified and reluctant when she was first pushed into power. No doubt many thought they could manipulate this puppet, this dumb doll, or slip of a girl as she was called among them. Speechless with fright in the parliamentary amphitheatre, she dealt with it just as another weak speaker, Charles I of England, had done in his time. She simply evaded it and bypassed its institutions. Instead she would come to rely on an inner circle of advisers. Centralisation and the dismantling of democracy were a long way off, but they began here. Having spent long years with the 'Free India' movement, her politics were left-wing and inclusive. She appealed to and reached the commonalty, especially the poor and underprivileged, to whom Indira became a dependable Mother Earth figure. She began in tune with her beliefs, dismantling privilege-laden hierarchies and introducing reforms designed to minimise disparities in wealth. The Green Revolution, aimed at creating self-sufficiency in food in the country, was given top priority. She was not burdened in these days with political self-interest and her principles were unsullied. 'I do not seek to retain office at all costs,' she said in 1969, when there were skirmishings and threats over the issue of the presidency. Six years later she could not have said the same.

The growth of her popularity and cult status as 'Mother India' promoted the malignant growth of narcissism. In the general election of 1971 she would state, 'I am the issue,' and prove it by permitting her image to be splashed massively on billboards in city centres, and minutely on badges made available countrywide. More reforms followed, but besides the radical ones there now crept in repressive measures: weakening of the judiciary and altering of the constitution so that individual rights were eroded. Meanwhile, in neighbouring Pakistan, democracy had collapsed with attendant murder, rape and mayhem. Indira supported the suffering East Bengalis of course, and the situation exploded into war: a one-sided affair which India won easily. Indira and democracy were triumphant, and her stock rose to dizzy new heights. She was the greatest leader ever, unassailable, a goddess. The narcissus bloomed in the sun. The Congress Party, always a broad church of opinion, had disintegrated with internecine squabbles into factions. The democratic process is ever tedious and turgid, buffered from extremes, frustrating to those who want instant results. More than ever Indira came to rely on her own cronies, willing to jettison those who crossed her, unable to see beyond the ramparts of her own views; views that were reflected back and reinforced by her circle of supporters and sycophants. Among these now numbered Sanjay, though he had no democratic authority whatsoever.

The insidious psychotic delusion that occupies the mind of the established great figure is nowhere so clearly etched as in the rise and rise of Sanjay by his mother's passive permitting. He was a spoilt brat, an indulged royal sprig with a hell-raising lifestyle who knew nothing of discipline, principle or restraint. Though his passion was for things mechanical, he failed to complete his Rolls-Royce apprenticeship, preferring to cause trouble and accidents speeding around in his Jaguar, or even thieving cars and joy-riding. Yet at 22 he was allowed a government licence to start a company to build a multipurpose car, the Maruti. Though funds poured in from business and banks, all with an eye to kickbacks, no product ever emerged, while Sanjay lined his pockets with an estimated fortune.

Ever contemptuous about government methods, Sanjay only became interested in politics during the state of emergency declared in 1975. His mother in the midst of many problems found herself charged with electoral malpractice, and her own election declared null and void. There was no real reason to suspend parliamentary democracy except that her own position was under threat. Now she declared that she would serve the people till her last breath, meaning that she would cling to power like grim death. This she did even before informing her cabinet about the emergency, though she roused them at 5 a.m. to receive the news of the *fait accompli*, the time of greatest vulnerability for the unprepared. Her son orchestrated the muffling of the media and the closing of the courts. Her opponents and challengers were arrested and imprisoned. The intimidating poster-portraits reappeared on hoardings, together with slogans – pearls of wisdom like those in Mao's little red book – about discipline, obedience and the rectitude of the leader. Indira used her emergency powers to negate the High Court ruling on her own election, and to annul other election results in Gujarat and Tamil Nadu which had gone against her. Censorship and secrecy were key features of this period.

Now Sanjay came into his own and, without any training, experience or democratic support, put into action a five-point plan under his mother's name. To give him some political credibility he was jockeyed into the executive committee of the Congress Party Youth Wing. This power-base evolved into a gang of thugs rather like Hitler's SA or Bobby Kennedy's drug squad, who would, under the guise of emergency policy, run amok with intimidation, extortion, even settling of old scores by harassment and murder. Even Indira, now steeped in her own authority, feared the son whom she could not control. He is reported to have slapped her face soundly and repeatedly, in public, without her resistance or response.

Two of the five points of the princeling's plan were slum clearance and sterilisation. He pursued them with the zeal and ruthlessness of a Cromwell with no thought for human rights. Tens of thousands were shifted on a whim from Old Delhi, at a moment's notice before the demolishers moved in; some were forced out at gunpoint. With his ill-conceived family planning he degenerated from a policy of incentives to quota systems to coercion. Young boys and old men were included simply to fill set targets. How bizarre, yet how horribly logical that this potential dictator should begin by emasculating his fellow countrymen.

Indira was ousted, yet she returned in 1980, and simply took off as if there had been no break in the continuum. 'I have always been India's leader,' she stated, as she erased the state governments where the Janata Party had prevailed. When Sanjay died, Rajiv was persuaded to step into politics. Indira listened less and less to anyone whose views were not her own. Her vision became dangerously monocular. The turbulence in the Punjab and the disastrous stand-off in the Golden Temple at Amritsar began the countdown to her own violent death at the hands of her Sikh bodyguard. She knew her likely fate just as any alpha male knows he will be toppled. She suffered depressions as a result and a sense of foreboding. Having no one to turn to, her mind engaged with superstitions, to performing pujas and avoiding eclipses, to practising yoga, and to seeking reassurance from her swami, Brahmachari. She placed more reliance on him and his spells and mantras than she did on her bodyguards. In the end neither saved her. Indira is not alone among the world's leaders in turning to religious practice when all else fails, as I shall do in my next chapter.

CHAPTER 12

The Church Militant

In some pockets of the secular world, religion seems to have little relevance. It can be well nigh impossible for inhabitants of that world to enter the mind of a fanatic, single-mindedly destroying himself and thousands of others, in order to achieve glory in a nebulous future. The doctrinal arguments of a past age that raised so much passion in their time now leave us cold. Yet religious devotion is an integral part of human behaviour patterns, and is even established in our genetic equipment, being partly determined by heredity. Sophisticated twin studies suggest that more than 50% of our inclination towards an organised religion is determined by our genes, though the precise allegiance is obviously cultural.

Investigation of our remotest past shows humans have always had an awareness of a non-physical life, of which the most clear-cut evidence is ceremonial burying of the dead. Aside from the sound practical reasons why this should be done even in Ice Age times, archaeology has revealed a host of practices that have no pragmatic explanation, such as weapons, beads, ornaments and domestic implements buried with the body. In some cultures, bodies were buried in the foetal position, which might indicate a sense of burying in preparation for rebirth. In prehistoric times in any small community, death must have seemed a common enough event. Few if any people would have died of old age. Infant and maternal mortality would have been commonplace, as would horribly painful deaths from injury and disease. Yet it obviously always happened to somebody else, not yourself. The more a man looked on such catastrophes yet was spared himself, the more he would believe he was immune.

The occurrence of epidemics of infectious disease within the community would readily be interpreted as evil-intentioned emanations. To an uneducated but intelligent mind, it would seem that these chancy events were avoidable. If their random nature suggested the malign influence of invisible spirits, then such spirits should be propitiated. The existence of spirits would have seemed self-evident. How else to account for the evaporation of a strong and forceful personality that had once occupied a body, now transformed in a matter of hours into a stone-cold and increasingly offensive corpse? The human mind, especially when primed by adrenalin and perhaps other mediators, does not readily accept chance as an acceptable explanation for random but mighty events, such as deaths and violent, natural phenomena, and here lie the seeds of superstition, of paranoia about witchcraft, and in a later age of blame and litigation for failed medical treatment.

The development of language and the capacity it gave humans for organised thought and mental manipulation of symbols, exchange of ideas and expansion of logic, must have transformed the mental concept a man has of himself. His egotism must have received a devastating challenge. Instead of being central to the universe, he would have begun to perceive that he was a body like any other, and that his days, like those of his community peers, would eventually come to an end. Of all the paradoxes and contradictions humans have to deal with, this single thought formulated in our brains, that we are going to die – whereas all our prehistoric instinct upholds the certainty that we are going to live for ever – causes most emotional pain and confusion. Out of that anguish springs religion with all its profound influence on behaviour patterns. And from the same source comes a masterly capacity for self-deception, of which the biggest delusion is that we can evade death and in some way become immortal.

Evolution's aims, if I may personalize briefly, are better served by a man who is oblivious of his own mortality rather than one who is cautious. Whether competing chimpanzee-style for the monopoly of the harem, or at least the pick of the women, or out hunting and warring with the lads, survival and propagation for the male are risky, confrontational undertakings. The very acme of this rash species is the Kennedy clan, as we've seen. Risk-taking gene packages are probably an assorted mixture, but in there a tendency to believe oneself sacrosanct is obviously a huge advantage to a model evolutionary pupil. And this is exactly what we see.

As all insurance companies know, the most accident-prone clients are young men from mid-teens to thirty, with the highest rates of road-traffic accidents and speeding offences. There is much individual variation of course, and women undoubtedly share in this youthful *joie de vivre* to a degree; though they experience a significant check to such kicking over the traces when children arrive. During their nurturing years their self-preservation is subsumed by that of the young ones. But most – if not all – of us have a certain optimistic complacency that bad things happen to the next guy and we ourselves are exempt. In the cameos within these pages I've described the exuberant showmanship of such young blades as Churchill and Franco, 'seeking the bubble reputation' and all that. Churchill actually wrote, 'I am so conceited I do not believe the gods would create so potent a being as myself for so prosaic an ending [as death in the skirmish line].' As often with him he neatly encapsulated in his prose a recognised credo. Churchill genuinely believed, and the belief grew on him, that he was anointed by the Almighty to fulfill some supreme task. He was not unusual in this, for every strong leader that ever was, certainly all those in this book, are firmly convinced of the same. When they survive a challenging event the belief is reinforced. Ronald Reagan, after the attempt on his life early in his presidency, believed that divine intervention had saved him for some big purpose. The idea of the hand of providence sending Ronald Reagan as a Messiah has a particular absurdity. Oliver Cromwell thought his successes in battle in the Civil War to be a sign of God's special favour and kept his ear delicately tuned to the voice that directed him to his subsequent atrocities. The kingdom of his god was certainly deep within him.

In parallel with this conviction that they are anointed, mighty leaders have a characteristically dogged reluctance to let go of the office they hold, a theme that will be explored in the next chapter.

Many are supremely reluctant to name or acknowledge a successor, as that would mean recognising their life was finite. Despots as disparate as Elizabeth I of England and Stalin of the USSR realised that nominated heirs are apt to become impatient for their turn. The primeval urge to cling to power is as indomitable a psychological force as any, it seems, as it can cause both men and women to kill off their own offspring in order to retain it. Though evolutionary immortality means passing on one's genes, a more cerebral perpetuation can be created by images, monuments, statues and whole cities named after oneself, as was practised on a grand scale in Russia and the USSR. Catherine the Great declined gracefully many personal honours, titles and even statues in her lifetime but allowed a plethora of portraits to be painted. Over five hundred are known. The 20th-century Bolshevik leaders lent their names to countless locations and buildings throughout the Soviet world. Money could be creamed off the budget for such purposes without reducing the commitment to arms, but never stretched as far as the people's welfare. Hitler had unbelievably grandiose plans for Berlin and Germany's other major cities, which obsessed him even during the war years. His plans for official show buildings were intended for his own eternal self-glory, as Albert Speer (his architect) records, and he was not in the least interested in social planning and welfare. And most great men have felt compelled to leave behind volumes of writing as legacy to lesser mortals.

The desire to reign eternal, which can be seen in the high and mighty, is present to a lesser degree in all of us. It is part of our self-confidence even though it is illusory. At the point in our history when it became apparent that death always came as the end, humankind had to make some fundamental adjustment. It was at this point, I believe, that religion was born. Human horizons have always had a limit, though it is ever expanding. Beyond that perimeter of our knowledge is a wild wood which can be peopled with spirits and filled with myth according to our prejudices. From there it is a relatively short step to belief; and in the natural hierarchies of man, to impose those beliefs on others in a more or less authoritarian way.

Religions are all manmade, and are designed to support and succour. At base they have nothing whatever to do with morality.

Many readers will violently disagree, and that is fine. I do not seek to remove those props that provide essential spiritual stability to some. Once long ago I allowed my religious beliefs to be demolished in an intellectual argument, and suffered agonies for a while, but I realised deep down that my brain had never condoned them. I had to let them go. In the first chapter of this book I took apart one of Robert Burns' famous lines. All of us can only sustain mental tranquillity by deceiving and blinkering ourselves to a degree, which is why human behaviour is such a taboo subject, why psychology has never developed beyond a capacity to mystify, and why all but the toughest-minded readers will have abandoned this book by now.

Religion ought to be a comfort to the individual, an exclusively personal affair; 'a love affair between a lonely soul and its god' was how one of my childhood mentors expressed it. Instead, the spiritual life has been hijacked for a multitude of purposes, some of them useful, some of them terminally destructive. In the development of all religions, the leaders have re-enacted some of the most primitive practices of animal-human behaviour.

The one feature all religions have in common is a construction of immortality, both retrograde as well as forward-looking, as if life should have no limits in any direction. That intellectually advanced people can and do cling to the irrational by blind faith, and consider themselves morally superior to non-believers, is in itself astonishing. In Judaism, with the emphasis on family life and investing in future generations, there is still a need to believe in resurrection of body and soul. Judaism postulates purgatory for one year to expiate sins, though while one is in there, intermittent relief comes on the Sabbath. There is also an ancient custom of cheating the Angel of Death when someone appears to be in extremis, by renaming the sufferer with a biblical name and thereby hiding him from the Grim Reaper.

The promise of Christianity is encapsulated in the gospel according to St John, 3:16: 'For God so loved the world that he gave his only son, that whoever believes in him should not perish but have everlasting life.' Central to the faith is that Christ's suffering and death have paid off everyone's sins. There are dangers in this removing of all responsibility, so that it was necessary to create a Hell for those irredeemably wicked. How a God of Love can tolerate the idea of eternal torment for some is never explained. The identifying of an enemy is a fundamental human activity, emphatically masculine, so God must have his polar opposite in Satan. This gives rise to theological problems about a second, equally powerful deity, which theology does not satisfactorily address.

Within the Roman Catholic Church, which is very controlling of its flock, purgatory is accepted as a threat and an incentive to sharpen up on good temporal behaviour. The Mormon sect, which is notably hierarchical, acknowledges three levels of Heaven, the third one reserved for the priestly caste and its hangers-on. There is a potential for evolution to god-like status (they accept multiple gods including some biblical prophets and their own founders).

Islam means submission to the will of God, due observance of which is rewarded at the Day of Judgement by a welcome into Heaven; or one of the seven heavens, where the faithful will live for ever in a state of bliss. This is described allegorically in the Koran as dwelling in gardens and vineyards with running streams, delicious fruit, fountains of (non-alcoholic) drink, reclining on soft couches placed conveniently for conversation, accompanied by chaste, dark-eyed virgins and high-bosomed maidens. The equivalent delight for women who enter Paradise is not specified. But the Koran lays much greater emphasis on the miseries of Hell than the delights of Paradise. Repeatedly you are reminded that Allah is compassionate and merciful, and maybe you need to be, for the fate of the irredeemably guilty is terrible indeed: pitch, chains, flames, rods of iron, filth, scalding water and eternal torment are the least of it for the hardened unbeliever. Nor are the wives of these villains given any chance of mercy for they automatically follow their lords to Hell. This is a religion that believes in sticks rather than carrots. Even the lowest level of heaven is supplied with comets and thunderbolts for use as missiles to fire at devils. And part of the joy of Heaven is to triumph over those you see below you burning in the eternal fires.

Hinduism is considerably more sophisticated than the monotheistic religions, being concerned with the individual's path to spirituality, and a recognition that the transcendent Absolute is to be found deep within oneself. It is at once the most diverse and the most tolerant, all-embracing religion. The Hindu concept of eternal life is bound up in the belief that life is cyclical, a series of births, deaths and rebirths, and that one's actions now determine the shape of one's next reincarnation. Goodly actions enable one to evolve as a happy human, but negative choices result in regression to a lowlier form of life. Much of the intricate and contradictory complexity of the pantheon of Hindu gods and myths reflects an appropriate though subliminal understanding of human nature and of evolutionary processes in this most ancient of religions. In particular they understand thoroughly the deep human need to cling on to what one has achieved, and not lose face or status. I have heard Westerners sneer at the Hindu notion of reincarnation to another life-form, yet accept without questioning the Christian depiction of Heaven beyond the stars, replete with feather-winged angels, harps and pious singing!

Sikhism, evolving in the Punjab where the original Guru grew up as a Hindu, familiar also with Islam, is a monotheistic religion that retains the Hindu belief in reincarnation and of meditative release from the cycle into a form of heaven-on-earth.

Buddhism also has its roots in Hinduism, and it is highly significant that the original Buddha (Siddhatta Gautama) sought enlightenment on account of an abrupt and shocking introduction to the problems of sickness, aging and death. His way of coping was to take a spiritual, mendicant, ascetic path. This is a semi-allegorical tale of the urge to escape reality, the reasons why we all need a spiritual way of life. Buddhists believe in the endless cycle of death and rebirth, and of use of free will to evolve into a better being the next time around. There are moral overtones, a notion that selfish craving causes the evil in this world, and an attempt to get beyond all that to a state of self elimination, or Nirvana. Nirvana achievers (called Bodhisattvas) stay around to help others do the same, while practising the six virtues. Because they counterbalance evil, Bodhisattvas are often portrayed artistically in ferocious, threatening forms.

Within an organised religion, eternal life is the big trade-off for all the other restrictions humans are prepared to have imposed on them. Accepting the spiritual life means that humans acknowledge vulnerability, and here opportunists have been quick to seize competitive openings, and to hoist theselves up the hierarchy into a position of authority. It is no surprise that the mega-religions of the world, Christianity and Islam, tend to split up into smaller sects as dominant figures intent on reaching the top, carve out for themselves an empire within an empire. Maybe too it is not so surprising that the religious world has given rise to more wars and bloody conflicts than any other. Our primitive tribalism too is responsible for much malevolence, and when the two fuse, all the furies of the bottomless pit are released.

During the time of the newly flowered Islamic State under Caliph Umar in the 7th century, which ruled half the then known world, the Middle East was a hotch-potch of religions of which the Islamic masters were mostly tolerant. Tribal loyalties at this time were emphatically fixed in one's religious sect – whether Jewish, Muslim, Coptic or Orthodox Christian or Zoroastrian – rather than one's nationality. The same is true of Jewish communities to this day. The religious history, culture and memory of past feuds keeps the Catholic and Protestant sects of Northern Ireland apart, and fixes many of them in mutual animosity. The creation of the National Jewish State of Israel in 1948 fomented hostilities between Jews and Arabs for which there is still no peaceful solution. Though all religions to a greater or lesser degree preach a controlled, ethical and peaceful lifestyle, not only is the dogma inadequate to restrain the population at large, but it is repeatedly and flagrantly defied by the self-styled leaders of the unguided flocks.

The Christian religion is the best example of this hypocrisy. Jesus Christ (according to the New Testament) was the very epitome of pacifism. His only recorded moment of temperament was when he drove the money-changers from the Temple. He did not burn them at the stake or mow them down with Kalashnikovs, yet this impetuous action is quoted repeatedly in justification of Christian offensives. The Crusades were particularly dark moments in the Church's history, which teachers today skate over gingerly, applying a veneer of glorious and colourful failure, and a distancing from their collective immorality. There has always been confusion in the

Christian Churches about militarism. Notably at the time of the Crusades, the Byzantine Church considered murder in battle a sin and banned offenders from Communion for three years. But the atavistic drive to fight and kill can easily be cloaked in pious rhetoric, and the Church in the West responded readily to Pope Urban's call to arms in 1095, in which he promised remission of sins and eternal life to anyone who should perish in battle:

> God exhorts you as heralds of Christ...to hasten to exterminate this vile race [the Turks]...Christ commands it.
> Oh what a disgrace if a race so despicable, degenerate and enslaved by demons should thus overcome a people endowed with faith in Almighty God.

Though the Crusades' ostensible purpose was to save Eastern Christendom from the Muslims, they did not achieve that aim. Indeed it hardly seemed they were trying. The holy city of Jerusalem was central to the spiritual inspiration of the First Crusade, yet on the way the lordly leaders were clearly more interested in seizing cities such as Antioch for themselves as well as lands and other wealth. Contemporaries from East and West testify to the most bestial warrior behaviour. For instance, at the city Maarat an-Numan, the inhabitants were divested of gold, silver and fine goods before being killed or sold into slavery. No one was spared and the streets rapidly filled up with corpses. So intent on looting that the food supply ran out, the poorer Crusaders began to chop up bodies to find hastily swallowed coins. They ended up by cooking and eating human flesh. No mercy was shown until the city was sacked and all the inhabitants dead or in chains...or consumed. The lords were prodded by the rank and file to desist from pillaging and move on to the gates of Jerusalem. There, after a considerable delay followed by a five-month siege, the city fell prey to the same mindless devastation. Jews and Muslims died by sword thrust, beheading or fire in an orgy of savagery that was unknown in the Middle East of the time. At the Dome of the Rock, it is recorded, men waded ankle-deep in blood on their way to seizing the gold and silver candelabra. Vast funeral pyres 'like pyramids' were required to dispose of the dead. Within the precincts of the Mosque, the Masjid al-Aqsa, normally frequented by devout and scholastic Muslims who passed their lives in peaceful meditative study, the crass Crusaders wiped out an estimated 70,000 persons who had fled there for sanctuary, men, women and children. The soldiers of Christ then went down on their knees in fulsome gratitude to God, that they had 'cleansed' the holy city. But the savagery of the Crusaders burnt into the collective memory, a permanent scar which polarised hostilities for centuries to come.

The invaders had been switched into battle mode by Pope Urban, not only permitting but encouraging, even enticing them to despoil and kill. Urban had his own motives for encouraging the mass military migration: the belligerent knights and barons now had some other object for their natural hawkishness than each other. More importantly, he stood to gain enormous prestige if the lands sanctified by the life of Jesus could be reclaimed. Human motives no doubt, and not very worthy, but he did not have sufficient psychological insight to foresee the devils he would unleash. 'Enemies of Christendom' is a broad and elastic definition and on the road to Jerusalem was applied without much discrimination or any mercy to Jewish groups in the Rhineland and even other Christian groups in Anatolia.

In the Third Crusade (1189), Richard the Lionheart of England captured Acre on his way to Jerusalem, acquiring an embarrassment of prisoners, about 3,000 Muslims. Though money could be raised by ransoming these, the process took time. Liberating them, as Saladin would have done, went against the grain. Richard selected the quick option and had them all slaughtered. They were mostly soldiers, he probably reasoned, glossing over the 300 wives and children in with the rest. Executions were a favourite couch-pastime, and maybe as historic illustrations suggest, he did indeed enjoy watching the proceedings from a comfortable grandstand.

In the Fourth Crusade (1203), as a result of trade rivalries, inter-ethnic conflict and shifting alliances, the Crusaders found themselves seizing Constantinople – the centre of Eastern Christendom and capital of the Byzantine Empire. Byzantium had always been a thorn in the long-suffering Roman papal flesh. The pope had decreed

that even Christians could be attacked if they hindered the Crusade –
another clever catch-all instruction from on high. Once Constantinople
was taken and the barons ensconced in comfort, the soldiers were
given the go-ahead for three days of rape and pillage, which they did
with professional thoroughness. The silks and silver of the exquisite
church, Haghia Sophia, were torn down for loot. Rape was visited on
women in their homes and nuns in their convents. All the riches of this
most splendid renaissance capital were up for grabs, and the clergy
were not behind in amassing their due share. Meanwhile, the
inhabitants were slaughtered indiscriminately. Blood lust when it is
aroused is not very particular, but fixates on the strange, the foreign, the
unrecognised.

Equally foreign was the war-cry that ululated from the Turkish
throats when engaged in battle: 'Allah al-Akhbar!' or 'God is great!'
The Crusaders matched them in tumult with 'God's will! God's
will!' At the time, only a celestial and dispassionate observer would
perceive that this was no holy war, just another tribal clash; and with
wonderful irony, in the name of the same nebulous Being. Primitive
superstition played a large part in directing events, as chance
happenings were attributed to divine favour, and defeats were a
source of guilt, usually attributed to sexual indulgence. Knights
would then restrain their loin-lust for a while, expel the women
camp-followers, and hope God would approve.

The Crusaders committed their fair share of rape against women
of all faiths in the Holy Land, their own included, true to their
military colours. But we may also recognise a manifestation of that
mysterious species, the military celibate, who combined their
knightly and monastic vocations, in the shape of the Knights
Hospitalers and Templars. Their initial function was to protect
pilgrims, particularly in undefended rural areas, and to care for the
sick, but their defensive role expanded in time to the only permanent
military body of the Crusades. Though they took vows of poverty
and chastity, the orders became wealthy, powerful and very
prestigious. The Templars even diversified to become bankers.
Eventually these orders, their high moral tone undermined by
wealth and power, became renowned for their greed and rivalry.

The notion that Christians turn the other cheek is as wide of the mark as the belief that dictatorship of the proletariat has actually been practised by communists. In the year 637, when Arabs captured Jerusalem from early Christians, the seizure was a strikingly different affair from that conducted by the Crusaders four centuries later, being marked by discipline of the army, dignity and respect, and above all for tolerance of other religions, especially those regarded as 'People of the Book', Jews and Christians. In 1187 when Saladin retook Jerusalem from the Crusaders, again it was done without frantic looting, destroying and bloodshed, though the ransom terms were extortionate enough, and the unransomed poor condemned to slavery. Yet Islam, in 636 a brand-new religion, had germinated in conflict and never had the same ambivalence about the use of the sword as Christians had. Holy war was a sacred duty, but only against non-believers, and for protection of the weak. Needless to say this restriction was ignored, and much Islamic conflict at the boundaries of the rapidly increasing Muslim Empire was directed against other Muslims of different ethnic cultures. Holy war became an accepted part of Islamic life, conducted for the usual political and secular reasons though justified as jihad. Yet war was not exclusively central to Muslim identity in its golden age, for the first five centuries saw a civilisation develop that was light years ahead of the uncouth West. In politics, law, a thirst for inter-ethnic learning, languages, travel, trade, literature, technology, education, philosophy, art, science, medicine, architecture, town planning, music, astronomy, they excelled with a creative vigour which counterbalanced pugnacity and induced tolerance, yet gave them much to defend. Their initial failure to withstand the Crusades was due to factional hostilities among themselves and an inability to unite against the greater foe.

The Crusaders galloped roughshod, blindly destructive, through all of this, still subscribing to the view, in their extreme arrogance, that their opponents were an inferior race with unsound beliefs. Such supreme haughtiness is to this day linked with the most successful hierarchy and dynasty that has ever existed, unsurpassed in its centralisation of power, its capacity to deceive, to obfuscate and to hypnotise a massive worldwide population. I refer to the Papacy.

For the first millennium of its existence, the papal succession had a turbulent history. Many of the earliest incumbents are reputed to have died as martyrs, but evidence is sketchy. The times were violent – what times are not? – persecution to be expected, and few popes seem to have died a natural death before the Emperor Constantine in the 4th century converted to Christianity. But the troubles were not then over because each emperor in his time expected the pope to yield to his will. Popes in their new security nevertheless grew into power and began to wield it. Damasus I in 366 employed a gang of thugs to massacre his rival's supporters and have himself consecrated. Rivalry and competition for the supreme clerical role became intense, with contenders using bribery and coming to blows, resorting to intrigue and corruption, issuing threats and soliciting favours. Displays of ambition, avarice and bargaining at papal elections were usual. Vigilius had a political compact adorned with valuable gifts made with the Empress Theodosia to secure the papacy, then blocked the fair trial of the man he deposed. Benedict I ensured many people owed him favours by appointing flocks of bishops. Gregory I, monastic and perhaps a little masochistic, was fixated on the pope's supremacy. He seemed to be obsessed by an unChristian rivalry over precedence with the Bishop of Constantinople. Discordance between papal and imperial powers was frequently an issue and at this time the emperor usually won. Popes could still meet with arrest, brutal treatment and assassination. Martin was tried for treason and subjected to public flogging and harsh imprisonment from which he died.

But people do not get to lofty places without a streak of brutality themselves. Hadrian III ordered a man to be blinded and a noble lady whipped naked through the streets. In the late 800s, Stephen VI, under the influence of a fanatical hatred of a previous pontiff, Formosus, ordered that holy corpse to be disinterred, clothed in ceremonial vestments, propped on the throne and tried for various papal violations. No worldly or celestial advocate sprang to the corpse's defence, and Formosus' papal acts were nullified. He was flung into the Tiber, no doubt having been divested first of his rich robes. But Stephen was deposed by his enemies, stripped of office, imprisoned and strangled, while Formosus' ghost stalked the land, performing miracles, it was said, through the short-lived reign of several popes, and may well have had a hand through the medium of his supporting factions in their deaths. Sergius III in 904 marched on the papal palace in Rome at the head of an army to overthrow Christopher, himself installed by a palace coup. Then he ordered Christopher and an ex-pontiff, languishing in jail, to be strangled. Some appointees owed their position to powerful families, such as Stephen VII and the Marozia, and so became the tool of family feuds. Although the law forbade a choice of successor during a pope's lifetime, this was violated by power-wielders in Rome as in the installment of John XII, who was only eighteen years old. Needing protection, he invited the German King Otto to come to Rome as emperor, then quarrelled with him, provoking civil unrest, bloodshed and even bloodier reprisals.

The era of Benedict IX was marked by violence and he was accused of simony (selling spiritual benefits), a sin to which a number of subsequent popes succumbed. After Urban II – who summoned the First Crusade – there followed an era of confusion when factions and schisms led to multiple popes, leaving historians much difficulty in determining the true line. Which names should be labelled popes and which consigned to anti-pope status? Let us hope their attempts at disentangling the claimants were directed by St Peter.

What of that other manifestation of power-holding, compulsive sexual activity? It was not lacking. To be honest, stern regulation of priestly sex lives was not attempted till after the first millennium. Damasus I in the 4th century had a 'disgraceful charge' brought against him, thought to be adultery. He certainly enjoyed the society of wealthy ladies and earned the name, 'the matrons' ear-tickler' by gossips observing his enjoyment of courtly pastimes as well as opulence. The next pope was also charged with adultery, but the charge did not stick. It was not unusual for popes to be the sons of priests: Boniface I, Felix II, Anastasus II, for a start. Boniface VI in the 9th century had a disreputable past, having been demoted twice for immorality. His succeeding as pope was more the result of civic rioting than due process of election as he had not even had his priestly status restored at the time. Sergius III, he of the armed coup, is reputed to have had a son (a future pope,

John XI) by the fifteen-year-old daughter of intimate noble friends. John XII, the eighteen-year-old incumbent, led an openly debauched life, known for coarse tastes and for creating a bordello within the papal palace. He lived life fast and furious, finally called by his Maker from the bed of a married woman (allegedly), where his exertions precipitated a stroke at the age of 27.

Bendict VIII spent much of his time at the head of armed forces, 'restoring papal authority' as it was called. He introduced canons prohibiting marriage or concubinage for all clerics, and condemned to serfdom existing children of such unions. Illegitimate children were treated as inherently wicked from inception by the Catholic Church, from this time to the 20th century, and duly punished. However, Benedict's main concern was for Church property, which he did not wish to see fragmented away among extended families. Leo IX (elected in 1094) displayed a reforming zeal against both simony and clerical unchastity.

A defining era came with the election of Pope Gregory VII (aged only 37) in 1037. Ordinary people had become utterly weary of the anarchy and violent lawlessness in Europe, where justice was simply the rule of brute force and strength. Though some turned with hope to the Church to relieve the prevailing inequalities, many realised that members of the Church did not behave any better than anyone else. Reforming movements began to spring up and, as is so often the case, they polarised and crystallized the attitudes of the existing establishment. Pope Gregory, no doubt sensing these peripheral rebellions, aimed at seizing supreme authority, by challenging the Holy Roman Emperor Henry on the issue of appointing bishops and abbots. There followed a furious war of words culminating in each deposing the other; but Gregory had the trump card. He could and did condemn Emperor Henry to eternal damnation.

Gregory won his case without further ado, as the terrified Henry yielded to him, and the pope gained a large following of temporal militants as a result. After the next incumbent, Urban II, who fully subscribed to his own over-riding greatness as he launched the First Crusade, the papal succession is a history of power-brokering of the most mortal, worldly and pagan kind. And the most Darwinian, for in the progressive emphasis on hierarchy, monopoly, overwhelming the opposition and controlling the masses by subjection to an immeasurably great and mystical leader, the Church has surpassed in its time all temporal contenders. In the 12th century, one of the reformist movements that reacted against the increasing corruption of the Roman Church was that of the Cathars in the south of France. They were Christian, but believed in taking back spirituality to a personal experience, thus rendering the ecclesiastical hierarchy and its appurtenances totally superfluous. They believed – not unnaturally, given the examples of sensuality and luxury the Church gave them – that mortal matters are inherently sinful and should be repudiated. They led simple lives in which wealth was rejected, and mutual respect and social virtues practised. In stark contrast, bishops and clergy of the time found multiple opportunities for money-grubbing, demanding fees for all offices from weddings to the Last Rites, selling indulgences to gullible sinners. They then spent their ill-gotten gains on riotous living, field sports, luxury, fine garments and the pleasures of the table.

Though aware of the shortcomings of his flock's sheepdogs, in 1207 Pope Innocent III, literally declared war on the reformers. Catharism had become so popular that it rivalled Catholicism. A Crusade specifically against Christians was launched with the co-operation of the King of France, raising an army of 15–20,000 for the purpose. Crusades were assured of the same soul-comforts as the Holy Land army had received, as well as the more material and bodily ones of plunder and rape. The first town to be sacked was Béziers, in which an indiscriminate massacre of 15,000 men, women and children took place. At first the soldiery could not distinguish the enemy: after all, Cathars did not wave green flags or wear yellow stars. The papal legate said, famously, 'Kill them all. God will recognise his own.' Mass panic ensued and, while some communities abandoned their homes and villages and fled, others tried to save their skins by denunciations. The 'heretics' were burnt in substantial numbers, and anyone who tried to save them was hanged. Some communities resisted, and Toulouse came under siege for nine months. By the mid-13th century, overt resistance ceased, but remaining Cathars simply went underground.

One astute observer of the paradoxical contrast between the saintly Cathars and the sensual clergy was a monk, Dominic, who started the organisation that evolved into the Inquisition, the Church's KGB. He fostered a roving network of ascetic, travelling and preaching monks (the Dominicans), trying to match the Cathars on their high moral pitch. Dominic himself practised self-flagellation and self-mortification, preaching hell-fire in words that could have come from the Koran: 'We shall...cause many people to die by the sword, will ruin your towers, overthrow and destroy your walls...The force of the stick will prevail where sweetness and blessing have been able to accomplish nothing.' The Dominican friars were given the role of unearthing and eradicating heresy by Pope Gregory IX in 1234, and the first Inquisitors were appointed in Toulouse. The Pope's edict permitted death sentences – by burning – on grounds of suspicion with no right of appeal. Never before had despotism had so ultimate an authority, so huge a capacity for holocaust. The Inquisitors could not be gainsaid. They had the papal blessing, their uncertainties were better than lesser folks' misgivings. Once under investigation, few could escape. If confessions were not forthcoming they would be forced out. Torture evolved for this purpose, of such cruelty and obscenity that few if any could hold out under its exigencies. In an extreme of mortal agony, virtually anything will be done or said to call a halt. The Inquisitors got past this theoretical objection to their methods by confirming the confession a day or two later. Inquisitors were oddly squeamish, and devised tortures that would not shed blood: the thumb screw, the rack, water torture. Likewise they kept their distance from performing the dirty work, until Innocent IV gave them *carte blanche* to inflict punishment in person. Nor did they lose any sleep if a troublesome detainee died or was permanently maimed under their hands. The blame was his/hers for not confessing.

Psychological intimidation and control were practised with great sophistication. The coming of the Inquisition to a community would be advertised in advance and the arrival would be conducted in an awesome display of processing clerical solemnity, usually accompanied by a threatening secular contingent, an armed escort. After a weighty sermon, potential candidates could either confess themselves or they could denounce others. Once under suspicion, the only way of escaping personal penalty was to betray others, and one may imagine how old scores and rivalries could be resolved by this means. Indeed, members of a family would sometimes offer up each other. The Inquisition understood the principles of divide and rule. The trials and subsequent executions were conducted in public for maximum impact. The downtrodden and terrified masses crept about in fear, not only of Church officials but also of each other. Solidarity, so essential for massed resistance, was removed at a stroke. Handwritten records of misdeeds and confessions were assiduously kept and could never be wiped clean. Ensnared like flies in a web, the humble folk could no longer even cling to the comfort of religion or a stable set of morals.

After the initial miltary campaign against the Cathars, 5,000 were burnt to death. Ambitious men with a sadistic bent naturally surfaced as Inquisitors, and some carried out their duties with a horrifying thoroughness and relish. Bernard Gui, one of the most notorious, between 1308 and 1322 in Toulouse discovered an average of one heretic a week of whom most were imprisoned and forty burnt at the stake. Lesser punishments included fines, and the spin-off for Inquisitors was that they could enrich themselves by this means. They were not above taking bribes. It became usual for a confessee's property to be confiscated, his family left in destitution, while the Inquisition became ever richer.

The Catholic Church was aware it had a job of work on its hands to keep the masses in poverty, ignorance and subjection because throughout Europe revolutionary new ideas were springing up which defied conformity and subordination. Refugee Cathars had spread to other parts, but spontaneous mutations were occurring also, in the far north (modern Ukraine), in Hungary, Italy, Bosnia, Switzerland and the Low Countries. One sect, the Brethren of the Free Spirit, followed a personal mystical path that had much in common with Oriental religions. More significantly still, philosophical books written in the common tongue began to appear. Leaders of these rebellious sects were at risk of falling foul of the authoritian Inquisition, such as Jan Hus of Bosnia who condemned Church wealth and the sale of indulgences. He was burnt at the stake for his outspokenness.

But the tide of liberation was not to be eradicated so easily. In time highly articulate reformers such as Martin Luther and John Calvin would initiate Protestant sects. Rome's tentacles had never gained a foothold in countries such as England and Scotland, who developed their own brands of Protestantism. Meanwhile the Holy Roman Church had some navel-gazing to do when King Philippe of France kidnapped the papacy and installed it in Avignon, where it spawned six generations of puppet popes with royal control. When eventually restored to Rome, the French continued to support their own candidates (anti-popes) in the great schism of 1378 to 1417. Then the powerful Knights Templar were becoming arrogant and mighty. Seventy-five were sent to the stake while the Inquisition dissolved the Order. A branch of the Franciscan friars showed an unhealthy anarchic attachment to poverty, and also required Inquisitorial correction.

In the 15th century, joint monarchs Ferdinand and Isabella of Spain undertook to cleanse their country of Moorish enclaves. They then installed their own version of the Inquisition in order to obliterate all varieties of worship other than the rigid brand of Catholicism they themselves favoured (with the papal blessing). Their Grand Inquisitor, the most notorious of all, the very epitome of fanatical sadism, Tomas de Torquemada, conducted mass executions. He was satirised by Dostoevsky in *The Brothers Karamazov* as a man who would condemn Jesus Christ himself as a heretic. Indeed one of the Spanish Inquisitors acknowledged that the whole process was nothing to do with soul-saving and everything to do with the control of the vulgar herd. In Spain, once the Islamic menace had been despatched, the Jews became the prime target for persecution. Wealthy Jews in particular were objects of interest because their riches could be appropriated. Inquisitors were farmed out to the New World, to Spanish colonies in the Americas where they amassed goods and assets, and conducted spectacularly showy *autos-da-fé* or public mass trials and pyrogenics.

The ancient Roman Church did not believe in witchcraft, and those who did were branded heretics. But in 1484, with a capacity for fact-fixing that would have done justice to communist leaders of the 20th century, by papal decree it became heretical NOT to believe in witches. Wise women and midwives then became objects for clerical misogyny, which condemned witchcraft as the very worst heresy of all because adherents aligned with and gave their love to God's enemy, the Devil himself. Two self-appointed experts, Dominican Inquisitors both, wrote an extraordinary book called *Malleus Maleficorum*, full of explicit diabolical-erotic fantasies which they adroitly foisted onto women. Priests, one step further removed than most men, could not understand women, so they feared them, blamed them, sought to disempower and even destroy them. As some modern government ministers still do, they poured rabid scorn on unmarried mothers but not their seducers. In France, Germany and Switzerland, hundreds were burnt to death, some villages being virtually depopulated of womenfolk. The paranoia later spread to Protestant communities, including Cromwellian England and Puritan colonies of New England.

None, however, matched the ferocity of the Inquisition in finding enemies to denounce, in a paranoid persistence that prefigured the Stalinist regime. The viciousness and the ingenuity of the torture methods, the dogged pursuit of abject confessions and the triumphalist, callous mode of execution at the stake, inflicting maximum suffering, are subjects one should dwell on only long enough to absorb that they were as sadistic as anything that has happened in 20th-century military or police states, such as Chile under Pinochet or South Africa at the time of apartheid. And they happened under the auspices of the Christian Church.

As Europe gradually awoke to knowledge and culture, the Church was put on super-alert, ready to shoot down in flames new monsters that flew into range like space-invaders in computer games. Humanists, artists and academics could find themselves accused of heresy. The Church had jealously guarded the privilege of knowledge, like a business with a patent, but they could not stifle all the sparks of intellect and individual thought. Many men of learning had rough encounters with the Inquisition, now rejigged as the 'Holy Office', of whom the most famous was Galileo Galilei. His clear and unequivocal demonstration that the world was not the centre of the universe ran counter to the Church's deluded belief and teaching. A censorship was imposed on knowledge by the creation of an Index of Prohibited Books in 1559, which was to be finally dropped from use only in 1966. Mystics and Freemasons earned the Church's bigoted hostility, likewise those who adopted scientific methods for extending learning. Darwin's *Origin of Species* was a body-blow for traditional theology, and it was more than a century before Pope John Paul II argued for an 'ontological discontinuity' between apes and men, in which humans acquired a soul (women as well as men – the Church had not always accepted that women had souls). The use of polysallabic words was no doubt a vain attempt to keep such matters above the bowed heads of the faithful.

By the 19th century, with revolutionary bush-fires springing up throughout Europe, the Church had lost its hold over life and death; but with dwindling temporal powers it sought to maximise its hold on spiritual survival. Popes have repeatedly resisted democratising attempts to subjugate their ultimate authority to a council; Pius IX was one such autocrat. Having centralised power and declared his aim of converting the whole world to Catholicism, he manoeuvred the first Vatican Council to declare him infallible.

The Inquisition (aka Holy Office) had such a sinister history that in 1965 it was renamed the 'Congregation for the Doctrine of the Faith'. It exists as before, if not empowered to act with the ruthlessness of yore, still to prop up papal power and quash any deviation from the path of approved Catholic thought. It is fascinating to note that many or most of the modern issues this body oversees are to do with sex and reproduction: the celibacy of priests, divorce and remarriage, co-habitation, contraception and birth control, sexual ethics, abortion, feminism, female priests, male dominance in the Church, masturbation and homosexuality. The prefect of the Congregation for the Doctrine of the Faith, one Ratzinger, believes the Church to be the 'mystical body of Christ'. He believes this as fervently and as militantly as Cromwell, or any other man of power, believed he had (or has) divine backing.

Bizarre and inexplicable though it may seem that a major branch of a spiritual organisation has committed approved mass murder throughout centuries, there is an explanation, in the form of archaic tribalism, which destroys without mercy anything foreign or threatening, and which promotes the reproductivity of its own kind at all costs. Indeed some Inquisitors probably made a more direct contribution to the Catholic population. In South America certain Peruvian and Mexican Inquisitors succumbed to the temptations of self-indulgent grandeur, living like lords and, just as Mao Zedong did, allowing themselves the sexual liberties for which their subjects would have been mercilessly punished. A Peruvian Inquisitor kept two sisters as mistresses while one in Bogota kept assorted women in his domicile and was known to treat them roughly. He was held in horror by the local convent because of his dirty talk. Another incumbent was simply sex-obsessed and made out with any woman no matter what her status, including his own near kin.

While so much devastation has been committed in their name since the time of the Crusades, how have popes comported themselves in that time? There were some certainly who almost attained the 'Angel Pope' iconism that the humble herd dreamed of, for example, Celestine V, a renowned ascetic who had lived in caves and was a healer and prophet. However, he was 85 when appointed and more given to fasting and praying than governing, and was simply a fish out of water. One may understand why such eccentrics appear at times in the lists, as reactions to the stereotype of which Nicholas III in 1277 was a true copy, given to nepotism and avarice. Boniface VIII had delusions of imperial grandeur and was obsessed by supremacy. John XXII acquired considerable wealth, though himself a man of simple tastes, and manoeuvred his relatives and close friends into the most lucrative clerical posts – nepotism on a grand scale, which was to be a recurring fault of the papacy, seemingly irresistible and incorrigible. It was a feature of Clement VI (also known for sumptuous high-living and sexual indulgence) and Boniface IX (also accused of financial irregularity). One of the contenders in the difficult years who claimed to be pope along with three others – but was consigned to anti-pope status – was John in 1410, who was as unprincipled in administrative habits as he was licentious in personal ones. Rumour claimed he had seduced 200 women in his legate years.

During the Renaissance, popes ruled like princes over a substantial area of central Italy. They held royal court in the Vatican in sumptuous style, and kept armies to protect their boundaries.

Sons of princely families destined for the Church would be given benefices while they were still children, in order (it was argued) to enable them to afford a suitable education. Cardinals drawn from the aristocracy expected to keep up their standards of living. They were given bishoprics and other lucrative offices – often at a consideable distance, even outside Italy – for which their proximity to papal power was supposed to give some degree of protection and patronage. There is no clearer demonstration of the cynicism of Church leaders, that they should condone such practice. The son of Lorenzo the Magnificent was created a cardinal at thirteen. Rodrigo Borgia became a canon and cathedral sacristan before he was eighteen and was allowed to use those incomes as a student, while living and working elsewhere. Like any secular rulers, popes allied themselves by marriage to other powerful and aristocratic families, so that the succession of St Peter was infiltrated and diluted by very worldly interests. Many popes preferred to father their own children rather than rely on such an uncertain dynasty. So acceptable was this practice that mistresses of popes were received with courtesy and their irregular offspring were used to cement alliances in extravagant weddings, often conducted within the Vatican. In the Renaissance of the 15th century, Pius II, Julius II, Innocent VIII and Alexander VI begat children, and so probably did Calixtus III, Sixtus IV and Pius III. To the last named, historical gossip accorded twelve children, though there is room for doubt.

Family backing was as important to the pope as to any other potentate, as much for his temporal protection as for the immortality of his genes. Characteristically, family members would be appointed to the College of Cardinals – a job and an income for life. Nephews, genuine or euphemistic, were the usual beneficiaries. Martin V, Eugenius IV, Calixtus, Pius II, Paul II, Sixtus IV, Innocent, Alexander VI and Julius II between them appointed 29 nephews to the college. Besides other Church offices, within the Papal States many secular and military posts, governorships of fortresses and captaincies of the Church army were up for grabs.

Rodrigo Borgia, a nephew of Calixtus III, was made a Cardinal at 25. He was a young man of promise, zesty, intelligent, proud and ostentatious, well connected and wealthy, good-humoured and self-indulgent, handsome and devilishly attractive to women. He was destined for great things. Having been successful in a minor military-cum-diplomatic skirmish, subordinating a rebel fortress, he was headily promoted to vice chancellor of the Church and commander of the papal army. Undoubtedly efficient at both these jobs, he was in a position to commandeer many other benefices that became available; and came to control abbeys and fortresses strategically placed around Rome, as well as the incomes from them. He was a big spender and built himself a huge palace – 'the Golden House of Nero' – where he lived in flamboyant style with lavish entertaining, though was notoriously mean in his household affairs. He was known as a sensualist, loved women and had a number of mistresses. He should have followed the rules of chastity but nobody did at the time. Still, his behaviour exceeded the rules, and a scandal arose when a baptism in Siena was followed by a celebration which degenerated into an orgy. His sponsor Pope Pius wrote a reproving letter, then back-tracked; he was no monk himself.

Even so, there was general surprise when Rodrigo Borgia was elected Pope (as Alexander VI) in 1492. The passage of four mules loaded with silver seen moving from Rodrigo's palace to his opponent's may have been connected. The new pope already had at least seven children by more than one mistress, and was to father one or two more in his primacy. The final child was very mysterious, labelled '*Infans Romana*' and the subject of two papal Bulls, the second acknowledging him as Alexander's son. The story of this papacy is a spectacular tale of secular violence with plotting and intrigue, shifting alliances, manipulation of power balance, extension of boundaries by military campaigns, vicious family feuds, political murder and even fratricide. Lucrezia, Alexander's daughter, was pressurised into three successive dynastic marriages. Her first husband was divorced when he was no longer useful, the second murdered. An inopportune lover of hers was also murdered.

Sensual pleasures were taken for granted, as when, in the run-up to Lucrezia's third wedding, a private supper party at the Vatican was graced by fifty Roman courtesans who danced naked with the servants, after which they were professionally available to the men present. The master of ceremonies, Burchard, looked on with detachment, but one wonders if he disapproved of these antics as thoroughly as the US White House staff have had cause to do in another time, another place.

Alexander's eldest surviving son, Cesare, known for treachery and ruthlessness, and the model for Machiavelli's Prince, may have murdered his brother Juan, Alexander's favourite. As exorbitant in his grief as in everything else, the pope mourned his youngest without reserve. He declared he would have given seven papacies if that could restore his son; I am sure he was sincere. He confessed openly that this was divine retribution for his wickedness, and set about personal and Church reforms. This behaviour casts a ray of honest light on the origins of guilt and morality which will be explored later. Regrettably, the introduction of any significant reform would have meant power-sharing, which no Borgia could accommodate, and he soon slipped back to his old ways.

Alexander may have been the most outrageously worldly pope ever to hold office, but he was not a total aberration. Paul III (elected 1534) was a hedonist whose noble mistress had borne him three sons and a daughter but who repudiated her when the pontifical office came his way. He conferred cardinalships on two grandchildren aged fourteen and sixteen. Julius III, his successor, was likewise a voluptuary who sponsored his relatives and whose infatuation with a fifteen-year-old street-youth caused gossipy outrage. This young man was adopted by Julius' brother and made a cardinal. Pius IV (elected 1559) was himself allied by marriage to a pope, had three illegitimate children, and did not become chaste after his own step up to the supreme office. He also practised family favouritism. Gregory XIII's loose living and love-child did not prevent him taking office and promoting his son's career in tandem. The most common and regular fault of the papacy through the centuries has been nepotism, and those who strove to react vigorously against the trend were mere punctuation marks. Aleaxander VII (elected 1655) tried to resist the lure but fell under temptation like the rest. Benedict XIV (1740) was devout and priestly and almost uniquely dubbed a 'pope without nephews'. Alas, Pius VI (elected 1775), yet another hedonist, was to revive the age-old family partiality.

Pius IX (elected 1846), he of the infallibility fixation, saw the papacy ignominiously shorn of its temporal power, as the Papal States were taken over by the irrepressible republican–nationalist Italian movement. He was restored, but diminished, though he might spit anathema at the 'outrageous treason of democracy'. Eventually all that was left to him was the present Vatican City. Pius' reign was remarkable for the indefensible kidnap of a six-year-old Jewish boy who had been baptised in extremis as a baby; Pius adopted him, ignoring the parents' pleas and world opinion. Pius' enclosed world isolated him to the point of becoming a little mad. He was insulated from reality, despotic, deluded. At the First Vatican Council, where he proposed (and had validated by vote!) his infalliblity, to those who protested or objected he stated, 'Witnesses of tradition? I am the tradition.' We have heard similar sentiments from the mouth of Indira Gandhi when her supremacy was challenged, and will hear it again in the next chapter.

Popes of the 20th century were 'men of prayer and meticulous conscience' claims biographer John Cornwell, and I do not doubt him. The excesses of the erstwhile papacy lasted only as long as their visible, palpable secular hold on power. But spiritual or virtual power seems to spin its own particular forms of grandiose delusions. Leo XIII (elected 1878) had begun to expand Catholic influence beyond Europe to North Africa, India, Japan and the US, and this reaching-out to pastures new is extending without limits. Apparently, a present-day Vatican think-tank is already considering how to react to extra-terrestrial races, should they be discovered. There is every reason to believe earthly missionaries would be galvanised into soul-saving in outer space, should this happen.

Leo also sought to free the Church from secular influence, to stand alone as a sovereign state, especially in its papal elections. He was an extreme autocrat who kept his distance from the plebs, liked the dissemination of his portrait worldwide (as dictators do), and expected earthlings to prostrate themselves at his feet. This disengagement from the evolving impious world was to lead the Church into all kinds of crises, which it could only resolve by stamping aggressively on modern thought, culture, knowledge and science. Pius X's fury at the Modernist movement was as intemperate in the context as Hitler's: 'They should be beaten with fists. In a duel you don't count or measure the blows, you strike as you can. War... is a struggle!' The Church was as determined as ever to exercise thought-control.

Religious antipathies legitimise a tribal state of mind in just the same way as political ones do. The Catholic Inquisition cum Holy Office had persecuted Jews in the past, as we've seen. On the occasion of the loss of the Papal States in the mid-19th century, Jews were vilified for supporting the revolution, and the resentment against them passed with the sense of humiliation down the generations of pastoral families. One such was that of Eugenio Pacelli, destined to become pope in 1939. His combination of Jewish antipathy, enormous personal ambition and fastidious spirituality led him along a career path of contradictions of such magnitude that his reputation lies in shreds as an enabler of Mussolini's, Hitler's and Franco's death-dealing dictatorships. He was undoubtedly a holy man whose highest ambition was sainthood – or Pastor Angelicus – but events got in the way.

As a youth he was highly intelligent and able, but also exaggeratedly pious. Priggish indeed, rigid and disciplined, according to his mother he had been born a priest. He owned an inbred, finely tuned sense of hierarchy and deference. Like Napoleon he was a loner who did not fare well in communal living, and always managed to have a mother-figure to care for his needs. As he grew in importance in the Church he contrived to cater well for his own comforts, whether travelling in Europe in a sealed, private, luxuriously appointed railway carriage with his own personal groceries, or retreating to a Swiss sanatorium when driven by stress and his nerves, which generally happened about twice a year.

Inevitably this true son of the Church would find himself in the inner sanctum of the papal court, helping to draft the Code of Canon Law which reshaped the hierarchy of the Church. This aimed to centralise power and to give the popes unchallenged authority at all levels. In 1929 the Lateran Treaty with Mussolini imposed this Code in Italy, and in exchange Catholics were required to withdraw from politics, dissolving the democratic Catholic Popular Party in the process. In 1933 he struck a Reich

Concordat with Hitler, designed – so he thought – to grant the schools and churches with special privileges. But in exchange they also had to back away from politics and dismantle the democratic Catholic Centre Party. In this Pacelli was aided by none other than the leader of the selfsame party, Ludwig Kaas, a legal expert and a priest. His position as spokesman for the German Catholic population was strange, to say the least, for he seemed to be in thrall to Pacelli, to the extent of becoming a close friend, confidant and even 'beloved companion' according to Pacelli's biographer. Indeed Kaas spent more time in the Vatican or traipsing off to the Swiss rest-cure establishment than he did with his own constituents. He was the equivalent of Rebozo to Richard Nixon.

So fixated was he on his own purpose, Pacelli did not perceive Hitler's tyrannical agenda or that the papal representative had rubber-stamped approval on his National Socialist activities and in particular the accelerating attacks on Jewry. The 23 million German Catholic population hitherto had opposed the Nazis and had to be emasculated in Hitler's view. The Centre Party dismantling and the Reich Concordat achieved that, and days afterwards the vicious attacks on Catholic gatherings of any social sort began, followed by waves of terror to stamp out all vestiges of democratic protest. Meanwhile, the persecution of Jews with social exclusion and deportations also accelerated. Pacelli weakly and ineffectively tried to protect Jewish Catholic converts. Then his nerves got the better of him and sanatorium treatment became necessary. After the 'Night of the Long Knives' he found it desirable to disappear on a diplomatic trip to South America. While maintaining his mystical detachment, he adored the adulation and worship he received, the fame, the crowds, even the high-speed drives with outriders, the honours, glory and hosannahs. Even he was secular enough to appreciate those things, as he was shown to the world as its future pope.

When Pacelli became pope in 1939 in a lavish ceremony that was broadcast worldwide, he became 'the father of princes and of kings, the ruler of the world, the Vicar on earth of our Saviour Jesus Christ.' There is an echo there of Idi Amin's titles. It occurs to me that no woman could ever become Pope. She would laugh outright at such vapourings.

Pacelli, now Pius XII, had made no protest about Hitler's murderous regime or Mussolini's invasion of Albania. As war broke out he continued his sterile notions of appeasement. He thought Poland should not be defended. He personally met and greeted Pavelic, author of racist and anti-Semitic atrocities in Croatia. As news of the Final Solution began to filter through he was conspicuously silent. After Reinhard Heydrich's assassination in Prague, reprisals extended to 13,000 murders including the entire male population of a village, Lidice. Yet Pius preferred to polish his own saintly image by entertaining first communicants than take a vigorous moral stand.

Pius' neutrality has been explained by anti-Semitism, of which there is no doubt he was guilty. He may have been hedging his bets, waiting to see which side won. Aware that condemnations sometimes led to worse reprisals, he excused himself: 'It is better to remain silent before the public and to do in private all that is possible.' That presumably was his interpretation of turning the other cheek, only it was not his cheek that got slapped. Even when the Warsaw Ghetto was razed to the ground with all its inhabitants, and when Roman Jews were being deported from his own backdoor under appalling conditions, straight to the death camps, he was supine. He was more concerned about the defence of the Vatican – with his own precious person in it – from attack by communists (partisans). I doubt whether he had had enough human contact to engender much true compassion. He was certainly tribal in his outlook and there is evidence that he held Jews, black people and communists in prim distaste.

Pius was a supremely wily kind of power freak who chose his own penchant, the spiritual way, to get to the top. He did not have the courage of a martyr and at base he did not care a fig about groups alien to himself, and so he vacillated. Historians point out that when the Church in Germany took a stand on euthanasia deaths in the 1930s, Hitler's regime backed down. When a concerted mass demonstration, week-long, of German non-Jewish wives had demanded release of their imprisoned Jewish husbands, they were successful. Moral courage, belief and true compassion were required for Pope Pius XII to do the same, but he lacked these qualities. If he had possessed them, he could well have mobilised sufficient public opinion to avert the Final Solution. But deep down he knew that power is nothing to do with morality and that his infallibility was a sham.

CHAPTER 13

Birds of Ill Omen

Karl Marx was not too wide of the mark when he labelled religion the 'opiate of the people'. Fundamentally, religion was dreamed up as a rampart against the intolerable realisation that we are not, in fact, immortal. He was wrong to attempt to demolish it though, just as wrong as psychotherapists have been in the past in their clumsy attempts to dismantle patients' defences against unbearable reality.

If religion is so necessary as a psychological prop, why has it diminished so markedly in importance and influence in the Western world? It could be because we have found other household gods in which we place greater (if equally misplaced) faith. One of those gods is medicine. I practised medicine for over one third of a century, during which time life expectancy increased significantly in the UK, and the boundaries of our knowledge and capabilities were greatly extended. Yet these have not kept pace with expectations, and there is a belief among the public that modern medicine and science can achieve anything, to the ultimate Elysian feat of conquering death itself. In my time I saw a revolution in communication with patients. They used to be shielded, 'protected' from bad news, fearsome diagnoses and the prospect of death. Now the etiquette favours truth-telling, but doctors do not in general do it well. In a culture where the immortal soul has no other avenues, an abrupt end to life is a terrifying prospect, as much for the teller as the told.

A doctor has many obligations to his/her patients, in accordance with the spirit of the Hippocratic oath, of which the first is to do no harm: '*Primum non nocere*' – in Latin it acquires a suitable gravitas. That is – or should be – the supreme intention, and rightly so, for most of the interventions we practise are capable of devastating damage if handled incorrectly. The public gives doctors enormous power and trust and, even in the present age of iconoclasm, enormous respect. Maybe even the reverence that used to be reserved for priests.

Coming towards the end of my medical career, I am uneasy about some of the trends. It seems that we have entered into a double-blind with the public in its belief that we will one day conquer all disease. In this modern era of transplantation, spare body parts and genetic engineering, it might seem that life-in-perpetuum is just round the corner. The consequences for an overcrowded, ecologically exhausted planet are horrific, but nobody thinks that far ahead.

My profession enters into unholy alliances with politicians in their short-term initiatives, which gull the public. I heard an announcement on the news recently that for the first time the heart-attack rate in Scotland had dropped. So, fine! But people are still obliged to die of something, and there are more unpleasant ways to go than a swift coronary. We enter into even more heathenish pacts with the pharmaceutical industry, to thoroughly medicalise every corner of people's lives, subscribing to the delusion that there is a 'pill for every ill', and inadequately preparing patients for the inevitable battery of unpleasant side-effects. We are often guilty of making the cure worse than the disease.

I feel uneasy when I hear of heroic bone-marrow transplant treatments for infants under one year old, knowing that child will carry through life the burden of immune distortion and its consequences. At the other end of the age spectrum, in the US you are seldom allowed to die peacefully with 'the old man's friend', pneumonia, when you have a terminal malignancy. You are more likely to find yourself on a respirator in intensive care, being brought back to life so that you can die a month or two later of your cancer. This argues a frantic need for the reassurance of life preservation. The public expect heroic cardio-pulmonary resuscitation for themselves and their relatives even though most people who die are not restorable by such means. The medical and allied professions connive with these deceptions because the public is so desirous of clinging to them. They have faith, just like the Crusaders of yore. This is one of the reasons for the spiralling costs of the NHS: public expectations and the profession's failure to be explicit about its limitations.

If ordinary humans have unreal expectations of medical power, the mega-heroes of this book will be the same, only on a much bigger scale. Leaders are acutely aware of the importance of appearing to the common herd to be in the very peak of vibrantly good health, and totally on top of the situation. The biological clock is not a perpetual time and motion machine on a rolling replacement programme, and these men tend to be of a certain age by the time they scrabble to the summit. Now the status quo must be fixed, the aging process halted. If health problems arise they can command the best to deal with them. The best? Well, yes, as they see it. The stuffy medical man, rigidly following the gold-standard rules, well honed by experience and audit, must understand that world leaders are above the laws that govern the hoi polloi.

Doctors who attend VIPs do understand this maxim without being taught it, as if by instinct or maybe long acquaintance with the dominance–deference, step-and-rise arrangement of the hierarchy ladder. One good example was Dr Zhisui Li, who attended Mao Zedong for the last 22 years of his life. Zhisui Li had idolised Mao, the revolutionary leader, from boyhood, when his brother had called Mao the Chinese Messiah. Li was appointed as Mao's personal physician in 1954, even though his background was decidedly politically incorrect, with links to the Guomintang and the bourgeoisie. But he was young, suitably pliant and deferential, a hard worker and utterly in thrall to the chairman. He was also 27 years younger than Mao. The usual doctor–patient relationship, which requires a modicum of respect from the patient and authority on the doctor's part, was never likely to be established. Mao was in no doubt that Li was one of his subordinates, a privileged member of the inner circle certainly, and like all the rest one who needed to 'eat bitterness' from time to time by being sent out to the country for a spell among the peasants, doing manual labour. Mao excluded himself from this obligation of course. He was a natural rebel and refused to be restricted or controlled by any laws, giving his bodyguards and medical attendants much headache.

When Li proposed a baseline medical examination, he became aware of what he was up against. Mao's blood counts from medical records had suggested he harboured a chronic grumbling infection, but Mao would only agree to a brief examination, hating to be prodded and scrutinised. Li discovered Mao's mouth to be the culprit, for he never cleaned his teeth apart from rinsing his mouth with tea. The teeth were covered with green slime, the gums infected. Suitable treatment was arranged, but after a brief enthusiasm for brush and paste, Mao dropped the routine and slipped back to his peasant habits. As far as he was concerned, he was only in bad health when he was in discomfort; preventive medicine was simply meddling. Li discovered that, in Mao's opinion, health was equated with an active sex life, and his prevailing concern at 62 was to avoid impotence, which he suffered from time to time, usually when under political storm and stress. His previous doctor had given him injections of an extract of ground deer antlers, but to no avail. Li's major role was to ensure Mao enjoyed an uninterrupted, vigorous sex life and lived to a grand old age. Mao subscribed to the ancient Daoist belief that one may achieve immortality by making love to a thousand virgins, and by this time he was busily notching them up, well supplied by lovely young maidens from various dance corps, cultural troupes and bureaux. He was easy prey to advertised aphrodisiacs and longevity potions, such as an injected drug called H3, marketed by a Romanian lady physician. Li discovered the active ingredient was Novocaine and permitted it; unsurprisingly it did nothing. He was considerably more vexed and alarmed at Mao's addiction to sleeping pills, mostly barbiturates (these are not nowadays approved because of their powerfully addictive capacity and other side-effects). Mao had a long-term problem with insomnia, perpetuated by his tolerance to barbiturates, requiring him to take up to ten times the usual dosage when one capsule was no longer effective.

Mao's sleeping habits were also related to his lordly personality. Hating restrictions, he ignored the clock and evaded routine, eating and sleeping when he chose. But like many such megalomaniacs he had a cyclothymic nature, responding to political events by extremes of ferocious drive and excited activity, or morbid anxiety with depression, causing a retreat to his bed for months at a time. He would cocoon himself when news of the terrible famine following the Great Leap Forward reached him, and he suffered loss of face. These episodes were difficult for Li to treat especially since psychological disease was not acceptable in communist China. Li would attempt with Mao's co-operation to wean him off the barbiturates and substitute a placebo, but Mao would revert to type when Li was away doing his stint with the peasants. Then Li would substitute a less harmful sedative such as chloral hydrate; but Mao would find that, mixed with Seconal, this provided a kick of euphoria, and would use this for a confidence boost before meetings or appearing in public, or even before his dance parties (where he did much of his wooing).

Dr Li became aware of how stultifying is the job of care of a single self-obsessed person, and he became a specialist in trivia such as Mao's bowel movements and frequent respiratory infections (Mao was an addicted cigarette-smoker). He knew that one day Mao would become seriously ill (which he did, with heart, lung and motor neurone disease), and worried at his own lack of hands-on, cutting-edge experience as the years rolled by. Meanwhile, his difficult patient would become impatient at minor discomforts, refusing to endure them and demanding quick fixes, and only too ready with blame and offensive remarks when relief did not happen. He did not persist with any treatment beyond symptom control, and refused to co-operate with more serious conditions such as venereal disease, an inevitable consequence of his gargantuan sexual appetite. He contracted *Trichomonas vaginalis*, which did not upset him, but spread like wildfire through the dancing troupe who were currently serving him. He would neither desist nor let himself be treated. He would not even take a bath – a waste of time – but had himself rubbed with hot towels. Meanwhile, the poor ignorant servile lasses were proud of being infected by the great chairman. At 73, Mao allowed himself to be treated for genital herpes with Chinese medicine, but his sexual contacts were too numerous and widespread by then for contact-chasing to be done.

Dr Li was never under any illusion that his job would be easy, but he had not foreseen how his illusions would be undermined, as the god he served revealed not just feet of clay but cloven hooves. He saw how Mao shared in the general belief of his supreme status, perceiving himself to be not only above the law of the land, but above morality too. Li saw how cold and callous his master was when faced with suffering on an individual or a massive scale; how he was unmoved by the prospect of the deaths of millions of Chinese, and even said so in a speech. We can always produce more people, said Mao. Li observed that his master openly identified more with the brutal, lust-obsessed Emperors of the past than with ideologies of Marxism or Leninism. Under obligation to celebrate Mao's 66th birthday, Li and other conscience-stricken leaders knew that, while they sat down to exquisite delicacies such as bird's nest soup with baby doves along with choice wines, the rest of the People's Republic were dying in their millions of starvation.

Mao's conscience may have atrophied as he reverted to seed, but he was increasingly tormented by the spectre that stalks in its stead: paranoia. He was fearful of death stealing up on him by poison or the assassin's knife. This was magnified by his addiction to barbiturates, under the influence of which many far-reaching decisions had been made, including events leading to the Great Leap Forward. He demanded the constant presence of bodyguards and elaborate protective measures. His paranoia would lead to the ready commitment to nuclear arms: 'No one should try to intimidate us. No one can lord it over us.' It would lead to him relying on Lin Biao, a man with a history of addiction to opiates and a severe personality disturbance, with exotic phobias, as military commander and heir apparent; then suspecting him of plotting and causing his flight in panic, maybe his death. It would lead to the chaos, violence and death that was unleashed by his need to preserve his cult status among the youth of China in the Cultural Revolution.

Finally it would lead to the farcical situation around his own death-bed. Even as Dr Li strove to do his best to keep alive the 83-year-old, disease-ridden ruin, he realised his own personal danger. The responsibility for keeping Mao alive was shared with a committee of doctors and nurses, with Mao's wife Jiang Qing, with the entire Politburo and, most influential of all, Mao's latest long-term mistress, Zhang Yufeng. She was aged about twenty and was the only one who could understand the disabled leader's indistinct speech. Inevitably this led to brawls around the bed. Elements of grotesquery included poor Dr Li having to write a report as to whether or not watching movies was good for the dying man, and being bullied into trying out exotic treaments and witchdoctory. Still more shocking was the experimental cataract surgery on forty peasant men with heart problems, as a practice run to restoring Mao's sight.

Even after Mao's death, the farce continued as the Politburo decreed that his body should be preserved for ever. The technology was not established, and attempts with injected formalin were aesthetically dreadful. It is probable that the body on show in the Memorial Hall in Tiananmen Square is a wax effigy rather than the real corpse.

Mao's cult status was so firmly entrenched that it long outlasted his death and even the exposure of the myth surrounding him. Similarly, the deifying of Lenin endured even when he was incapacitated by his final illness and beyond. Never fully diagnosed in spite of the collection of top-class Russian and German doctors who attended him, Lenin's neurological illness may have been due to a series of cerebrovascular accidents, or neuro-syphilis. He died at 52, intending to block Stalin's graduation to leader but being overtaken by events. We should not mourn this twist of fate unduly: if Stalin's career had been scuppered there were plenty of others, Trotsky maybe, with the potential to evolve in similar ways. Meanwhile, Lenin's reputation survived more or less intact for the best part of a century. Such endurance reflects the collusion of the public in myth maintenance, for nations expect and demand that their heros – and their claims to fame – are indestructible.

In Franco's Spain, his legitimacy to rule was based on his supposedly transcendental mightiness, and when his health began to fail the spin doctors got to work along with the medical ones. Dark jokes about Franco's immortality went the rounds rather desperately, while signs of Parkinson's disease began to appear; maybe, it is suggested, worsened by enthusiastic medication on the part of his physicians. He refused to name a successor or to acknowledge his physical decline. He would burn himself out in the name of duty, he protested. Meanwhile, when admitted to hospital for phlebitis, his medical adviser of forty years' service was despatched after a fist fight with Franco's doctor son-in-law. Passions ride high and primitive in terminal power struggles. Probably, Franco's life-long paranoia and incipient senility did not need the diamorphine – inappropriately prescribed for his Parkinson's disease – to propel him into his final acts of repression: death sentences for Basque and other terrorists, carried out in spite of international pleas for clemency.

Franco's terminal event was a highly allegorical one: a massive intestinal haemorrhage that flooded his bed, the floor and even the walls with gore. Yet he was not allowed to die. They plugged him into a life-support machine and gave him continuous blood transfusions, with the doctors too terrified to allow him a dignified end until his daughter eventually sanctioned his disconnection.

Many of the great ones in their terminal spasms acquire too many doctors, which is not a good idea from the patient's perspective, because doctors never agree, and never approve any methods that differ from their own. They are acutely conscious of their own professional prestige, and in groups can be tediously point-scoring. No doctor attending a dictator would be courageous enough to face his task single-handed; but the converse, treatment by committee, can be disastrous. The Shah of Iran when he died in exile was surrounded by eight medical teams from five different countries (France, the United States, Mexico, Panama and Egypt). The difficulty in coming to concerted decisions must have been immense. His usurper, the 86-year-old Ayatollah Khomeini died under the ministrations of forty arguing Iranian physicians.

These morbid tales have elements in them that are characteristic of the medical histories of leaders, and are by no means confined to tyrants in totalitarian states. The choice of physician is usually made on the basis of political or social imperatives, and he is frequently so much in awe of the great man that he never acquires sufficient authority to assert his expertise and experience. Frequently, the doctor compromises on good management for political reasons or even colludes altogether with the patient's view of what is needed. Permitted problems of addiction are astonishingly frequent in our political leaders. Secrecy is a vital element in the leader's view, first on whether he will admit he is ill at all, and second, on how much to admit, and to whom. It is clear that his health and potency must be in evidence to the people, even if that is for the moment illusory. Virtually every biography I have read of top people, male and female, refers to significant and disabling episodes of depression, usually precipitated by failure and loss of popularity, also accompanying aging and declining vigour, and certainly with loss of office if that happens. For those who have led a life of violence there lurks the demon paranoia, fear of one's shadow, isolation, the misery of a hollowed-out personality incapable of giving love. The final invariable theme is that none of the greats can relinquish their hold on power. Very few go voluntarily, and when they do appear to, it may be under the pressure of behind-the-scenes threats, blackmail or deals.

The supposed assurance of having a personal physician – or several – in permanent attendance, an extension to the bodyguards, is illusory, for such a doctor becomes deskilled as speedily as he becomes politicised. Lord Moran, Winston Churchill's doctor, wrote that his job was to see his patient stay in power and in office as long as possible, even while he knew that Churchill's mind had been failing since the end of the war, and that he was not up to the job. This remarkable statement opens up a whole battery of questions as to the prime duty of a doctor in such a position. Moran's perception of how to do his best for the patient was accurate: Churchill lived for his position rather than his work. But was the national welfare not due any consideration? And if not by Moran, then by whom? Moran's attitude shows yet again an innate belief that great men have rights that supersede those of the common herd. Our archaic instincts perpetuate the alpha male, the one who has much and to whom more will be given.

Franklin D Roosevelt's doctor behaved in exactly the same way when the president chose to stand for a fourth term of office in 1944. Dr (Admiral) McIntyre was well aware that everything – not excluding the conduct of the war – was subjugated to winning that magnificent fourth goal. McIntyre was a classic example of a physician chosen for non-medical qualifications: by being an acquaintance of a previous White House physician, and for his beliefs in the primacy of presidential confidentiality. His training as an ENT specialist hardly fitted him to deal with Roosevelt's particular heart, lung and circulatory troubles. Roosevelt had been seen by a heart specialist in 1944, who gave an in-depth report of life-threatening cardiovascular disease; but McIntyre interpreted this in falsely optimistic language, and suppressed the graver aspects, using his senior rank to quell dissent from colleagues. Records even went missing. So, Roosevelt's malignant hypertension progressed unchecked, inadequately treated and monitored. The results became progressively evident even to lay people, as the president's mind clouded and his systems failed, and he was clearly not up to the job, a wreck of a man falling asleep at the crucial Yalta Conference at the end of the war. He died soon after.

Pope Pius XII chose as his doctor an eye specialist, Professor Ricardo Galeazzi-Lisi, who remained with him for twenty years. In the late 1930s, Galeazzi-Lisi had, in supplying new spectacles, created an impression with a display of medical patter. His working knowledge of general medicine must have been minimal, but he was supposed to draw in other specialists as needed. Protected by the approval of the Pope and his carer Mother Pasqualina, the doctor resisted the attempts of the papal court to throw him out as an incompetent charlatan, and drew in other fellow leeches to practise alternative therapies on the hypochondriacal pontiff, who had always had a troublesome stomach. The treatments included the poison chromic acid for teeth and gums, which probably enhanced the stomach complaint. A fashionable Swiss therapist, popular among secular leaders and showpeople, was called in to administer cellular therapy. This consisted of foetal brain from sheep and monkeys. It sounds similar to the quack remedies used by Christiaan Barnard and Mao Zedong, and indeed claimed the same magical powers, including postponing aging and improved sexual function. Presumably the pope was not interested in those aspects, but the treatment claimed benefits for assorted disorders, on a you-name-it basis. Maybe faith was a vital ingredient.

Pius XII was almost pathologically solitary, yet he loved the adulation of crowds and considered himself a dead cert for canonisation. He backed away from the passion of anger and violent confrontations, and was fastidious to the point of girlishness about contact with humanity in the raw. His silence on the horrors of the Holocaust may have had no more profound an explanation than this. After being rough-handled by gangs of Fascists in Rome during the war, he kept himself virtually imprisoned in the Vatican for the duration. He was terrified of communists. Yet he was as autocratic as any pope has ever been, and his capacity to wax prolix on an enormous range of subjects bore evidence to a total breach of contact with reality, to the point of delusions of omniscience. He would discourse on dentistry, gymnastics, aeronautics, cinemato-graphy, psychology, psychiatry, agriculture, plastic surgery, central heating, newscasting. He was so arrogant that he lectured T S Elliot on the subject of literature. He truly believed he was wiser than any man living (the sagacity of women never entered his thoughts). Meanwhile, in keeping with his expected infallibility, he would brook no contradiction, alternative or new thinking on his own intellectual patch, theology. Modern ideas were quashed, along with the thinkers, including the intellectual Teihard de Chardin. His isolation may have rendered him more than a little mad, for he began to have visions and hallucinations along with phobias about his health. The most bizarre anecdote about Pius XII was his reaction to his secular impotence against Hitler. He would conduct nightly ceremonies alone in his private chapel in the ghostly small hours, trying to exorcise the demon occupant of Hitler's soul. And no doubt he believed he had succeeded.

When Pius XII died, his devoted Dr Galeazzi-Lisi, ever courageous in his ignorance, attempted to embalm the body according to a new untried formula. It failed and the cadaver began to pop and crackle as it rapidly decomposed and fermented in the Roman heat, turning green and giving off an unholy stench. Pius' corruption was on a par with that of his peers, the lordly ones, even those without a heavenly sponsor.

Secrecy is a usual attendant when an influential person falls sick. The charisma of handsome, unalloyed health is vital for political survival. Jack Kennedy's disastrous medical history in his youth was not allowed in the public domain and he denied that he suffered from Addison's disease (in which he was backed by Janet Travell, the White House physician). He was also in long-term denial over his venereal disease, especially non-specific urethritis, which resisted eradication right up to his death. Earlier in his career in the war years, his father had pulled strings for him to get into the navy, from which his medical records should have debarred him. Father Joe had a word to the wise, namely the director of Naval Intelligence, who advised the naval doctor examining Jack to tone down the history of his past medical crises. That way, Jack was able to build up his heroic reputation in sea-going exploits, and burnish his image as a coming man and a future president.

At Christmas 1941, Winston Churchill visited President Roosevelt to strengthen Anglo–American bonding for the war effort. One night in bed, feeling hot and uneasy, Churchill got up to open the window. Suddenly he felt breathless and a pain developed over his chest, travelling down the left arm. The next morning Lord Moran was summoned. Such a history leaves little doubt that this was a heart attack or severe angina, but even as he listened down the stethoscope, Moran was making up his mind to say nothing to anyone. With America just engaged in the hostilities, Churchill could not be physically and mentally crippled. He was advised simply to avoid unnecessary exertion. Lord Moran would adopt the same softly-softly approach in later years when Churchill suffered repeated strokes.

History is full of such stories that generally come to light only in after years. The Shah of Iran developed a low-grade lymphoma in the early 1970s, a malignancy that imposes a limited life-span, and which requires specialised treatment to control it for as long as possible. French specialists were imported under maximum secrecy. Even the empress did not know the diagnosis for several years. The shah continued to rule while on debilitating chemotherapeutic drugs, steroids (which affect mood and judgement), anxiolytics and anti-depressants. Under these circumstances it is grindingly difficult to do an ordinary clerical job, never mind govern a country.

In 1972, President Pompidou of France developed multiple

myeloma, a form of bone-marrow cancer. Again his wife and the public were not informed, as he wrestled with chemotherapy and its weakening side-effects, disappearing from public view as needed. The gaps were covered by sophistries about flu and virus infections, while serious illness, on display in his behaviour and appearance, was hotly denied. When President Ronald Reagan was shot non-fatally in the lung, his press advisers presented him as recovering heartily in a few days. In reality he was a broken disorientated invalid for fully six months.

When President Eisenhower had his heart attack in 1955, his doctor treated him quite as cavalierly as Churchill's had done. Rather than transfer his vulnerable patient to hospital urgently as would normally happen, this doctor's instinct was to administer first aid himself and initially to lie to the press. Ike's stroke two years later – potentially more damaging to his intellect and hence his public image – was concealed even more obsessively.

In an earlier era when the press was less powerful (or less courageously intrusive), President Woodrow Wilson suffered a paralytic, disabling stroke which left him virtually helpless. His doctor, wife and political aide ran the country on his behalf, standing like three-headed Cerberus at his bedroom door and making a play of consulting him. Dr Grayson, Woodrow's physician, had been selected for social connections and suave manners, and because Woodrow found him congenial. His experience was mainly in obstetrics and gynaecology! Dr Grayson refused to admit his patient was seriously ill. Words like 'exhaustion' and 'depleted system' were bandied around. Secretary of State Lansing confronted the trio with the US constitution, which provides for the vice-president to act up under such circumstances. This was construed as an act of disloyalty, and Wilson later required Lansing's resignation on that account. There is no better evidence than this that the universal human subliminal perception holds the leader to be greater than the collective led. The rationalisation excusing such secrecy often included a desire to avoid 'public panic'. The real reason is a wish to cling to power, both on the part of the incumbent and his surrounding courtiers, the limpets who are themselves on the make.

The theme of addiction and harmful medication is found too often in the lives of the powerful to be dismissed as mere chance. Power is itself as addictive as any chemical comforter, working as an energy stimulant, an aphrodisiac, and through intense magnetism. Acceptable creature comforts like smoking (Churchill, Mao Zedong, Havel) and eating (Edward Kennedy, Robert Maxwell, Napoleon Bonaparte, Hermann Goering, Churchill, Stalin) scarcely distinguish leaders from the common herd. Yet at times of scarcity they do not go without. Descriptions of Churchill's wartime fare, while everybody else tightened their belt on strict rations, are lavish. Lord Alanbrooke described a *tête-à-tête* dinner with the prime minister in 1943: plovers' eggs, chicken broth, chicken pie, chocolate soufflé, a bottle of champagne, port and brandy. Stalin's feasts were more spectacular still. Once alone with Churchill (who was on a negotiating visit), the two sat down to sucking pig, two chickens, beef, mutton and a huge variety of fish, besides abundant garnishings – enough for thirty people it was said.

Alcohol presents problems because its abuse is so insidious, because in many cultures it is associated with macho resilience, and because it is desperately damaging even in small, regular amounts to physical and mental functioning. Where it is not part of the accepted culture, the long-term effects can be terminal before even recognised, as in Atatürk, the founder of modern Turkey. Late in life he complained of a severe itch, for which his own attendants could not find a cause. They looked assiduously for external factors such as biting insects. It was left to a foreign physician, presumably less blinded by awe, to recognise the clinical features of end-stage alcoholic liver cirrhosis: jaundice, swollen belly and legs, skin marks called 'spider naievi'.

The fact that alcohol is forbidden in Islamic teaching is frequently ignored by wealthy, upper-crust, male society. Osama bin Laden, when he was the son of privilege, a scion of a *nouveau-riche* Saudi family, was sent to school in cosmopolitan Lebanon. At sixteen he discovered beer and other innocent student joys, girlfriends, partying, the cinema, skiing. With his wealth, in the *beau monde* that Beirut became in the early seventies, owing to the oil-boom, Osama was soon into the more serious pleasures of lavish spending, gambling, heavy drinking and prostitutes. His asceticism and reclusive ways were exchanged for a fast, glamorous, indulgent, playboy lifestyle. For a time he drank so heavily that he became an embarrassment, as much for his sexual propositioning as his drunken trouble-making. This lifestyle was interrupted by the 1975 Civil War. Back in Saudi Arabia, alcohol was strictly illegal, though as ever the seriously wealthy families were above the law. Osama continued his anaesthetising intake of whisky on a daily basis as a student in Jeddah, until some road-to-Damascus revelation appeared to drag him back to the sober ways of religious enthusiasm in his twentieth year.

John Curtin, Prime Minister of Australia during the Second World War, had a long-standing drink problem of which the press was aware but chose not to make public. Boris Yeltsin was not so favoured, and the whole world has seen the ridiculous and undignified dregs of a man with a long-term addiction, eroding all his systems, especially his mind. How tragic that the first freely elected head of state in Russia's last one hundred years should come to this. He had suffered from insomnia during his punishing, overloaded schedules, for example a trip to America in 1989, and would befuddle himself doubly by mixing sleeping pills with alcohol.

President Richard Nixon was a man of shocking instability, teetering on the brink of nervous collapse at moments of crisis, and betraying his emotional ineptitude to a fascinated press by episodes of freakish behaviour. He used alcohol as a prop for his stressed personality, and came to depend on it. Insomnia plagued him during the obsessional, fast-track times, and alcohol helped at first with this symptom; but soon he progressed to sleeping pills, then to a combination of both. Nixon chose as his personal doctor a flamboyant and fashionable man, Arnold Hutschnekcker, who professed to be an expert in psychosomatic medicine. He started Nixon on sedatives but recognised that underlying depression was a major problem. Nixon's relationship with his therapist was totally hush-hush: he didn't want people thinking he was 'cuckoo' or 'seeing a shrink'. Nixon was halfway 'cuckoo' before he became president. In the early 1950s he had been in the habit of releasing tensions in hard-drinking recreational nights with the boys, but also in facing his daytime problems as vice-president. At some point, possibly when he had become president, he was introduced to the anti-epileptic drug Phenytoin by a friend and sponsor, Dreyfus, who used it as a magic elixir-cum-universal-panacea. Dreyfus was a millionaire, and handled the advertising of the drug, so was in a position to deliver liberal supplies to Nixon, who took it in large quantities for many years, ostensibly for depression – for which it is not licensed. It is however, mind- and mood-altering.

The White House doctor of the time, Walter Tkach, was a yes man who did what presidents told him. He would even rubber-stamp and sign an immunisation programme without actually giving the injections, according to Ehrlichman, Nixon's aide. He was unlikely to take a stand on Nixon's pill-popping and Scotch-swilling. On Phenytoin and sedatives (Seconal, a barbiturate), even a single drink could lead to disorientation, confusion, speech-slurring, insomnia and tremulousness as the chemicals perilously reinforced each other. Nixon's decreasing capacity for drink and his bizarre behaviour even in public and in front of the camera were well recognised. It was suggested by one of his spiritual advisers that he had resorted to amphetamines also, needing a stimulant to counter the suppressants. Often at night-time during his presidency, Nixon was unavailable for decision-making, being unrousable. During the 1973 Middle East War he was perpetually under the influence, and Henry Kissinger was in charge.

Jack Kennedy's use of feel-good drugs may have stemmed from his many episodes of medication in his youth. In 1944 (in his twenties) he had spinal surgery which was not successful and for some weeks afterwards he required 'fairly large doses of narcotics' to keep him comfortable. Addictions often do start in this way. When his Addison's disease was at last diagnosed he required replacement steroids, in huge doses. However, it was rumoured that even before his presidency he had an episode of steroid psychosis (that is, overdose). In the White House, Jack engaged the fast set's fashion physician, Dr Max Jacobson, dubbed 'Miracle Max', to supply vials, needles and syringes to him and his wife. Jack used these six-hourly, on the dot. The contents were unknown to the users, but they were analgesic, mood-lifting, energy-giving and addictive. Jack said, 'I don't care if it's horse piss. It's the only thing that works.' He would use the shots to ease his back pain and to shepherd him through televised debates and state visits. To the dismay of White House staff, Jacobson took to travelling with the president. Bobby Kennedy eventually had the contents of the unlabelled vials analysed by the FBI laboratory. Jacobson had concocted a hell-brew of human and animal tissue extracts, placenta, bone, liver and stuff from eels and elephants. Probably the only active ingredients, both highly dangerous in terms of mind- and mood-bending, were high-dose amphetamines and steroids. Jacobson was to forfeit his right to practise medicine in 1975. In spite of his nannying of his big brother, Bobby Kennedy was also reputed to use drugs: coke, opium and marijuana, which he stole in the course of his duties on the drug-busting squad.

Dr Jacobson was not the only doctor attending the highly placed who prescribed dangerously addictive, mind-altering drugs. J Edgar Hoover himself, the sinister chief of the FBI, in his seventies received a daily injection of some stimulant at 9 a.m. every day. He would immediately take off like a rocket in frenzied activity, but ran out of steam after lunch when he would crash out in sleep until the end of the working day. Hoover never consulted with Jacobson, but he was a hypochondriac who furtively saw many doctors in New York and Washington. From his analysis he would have known the contents of JFK's pick-me-up injections, and perhaps persuaded some compliant doctor to fix it for him. Hoover instructed one of his staff to investigate medicines that would prolong life and rejuvenate him.

Perhaps the most omnivorous pill-popper of them all was Adolf Hitler. He was introduced through the grapevine to Dr Theodor Morell, a flamboyant character whom Albert Speer described as 'not an out-and-out quack – rather a bit of a screwball obsessed with making money'. Articulate and plausible, Morell put a specious logic on his untested methods, which Hitler swallowed – as also did assorted crown princes and other celebrities. At first, the treatment consisted of vitamins, hormones, phosphorus and dextrose. Then Hitler received capsules of intestinal bacteria called 'Multiflor', and injections made from bulls' testes. Hitler, who suffered from recurrent abdominal pain and insomnia, worried about how long he would have on earth to achieve his ambitions. On Morell's treatment he experienced a dramatic improvement in health, which was possibly a placebo effect, as it was only temporary. At least Morell kept medical records (which is more than Jacobson seems to have done), and recorded 73 different medications given to Hitler. These included sedatives, hypnotics, stimulants, tonics, a cardiac stimulant, belladonna (atropine), barbiturates, corticosteroids, hormones from placentas, laxatives and enemas, tablets containing caffeine and amphetamines and an injected narcotic of equivalent potency to morphine for Hitler's belly-ache. As with all witchdoctors who treat symptoms rather than underlying conditions, Morell made his mark and his patient became dependent on him as well as his treatments. He was not approved among the medical brotherhood of the time, and Hitler's associates were uneasy (Albert Speer reports) about the increasing frequency of the injections. Then in 1944 Hitler acquired a further addiction, to cocaine, which he applied in liquid form to his nasal linings, and inhaled twice daily. When first introduced to practice, this demon drug was hailed as a wonder restorative, its dangers unrealised. In the war years, Hitler was a walking drug-den, high on a mixture of horse, crack, speed and barbs, with a few others tossed into the brew. They did not make him what he was, but enhanced his most dangerous traits of paranoia, megalomania and tribal hatred. His colleague Reich Marshall Goering was a morphine addict who could oscillate from bombast to torpor within minutes.

Winston Churchill drank a staggering amount of alcohol in his prime ministerial years and before. This was no secret, and men of his class were accustomed to indulge themselves without restraint. In 1911 he had written to his wife that the Liberal prime minister, Herbert Asquith, was embarrassingly drunk in the House, scandalously so. Asquith earned the nickname 'Squiffy', and Churchill opined that only loyalty prevented scandal. 'What risks to run,' he wrote. Yet the same problem and the same lack of insight affected him as the years rolled by. At the British Embassy in Cairo in 1943, he demanded a glass of white wine at breakfast, informing his hostess that he had already downed two whiskies (the time being 7.30 a.m.). At lunch he would take whisky and brandy; at dinner, champagne, wine and brandy. Churchill was an exceptional man who kept his wit and drive and his incredible dominance into ripe old age, yet it was apparent to those around him that his nuisance potential, capacity for time-wasting and irrelevant enthusiasms were a serious hindrance to the speedy end to the war. Few realised that, in addition to his gargantuan alcohol intake, he took sleeping pills – barbiturates again. In fact from his letters it is apparent that he had started the barbiturate habit for sleeping in his mid-thirties. He took a variety of mind-altering medications in the war years, all with the concurrence of his slavishly deferential doctor, Charles Wilson aka Lord Moran, whom Churchill intimidated as effectively as he did everyone else. Moran's account of Churchill petulantly resisting anti-malaria treatment in 1944 when on his travels, and defying restrictions after pneumonia, make him sound like a blood brother of Mao Zedong. But symptoms that interfered with his chosen activities he expected to be relieved. Sleep he wished to summon like a servant, and so the red pills – barbiturates – would be taken at night; one or two as occasion demanded, and even for an afternoon sleep if he needed an active evening mind. He also took them before a major speech in the House of Commons. One of his ministers gave him a new sedative – a fashionable one called Supponeryl – when the red ones were not sufficiently effective. Churchill took double the dose, and was found semi-stuporous the next morning. In his memoirs, Moran did not mention the active ingredient, but it was supposedly four times the strength of his usual powerful narcotic.

Moran lists the tablets that sat on Churchill's bedside table: apart from Disprin, in Churchill-speak they were, Lord Morans, majors and minors, reds and greens, babies and midgets. Taken in the context, one may surmise that most of these were mood-adjusting. In 1944, on one of his busy flights around the world, Churchill was overheard discussing with Anthony Eden the merits and doses of barbiturate sedatives. Churchill said, 'I'm a hardened case,' but Eden became no less so. In the early 1950s he was seriously ill with painful biliary colic, and by mismanagement of his pain control became dependent on powerful analgesics. His biliary problems became chronic (allegedly), and so did his pill-taking. He would carry around a box of medicines which included morphine. Then during his short time as prime minister he was plagued with political crises, including the Suez affair. He apparently persuaded his doctors that he needed longer waking and active hours, and so started his addiction to amphetamines – the most dangerous drug of all for leaders. The initial effects seem brilliant to a hard-pressed statesman: clarity of thought, less need for sleep, increased energy. But too much of a good thing results in euphoria, loss of touch with reality, irritability and over-paced thinking, then confusion, paranoia and delusion. Eden acknowledged his dependence on Benzedrine, and onlookers observed his state of mania bordering on hysteria as the Suez fiasco unfolded.

Mao Zedong was not the only communist leader to depend on sleeping aids. Leonid Brezhnev suffered from insomnia and began taking night sedatives in increasing doses, eventually becoming addicted. His nurse encouraged this trend, and an associate suggested knocking the pills back with zubrovka (coloured vodka). As an ex-smoker he craved tobacco smoke and would have smoker minions breathe fumes over him during the night when all else failed.

Depression is so common among leaders of states and nations that it might be considered an occupational hazard of almost 100% risk. How ironic then that political dirty-tricks campaigns can destroy a man's chances of high office if a history of depression is unearthed, as happened with Senator McGovern's running mate, Michael Dukakis, in 1988. Had these men known their American history they would have been able to observe that Abraham Lincoln himself had periods of depression, despairing over the loss of life in the Civil War and 'almost ready to hang himself'.

Consider the following catalogue of mental disease among the world's acknowledged great men of the past. Overwork, anxiety and strain were the triggers for Lord Nelson's episodes of melancholy, and also for his hypochondria. He may have been frankly manic-depressive. His worries were somatised and gave him further cause for gloom because he was desperately ambitious, and feared death would cut short his achievements. Oliver Cromwell had a period of youthful mental crisis, marked by psychosomatic illness in which he took to his bed and suffered the profoundest melancholy. He had curious delusions at this time, including one in which he saw himself as the greatest man in the kingdom, suggesting that his black mood emanated from a furious frustration that his sense of destiny was not going to be realised. As described earlier, his later success in battle coincided with a swing to hypomania, whereas doubts and drawbacks always plunged him into a pit of gloom.

Napoleon was a surly misfit at school, with behaviour oscillating between sullen withdrawal and violent aggression. He had a depressive illness at age sixteen, laced with an obsession about suicide and morbid defeatism. The depressive tendency returned at the end of life when his star was on the wane, accompanied by lethargy and indecisiveness to an extreme of psychotic paralysis. When he had abdicated, he seems to have made at least two attempts to do away with himself. His contemporary and opponent Tar Alexander VI, with whom Napoleon experienced strong male-to-male attraction and even love, also suffered violent mood swings amounting to manic-depressive extremes at the time of their negotiations and Napoleon's victories.

Benjamin Disraeli had an indolent and melancholy side to his flamboyant, egotistical personality. Descriptions of his powers of oratory from his contemporaries – like a racehorse approaching the winning post, full of energy, grace, power and expression – sound as if he bordered on the hypomanic. The converse was a tendency to depression. The most protracted occurred in his youth in 1827 when everything he had turned his hand to had failed disastrously. He was left with appalling debts, and with condemnation and abuse from those who had previously loved and eulogised him. He withdrew from society, and suffered psychosomatic illness, which he correctly attributed to thwarted ambition. Later, depression occurred at disastrous setbacks, notably his maiden speech in the House of Commons; and more gentle melancholy when at the end of life he had everything but no longer the means to enjoy it.

William Gladstone was inclined to be morbid and preoccupied with his own mortality, which he balanced with religiosity. He practised solitary self-flagellation, which implies guilt, maybe over his rescue activities with prostitutes, into which it is clear he channelled much displaced sexual energy. He seems to have been too energetically self-disciplined to sink into anything like the depths of gloom of his rival Disraeli.

Lenin, like most men, hated to admit to illness, and responded to his physical decline in 1921 with severe depression. At first his tiredness, insomnia and headaches were attributed to his work overload since 1917. He admitted to strange obsessions and began to wonder if he was going mad. Now over fifty he gloomily complained his song was sung, his role played out. He considered suicide, and even engaged Stalin to acquire poison for him; and after his stroke had incapacitated him, he begged his wife and sister to do the same. Mao Zedong's depressions, in which, like Cromwell, he shut himself away from the world for months at a time, not leaving his bed, also coincided precisely with failure, and with loss of face and self-esteem.

Vaclav Havel had an episode of post-prison blues when he emerged to find his wife Olga, to whom he had been repeatedly unfaithful, had herself had an affair and toyed with the idea of leaving him. He isolated himself and sank into unredeemed misery while drinking heavily. He was prone to unstable mood swings later in life when, as the Czech leader, he had made an injudicious second marriage and become the butt of his people's ribald jokes instead of their worshipful adoration.

Hitler's dropout years, tramping and dossing in the streets of Vienna, were marked by cyclothymic swings, varying from moody, surly and reclusive indolence to excited tub-thumping and eccentric oratory. He behaved similarly in his army years in the trenches. His narcissism and hypomania fed hungrily on adulation in his successful years, but later when his magic powers left him and his war plans backfired he would drop into mental torpor, evading company, unable to reach decisions, irritable and even – wonder of wonders – silent! Mussolini, when he was dictator, Il Duce, surrounded by adulation and adoring women, would endure periods of gloom when he droned on interminably about his loneliness and lack of friends and intimates. During the first three years of war, his mood swung from euphoria to despair in line with his vacillations, or his plans and expectations contrasting with the evidence of reality.

Franklin Roosevelt became depressed when aware in the early 1940s of his failing physical health. To buoy himself up he would invite his erstwhile mistress to dinner when his wife Eleanor was absent, seeking rejuvenation in her presence. Churchill's 'black dog', as he called his periodic plunges into melancholy, plagued him throughout life. He was particularly susceptible (as were several generations of Churchills before him) and there were certain triggers, such as hospital and vapid characters. His episodes were also associated with failure, with periods out of office, and when he faced a hostile House of Commons yelling at him to sit down or get out. Before his restoration in the Second World War he would glumly state, 'I'm finished,' to his cronies twice a day. In the 1945 general election Churchill was put out of office – a monumental snub – and a Labour government welcomed instead. Struggling to accept this bravely and philosophically, he was obsessed by his rejection, and could talk of nothing else. He lived in the past, and found difficulty in filling his day. Physical symptoms cropped up. He awoke in the night and took an extra 'red'. He no longer commanded everyone's attention as the most royal of royals. Lord Moran described the ugly scar that the election result had left. He was seventy, and the repulse hurt and humiliated him as if he had been in his prime. He returned to office of course; but after his final resignation, he prayed daily for death.

Menachim Begin's ambition, for which he believed he had been specially chosen by God, was to establish the Jewish homeland in Israel. He was a supreme narcissist, identifying himself with his nation and his cause. After four years as prime minister, his arrogance raised questions about his democratic support, but a successful election in 1981 sent his spirits into orbit again. The expected flip-side of this character-type was there, recorded in history: clinical depression in 1939, 1951 and 1978. His episodes of depression were of such a severe order that onlookers thought he was a terminally sick man. Yet success ensured his recovery. In the middle of his second term as prime minister, his wife, who had been his rock and support, died. This precipitated a depressive crisis of such durable severity that he resigned and became a recluse.

Richard Nixon's depressions were on display when he failed or feared failure, even in student elections. However, his daughter Julie recorded in her diary in 1967, when he seemed to be a political has-been, weighing the chances of a further run for the presidency, that he was depressed in a way she had never seen before. Later his tendency to mood swings was exaggerated by the highs and lows of his addiction to power as well as to more palpable intoxicants.

Bill Clinton's depressions coincided visibly with failure. One of the most catastrophic downfalls, following which the balance of his mind was seriously questioned, was when he failed to be elected for a second term as governor of Arkansas in 1980. He had only been in office for two years, but the magnitude of his emotional collapse and obsession with his failure were way beyond one of life's little hiccups. After total withdrawal from press and public, and tear-choked speeches to his own camp, he set about blaming everyone, even his supporters, but most particularly the electorate, whom he and Hillary lambasted in derogatory terms. In his brooding, bitter depths of despondency he connected with preachers, as if needing forgiveness. He became apologetic, abject, wandering around like an Ancient Mariner, relating his life's story as if he was at the end of everything, begging to be loved again.

One of Boris Yeltsin's aides observed astutely that democratic politics is too slow to achieve results. Most crucially, approval ratings are very hard to push up, needing more hard graft than showmanship. Under these unstimulating circumstances, Yeltsin would become gloomy and inert. He was always best in a crisis, depressed and apathetic in the aftermath.

Slobodan Milosevic suffers from bipolar mood swings, and in that pattern which should now be recognisable his depressions have followed severe reverses, such as in 1992. During this watershed year, Serbia was isolated by sanctions imposed by the West, and Milosevic was incredulous at the virulent intensity of local opposition. He vanished into isolation, his moods showing cycles of 'angry elation and manic depression', according to a senior aide. After fraudulent elections in 1996, the opposition protested vocally and visibly in Belgrade. His mood spiralled down and down, helped on its way by the contents of a whisky bottle. And finally it hit rock bottom when the chief prosecutor of the UN War Crimes

Tribunal issued a warrant for his arrest, charged with crimes against humanity.

The reader will I hope forgive me for labouring this particular point in a far from complete list. Pathological depression as a response to failure, loss of power, loss of prestige and above all, loss of adoration, is such a regular observation that it confirms, if there were any doubt, how profoundly addictive and even irresistible is the quest for power. This is particularly so after one has tasted the elixir, or if one is by inheritance specially predisposed to do so. This observation is reinforced by the final theme of this chapter: an inability to relinquish power, even among those who rule in democratic states with constitutions and safety clauses.

The belief in a personal divine mission, decreed by the gods, or fate, or whoever, seizes hold of a new incumbent in office. Once that belief is entrenched, intercurrent illness or disability seems to come as a contradiction. The chosen one considers his options, teetering on the brink of depression. But then he sees this malady as an obstacle to be overcome. He will sacrifice himself on the cross of duty; he will devote himself to the people who adore him. He will not let them down; they will not let him go. And amazingly, especially if he has got his publicity right, they will not.

This chapter has dealt with many sick leaders who did not perceive that because of their poor health they were incapacitated, indeed crippled, not only by disease but by its treatment. The Shah of Iran, on his debilitating steroids, chemotherapy and anti-depressants, probably never dreamt for one moment that he should hand over the job to someone else. His task of modernising the country was not yet complete. Ferdinand Marcos as a young man developed kidney disease and was to be eventually diagnosed with systemic lupus erythematosus. At 47, after a career working up the political ladder, he became President of the Philippines. But his ailment was pursuing him relentlessly, and he learned that his time was limited. Meanwhile violent disturbances in the country by communists gave him an excuse to suspend the democratic institutions and impose martial law. He needed to assure himself of his grasp on power. As his renal disease progressed to a stage where he could no longer conceal it, so his dictatorship became more authoritarian. On dialysis and awaiting kidney transplant, he was a terminally sick man, refusing to let go. Acts were created to give him extraordinary powers, while the government and the army were purged of contenders. After a failed kidney transplant, with all the attendant immuno-suppressive medication, requiring isolation because of the hazards of any infection, Marcos announced he would run for re-election. His repeated violation of democratic rights, his interference with justice and his political murders were compounded by election fraud in the snap election of 1986 which Corazon Aquino rightly won. Marcos went down at last in a bloodless coup and fled the country.

The longer a man remains in power, the more he is convinced of his right to rule for ever. Habib Bourguiba ruled Tunisia for 31 years. Although at first planning institutions to protect people's rights, he then rapidly sank into autocratic leadership. He defied his own laws, saying, 'The system? I am the system' (remember Indira Gandhi's similar statement, and that of Pius IX). He suffered a series of heart attacks, one nearly fatal, and was incapacitated for long spells. His brain became affected by poor circulation. He agreed to step down, then retracted, proclaiming himself President for Life.

Idi Amin of Uganda – 'Lord of All the Beasts of the Earth and Fishes of the Sea and Conqeuror of the British Empire in Africa in General and Uganda in Particular' – always felt insecure and vulnerable because of his limited intelligence. Insecurity plus power equals tyranny with paranoia, and his became pathological. Like Stalin he simply purged inconvenient groups, including his country's intelligentsia. He likewise proclaimed himself president for life.

Deng Xiaoping had a troubled life under Mao Zedong's leadership of China, seeking to limit Mao's personal excesses and undermining his own position in the process. As China's national leader after the revolutionary extremis, he was praised for fostering the country's economic and international development. He removed labels of 'class enemies' from those unfortunates stuck with them under the Mao years. He recognised the limitations of the individual, and in a Politburo of septuagenarians and a party of veterans, vigorously encouraged the elderly to resign or retire. Age limits were set, 65 for Ministers, 60 for officials. Deng was 82, and did not extend the rules to himself.

Yet in old age as well as in positions of unrestricted power, propensities merge into pathologies. Deng's fear of capitalism, and his terrible traumas in the violent Cultural Revolution at the hands of China's youth, contributed to the paranoia that released massacre on the pro-democracy protesters in Tiananmen Square in 1989. Deng, with other top leaders Li Peng and Jiang Zemin, were convinced that CIA agents had infiltrated the student body. In the face of worldwide horror at the geriatric murderers, Deng spoke of the young students and workers of his country as 'the enemy', the scum of the nation who did not merit his mercy or forgiveness.

History is littered with leaders who pass their sell-by date. Pik Botha of South Africa at seventy-three suffered a stroke that left a partial paralysis, yet he clung to office for the next seven months, feeling he had unfinished business, and resisting calls for his resignation. US Secretary of State John Forster Dulles refused analgesics and sedatives for his terminal bowel cancer, which caused severe pain and intestinal dysfunction. Rather than admit he was ill and leave the vital task to a fit man, he soldiered on, making decisions that affected millions of people, not balanced enough to know when to go.

Vaclav Havel's lung cancer (the result of his lifelong heavy smoking) was diagnosed when he was negotiating Czech entry into NATO – no time for a leader to be indisposed. But no time ever is convenient. Secrecy was paramount and his disappearance from public view had to be stage-managed and speedy. After a four-hour operation to remove the tumour and half a lung, President Havel was rushed to an intensive therapy unit. He developed pneumonia, respiratory failure and heart problems. Following heroic treatment he was slow to recover, subsiding into depression partly because of tobacco and alcohol withdrawal. He then tried to recover his lost youth by marrying his actress girlfriend, and staggered on in office. He became aloof, distancing himself from any who might suggest his time was over, comforting himself with displays of pomp and ceremony, buffered by an enclosing circle of lackeys who kept out his critics. The truth seemed to be that he could no longer risk being seen or accessible, for then the population would have its fears verified, that this mortal man really was past it.

In the UK we have had two octogenarian prime ministers in the past two centuries. William Gladstone was an extraordinarily capable man on anyone's scale of abilities, holding that office for four sessions in a parliamentary career lasting over sixty years. He had been chancellor of the exchequer under three other premiers, and once held that post concurrently with prime minister. In 1882 he noted his own decline, with flagging energy and disinclination for work. He observed then that he should not hold the stage as a 'half-exhausted singer, whose notes are flat and everyone perceived it but himself'. A year later, he observed, 'A strong man in me wrestles for retirement: a stronger one stands at the gate and forbids it.' He gave in to the stronger, and went on for another twelve years. He was beginning to suffer from an assortment of age-related infirmities, and earned the nickname 'Grand Old Man' from his colleagues as well as a protecting cocooning by his womenfolk. Always a great talker, he became voluble, verging on the garrulous. In 1886 he took his third stint as PM. He might protest that other, younger men should take over; but he certainly did not give way to them. There was always some new fight, the last... and then another. By 1892 (at 83), many thought he was finished, but his fourth prime ministership began then. Partially blind with cataracts and with disabling deafness, he was not able to conduct his supreme office without considerable tolerance and adjustment on everyone's part. His final *tour de force* – a speech on Irish Home Rule, which he knew was doomed – was his swan song. He resigned at 85. Definitely he hung in there too long, but his reputation was remarkably intact. No one had dared challenge him, this towering man of gravitas, but his departure left a hiatus in the Liberal Party that could not readily be filled – a regular phenomenon after a particularly strong leader, an inertia that endures with the deference due.

The same was not true of Winston Churchill, whose mental powers were in serious decline even in 1943, according to Lord Alanbrooke, Churchill's chief of Imperial General Staff. Churchill's cerebral arteriosclerosis was hastened by his addictions, and seriously hindered war-time planning. His reasoning was unbalanced; he became obsessed with trivia, unable to see the big picture or overall strategy. He was a past master at time-wasting, spending hours discussing, rambling, incoherent, unable to reach decisions, and on occasions was obstinately obstructive. He would be motivated by petty jealousies, wanting always to be at the centre of the action. Lord Moran noted in his diary the PM's mental weakness in 1944, with undue tiredness and lack of concentration. In 1949, Churchill had a stroke followed in the next two years by 'stuttering' or mini-strokes. Yet in 1951 he was returned to office as PM in a Conservative administration. He had multiple pathologies affecting all his systems and at 76 was burnt out. Anthony Eden, the foreign secretary, attempted to lead from behind but was himself struck down with illness. In 1953, Churchill had another major stroke. He was incoherent and could barely walk, drooling and with a paralysed left arm, yet insisted on taking the Cabinet meeting that day. As the stroke became denser, Churchill agreed he should resign. But anodyne press statements about 'needing a rest' covered his back, and he decided to hang on. From this dispassionate distance in time, it seems astounding that no one dissuaded him. While he rested he wrote his memoirs, with assistance and the usual enormous quantities of champagne and cigars. And amazingly, this scarred and ancient dominant was able to get up and speak for an hour at a party conference and in the House of Commons without anyone realising how much of his brain had gone soft. His success encouraged him to resist pressure to step down, which now came from all sides, particularly the press. To direct approaches from both Eden and Macmillan, Churchill wrote platitudes about not failing in his duty and about using his influence for... 'the causes we both have at heart, crisis and tensions in world affairs'. Meanwhile, without the Cabinet's concurrence, Churchill decided that Britain should develop its own H-bomb. His attention and capacity for work were minimal. Yet he continued to coquette, to vaguely plan his retirement, then find there was yet another job he should accomplish. He was eventually ambushed, and left office in 1955 at the age of 81.

The United States Constitution, with its 25th Amendment, is far ahead of any other democratic nation's self-regulation, in decreeing that power is limited to only two terms in office as president, and that the machinery is available to replace a disabled man in office. The voluntary relinquishing of presidential control on a temporary basis has never happened, even though it should have done so, for instance when Reagan was wounded and when he had cancer surgery. There is no case on record of a doctor to a VIP, aware of his patient's incapacity, seeking to persuade his colleagues to remove him.

Since power is addictive, it is absolutely vital that it is parcelled out in minute quantities, for short periods of time, and shared around with all the citizenry, who should learn to maintain respect while stifling their instinctive deference.

CHAPTER 14

Of Blood and Brains

It is curious how the nature–nurture – or genetic–environmental – debate polarises people along political–ideological lines. Even in the face of incontrovertible evidence to the contrary, environmentalists' views have held sway in the popular mind in recent decades, when every biographer has to become an amateur psychoanalyst. With a claim to Freudian insights, adult frailties are attributed to childhood traumas. All men and women start off equal, they say. Communists, socialists, liberals like to believe this is true. By contrast the suggestion that men and women are born decidedly unequal, and that much of their personality and attributes are defined before birth, the province of the behavioural geneticists, has raised such passion and fury among radicals that some scientists have had their lives threatened and their research vilified as bigoted and evil. The emotional reaction against Darwinism is a measure of the grandiose delusions we have about our own status in the animal world. For we are not a peak or a triumph of evolution, but merely an offshoot, and a highly dangerous experiment rather than a design of perfection. We dominate now, but may be brought down in a matter of decades by a virus. I would guess there is an excess of men among anti-Darwinists. George Bernard Shaw was one of them. On the subject of Darwinian theory, he wrote, 'When its whole significance dawns on you, your heart sinks into a heap of sand within you. There is a hideous fatalism about it, a ghastly and damnable reduction of beauty and intelligence, of strength and purpose, of honour and aspiration.'

266

The confrontation arises because we confuse What Is with What Should Be. Morality really does get in the way at times. There is no morality in nature whatsoever, and when we try to understand ourselves as part of the natural world, we must divest our thoughts of moral overtones – for a time. Morality is real and must be faced, as it will be in the last chapter of this book. The way we are does not fit with notions of democracy, compassion, philanthropy or human rights.

But that does not mean we should cast aside those holy principles.

I have never been at heart an environmentalist, have always felt human nature must have a more deeply rooted anchor than the winds of chance. Yet I have not held to a Hitler-type philosophy that conflict is what should be, and the top trampler has rights canonised by virtue of success. This book is all about the deplorable conceit of unbridled ambition, and I really do want to see more equality and fairness in society; but the only way to reach that is to recognise just how far from achieving it we are in our natural state. Having said that, the challenge is, should we even attempt to alter what seems to be unalterable? All the sinister experiments of the 20th century, to adapt and control humankind, have failed abysmally and left a trail of destruction. The struggle meetings of Maoist China, the brainwashing of the USSR, the terror control of totalitarian regimes, the huge power-base built up by Freudian psychoanalysts in the States to subdue erratic and antisocial natures; all of these have admitted defeat at last. They have shown what modern behaviourists know thoroughly from twin studies and indeed from simple observation: that we are born with a well-defined set of personality features and behaviour patterns, and these we will carry throughout life.

But that does not mean we are robotically programmed by our genes. This study of mine has opened the door a crack onto the complexities of human nature, indicating that the tangling of inner and outer influences is so intricate that it eludes analysis by our stumbling experiments. I have peered down the microscope at a selected sample of humans about whom much has been written and, fortuitously, whose behaviour patterns are remarkably consistent. Many of their biographers describe these men as 'complex' because so much about them is contradictory. But they are not complex: they are very simple and amenable to understanding.

I have at my finger tips a beautiful analogy for behaviour patterns, but this necessitates a brief digression into the world of blood and immunity. I shall keep it very simple because I really want to carry you, the reader, with me. As a doctor, one becomes most keenly aware of how effective and sophisticated our immune capacity is when you see what happens where it breaks down. If the system in a young baby adopted a blank-sheet, wait-and-see policy, totally unprepared for the invading hordes of infectious organisms ready to bombard the infant, it would be carried away to its ancestors in next to no time. On the contrary, the infant has a huge battery of defensive weapons – an almost infinite variety, but all individually in small numbers. In the interests of safety, she must be prepared, but in the interests of economy she must not overproduce any one immune capability until it is called for. Flexibility, a broad spectrum of capacity, and rapid response times are the watch words. A note of caution here: all this implies forward-planning. But evolution has no foresight. This degree of preparedness has come about through natural selection. We do know that the immunity in a population is tailored to the infections prevalent in that geographical area. Where measles has been introduced anew into populations, for instance the South American Indians, those populations have been virtually wiped out with frightening speed. In West Africa the indigenous people have a high frequency of a gene (HLA B53) conveying protection against a lethal form of malaria (quite apart from sickle cell and other blood variants that give a measure of cover). Our immunity is specifically geared to the population into which we are born.

Let me introduce you to lymphocytes: small, round, unremarkable-looking 'white' cells that circulate in the blood and permeate the various organs and tissues through lymphatic channels. They are the KGB or the FBI of the body, policing tissues for any sign of invading aliens or subversive activities. There are billions of lymphocytes in a body, each one belonging to a small clone with a very specific enemy-fixation. The foe for which a clone of lymphocytes is armed may never be encountered.

Indeed most virgin lymphochytes will die off, never having achieved their destiny.

The weapons that lymphocytes carry are called antibodies and, by a clever freak of economy, these antibodies can function as antennae, or radar, or whatever sophisticated signal-receiver analogy you fancy. Their busy mobility gives them every chance of encountering their particular Moriarty, if he is at large. It is their predestination and yet their high chance of expendability that is so remarkable. Even more mind-boggling is the juggling that goes on in the genes of virgin lymphocytes to ensure that the body is equipped with the standard, unimaginably vast repertoire of defence capabilities.

Let us miniaturise even further, shrink down to the size of chromosomes, and the vital antibody-making genes they carry. The genes that are the instruction manual for the business end of the antibodies are complex. They consist of segments of three types (VD and J) . In a new lymphocyte, a single segment from each category is selected (by a process that looks random, but almost certainly is not) and the three are spliced together as in a tape or roll of film. This is how the blueprint for each part of the antibody is constructed, which will determine the defence profile and which future progeny of the cell will carry. If the cutting and pasting process does not succeed, there is another chance to get it right using the second chromosome of a pair – rather like having two serves at tennis. The DNA map is prepared in this manner for all the parts of the antibody before assemblage actually begins and the antibody appears at the cell surface, ready for surveillance work.

Lymph nodes act as police stations where lymphocytes report back from their beat, and hope to meet scavenger cells carrying their own specific opposite number – an antigen – a felon who has been captured, lurking in the tissues somewhere. There has to be an exchange of passwords between co-operating immune cells to ensure no attacks are made on the body's own tissues. Only now, after meeting and being primed by its destined enemy, can the lymphocyte mature into a fully fledged fighter. Moreover it proliferates, self-replicates rapidly to produce a suitably sized army of lymphocytes, ready to charge out and set about eliminating the hordes of infectious intruders. Some of its progeny form long-living 'memory' cells, to provide an even swifter and more bloodthirsty response should a future attack by the same bug occur. The primed lymphocyte activates a 'hypermutation' mechanism in some of its own rearranged antibody genes, which may well be random, and serves to extend on the hoof, as it were, the killing capacity of its arms: broadening the spectrum of capability still further, in case the cunning invader has also taken another step in the arms race, and has new, hidden weapons

This is a grossly oversimplified account of a mind-bendingly complicated system. The immune system is beautifully tuned to prepare the body for (almost) any eventuality by permutation and combination at the genetic level; but only allowing that particular response where the external conditions are right, the correct button is pressed, the specific enemy targeted. Nature provides the potential; the environment acts as the trigger.

Where evolution has devised one mechanism that functions well, that mechanism is likely to be seen in other contexts. This system of inborn potential released by environmental triggers is, I believe, the mechanism underlying much of human behaviour. It certainly seems to be relevant to the great men in this book. Their behaviour patterns seem to be particularly simplistic because, once ensconced in splendour, they revert to a state of atavism. I have mentioned elsewhere the similarities between gene 'behaviour' and that of powerful people. The trigger is the perception of power in one's own control, and simple anticipation can sometimes set things in motion. The pattern responses recall adaptations from a remote past, millions of years ago, when our ancestors conducted jungle-style harems with an alpha male in charge. More common in present-day leaders are reminiscences of our pack-hunting, territorial forebears. But there are vestigial remnants of both living styles, with their associated sexual strategies.

Although Darwin's theory of evolution and its subsequent sophistication, notably Mendel's discoveries and Dawkins' selfish-gene theory, are accepted as scientific lore, there are plenty of Creationists around today, even in the scientific community, who argue that some Supreme Being must have designed all this, and remain in overall charge. I do not deny them their will-o'-the-wisp fantasies, for everyone needs myth to survive this troubled life. But no thinking person can seriously doubt that a good measure of human behaviour is inherited. The problem is to discover the chemical links between genes or gene clusters and the resulting behaviour pattern. Dawkins defines genes as the policy-makers, with brains as the executives. Brains control considerably more of my day-to-day behaviour than they do in my cat for instance. While I am puzzling away and writing about human oddities, she is sleeping at my feet or wheedling for her next meal. Dawkins argues that human brains may become so sophisticated that one day they will simply receive an instruction from the genes to do all that is needed to keep them alive. We are a long way from knowing what is best for us though, and our brains supremely bad at learning from history.

In experiments with animals, bees for instance, it can be shown that certain quite complex behaviours can certainly be passed on in a Mendelian way. Though the same experiments cannot be conducted in humans, it is clear from simple observation that, even in infancy, certain innate behaviours are established: the need to feed for instance, and the need to communicate very loudly if discomforts are felt and not immediately corrected. Communication in humans is a very good example of the nature-plus-environmental-trigger scheme I have described. All children have a capacity for learning languages (as well as a voice box). But unless they are in daily contact with speakers, they will not learn a language. Chimpanzees do not have a language centre in their brains. They have not evolved that ability, and no amount of earnest human input has been able to teach them to speak or to communicate meaningfully in words. So in humans it is legitimate to talk of a 'gene for language' even though that gene is virtual and we have no idea what it is.

There may be some people sceptical about a genetic capacity for behaviour being conserved over millions of years, as I have assumed that the capacity for alpha-male behaviour is, for instance. For those Doubting Thomases I will digress once more before returning to the heroes.

One of the examples of biological complexity that superficially looks as if it *must* have been purposely designed, is the eye. In fact, the evolution of a box-camera eye is not all that difficult, as Dawkins outlines in *Climbing Mount Improbable*. But the most intriguing part of this account relates to the light it casts on our common ancestry. In the mouse is a gene called 'small eye' that instructs the developing mouse to 'create an eye'. If the gene is absent or defective, the poor creature will be eyeless. An almost identical gene is present in humans and in the fruit-fly (and in molluscs, marine worms, sea-squirts and others) – identical in terms of DNA sequence. This is testimony to a common ancestor of all these animals (including ourselves) if you go back far enough. Scientists have removed the mouse 'small eye' gene and introduced it into developing fruit-fly embryos, on the leg instead of the head. Amazingly, the fruit-fly embryo obediently developed an eye on its leg. Even more amazingly this was not a mouse eye, but a compound insect eye.

Let this remarkable fact sink in. This particular mouse gene had been literally passed down from generation to generation for countless aeons until some meddlesome human transplanted it. It had been instructing creatures in those mega-ancient times, the times we cannot fathom even in imagination, when fruit-flies, humans and mice did not exist but their common ancestor did, to whom the 'small eye' gene said, 'Make a light-sensitive organ.' It did not carry the instruction manual, but simply the command to open it at the right page and get on with the job. It was around when eyes were presumably very simple affairs of specialised light-sensitive tissue, long before they had evolved to compound or camera-type eyes, or their various sub-varieties. This signal has been conserved for at least six hundred million years, and is still able to be interpreted in a modern context. It is therefore reasonable to suppose that an archaic gene for behaviour can also be so interpreted; and to be conserved over a mere six million years would be very small beer indeed.

In Chapter 4, I described the qualities that are recognised in young people that give them potential for leadership. Although there are some common defining features, the young versions of great men are marked by a fair amount of diversity. By contrast, look at the specimen at the peak of his powers and beyond. The arresting features here are the similarities rather than the contrasts. They are as startling and as mystifying as the similarities between identical twins. This first dawned on me when I read the book *When Illness Strikes the Leader* by Post and Robins, a truly insightful account which should be required reading for any politician or statesman. In the next chapter I shall assemble a prototype of a leader, gathering his parts from several examples. You will recognise him readily. He is not a clone, rather a sample of convergent evolution, and – would you believe it? – he is not actually very interesting, except as a specimen. Egocentric people are often, if we will but admit it, very boring to be around.

The central quality of leaders is selfishness. That has come through again and again in the stories in this book. Cosseted genes within our bodies pass this out as the most fundamental instruction. Our brains and our capacity to learn give us a multiplicity of other more sophisticated instructions, particularly how to cope in a highly socialised situation, replete with an overwhelming barrage of lifestyle choices. Morality is born at the social level, and is nothing to do with sex, everything to do with mutual back-scratching. In *The Selfish Gene*, Dawkins discusses how by means of game-theory, even with our innate selfishness, mutual kindness and co-operation can win out. While this is very comforting to know, there is the uncomfortable realisation that, wherever a power gradient develops – or even is perceived to be desirable – game-playing is ditched, and atavism takes over. Leaders abandon their brains as they grab the reins, and let their ancient genes direct them.

Yet leaders must work nonstop to maintain their position, and easily fool themselves that the grinding hard work is their response to duty, an indicator of altruism. Next to selfishness, deception (including self-delusion) and its close kin, secrecy, are hallmarks of the reversion to seed. Ruthlessness replaces competitiveness; eminence replaces charisma. Misogyny and nepotism supersede lust; cronyism takes over from alliance-making. A social conscience turns into tribalism. Pragmatism wins over principle. The metamorphosis is complete.

CHAPTER 15

Reverting to Seed

We accept rather too readily that our governments will be more or less corrupt and deceitful. The fact that we don't shout and get indignant is part of our lingering deference to the great ones. There is a league table in which some are manifestly worse than others, and though Western-style democracies are designed – more or less – to keep things on the straight and narrow, they fail. Much is done in secret, the electorate effectively excluded. Sometimes even the executive is excluded. We find out too late who the murderers and sinners are, like Richard Nixon and his secretary of state, Henry Kissinger. It was Kissinger's obsessional protection of his own secrecy that recommended him to Nixon's twisted mind. Kissinger, once labelled 'Mr Clean', is at some risk of being brought before a war crimes tribunal, for his part in the Vietnam war, the Pinochet coup and the Indonesian invasion of East Timor, but perhaps his worst crime of all was to collude in the deception of the American people that the president was a man of peace. Nixon was a mentally unstable disaster who seriously proposed using the nuclear bomb on Vietnam.

Italian Prime Minister Silvio Berlusconi is a wealthy businessman who controls Italy's three main private TV networks, owns its biggest publishing house, a major newspaper and the leading soccer team; a conglomerate of financial media and political muscle which his countrymen do not seem to view as anti-democratic. He does not sit on his companies' boards, but family members do. Berlusconi is familiar with charges of fraud, bribery, corruption and tax evasion, as in the course of his complex business life he has faced twelve; but none have stuck for a variety of reasons.

President Chirac of France has faced allegations of misuse of public funds to finance his summer holidays as well as enlarging his country estate. Various reports put the amounts at around three million French francs between 1992 and 1995. No proof of the reports is available because Chirac declined to answer judicial questions, as a president is entitled to do.

In Germany, Helmut Kohl, veteran chancellor of seventeen years faced allegations of financial impropriety a year after he had been voted out of office. He was forced to admit that he had circumvented the proper procedures in handling a network of secret accounts. These were not for personal gain, but donations to his party, the Christian Democratic Union Party. He admitted to receiving one million pounds on its behalf. The source and purpose of these moneys was not revealed. Further scandal surfaced in the shape of accusations that François Mitterand and the French government had handed over cash to keep Kohl in power; to maintain the strong Franco–German axis within the European Union. Kohl denied this. Mitterand's name was also linked with corruption scandals relating to a French oil company. The patrician Valery Giscard d'Estaing, recently reincarnated as head of the EU Convention, was not free from scandal in his presidential years. He liked to go big-game hunting with a murderous African despot, from whom he allegedly accepted a gift of diamonds without declaring them. This may have contributed to his defeat in the presidential election of 1981.

There is much secrecy surrounding the sale of British arms, which occupies 20% of the world's market. In spite of the vocal anti-arms lobby in the UK, and pious declarations about an ethical foreign policy, in 1999 Britain was still selling the British Aerospace Hawk jet trainer, a versatile craft that can be used for repression, as part of a three hundred million package to Indonesia, and more was planned. We have had other scandals: the Ecclestone money and tobacco advertising, the Hinduja money for passports, the Enron money for influence and the Mittal money for backing dubious steel business. The trouble is, when politicians plead they were not aware of a conflict of interest, I believe them. They simply lower their moral standards to accommodate those things they want, or find good excuses for them. We are all past masters at justifying our own ambitions, and stratospheric ones cause all else to pale into insignificance.

In opposition, politicians can afford to be people-orientated, to take up issues, to wholeheartedly support universal rights. But once in power, a man progressively loses touch with democracy. His inherent self-belief ensures this will happen. Self-belief rapidly transforms into a sense of mission, of fate, of walking with Destiny to a Great Future. If he is religious he will open a hotline to God. He will be convinced he has a job of work that only he can do; 'Miles to go before I sleep' believed Robert Kennedy of himself and all his clan. The path they walk is no longer the mundane one of social equality. They receive a blinding insight that their calling places them above the ordinary limiting laws.

Their calling necessitates them being more brilliant at everything and anything than any other person, and they become progressively less able to take advice, as Reagan was after his gun-shot wound. Democracy is no longer giving ear to the people you serve; it is convincing them of your superior capacity to know what is best for them. When the Conservatives in 1997 lost every seat in Scotland and Wales, the reason was apparently that those nations had not received the Tory message properly. Prime Minister Tony Blair has a distressing habit of lecturing like a public-school prefect when we, the people, are not on message, for instance over the safety of the MMR vaccine and GM foods. When issues are pushed so hard, we recognise there is another agenda, usually one of financial or prestigious significance. When professional groups prove stubborn for perfectly good reasons, they are given a tongue-lashing with labels such as 'wreckers' applied. This is the same tactic as that used in communist countries: 'enemies of the people', 'running dogs of imperialism', and 'capitalist roaders' ring ominously in the mind. Perhaps more dizzyingly out of touch in his halo of isolation, Pope Pius XII surrounded himself with reference books so that he could outsmart any expert in knowledgable discourse. Kruschev, simple and uneducated, yet overblown with flattery, believed in his own infallibility every bit as much as any pope, in his arbitrary decision-making and opinion-vaunting. Stalin simply purged anyone who was better than him in any capacity. Idi Amin did the same, with a particular penchant for intellectuals because his own learning was so meagre. In this book we have seen leaders unleash armies against their own people to establish their own personal power: Franco in the Spanish Civil War, Pope Innocent III against the Cathar heretics, Deng Xiaoping in Tiananmen Square. Confrontation may happen in more measured ways in democratic countries, but it is only a watered-down version of the same lordly delusion. Edward Heath faced the striking miners in 1974 and called a general election on the theme: 'Who governs the country?' The people considered he should have asked, 'Who elects governments?' and they showed him who did. Even in democracies, leaders have the power to disempower the electorate for their own reasons, as Indira Gandhi did. They can more subtly disenfranchise the voters by surrounding themselves with unelected, unaccountable cronies like Tony Blair's chum Derry Irvine, the lord chancellor, his press secretary Alastair Campbell, and the multiply resuscitated Peter Mandelson. And from Robert Mugabe with intimidation, to George W Bush with sophisticated electronic vote-losing, it appears to watchers that the wily wannabes find ways to bypass even the election process itself.

Once in place, a ruler rapidly acquires accretions, like a caddis-fly, of clinging loyal supporters. Some he will have carried with him through the difficult times. As time progresses, the honeymoon period is over – sooner in the democracies than in totalitarian states – and the leader gets a distressing feedback. As we've seen in Chapter 13, such an event signals a slump into depression, so the courtiers come to surround the great man, shield him from the worst, filter out impurities, feed him what he wants to hear. He loses touch with the people, becomes distant. The contrast is particularly regretted when he has been a long-term charismatic leader, a man of the people, such as Vaclav Havel had been. The cocooning of such a man happens physically as well as metaphorically: Presidents in their palaces, Popes in the Vatican, Mao Zedong in his swimming-pool suite in the Forbidden City, Hitler in his Berlin bunker. All of them acquire a set of bodyguards and chauffeur-driven cars, ostensibly for protection from assassination attempts. In reality the protection is more powerfully effective for the ego than the person, as I can testify from my three months as foreign secretary's wife. The psychological boost from being nannied in this way gives one an incredible sense of priceless untouchability.

Many leaders have discovered in their humble days, as Milosevic did, that the ability to move a crowd by oratory is intensely rewarding, heady and inspiring. It can be a one-shot habit-former, as it was with him. Those who discover, as Hitler did, that they have unexpected pulling power, make their whole career on that basis. Here begins narcissism, if it was not there to start with. Hitler, who wooed his crowds like a woman, had no love for them himself; the power and expression of adoration came entirely from them. In time, with recurrent recourse to the mass adulatory fix, a man becomes progressively empty of ability to love back. Those surrounding Hitler described him as almost robotic in his emotional responses; yet they went on servilely worshipping him. Albert Speer, travelling with him on a train during the war, described how they were seated at a dining table enjoying a sumptuous meal, immune from wartime austerity. At a station, a troop train drew alongside, jammed with injured, weary, hollow-eyed and hungry fighting men. Panic-stricken, Hitler peremptorily ordered the blinds drawn down. He was no longer the omnipotent deity, and returned no warmth of compassion.

Those who loved Jack Kennedy, men and women alike, observed how shallow was his own reaction to any person. Mao's doctor learned that he had no core of warmth, no feeling of relatedness or love for his people. Stalin had no compunction whatever about the lives he wasted. His nemesis for such coldness was stifling paranoia. Lenin even shocked his own family with his ruthlessness as he decreed that peasants could expect to starve to relieve towns and factories, in support of his New Economic Plan. Napoleon once admitted he sacrificed his men in the Italian campaign to show off to his latest lady love. Yet these stone-cold men could shed easy tears when moved by their own oratory or some banal display of kitsch sentiment – true of Franco, Cromwell (tagged 'a greeting devil' by a cynical Scot), Clinton, J Edgar Hoover and Robert Maxwell.

Most of the characters in this book have been convinced to a variable degree of their messianic status. Trouble looms when one world saviour clashes with another, as happened in the Second World

War, when Churchill and Roosevelt busily stoked each other up in a secret correspondence denigrating Charles de Gaulle. He was too absorbed in his own personal career, they wrote, unconscious of any irony, exalted as he was to hero status by his BBC broadcasts to Occupied France. Narcissism was a key feature of all the Soviet leaders of the 20th century, reaching ridiculous extremes in a culture of fawning and flattery, no different from the courts of absolute monarchs. Gorbachev the reformer struggled to rise above all that, refusing medals and the more syrupy extremes of leader-worship. Yet like his predecessors he loved to see his speeches in print, and his collected works (even those of a functional nature) appeared almost overnight in multiple volumes in beautiful leatherwork covers. Hundreds of thousands of unread tomes from previous leaders already languished unread on bookshelves, but one's own work has special status. Gorbachev loved to walk with the other world statesmen, and in their company spoke – but did not listen. He considered himself a king of kings. The praise and column inches accorded to him in Western media certainly turned his head. He became boastful, savoured his elevation, and engaged in a vicious, jealous struggle with the rising, unburdened Yeltsin. He began to see enemies in society. Confrontational labels began to appear in Politburo-speak: 'opportunists', 'radicals', anti-communists', 'regionalists'. Such a man is so absorbed in his own perorations and their effect that he loses his listening capacity altogether. He is increasingly distanced from the warmth of human contact. Two-way conversations are our form of grooming after all, and I suspect the seeds of depression lie sprouting there.

Narcissism leaves the great one open to ridicule. Hitler and Mussolini both needed reading glasses, but hated to be seen wearing them. Robert Maxwell dyed his hair and powdered his face. Once when not greeted with sufficient éclat and limelight at Jeffrey Archer's London penthouse, Maxwell stalked off in a huff after ten minutes. Lord Horatio Nelson's vanity was peculiarly naive for he craved honours that would be conspicuous to the eye, such as the Order of the Bath, whose visible expression was a shiny, showy star. Titles he loved, even more than the income they brought, but the decorations pleased him most. He went on to collect a glittering galaxy of medals, ribbons and bows, emblems, crosses, gold braid, crowns, pips and brass, his favourite a spray of Turkish diamonds. A contemporary wrote caustically that he sat to every painter in London. Nelson adorned himself with his decorations at the Battle of Trafalgar, making himself an eyecatching target for even a modest marksman, probably bringing about his own death. The vulgar delight in gaudy gongs was shared by Soviet leaders, especially Brezhnev and Chernenko, and by Saddam Hussein, who has awarded himself every civil and military medal Iraq has to offer. He is said to be very sensitive about his image in the Western media, and foams with rage if lampooned in unflattering cartoons.

A love affair with one's own voice is common to leaders, and many gauge their personal influence by the media response, others by the length of their speeches. In power circles, speaking is vital. Silence is taken for submission. One exploiter of that principle was William Gladstone, whose speeches in the House of Commons could last four hours, and who in old age could lose touch with time altogether. Disraeli's first budget speech as chancellor of the exchequer lasted five hours. Kruschev's monologues to visiting communist groups could last six hours or more, and Fidel Castro in his seventies spoke for seven and a half hours to an Irish human rights delegation. Interruptions are often direct, gladiatorial challenges. Gorbachev would try to destabilise and cow Yeltsin by repeated interruptions in the Politburo. But this is only one of several ways that leaders invade and domineer the time of lesser mortals. Hitler's famous 'table-talk' and Churchill's dinnertime monologues have been mentioned. According to Lord Alanbrooke, Churchill was frustratingly prone to commandeer and occupy everyone's time, with frequent phone calls, instant changes of plan, creating of superfluous yet urgent work, and calling of meetings at a moment's notice at the most awkward possible times. Making calls in the early hours of the morning is a useful ploy for gaining a psychological advantage, as Indira Gandhi used to her advantage to announce the emergency to her cabinet. Mussolini would keep his cabinet up through the night till 5 a.m. to gain some trivial point. Bill Clinton was renowned for habitual lateness, unable to discipline himself and heedless of the disruption to everyone else. Albert Speer found himself summoned urgently to Hitler's presence even from distant holiday locations, only to find after a difficult journey that the pressing conference had been postponed.

The overwhelming need to get big results instantly, a reprehensible facet of politics generally, is seen in individuals. Cromwell, Napoleon and Lenin were all of a choleric and impatient type, sometimes taking too many projects on simultaneously so that plans were dropped, botched, half-completed, stripped apart but not restructured. Yet many great ones had a short attention span, born perhaps of doing things in a tremendous hurry – Kruschev for instance. Joe Kennedy and his son Jack were both quickly bored, seeking the excitement of change and conquest. Mussolini and Napoleon were restless, with low boredom threshholds and limited concentration spans. Churchill's fidgety globetrotting as wartime PM was of a similar nature, and Robert Maxwell's jet-setting was as much propelled by *ennui* as by narcissism. These themes are not contradictory: the great man's time is infinitely valuable, whatever he chooses to do with it; everyone else's can be dispensed like Smarties.

The competitive instinct, fundamental to all life, does not wither when the rising star becomes the ruler, but may have a different expression. The regicides no doubt felt that, after toppling a king, who could challenge them? Some pursued a scorched-earth policy, as Stalin did. Napoleon sent impudent challenges to the pope, demanding he renounce his temporal power, and arresting him when he refused. There can be cross-global skirmishing by contenders who never meet, as we have seen with Churchill and Hitler. The media giants Rupert Murdoch and Robert Maxwell in 1968 engaged in legal acrimony in their bids to buy the *News of the World* newspaper.

The worst near-fatal confrontation of the 20th century grew out of the fear by various American administrations of Fidel Castro and Cuba; the horror of having communists in their backyard. Cuba became a political football in the 1960 presidential election, which Kennedy, scandalously irresponsible, used to whip up tribal terror. Castro made things worse by predicting a full-scale American invasion of Cuba. During the Cold War, capitalist–communist battles tended to be fought out in Developing World territory in a manner analogous to wild animals engaging by intimidation rather than head-on. People in power like to feel good in themselves and to see that feeling reflected in their own people's eyes, so if dirty deeds must be done, they are best carried out at arm's length. So Jack Kennedy permitted the plotting of Castro's assassination (via the Mafia apparently) concurrently with an invasion of Cuba by specially trained Cuban exiles, at the Bay of Pigs. It was a humiliating disaster for Kennedy, and prompted an obsession with Castro, a desire for revenge ('Don't get mad: get even,' was his father's invariable advice), which Bobby Kennedy fostered even more hawkishly on his brother's behalf. Contemporaries agree that the Kennedy fixation on Castro was disproportionate, and more of a personal vendetta than a legitimate presidential concern. American hostility drove Castro into closer liaison with the USSR, forging trade, ideological and military links with them. Meanwhile, an unprepared Kennedy was bullied by a harsh, combative Kruschev at the Vienna Summit in 1961, over the issue of the brain drain from East Berlin to West. While Kruschev ever had to watch his back and deliver the goods, Kennedy only associated such blatant, in-your-face confrontation with his father, not his equals.

The Kennedy brothers were indeed steaming ahead, planning in secret for a full-scale invasion of Cuba. Operation Mongoose was an ill-conceived, ill-starred project, which luckily was overtaken by other events. It was not as secret as it should have been, and it ought to have been no surprise to find that Kruschev had been delivering and installing nuclear missiles on Cuba. The world watched and trembled with fear as the two giants faced each other, high on adrenalin and testosterone. Kruschev and Kennedy both knew that to back down safely, each had to save face. In the event, Kruschev removed his Cuban missiles (to the fury of Castro, who had become a bit-player), while Kennedy removed some antiquated weapons from Turkey. Back home, Kennedy's image machine worked to create a tough, gallant, dragon-slaying Galahad. Reading accounts from aides of each Big K, one is struck anew by the mirror-image of conduct on both sides during the stand-off. The steely determination of each man for apparent head-on collision could not be deflected by his subservient colleagues. The deference due to the totalitarian dictator in his supposedly egalitarian state, and the reverence given to the iconic president in his nominally democratic country, were matched in every way. Even the downfall of each man, two or three years later, may well have been the end result of a chain of events that started here.

Men of power are seldom satisfied with ruling in their own countries. Their fix needs to increase in dosage; their influence seeks to extend to other lands. There is not a single national ruler mentioned here that has not set his sights on distant horizons. Napoleon, that mega expander, even had an Oriental complex. Franco dreamed of restoring the old Spanish empire. Saddam Hussein aspires to dominate all Arab nations. Mrs Thatcher had her moment of reflected glory in the Falklands. John Major had his in the Gulf War. Tony Blair's most sacred and exalted mission so far has been in Afghanistan. Kennedy's posturing against Castro and Kruschev was a trigger for his increasing involvement in Southeast Asia, with the creation of a secret Vietnam Task Force. No rationally argued international judgement this, as a number of his close aides observed – it was a visceral response to all that had gone before. The war was handed like a live grenade to the next two Presidents, L B Johnson and Nixon.

An assessment of Kennedy's historical perspective was made by a contemporary Harvard historian, David Herbert Donald, who met the president in 1962. To Kennedy, American history was a distillate of great men and their doings, and how he would stand shoulder-to-shoulder among them. Kennedy idolised Lincoln and F D Roosevelt because, he said, to be a great president you have to be a wartime president. Donald not unnaturally found this scary. But the lure of miltary glory seems to be specifically irresistible to an individual in power. The Second World War happened at the behest of one man – Hitler. Oliver Cromwell's motto was 'Let Peace be sought through war'. Charles de Gaulle was a soldier through and through and glorified the military life as a supreme end in itself. Churchill's adoration of 'glorious, delicious war' was legendary. And Henry Kissinger, in a moment of rare honesty, admitted that Indochina was bombarded during the Nixon administration because 'a sudden withdrawal might give us a credibility problem'. We are back to face-saving, for which, in this war, over twenty thousand American servicemen died, not to mention the half-million 'enemy' and over three million civilians (at a conservative estimate). To men of power, military honours are carried like trophies, like Nelson's bullet-guiding baubles, visible expressions of their manliness, their dominance, their extended phenotype. Make your ears deaf to their justifications. This – as Henry Kissinger owned – is what it is all about.

To become a leader stereotype, an individual must undergo a degree of change. To those who, like Churchill, sparkled with singularity from the word go, little adjustment is seen. But some leaders must metamorphose as radically as any insect, and this is remarked on in biographies. We have seen how tragically Vaclav Havel fell away from being a man of the people. Another such is Boris Yeltsin. By the time he trod the world's stage, we saw a harsh and overbearing type, struggling with illness and an undignified drink problem, oblivious of his steep decline, more buffoon than statesman. He finally departed like a soldier in retreat, covering his back and his getaway by skin-saving shady deals. Yet at his best he had been an honest, dependable fellow, a dynamo, a populist, a man content with his hands-on role as provincial Party chief, and who resisted being drawn into the Moscow rat-race. When he became Moscow Party boss he could still be seen travelling on buses and standing in queues at the market. He stopped the senior privileges, quashed the black markets and the corruption, and declined a luxury villa and a personal plane. He dared to defy entrenched venality, dared even to criticise the steep, subservient hierarchy with Gorbachev at the top. The confrontation between the two men propelled them both towards the stereotype.

As the Russian Republic's first president, Yeltsin's inherent weaknesses became manifest. Inevitably there were economic problems which were used to make challenges against him. Then came his Waterloo in the shape of Chechnya. Can any leader resist augmenting his reputation by feats of arms? Yeltsin could not, even though his people opposed it. He had passionately advocated greater autonomy for the Soviet Republics, yet brutally sanctioned military suppression of the Chechnyan breakaway. This was a war in which neither side was right; it was messy, savage, unwinnable. And Yeltsin could not cope. No longer the honest, sturdy saint, he isolated himself, hid from public view and learned to lie to wriggle out of painful inquiries. He became introspective, depressed and lethargic. Suddenly his drinking became an issue. He had always consumed like a Russian, probably more than was good for him, but never before in such a destructive way. He became clownish, an object of ridicule and shame. His brisk energy translated into bearish bad temper, frank ill-humour. He began to treat underlings with crushing condescension. Secrecy, intrigues, the exploitation of power, summary demotions and dismissals, the trappings of an autocrat – all these became his new ways.

Metamorphoses of similar suddenness have been seen in the lives of Milosevic, of Osama bin Laden, of Oliver Cromwell and Vladimir Lenin. Bill Clinton's nemesis seemed to come after his 1980 defeat for a second term as governor of Arkansas. One colleague said that at this point he lost his guts; from then on his sole aim was to get and stay elected. 'He made his deal with the devil.'

In 1973, Augusto Pinochet and his wife Lucia wrote a letter of treacly affection and eternal friendship to a couple, José and Victoria Morales de Toha, with whom they were on regular visiting terms. The Tohas were high in the Allende government circle. Two months later, four days after the coup that deposed Allende, Pinochet sent José Toha to a remote prison island where he was treated with contempt, forced to do manual work, and exposed to the harsh elements. He died within a few months, of possible suicide, illness or murder. This betrayal of fellowship coincided with Pinochet's own diabolical pact. Napoleon's emergence from transitional to supreme autocratic status came after the Battle of Austerlitz in 1806. And few match Mussolini's Mephistophelian capacity for political opportunism, transforming himself from socialist, anti-bourgeois, anti-military revolutionary to fascist dictator and henchman of Hitler, as chance decreed.

The capacity for metamorphosis is only one of the inconsistencies that we've seen. Other examples are Cromwell's extremes of tenderness and ruthlessness; Napoleon's imperial aspirations and yet his belief in the rights of man; Martin Luther King's florid sex life in the midst of his unsullied pious reputation; Pope Alexander VI's spending wantonly on visible expressions of splendour, yet mean as a Lenten fast towards his own household.

Make no mistake, the transmutated animal is not at all a nice or charming animal. Any charisma he once possessed has been turned to more practical use: as an aura of fear, as in the case of Saddam Hussein. Stalin had the same. Osama bin Laden, silent and shy, is said to carry a threatening miasma around him, born of his reputation for inflicting unlimited terror. Others with less confidence or less ruthlessness draw attention to themselves through sheer size: for example, Robert Maxwell, all 22 stone of him. His bulk was a manifestation of his conspicuous consumption – of smoked salmon, lobster, caviare, Krug champagne and port, besides more durable luxuries such as yachts, planes, royally grandiose apartments, and other people's money, even his own employees' pension funds.

Riches are used to vaunt as well as indulge oneself, as was the Shah of Iran's re-creation of ancient Persepolis in the form of a fabulously luxurious tented city in 1971. Here he threw a bash for half the world's heads of state – the richer half of course – costing around £165 million, at a time when most of his countrymen were mired in poverty. The ostensible reason for the celebration was the 2,500th anniversary of the first Persian Empire, with whose roots the Shah wished to align his own origins. The tents were furnished with all the finest-quality carpets, drapes and fittings by a Paris designer. Crystal, linen, caviare and champagne came from the most expensive sources.

In the reign of the geriatric leaders of the USSR, Andropov – in accordance with the metamorphosis principle – had at first tried to obliterate privilege. But Chernenko soon worked him round to approving high pension rates, the best of medical care, and use of the black stretch limousines and suitably appointed country dachas for the elderly top brass. Jack Kennedy's Air Force One plane was described as 'plush as a mansion' with a presidential bedroom suite suitable for his style of entertaining. In Hitler's entourage, the greed and the hedonism in 1944 was such that the Gauleiters were building themselves hunting lodges and palaces, diverting labour

and material from the war effort, and when ensconced in splendour
enjoying a well-stocked board and choice wines, untroubled by
rationing. Their protection diverted further desperately needed
stocks and labour to build rabbit warrens of bunkers with roofs
several inches thick. Goering's birthday that same year brought him
cartloads of valuable gifts – gold bars, luxury cigars, famous works
of art – which were extorted from colleagues who knew better than
to refuse, even in the desolate waste that Germany had become.

Like Boris Yeltsin, the seasoned leader often has a short fuse and
a ferocious temper; it is unwise to cross him or provoke him too far.
Bill Clinton was known by his house staff for his 'purple fits'.
Napoleon, Saddam Hussein, Adolf Hitler, Sam Giancana the
hoodlum chief, all worked themselves into spectacular, intimidating
histrionic and often bogus rages. Oliver Cromwell could crank up
his righteous indignation to a state of near-dementia in which he let
rip with the most unparliamentary language. Lenin in a bad mood,
nervous the day before a major speech, would terrorise even his
worshipful sister by his bad language and loss of control. Kruschev
was boorishly aggressive, Gorbachev a steam roller in contentious
debate who used curses and colourful language to flatten opponents.
Robert Maxwell liked to bark his orders in his deep powerful voice
over intercoms and telephone lines, terrorising employees,
demanding their instant compliance and cutting short any feeble
response. If required, he too could explode volcanically. Mussolini
seemed a master of rage and invective until he met and was
outclassed by Hitler.

All this is supremely primitive behaviour, straight from the ear-
shattering, intimidating display of the alpha male ape. The awesome
histrionics rely on both visual and auditory impact, and humans can
augment the performance by the choice of coarse and obscene
language, shocking their victims by gutter-speak in exalted places.
Mussolini and Jack Kennedy could be verbally abusive when their
women displeased them, and Mussolini liked to shout and talk dirty
as he made love. L B Johnson's choice of words could be earthy and
obscene, especially when drunk. He had no compunction about
contravening all the laws of measured social behaviour. Once as
president, and anxious to hold on in the face of a possible new

Kennedy threat, he felt challenged to the core on the subject of JFK's sex exploits. In the presence of the prim and inhibited J Edgar Hoover and other FBI agents, he unbuttoned, extracted his penis and displayed it on a glass-topped table, asking if Mr Kennedy could have 'measured up to the size of that motherfucker?'. Courtesy is often coded deference, and such boorish behaviour is the opposite, a coded put-down. Cleopatra's father was similarly humiliated by the Roman statesman and orator Cato, being received by him just as he was in the process of receiving his enema.

These high-ranking people had other astonishingly similar habits. It is remarkable how many of them have been inept to the point of helplessness in everyday activities. Others were no doubt protected from their own inadequacies by the army of women surrounding them. Hitler's personal appearance in his ruling years was immaculate, but in his struggling and lonely era in the streets and dosshouses of Vienna he could not be particular; and during the crumbling of the empire, in the Berlin bunker, he would show signs of recurring slovenliness. Mussolini, in his youth gladly adopted the Bohemian image, dirty, unkempt, with several days' growth of stubble on his chin. Even when he became head of state, on visiting terms with royalty, he neglected to shave (a task that he never mastered). His collars were dirty, he didn't change his shirt, never found a regular bath necessary, and was ever reluctant to clean his teeth. He would souse himself in eau-de-Cologne as an alternative to washing, and his apartment stank of the cloying scent. He did not perceive the shabbiness of his garb, his unpressed trousers, dilapidated shoes, frayed linen and scruffy hat. Even in uniform he was splattered with food residues. Mao Zedong's distaste for bathing and teeth-cleaning has been noted, and he also disliked formal dressing (he received Kruschev in his swimming-pool area, clad in his bathrobe). Cromwell in his early parliamentary career was as untidy and unkempt in dress as he was rude in speech. Bill Clinton's style as he emerged from academe to the real world in the seventies was of scruffy, untidy informality: dirty jeans, a profusion of disordered curly hair and a beard. After the Arkansas defeat he smartened himself up considerably. But when at home in the White House, his domestic gear was casual to say the least, with sweat clothes, sporty gear and baseball caps.

Robert Maxwell's maids had much to put up with, for his personal habits were deliberately disgusting. He would blow his nose into a napkin, and after solitary TV suppers the food remainders would be tossed down on the floor along with soiled clothing. He would leave the toilet unflushed after use, and wipe his bottom with new face towels, discarding them on the floor. One does not have to go far back in nature to find arrogant, dominant male animals marking their territory with their excreta and body smells. It is only subordinate animals who cover up their ordure.

David Lloyd George as a young parliamentarian, staying on his own in a London flat, worked on his wife Margaret to come and look after him by magnifying his domestic incompetence. He would forget to send his laundry home and not change his underpants for weeks. Letters home are full of complaints about his hard bread and chaotic flat. Yet he managed to gain a reputation for his sleek, smart appearance. Those close to him, including his wife/mistress Frances Stevenson, observed that he was astonishingly helpless in little ways, like finding socks, and she, of course, pandered to this incapacity. When installed at 10 Downing Street, he could never open windows, and the dining-room doorknob defeated him altogether. To prevent him losing his temper, a minion had to leap forward and do it for him. As a traveller he was forgetful, leaving a trail of belongings at each stopping-place. I sometimes wonder if my ex-husband Robin Cook is a reincarnation of Lloyd George, for there are uncanny similarities. Napoleon, whose supporters worshipped him as totipotent, was clumsy and incapable at all the fundamental techniques of the military life. He was an incompetent horseman, falling off his horse three times in one campaign. He was bad at target shooting and failed dismally as a naval commander.

Men such as Bill Clinton who hold positions of authority at a young age, enjoy and exploit the capacity to blur the margin between their own and government resources. In the governor's mansion at Little Rock, the domestic staff came with the job: a liberal supply of cooks, housekeepers, maids, nannies, chauffeurs and the local prison inmates were put to work in the garden as well as on Bill's own property. But Bill was apparently a freeloader from youth on, forgetting to pay his bills as a student and sponging off his friends, never carrying cash so that someone in his entourage had to pick up the tab for petrol, coffee and snacks. Later in official life, such habits were ingrained. He could not cope with practicalities that ordinary mortals perform in their sleep: writing cheques, maintaining cars, percolating coffee, balancing the books.

This quirky shortcoming, which surprisingly seems to have gone largely unchallenged by his friends, disguises a more ugly meanness, greed and acquisitiveness, and Bill was not unique in that respect. He shared it, as so many things, with generations of Kennedys. Joe Kennedy, who would lavish money on his own comfort and his family's advancement, was as mean as they come in other ways. He liked to buy and own huge houses but never bothered to maintain or adorn them. His Palm Beach home was crumbling and shabby with economy-style furnishings. As with Thatcher, society was an alien concept to him. There was no sense of duty, of owing and giving back; society was simply something to be trodden underfoot in the race to get there first. Robert Kennedy as attorney general expected his minions to pay cabs, tips and bills when travelling. His brother Jack's stinginess was legendary, for he never carried money or expected to pay his share in restaurants and bars. Official aides of both brothers learned eventually to carry around books of blank Kennedy cheques, and insist on a signature as needed.

Mussolini had a spurious reputation for generosity, but only with government funds. With petty expenses he tended to borrow and forget to return, or just let other people have the privilege of paying for him. Il Duce identified himself with the state, and its funds therefore became his own. At Fascist rallies, a policeman would follow with a bag of largesse, which he would throw to his supporters. He lost touch with the value of money, and had no idea of how much it cost to live. He was penny-pinching with his mistresses, though Claretta Petacci circumvented the problem by relying on his name for credit. Lenin, who relied on his family for his keep, was cheese-paring when it came to giving presents to them.

Gladstone, Disraeli and Churchill were not at all averse to freeloading on a magnificent scale, and behaved as if the paid holidays and string-free loans they attracted were their due. Disraeli and Churchill were extricated from major financial embarrassment this way. Churchill was also noted for his parsimony with praise and gratitude to those close to him, as Lord Alanbrooke observed.

Leaders also have remarkably similar leisure interests; not that they have much time to relax. Someone – was it Nicky Fairbairn? – once said that television is not something you watch, it is something you appear on. Nevertheless, the fascination with cinema is common to a great many, that medium with its capacity for flights of fancy – among modern men at least (in Disraeli's time, the theatre occupied the passion for spectacle). Ronald Reagan, himself an ex-B movie star, sometimes had to be dragged, disgruntled, from his cowboy films to sign state papers. J Edgar Hoover had similar tastes in westerns. Mao Zedong enjoyed war films from the US and those with a martial-arts theme. As his health failed, cinema equipment was set up near his swimming-pool base, and all his staff were compelled to watch as long as he did, to the small hours of the morning. Now he could only satisfy his libido by watching explicit rape scenes. Movie-watching was staple after-dinner entertainment for Hitler's entourage, mainly frothy trivia, reinforcing the banality of the cultural level. Stalin had projection equipment in the Kremlin and in his dacha, where he watched one or two films a week, for escapism as he recognised. The soldier Franco preferred films to his military duties, and they continued to feed his fantasy life. The Kennedy tribe were intimately connected at many points with the glittering world of Hollywood, which had for them a moth–candle attraction, as it did for their contemporary and alleged supporter, Mafia murderer Sam Giancana. Robert Maxwell assuaged his need for indulgence and his loneliness by watching adventure video films on board his yacht *Lady Ghislaine* and his jet.

For their sports preferences, these warriors choose, in the main, hunting and swimming. A passion for blood sports has been remarked in several lives, including those of Cromwell, Lenin, Mussolini, Franco, Churchill and Eisenhower. The regularity of a water fetish is a possible coincidence, but I think not. Maybe this too can be attributed to an archaic pattern of behaviour. All mammals, ourselves included, show they spent some time in a watery medium by traces of gills in embryonic life. Matt Ridley argues that many things hint at a watery interlude in our distant ancestors' lives: our capacity to swim, to devise and practise watersports, our dependence on water, our recourse to a fishy diet, and our love of beaches. Some fossil evidence suggests the human hand has evolved from the fish fin. Swimming has been a preoccupation of Gladstone, Mao Zedong, Lenin, Brezhnev, Mussolini, Jack Kennedy, Richard Nixon, Bill Clinton and Robert Maxwell. Napoleon loved to luxuriate in hot baths; Jack Kennedy would shower five times daily. Churchill's bath-times were as much of a ritual as those of a child, and he seems to have spent hours in there, expecting vast quantities of hot water even in the most remote places.

Confrontation and competing being the life-blood of the successful ones, inevitably risk-taking is a major facet of their daily lives. It appears in several forms: financial (Disraeli, Joe Kennedy, Robert Maxwell), fast driving (Jack and Robert Kennedy, Bill Clinton, Hitler, Mussolini, Pope Pius XII), scorning safety measures (Franco, Churchill, Nelson, Robert Kennedy) and sexual (the Kennedys, Clinton, Gladstone, Asquith, Lloyd George and many others). Yet, paradoxically, many are seized with paranoia and take excessive precautions for their own safety, as Saddam Hussein does. His thousands of guards, recruited at fourteen or fifteen from his own area of Iraq, are indoctrinated with loyalty at an impressionable and submissive age.

Leaders' family relations follow well-defined patterns. A number show unexpected fondness for children, and pleasure in their company; this is true of Cromwell, JFK, Pinochet, Lenin, Hitler, Pope Pius IX and J Edgar Hoover. By contrast, a nasty streak of misogyny is too readily apparent. Both Napoleon and Cromwell would semi-accidentally spill drinks or coffee over a woman's dress, destroying her finery – a recognised form of not-so-subtle aggression. Napoleon's ambivalence took many forms, flowering in the Napoleonic Code, which delivered a belly-blow to the incipient emancipation emerging from the Revolution. In it the woman was disadvantaged in marital relationships, divorce, charges of adultery and autonomy. Nixon, Churchill and Franco have already been seen to be averse to women – or frightened of them. Pope Pius XII looked down from a great height on women's humble status, decreeing that 'the female person' should never presume to approach the High Altar. Both Lord Nelson and Lloyd George kept a wife and a mistress simultaneously and treated their respective wives with spiteful hostility, blaming them for neglect and lack of appreciation of their spouse's genius. Nelson's viciousness towards his wife escalated after his daughter was born to his mistress, Lady Hamilton, and extended to her son by a previous marriage. Vaclav Havel was unkind to Olga, his wife, and his letters show him to be a master of the art of put-down and back-handed compliments. Olga had a facility for writing which contrasted with Havel's own, and he was jealous. He would flaunt his conquests, sending love to his girlfriends in his letters to her.

Misogyny at first sight, in the evolutionary order of things, seems strange. Again we must not be misled into thinking of evolution as some benign, marian, forward-thinking deity. In biology, misogyny is common and is explained on the basis of sexual selection and sexual conflict. In the insect world a male would-be copulator has to compete with other contenders not only for access to a given female, but for his sperm to succeed in fertilising her. The longer he mates, the more probable his success. Male genitalia of insects have developed all kinds of elaborate mechanisms in the arms race that is the gender war, 'designed' to lengthen copulation (spines and hooks to cling on) and to clear out other sperm (lengthy penises). The prickly appendages damage the female and may cause her early demise, though only after she has produced her eggs. In other species (hamadryas baboons for instance, who are relatively close to us in evolutionary terms), damage and pain inflicted in love-making is common, and the purpose seems to be to deter females from seeking other mates. In humans, crass, insensitive coupling and rape have their origins here, but also in the male fear of being overtaken by other men, and the desire to control and diminish women.

Last in the theme of family relationships is kin selection. As if to verify Dawkins' 'selfish gene' elaboration of evolutionary theory, the history of the papacy has been a story of nepotism, whether the nephews were genuine or a euphemism for sons born on the wrong side of the blanket. But there have been plenty of non-clerical examples, too. Within the Kennedy clan, amid all the dynastic self-seeking, the appointment of Bobby Kennedy as Attorney General was particularly blatant. Cromwell engaged as his closest henchmen those many men related to him by marriage. Napoleon ejected the Bourbons from France and Italy and installed members of his family to govern parts of his empire, which stretched at its peak from the Atlantic to the Russian frontier. They ruled (in his name) parts of Switzerland, Tuscany, the Kingdom of Italy, Naples, Spain, Holland and Westphalia. Saddam Hussein has followed an obsessive formula of making family members his political allies, which has not necessarily saved them from falling painfully out of favour, or him from lapses of loyalty. Richard Nixon in his grandiose plans at the start of his second term in office was probably trying to emulate the Kennedys as he planned for his brother and his two daughters' husbands to run for Congress.

Tribalism is a heritage from many layers of our past, perhaps most particularly from the hunting era. For primitive peoples in a community of maybe 150, even the people in the next valley were hostiles, and wandering a few miles from home into alien territory could invite swift annihilation. Recognising your own clan and the limits of your own territory was vital to survival. Small wonder that we see elements of it in modern behaviour, etched most acutely in those who live on the edge, standing out from the crowd, courting danger: the leaders of all authoritative institutions.

But strong tribal instincts have as their inevitable flip-side, racial prejudice – 'racial' interpreted in the widest possible sense. There have been plenty of examples already in this book; now I am drawing the threads together. Lenin has been called a 'social racist', and the same apellation can be applied to any protaganist of a single ideology, a single class of society, a single religious credo. We have seen how ruthlessly Pope Innocent III, Lenin, Stalin, Franco, Hitler, Pinochet and Osama bin Laden exterminated people of the class they hated, using the language of purification – ethnic cleansing, racial purity, crusade, holy war. The same rhetoric is current in the Balkans, the Middle East, Northern Ireland, Iraq, among all Islamic fundamentalists.

Yet tribalism can be sinister and freedom-eroding even when

practised in more subtle ways, and most especially by those with sufficient power to be discriminatory. The first step is to besmirch people with labels, a technique used to effect in communist states – enemies of the people and the rest. Labels of any sort are meant to be demeaning: Yids, niggers, Pakis, Chinkies, dykes, queers, Proddies... wreckers. The facility of us all to divide the world into 'us and them' is something we have to work to get past. Abraham Lincoln loathed slavery, yet he never believed that blacks were equal to whites, and favoured segregation. He was only partly emancipated in his understanding. Those modern leaders who never – or hardly ever – leave their own countries keep their tribal instincts intact and sensitively tuned – Thatcher, Mao, George W Bush, J Edgar Hoover. They are the ones who should be last in the queue for ruler or director status. Those religions that practise the highest degree of exclusivity are simply organised tribalism in another guise: most particularly Roman Catholicism and some forms of Islam.

One of the most archetypal tribalists to swagger in recent times was J Edgar Hoover, director of the FBI for nearly fifty years. His principle characteristics were two-fold, territoriality and an obsessive enemy fixation. He held his directorship against many challenges till his death at 75, and expanded his domain with far-reaching tentacles of illegal and sinister powers. Anyone who crossed or defied him was victimised. Much was done in secret, and all justified on the pretext of the protection of the American people against the enemy within. In early manhood, Hoover was convinced of his calling to separate right from wrong. Unfortunately, as with every one of us, his perspective of morality was a personal one with himself at the centre, the still reference point of the world that turned on his own axis. And like so many men before him, led by their archaic drives, he did not distinguish between the 'sin' and the 'sinner'. In the context of modern free America, he did not send them to the guillotine or the stake, but his undercover vendettas led to despair, shattered reputations and careers, ruined marriages and to suicide. How close he was to the criminal underworld of the Mafia is a subject for speculation, because he never made an enemy of them, never targeted them, and for decades denied that organised crime existed in America. There is evidence to show that, by rapidly 'solving' the assassination of J F Kennedy, he obstructed the course of true justice and may have actually covered up the Mafia involvement in this murder, and those of Robert Kennedy and Martin Luther King.

Hoover's career in the FBI in the early days was strongly influenced by the upheaval of the Russian Revolution, when radicals and Russian immigrants in the States became the focus of much national paranoia and harassment, labelled 'alien filth'. Hoover's first enemy, on whom he opened a file, was a Jewish attorney who had objected to the institutional violence in those Red raids. From the deporting of anarchists, radicals and communists to the 'Reds under the bed' activities of Senator Joseph McCarthy, and thence to the anti-war campus protests of the sixties, Hoover identified communists with all that was evil and disruptive in society. He kept files on all potential subversives, and these were nearly all political rather than security risks. He kept a spectacular 'enemy list' on whom he squirrelled away scurrilous information. Such material was power, and he used it ruthlessly to manoeuvre and to blackmail. Besides communists, Hoover had phobias about Jews, blacks, the United Nations, the English – any foreigners in fact. And about homosexuals or protesters of any hue – gay lib, women's lib – any who opposed him, crossed him or offended him. He was also neurotic about germs and flies! In time he would keep information on friends too. Prominent names who earned fat files were Bill Donovan (founder of the Office of Strategic Services), First Lady Eleanor Roosevelt, Secretary of State John Foster Dulles, Head of the CIA Allen Dulles, presidential candidate Adlai Stevenson, President Truman, Secretary of the Treasury Henry Morgenthau, black activist Martin Luther King, all the Kennedys, and the 'three Judases', seniors in the FBI who fell foul of him. The third 'Judas', Sullivan, responded to his accusation, 'I am not a Judas, Mr Hoover. And you certainly aren't Jesus Christ.' One well-connected lady earned his wrath by simply referring to him as 'Virgin Mary in pants'.

To obtain his information Hoover and his agents used illegal methods of telephone-tapping and hidden microphones, breaking and entering, spying, burgling and mail-opening. He dabbled in the sink of human nature and seldom found it spotlessly clean. His methods were spiteful and vicious, as when he blackmailed a publisher with photographs of his wife caught unawares in an act of fellation with her black chauffeur. When compromising information was not forthcoming, it could be invented. Smears and innuendo stick and damage even when not true. Simply sending gossip over the grapevine that someone was a communist could disrupt job, marriage and social life. Hoover's tenure lasted through ten presidencies, and he had files on each incumbent of the White House. Richard Nixon fully intended to sack Hoover, and called him into the Oval Office twice with the intention of doing so. But Hoover emerged unscathed.

The home territory for Hoover was the FBI he had created, and it made up the whole of his life. He expected his staff to give the same unconditional loyalty and unstinting endeavour, and their families suffered. No Catholics, Jews, blacks, women or foreigners could expect to be employed as agents. Under President Roosevelt the FBI expanded hugely, in size, power and influence. Sparring with the other state departments, Hoover spread his authority even to foreign intelligence. He aimed to extend to nothing less than a worldwide secret intelligence-gathering bureau.

If Hoover's behaviour patterns were primitively tribal, his ambitions were even more archaic – to quell and bend to his will all men in his own community, and destroy one way or another all those beyond the pale. Yet the forebears who first lived in tribes had comparatively small brains and contracted horizons, whereas Hoover's modern massive brain nurtured ambitions on an exponentially vaster scale.

Hoover, my last rogue elephant, shared many features with the others. Like the military celibates he was not interested in women, never married and made his most significant friendships with men. His closest long-term relationship was with his deputy, Tolson, with whom he had an affectionate closeness, similar to that of Nixon with Rebozo. Hoover had a huge presence (though he was short-statured) and a steam-rollering voice that could mow down presidents. After his regular morning fix it could come at you like a salvo of machine-gun fire. He dominated any conversation in monologues. He was addicted to stimulant injections. He was guilty of vast deceptions and invasions of human rights on a nationwide scale, as well as petty thieving and misuse of government funds for his own purposes. He was determined to hang in there for ever, and avoided grooming a successor. And he had his bid for immortality in the shape of a new gigantic FBI headquarters, which was named after him – the J Edgar Hoover Building. In spite of his partial demythologised status after death, the name has not been changed. His ghost still stalks the corridors of the modernised FBI, perpetuating a distinct malevolence towards anti-establishment activists.

CHAPTER 16

The Moral High Ground

So there he stands, the variegate mongrel in motley garb. No wonder he's misconstrued as complex. The part of his imperial robes I am about to strip off and examine is what passes for morality. He does not have much of the genuine article, but synthetic shoddy makes up for the deficit. Always suspect and treat warily the great man whose religion is worn on his sleeve, part of his political persona: he confers with God among the clouds on Mount Sinai, way above the heads of his colleagues, until his identity merges with that of his autocratic idol. Don't be gulled by the nonstop schedules, the extended working hours, the charade of commitment to duty: a politician's lifestyle has become jam-packed because of an arms-race type of escalation which means the top man cannot rest, or the senators' plots may come to fruition. When he gains a formidable reputation on the international stage, don't succumb to national pride: he is simply on an ego trip.

Moral rectitude has a slippery quality when you try to define it. To say what it is not is far from enough. Throughout this tale of stupendous egocentricity, little beacons have flashed in the murk like will-o'-the-wisps, saying humans are not rotten to the core. The natural world, from which we illogically hold ourselves one step removed, has clearly defined laws but no ethics whatever. There is no gold standard for goodness and mercy to be found, though there is co-operation and there are trade-deals and plenty of examples of social interaction and mutual support. We warm to the chimpanzees and the bonobos in their small communities, in their habits of caring for their young, adopting orphaned infants, two-way grooming, relaxed companionable contentment and capacity for collective fun. We react in horror when we read accounts of their savagery to solitary wanderers, the rare instances of infanticide and cannibalism, the pitched battles to death between alien groups. We are ambivalent about their ruthless hunting techniques and their uninhibited and sometimes violent sex.

Leaving aside the grey areas of hunting and sex, most if not all people would mentally mark approval of the sociable behaviours and disapproval of the destructive ones. We have a mental module that, in a quiescent and non-provocative environment, says it is good to be at peace and to make common cause with the neighbours. This judgement, which is inherited, is vital to prevent decimation among groups of savage animals, and is a baseline for behaviour. We are tempted away from it by prevailing circumstances to a varying degree; but small communities can usually find the level again after intermittent mayhem.

As our brains grew clever enough to cope with abstract thought, we realised – some aeons ago – that this wholly desirable state of peaceful, neighbourly co-existence equated with individual ways and disciplines which were defined as 'good' and 'moral'. It is a minimal definition compared with what those words usually embrace. The question it begs of course is, what do you then accept as a neighbourhood? Where do you draw the line? That definition has changed hugely from the days of those communities of 150 or so to our present potentially global outlook. Within the world population are whole countries as well as individuals who are considerably more insular than others. With Margaret Thatcher, George W Bush, Hoover and Mao Zedong, once they had established their power-base, their complacent tribal instincts, held so passionately, were immutable.

Probably the imprinting comes in childhood, when attitudes are impressed by witnessing how one's own adult mentors behave. Abraham Lincoln had an innate sense of social rectitude on the question of slavery, but he could not get past the notion that blacks were inferior to whites, because that was imprinted on his mind at the receptive age. In immigrant ghettoes in modern cities in the

States, the UK and elsewhere in Europe, the people are manifestly poorer and socially more disadvantaged than the indigenous folk, a pattern that must seem irreversible to onlookers. Indigenous children in particular, growing up and observing the contrast, nurse a feeling that this is the natural and correct order of things. Later in life, such a belief is difficult to eradicate. Anti-discrimination laws move in the right direction but not far enough. Mingling on equal terms from infancy up is what is required. Children to the age of ten have an incredible facility for learning languages, which ability becomes progressively attenuated thereafter. It would not surprise me to learn that a child's capacity for imprinting the features of strangers and other nationals diminishes on a similar timescale. The difficulty may be overcome by culture, education and travel to a degree; but those desirables are not always available.

I can call again on my micro-colleagues the lymphocytes, the embodiment of immunity, to set a precedent. In the nurturing period, lymphocytes undergo a complex induction process to enable them to distinguish between 'self' and 'non-self'. It is vital that they do not unleash horrors on the tissues in the body they exist to serve (this powerfully held distinction must be overridden in order to get a tissue transplant to 'take'). Some similar distinguishing process is at work in the minds of children everywhere and, in the name of greater inter-ethnic tolerance, we should watch this phenomenon urgently, and learn how to harness it in the name of peace. People of my generation will remember the song from the musical *South Pacific*:

> You've got be taught, before it's too late,
> Before you are six, or seven, or eight,
> To hate all the people your relatives hate,
> You've got to be carefully taught.

Children don't actually need to be taught to be hostile or friendly: they observe, and learn by both precedent and default. All they need is the right example.

In an ideal world, everyone would respect and tolerate everyone else, live cheek by jowl in harmony, taking up one's allotted fair share of the earth's surface and produce. Everyone would have a stake in ensuring that no groups, however distant, starved; and no individual gained a disproportionate share. This might have been, and may still be, achievable in small communities. How to make it happen worldwide is the problem. How surprising it is that this ideal of levelling out, of revolutionary democracy, is held in a race (ourselves) that is innately so competitive and has such a hierarchical history. Yet revolutions aplenty there have been, with this core egalitarian ideology, whether based on social class, religion, race or sex – wherever ambitious lords have made power their business with deplorable results. Equality is a fast-moving force and is still smashing idols. Witness the erosion of deference to establishments in the last thirty years – a healthy sign.

Reputations should be acquired by genuine worth, say the modern icons. No crowns, palaces, military-style parades, robes of state, pedestals, hypnotic speechifying and hereditary mystique have power over the people any longer. In a way we have come full circle to those co-operative communities in the savannah, hundreds of thousands of years ago. In those communities of one or two hundred, your reputation was vital, for there would be little chance of deceiving. As in country villages, everyone would know everyone's business; nothing would be secret. The only way to maintain a name for honest dealing, care of one's family, fidelity to one's spouse, open, overhanded ways, was to actually practise those virtues. In a modern context, a good name is likewise valued, as we seek character references and certificates of ability before appointing someone to a job: trade standards, trademarks, gold stars, guilds and registers, evidence of a clean licence, a spotless past. Politicians stand or fall by their reputations, which is why they are so eager to establish solid family credentials. Hoover, that quintessential tribal throwback, showed how vital an honourable name was as he destroyed the scaffolding of those he threatened and exposed. He could have toppled any president he chose, and many other big names too. When Martin Luther King's exotic sex life had been discovered by the FBI and partially leaked, he spiralled down into a state of morbid depression, as continuing surveillance taps revealed.

Morality is that set of standards on which reputation is based; just that and no more. It is often more easily manufactured than acquired by true worth, which is why leaders are so secretive. In a society, certain standards of behaviour are the norm and, if you want to belong, you must live up to them. Those standards can vary according to time and culture. Until the sexual revolution in the sixties, in Western societies the concept of fidelity within marriage and chastity without was generally held and almost universally flouted. It is nearer to the female sex strategy than the male's. In times past it was accepted that you could stray within marriage, but must do so in secret. It is all too horrifying that women and children in the past who begat or were begotten without social approval suffered vastly more than men. Whole peoples adapt very swiftly to a prevailing pattern of behaviour, as did the German population in the Nazi era. Even traditional 'carers', psychiatrists and doctors made wholesale transformation of their ethical standards to accept the institutional murder of 'defectives'. When they faced the horror of the rest of the world, the pain of facing their own moral degeneracy was too much to bear, and the collective guilt remains to this day. No wonder morality is as difficult to pin down as water, for there is no absolute reference for it.

Nevertheless, as Hoover's depredations show, the sense of standard practice that prevails in a society is a powerful factor for keeping a harmonious community. As such it is all too easily hijacked for ambitious purposes. Religious orders and governments from time immemorial have used this covert mutual supervision of neighbour by neighbour to maintain stability. The most blatant example of this rule by reputation, or fear of losing it, was in the communist societies of China and the Soviet Union. In this context it can again be seized to damage enemies, settle scores, and further one's own standing by spying.

Yet the desire to stand well among our fellows is the best force we have for 'good' in society, and the only counterbalance to the darker side of our selfishness. The innately ambitious man will exaggerate this quality, as he does so many, till it becomes narcissism. Yet this too can be a force for good, as we've seen with Churchill when, in the darkest hours of the Second World War, he imbued the entire country with his own invincibility (and please note, this was not good from our enemy's point of view). The same drive keeps men determined, committed, creative, influential. It is reinforced by the competitive instinct. These powerful inducers lead men to excel in many fields, including the creative arts and architecture. They propel him in the professions too, including the caring professions such as medicine. I know an eminent London professor who made it to the top by specialising in treating the untreatable, a risky practice on which to base your reputation. Men's working lives are marked by a need to be seen to be excellent. They flaunt their fame with sparkly medals, honours, merit awards and knighthoods. Women have in the past been more content to be a vital cog in the machine, gaining satisfaction from a job well done, though within that niche there is essential gratification and wellbeing from local approval and trust.

The purpose of these meanderings is to attempt to define a type of society that accommodates our complex needs from the past, yet does not allow the worst of destructive behaviour patterns to prevail – giving an eye also to long-term sustainability of the planet and leaving as rich a heritage as possible to future generations.

One fact stands out in crystalline clarity: the power wielded by any one person must be limited in time and extent. But then, who is to exert control? It must come from every member of society; all should be vigilant. Can we design a society motivated by positive 'good things' without creating too much potential for competition and self-serving? For maximum openness, units of community structure should be relatively small. Federalism is suspect unless we can make links without a president. Wily people can so easily manoeuvre into potent positions by stealth, as Hoover did, where he gained an ascendancy from which he was dislodged only by death. If we cannot rule ourselves without some nominal leader, then there should be a brief period in office – maybe three years – with low-key appurtenances of rank and privilege, and an expectation that such a person will not rest on their laurels, collecting huge fees for appearances, but go on serving the community. I would have any future leaders behaving like Mary Robinson, ex-President of Ireland, who used her feminine tact to spread new tolerance and build bridges, and who went on to become UN Commissioner for

Human Rights. It goes without saying that, in my ideal world, women will rise to their full potential, which, though lying dormant for millennia, has an untold capacity for dissemination of peace and defusing of aggression.

In my particular design for a Brave New World, I would positively welcome immigration. In the UK our ethnic minorities should be absolutely vital to training British-born children towards tolerance. Already I see contradictions; my designer world requires children to encounter as wide a spectrum of people as possible, yet adults potentially behave better in small communities. Before all else I would veto any coercion into an ideological or fashionable set-pattern. Progress must be slow, and achieved only over generations. Children above all should be secure and happy. Untold misery, ineradicable misery, has been caused by left-wing theory that children did not need families and could be brought up in collective nurseries or communes. We only have to look at the problems of 'care' upbringing to know how vital to children the family is. A child has no status outside that of her family, and is as vulnerable as a lone, wild, young animal. Yet the family is of all units the epitome of inequality. For many the power gradient from parent to child is benign and loving, and diminishes with time when the inevitable frictions help to speed the youngster on her way. It does not always work like that of course.

There will always be conflicts and contradictions between society and its supervisory systems. We value our individual liberties, yet because of others' equal rights, some of our own must be restrained. For the collective good we must all cough up a certain amount of income for taxes to run the show. That is tough and always some will try to buck the system, so there must be laws and a coercive force to police them. Coercion brings a power gradient – it must to be effective. But somehow we must learn to put effective brakes on power, because nature has hitherto not designed any for us.

Concessions must be made to competitive drives, simply because they are there, compellingly so, and must have some safe outlet. Already those release valves are established in the shape of sporting events and creative endeavours. In recent years in the UK there has been a visceral and vocal anti-hunting lobby. Humans and their antecedents have passed much evolutionary time surviving on the basis of their hunting skills, and it is not coincidental that many of my rogue leaders have had a taste for it. Moreover, hunting and militarism are twinned behavioural developments. It would be in the interests of peace to have some recreational outlet for it. Already there exist activities, such as drag-hunting and clay-pigeon shooting, which do not depend on the slaughter of any living thing, and it is well within our imaginative capacity to devise more mock-hunt models. War games of the paintball and laser-quest variety provide further outlets for male (and female) aggression. We may have to devise political games too, perhaps community debates of the *Question Time* style, which could be an excellent forum for testing public opinion. But more complex and realistic drama games are conceivable, with capacity for one-upmanship, deceit, secrecy, belligerent determination and utter ruthlessness. The more sophisticated board games already have some of these elements. I remember how popular they were among the men of my family, and how one Christmas Eve a game of Monopoly released such merciless cut-throat ambition to win that the Christmas spirit was temporarily in abeyance, and I was furious. I determined never to play the game again, and never have. While my alarm was well founded, my reaction was illogical. Such traits need to be sublimated and it is far better to do it in recreational life than for real.

It goes without saying that in the new democracy there is no place for royalty or hereditary titles and privilege. But no revolutions please. The royals and the aristos should be phased out, their wealth gradually brought down to size by long-overdue taxes. We would attempt to shed our unwieldy baggage of exorbitant deference, and substitute a culture of uniform courtesy. I would apply a ruthless degree of control over business so that no single man acquired wealth beyond a certain ceiling, and all employees would have a proportionate stake. There is some evidence to show that the more equal societies are healthier societies, and there is less discontent and damaging envy.

Speaking of game-playing, in *The Selfish Gene*, Richard Dawkins describes a wonderfully simple behaviour game involving two players, a system of rewards and fines, and in any one round a choice of two options – co-operate or defect. The rewards and fines depend on the combination of outcomes. The real interest in the game becomes apparent on repeated playing, as the players gain an insight into each other's strategy. It is very apparent that all life – not just human – is vibrantly engaged in this very game. In human terms we can gain enormous advantage by mutual co-operation. If a tradesman comes to your house and does a good job, and you pay him promptly, everyone is happy. If you refuse to pay him, he loses out, feels a sucker, and you appear to be the gainer; but you will find yourself in court eventually, and will get a name for being dishonest. If on the other hand he does a shoddy job, he may save on this occasion but will gain a poor reputation and will get no business. If he fails to turn up and you badmouth him, nobody is a winner.

The game can be played according to a number of strategies, which have been analysed by computer model for their reward potential in competition with each other. Strategies can be categorised as 'nice' or 'nasty' according to whether defections occur only as retaliation, or when unprovoked. Another quality that becomes apparent is 'forgiving': a short memory for defection so that runs of mutual revenge are avoided. Amazingly – and joyously – it was found that those strategies that incorporated niceness and forgiveness were the most successful in terms of point-scoring. It was also shown that envy – trying to prevent the other guy from point-scoring – was a damaging strategy (so let's reject Joe Kennedy's philosophy of 'get even'). Another significant observation was that 'nice' strategies could get drowned if pitted against a majority of 'nasties'. Therefore, in the context of the equivalent of Nazi Germany, you can expect martyrdom if you go against the prevailing mood. These analyses show very clearly how apparent altruism and mutual harmony *can* emerge in a predominantly selfish world. On the assumption that 'success' in the human context translates into better reproductive fitness, creating such a harmonious environment should foster the spread of 'nice' qualities to future generations.

One moving example quoted by Dawkins is the forbearance that German and British soldiers showed each other, as they dwelt in their trenches in the First World War, face to face across No Man's

Land. These mutually beneficial intervals of *pax vobiscum* enabled parties to collect in their wounded soldiers in relative safety, run messages, do vital maintenance work, all based solely on mutual unspoken trust, grown out of non-verbal behaviour. Patterns of ritualistic firing and shelling grew up, so that either side could predict with some assurance the quiet spells and move about with confidence. One brave German soldier actually stood up and apologised for a trigger-happy episode when someone breached the code. These soldiers had more in common with each other than with the high-ups on their own sides, who tried their best to scupper this behaviour, which was not likely to win the war. This theme, that a stable strategy of mutual co-operation can be wrecked by a power-monger, has been amply illustrated in these pages.

In more hawkish circumstances at the Western Front, when compassionate attempts to rescue the severely wounded had prompted many men to their heroic deaths, it was later found that men lying dead in the mud had forced their fists into their mouths to stop themselves crying out, trying to prevent further waste of life. Both types of behaviour approach pretty close to pure altruism.

Within communities of like-minded individuals, with similar needs, lie our best chances of a happy life. In those situations, examples of apparent altruism abound, though the givers expect to receive in their turn, even if that event may be deferred. It seems to me that, even if virtue in our imperfect world never constitutes its own reward, the sense of sitting well with your peers gives a glow, a sense of security, an absence of guilt, which is assuredly part of that reward. It's rather like the pheromone burst following vigorous exercise. That feel-good factor is one you want to repeat, so you plan to play the 'co-operate' card again. No doubt evolution has capitalised on this and favoured those who respond with the after-glow, at least where they live in social groups. Many examples of stunning altruism in civilian life can be cited. One of the biggest ever was the creation of the British National Health Service. For the inspired genius whose baby it was, Nye Bevan, the rewards were reinforced by a tremendous boost to his reputation, his prestige, his gravitas. Kindly minded people do tend to gravitate to the NHS to work and spend their lives, which has as a consequence resisted attempts hitherto to inject business methods into its soul. I have known staff who left better-paid and quieter jobs to work in the hectic, impoverished service and never regretted it. The person-to-person warmth and gratitude really do make the effort worthwhile. I remember an elderly, self-effacing grandmother who had spent some days ill in our hospital. She said in tones of genuine wonder, 'I have never, in all my life before, received so much kindly attention.'

It is important to write a happy ending, and this is an optimistic one if not a metaphorical high peak, which I have learned to mistrust. Nor may it be a recipe for living happily ever after, but if it inspires some creative ideas about how our collective brains can control our lusts and our dark, dark genes, this book will not have been written in vain.

Bibliography

The Hutchinson Encyclopedia of Modern Political Biography. Oxford, Helicon, 1999.

Abse, Leo. *The Man Behind the Smile*: *Tony Blair and the Politics of Perversion.* London, Robson Books, 1999.

Alanbrooke, Field Marshal Lord. *War Diaries 1939–1945.* London, Weidenfeld and Nicolson, 2001.

Alexander, John T. *Catherine the Great: Life and Legend.* Oxford University Press, 1989.

Andersen, Christopher. *Bill and Hillary.* London, Warner Books, 1999.

Aron, Leon. *Boris Yeltsin: A Revolutionary Life.* London, HarperCollins, 2000.

Baigent, Michael and Leigh, Richard. *The Inquisition.* London, Viking, 1999.

Bellonci, Maria. *Lucrezia Borgia.* London, Phoenix Press, 2000.

Betzig, L L. *Despotism and Differential Reproduction: A Darwinian View of History.* New York, Aldine, 1986.

Birkhead, Tim. 'Penis Power'. BBC *Wildlife Magazine*, April 2002.

Bower, Tom. *Maxwell: The Final Verdict.* London, HarperCollins, 1996.

Boyd, Don. 'A Suitable Boy'. *Life, The Observer Magazine,* August 2001.

Buchan, John. *Oliver Cromwell.* London, Reprint Society, 1941.

Bullock, Alan. *Hitler: A Study in Tyranny.* London, Penguin Books, 1990.

Bullock, Alan. *Hitler and Stalin: Parallel Lives.* London, Fontana Press, 1998.

Clarke, Peter. *A Question of Leadership: From Gladstone to Blair*. Penguin Books, 1999.

Concepcion, José Luis. *The Guanches: Survivors and their Descendants*. Tenerife, José Luis Concepcion, 2001.

Conquest, Robert. *Stalin: Breaker of Nations*. London, Phoenix, 1998.

Cornwell, John. *Hitler's Pope: The secret History of Pius XII*. London, Penguin Books, 2000.

Costello, John. *Love, Sex and War: Changing Values 1939–1945*. London, Collins, 1985.

Curry, Patrick, and Zarate, Oscar. *Introducing Machiavelli*. Cambridge, Icon Books, 1997.

Dawkins, Richard. *Climbing Mount Improbable*. London, Penguin Books, 1999.

Dawkins, Richard. *The Selfish Gene*. Oxford University Press, 1999.

Dawkins, Richard. *The Blind Watchmaker*. London, Penguin Books, 2000.

Debaine-Francfort, Corinne. *The Search for Ancient China*. London, Thames and Hudson, 1999.

Diamond, Jared. *The Rise and Fall of the Third Chimpanzee*. London, Vintage, 1991.

Doder, Dusko, and Branson, Louise. *Milosevic: Portrait of a Tyrant*. New York, The Free Press, 1999.

Evans, Dylan, and Zarate, Oscar. *Introducing Evolutionary Psychology*. Cambridge, Icon Books, 1999)

Evans, Richard. *Deng Xiaoping and the Making of Modern China*. London, Penguin Books, 1997.

Foot, Michael. *Aneurin Bevan*. London, Indigo, 1997.

Fowler, J, Fowler, M, Norcliffe, D, Hill, N, and Watkins, D. *World Religions: An Introduction for Students* Brighton, Sussex Academic Press, 1999.

Frank, Katherine. *Indira: The Life of Indira Nehru Gandhi*. London, HarperCollins, 2001.

Franks, Suzanne. *Having None of It: Women, Men and the Future of Work*. London, Granta, 1999.

Fraser, Antonia. *Cromwell: Our Chief of Men*. London, Arrow, 1999.

Fraser, Antonia. *The Warrior Queens: Boadicea's Chariot*. London, Arrow, 1999.

Freely, John. *Inside the Seraglio: Private Lives of the Sultans in Istanbul*. London, Viking, 1999.

Gentry, Curt. *J Edgar Hoover: The Man and the Secrets*. London, Norton, 2001.

Gilbert, Martin. *Churchill: A Life*. London, Pimlico, 2000.

Gonsiorek, John C, and Weinrich, James D. *Homosexuality: Research Implications for Public Policy*. California, Sage Publications Inc., 1991.

Goodall, Jane. *Through a Window*. London, Phoenix, 2000)

Grigg, John. *The Young Lloyd George*. London, Methuen, 1995.

Guevara, Ernesto Che. *The Motorcycle Diaries: A Journey around South America*. London, Fourth Estate, 1996.

Hamilton, Nigel. *JFK: Reckless Youth*. London, Pimlico, 2000.

Harvey, Robert. *Clive: The Life and Death of a British Emperor*. London, Hodder and Stoughton, 1999.

Haste, Cate. *Nazi Women*. London, Channel 4 Books, 1999.

Hazlewood, Nick. *Savage: Survival, Revenge and the Theory of Evolution*. London, Hodder and Stoughton, 2001.

Hersh, Seymour. *The Dark Side of Camelot*. London, HarperCollins, 1998.

Heymann, C David. *RFK: A Candid Biography of Bobby Kennedy*. London, Arrow Books 1999.

Hibbert, Christopher. *Nelson. A Personal History*. London, Penguin Books, 1995.

Hitchens, Christopher. *The Trial of Henry Kissinger*. London, Verso, 2001.

Hitler, Adolf. *Mein Kampf*. London, Pimlico, 1999.

Hodges, Gabrielle Ashford. *Franco*. London, Weidenfeld and Nicolson, 2000.

Hoffbrand, A V, Lewis, S M, Tuddenham, E G D. *Postgraduate Haematology*. Oxford, Butterworth Heinemann, 1999.

Jackson, Guida M. *Women Rulers Throughout the Ages: An Illustrated Guide*. Oxford, ABC CLIO, 1999.

Jandl, J H. *Blood: Textbook of Haematology*. Toronto, Little, Brown and Co., 1987.

Jenkins, Roy. *Gladstone*. London, Macmillan, 1995.

Jones, Terry, and Ereira Alan. *Crusades*. London, BBC Books, 1994.

Keane, John. *Vaclav Havel: A Political Tragedy in Six Acts*. London, Bloomsbury, 1999.

Kelly, J N D. *The Oxford Dictionary of Popes*. Oxford University Press, 1986.

Kessler, Ronald. *The Sins of the Father: Joseph P. Kennedy and the Dynasty he Founded*. London, Hodder and Stoughton, 1997.

Kohn, Marek. *As We Know It: Coming to Terms with an Evolved Mind*. London, Granta Books, 1999.

Li, Zhisui. *The Private Life of Chairman Mao*. London, Arrow, 1996.

Longford, Elizabeth. *Victoria R I*. London, Abacus, 2000.

Machiavelli, Niccolo. *The Prince*. London, Penguin Classics, 1999.

Macintyre, Donald *Mandelson: The Biography*. London, HarperCollins, 1999)

Mallett, Michael. *The Borgias: The Rise and Fall of a Renaissance Dynasty*. London, The Bodleyhead Ltd., 1969.

Marx, Karl, and Engels, Friedrich. *The Communist Manifesto*. London, Penguin Books 1985.

Maurois, André. *Disraeli*. London, John Lane The Bodley Head, 1942.

Maynard Smith, John. *Shaping Life: Genes, Embryos and Evolution*. London, Weidenfeld and Nicolson, 1998.

McKie, Robin. *Ape Man: The Story of Human Evolution*. London, BBC Books, 2000.

McLynn, Frank. *Napoleon: A Biography*. London, Pimlico, 1998.

Monelli, Paolo. *Mussolini: An Intimate Life*. London, Thames and Hudson, 1953.

Moran, Lord. *Winston Churchill: The Struggle for Survival 1940–1965*. London, Sphere Books, 1968.

Morris, Desmond. *The Naked Ape*. London, Corgi 1969.

Morris, Roger. *Partners in Power: The Clintons and their America*. New York, Henry Holt and Company, 1996,

O'Leary, Olivia, and Burke, Helen. *Mary Robinson: The Authorised Biography*. London, Hodder and Stoughton, 1998.

O'Shaugnessy, Hugh. *Pinochet: The Politics of Torture*. London, Latin America Bureau, 2000.

Palmer, Douglas. *Neanderthal*. London, Channel 4 Books, 2000.

Parris, Matthew. *Great Parliamentary Scandals: Four Centuries of Calumny, Smear and Innuendo*. London, Robson Books, 1997.

Parris, Matthew. *The Great Unfrocked: 2000 Years of Church Scandal.* London, Robson Books 1999.

Parsons, Stephen. *Ungodly Fear.* Oxford, Lion Publishing, 2000.

Partner, Peter. *God of Battles: Holy Wars of Christianity and Islam.* London, HarperCollins, 1997.

Pearce, Edward. *Machiavelli's Children.* London, Victor Gollancz, 1993.

Pitt, H G. *Abraham Lincoln.* Stroud (England), Sutton Publishing Ltd., 1998.

Post, Jerrold M, and Robins, Robert S. *When Illness Strikes the Leader.* New Haven, Yale University, 1993.

Ramadan, Mikhael. *In the Shadow of Saddam.* London, GreeNZone, 1999.

Rentoul, John. *Tony Blair.* London, Warner Books, 1997.

Ridley, Jane. *The Young Disraeli: 1804–1846.* London, Sinclair-Stevenson, 1996.

Ridley, Matt. *The Red Queen: Sex and the Evolution of Human Nature.* London, Penguin Books 1994.

Ridley, Matt. *Genome.* London, Fourth Estate, 2000.

Roberts, J M. *History of Europe.* London, Penguin Books 1999.

Robinson, Adam. *Bin Laden: Behind the Mask of the Terrorist.* London, Mainstream Publishing, 2001.

Rosenbaum, Ron. *Explaining Hitler: The Search for the Origins of his Evil.* London, Random House, 1998.

Runciman, Steven. *A History of the Crusades Vol. I, The First Crusade.* Cambridge at the University Press, 1962.

Sardar, Ziauddin, and Malik, Zafar Abbas. *Introducing Muhammad.* Cambridge, Icon Books, 1999.

Service, Robert. *Lenin: A Biography.* London, Macmillan, 2000.

Shaw, Karl. *Royal Babylon: The Alarming History of European Royalty.* London, Virgin Books, 1999.

Sherman, Paul W, and Alcock, John. *Exploring Animal Behaviour.* Massachusetts, Sinauer Associates, 1999.

Short, Philip. *Mao. A Life.* London, Hodder and Stoughton, 1999.

Silvester, Christopher. *The Pimlico Companion to Parliament: A Literary Anthology.* London, Pimlico, 1997.

Speer, Albert. *Inside the Third Reich.* London, Phoenix, 2000.

Spence, Jonathan. *Mao*. London, Weidenfeld and Nicolson, 1999.

Stafford, David. *Roosevelt and Churchill: Men of Secrets*. London, Abacus, 2000.

Stephenson, Pamela. *Billy*. London, HarperCollins, 2002.

Summers, Anthony. *The Arrogance of Power: The Secret World of Richard Nixon*. London, Victor Gollancz, 2000.

Tate, Georges. *The Crusades and the Holy Land*. London, Thames and Hudson, 1999.

Tattersall, Ian. *Becoming Human: Human Evolution and Human Uniqueness*. Oxford University Press, 2000.

Taylor, A J P. *British Prime Ministers*. London, Allen Lane/The Penguin Press, 1999.

Thackrah, J R. *Politics Made Simple*. London, Heinemann, 1990.

Trudeau, Margaret. *Beyond Reason*. London, Arrow Books, 1980.

Volkogonov, Dmitri. *The Rise and Fall of the Soviet Empire*. London, HarperCollins, 1999.)

Waal, Francis de, and Lanting, Francis. *Bonobo: The Forgotten Ape*. University of California Press, 1998.

Weir, Alison. *Elizabeth the Queen*. London, Pimlico, 1999.

Wilson, Derek. *The King and the Gentleman: Charles Stuart and Oliver Cromwell 1599–1649*. London, Hutchinson, 1999.

Wilson, Glenn. *The Great Sex Divide: A Study of Male–Female Differences*. London, Peter Owen, 1989.

Wright, Lawrence. *Twins: Genes, Environment and the Mystery of Identity*. London, Phoenix, 1997.

Young, Hugo. *One of Us*. London, Pan Books 1993.

Index

addictive mind-altering drugs 249, 252, 254
adult mentors 300
Aerospace Hawk jet trainers 275
Africa, communities 34
agriculture, socio-sexual revolution 126
AIDS 144
Aitken, Jonathan 95
Alanbrooke, Benita 140
Alanbrooke, Field Marshall Lord 140, 249, 263, 280, 291
alcohol 249–50, 253–4, 257
Alexander the Great 147
Alexander I, Tsar 139, 187–8, 256
Alexander VI, Pope 25–6, 228–30, 286
Alexander VII, Pope 230
Allende, President of Chile 112, 117, 285
Allied Bomber crews 136
Alliluyeva, Nadezhda 110–11
alpha males 59, 71–96, 123, 129, 155–6, 182, 270
Alphnso XIII, King 170
altuism 308
amazons 181–205
Amin, Idi (Uganda) 47, 233, 261, 276

Amos, Alan 149–50
Anastasus II, Pope 219
Anatolia, Christian groups 215
Anderson, Christopher, *Bill and Hilary* 86
Anderson, Jock 69
Andropov, Yuri 165–6, 286
Anglo-American bonding 247
animal behaviourists 18
animals 142, 157–8
Anthony, Mark 186–7
Anti-discrimination laws 301
Anti-hunting lobby 305–6
Antioch 214
aphrodisiacs and longevity potions 239
Aquino, Benigno 183
Aquino, Corazon 182–3, 261
archaeology 206
archaic behaviour 71–2, 226–7
Archer, Jeffrey 279
Archer, Mary 94
Arizona, Indian art and culture 98
Armand, Inessa 120
armed forces
    homosexual behaviour 145–6
    leaders 169
Arvad, Inga 81
Aryan master race 13, 104–5, 177

Ashanti 35
Ashby, David 149
Asquith, Herbert 47, 115, 253, 292
Asquith, Margot 115
assassination attempts 277
asylum seekers 169
Atatürk, Mustapha Kemal 249
Atherton, John (protestant bishop)
   150–1
Attlee, Clement 47
Augustus II, King of Poland 32–3
Aurelian, Emperor 195
Auschwitz 13
Austerlitz 187, 285
Austrian Social Democrat leaders
   63
Avignon, papacy 224
Azaña, President Manuel 170
Azande (Sudan) 35
Aztecs, empire of 31, 34

Babylon 31, 34
Bacon, Francis 148
Baden Powell, Lord 139
Bai, Lakshmi 185–6
Baldwin, Stanley 64
Balkans, exterminations 294
Bandaranaike, Chandrika 182
Bandaranaike, Sirimavo 182
barbiturates 254
Barclay Castle 100
Barnard, Christiaan 95–6, 245
Beaverbrook, Lord (Max) 77, 116,
   176
Bechstein, Frau 101
Begin, Menachim 258
behaviour patterns 268, 304
Benedict I, Pope 218
Benedict VIII, Pope 220
Benedict IX, Pope 219
Benedict XIV, Pope 230
Benn, Tony 153
Beria, Lavrenti 92, 162–3

Berlusconi, Silvio 274–5
Bernard Shaw, George 268
Betzig, Laura 34–6, 84, 89, 123–4,
   126
Bevan, Aneurin (Nye) 149, 175, 308
Béziers, France 221
Bhutto, Ali 182
Biao, Lin 241
Billings, Lem 81, 83
bin Laden, Mohammed 71
bin Laden, Osama 91, 249–50,
   285–6, 294
birds of ill omen 236–65
bisexuals 144–5, 156
black people 137, 234
Blair, Tony 9–10, 37, 40–1, 47, 155,
   159, 276
   Afghanistan 283
   campaign against terrorism 168
   flirtation with the Church 46
   J McMurray 46
   Mandelson 153–5
   Ugly Rumours 43
Blitz 76
blood and brains 268–73
Blount, Charles, Earl of Devonshire
   198
bodyguards 277
Boer War 50–1
Bolshevik 162
Bolshevik leaders 209
Bonaparte, Josephine 92, 127
Bonaparte, Napoleon 39, 44, 46–8,
   92, 114, 129, 139–40, 187–93,
   232, 281
   Battle of Austerlitz (1806) 285
   Bonaparte, Napoleonic Code 292
   challenges to the pope 281
   clumsyness 289
   depressive illness 256
   eating 249
   empire 294
   military service 48

oratory 278
rages 287
sexually prudish 131
women 127
Bonaparte, Pauline 92
Bonaparte, Stephanie 92
Boniface I, Pope 219
Boniface VI, Pope 219
Boniface VIII, Pope 227
Boniface IX, Pope 227
bonobos 141–2, 299–300
Borgia, Rodrigo 228–9
see also Alexander VI, Pope
Boston 71–2
Botha, Pik 262
Boudicca 184, 186, 190–1
Bourbon kings 33
Bourguiba, Habib 261
Boyd, Don 179
Brahmachari 205
Braun, Eva 100, 103, 140
Brave New World 305
Brenner Pass meeting (1940) 128
Brethren of the Free Spirit 223
Brezhnev, Leonid 139, 163–5, 255, 280, 292
Britain
  aristocracy 150–1
  arms trade 275
  army, sexual activity 135–6, 144–6
  class system 13
  ethnic minorities 305
  gay MPs 148
  illegitimate birth rates 137
  National Health Service 238, 308–9
Brittan, Leon 192
Brooke, Charles and Vyner 93
Brown, Gordon 37, 153–4
Brown, Michael 150
brutality 218
Buchan, John, *Oliver Cromwell* 59

Buddha (Siddhatta Gautama) 212
Buddhism 156, 212
Bukharin, Nikolai 108–9
Bulgaria 65
Bunin, Ivan 161
Burns, Robert 1–2, 8, 210
Bush, George W 168, 277, 295, 300
Butto, Benazir 182
Byzantine Church/Empire 214–15

Caesar, Julius 25, 32, 186–7
Calcutta, Black Hole 92
Caligula, Emperor 32
Calixtus III, Pope 228
Callaghan, Jim 149
Callipoli fiasco 115
Calvin, John 224
Cambodia 34, 111, 144
Campbell, Alastair 7, 113, 277
Campbell, Judith 82
Canning, Lord 46
Canterbury, Archbishop of 138
Capone, Al 74
Cardinals, College of 228
caring professions 304
Carrington, Lord 192
Carter, President Jimmy 190
Casement, Sir Roger 147
Castlereagh, Lord 151
Castro, Fidel 82, 112, 280–2
Cathars 221–3, 277
Catherine the Great of Russia 195–8, 200–1, 209
Catholic Church *see* Roman Catholic Church
Cato, Marcus Porcius, the Elder 288
Celestine V, Pope 227
Cerberus 248
Chamberlain family 39
Chamberlain, Prime Minister Neville 64–5, 174
Chappaquidick (1969) 67
charisma 43–4

Charles I, King of England 29,
    53–5, 57–62, 118, 202
Charterhouse 178
Chernenko, Kostya 139, 164–7,
    280, 286
Chernobyl 166–7
children 176–80, 292, 301, 305
Chile, Pinochet 225
Chilperic, King 201
chimpanzees 18–21, 23, 26–7, 30,
    33, 271, 299–300
China
    communism 13, 303
    Cultural Revolution 241, 262
    emperors 35, 105
    empire of 31
    Forbidden City, swimming pool
        89–90, 277, 288
    Great Hall of the People 89
    Great Leap Forward 240–1
    Maoist 267
    terracotta warriors 2–3
    Tiananmen Square 112, 266, 277
    Memorial Hall 242
Chirac, Jacques, President of France
    275
Chotiner, Murray 113
Christendom, medieval 35
Christian Churches 23, 150–2,
    206–35
Christians 32, 216–17
Christie, Agatha 125
Christopher, Pope 219
chromosomes 145, 269
Churchill, Clementine 115–16
Churchill, Lady Randolph 49–50
Churchill, Winston 42, 97, 140, 145
    alcohol 253–4
    ambition 50–1
    Anglo-American bonding 247
    bath-times 292
    belief that he was anointed by the
        Almighty 208

'black dog' 258
bravado 131
company of men 116
Conservative candidate for
    Oldham 51
cross-global skirmishes 281
dinnertime monologues 280
eating 249
egocentricity 175–6
expansion of German Navy 64
exuberant showmanship 208
favours 155
First Lord of the Admiralty 65
freeloading 290–1
globetrotting 281
Hitler's power 65
Holy Orders 46
homosexuality speculation 139
likes and antipathies 116
memoirs 264
menace of Hitler 115
mental powers 263–4
military celibate 114–15
military service 48–52
peace-monger 64
risk-taking behaviour 292
Roosevelt 278
Second World War 303–4
self-absorption 52
size 129
smoking 249
wars 279
wartime fare 249
wartime prime minister 65,
    115–16
wife and family 116
women 292
Civil War
(1648) 53, 58
first (1642) 55
Clark, Alan 95
Claudius, Appius 32
Clay, James 94

Clement VI, Pope 227
Cleopatra VII, Queen of Egypt
  186–7, 194–5, 288
Clinton, Bill 39–41, 43
  appearance 288
  depressions 259
  eagerness to please 101
  freeloader 289–90
  habitual lateness 280
  hypothesis about why men go
    into politics 88
  JFK 46
  Lothario lifestyle 86–7
  lovers 45
  male bonding 45
  military service 48
  mood swings 48
  nemesis 285
  oratory 278
  purple fits 287
  reproductive strategy 123
  risk–taking behaviour 48, 292
  sex drive 122, 196
  stinginess 52
  swimming 292
  vested interests 155
  wild-type of behaviour 88
Clinton, Chelsea 87
Clinton, Hillary 86–8, 186, 259
Clinton, Virginia 39
Clive, Lord, of India 48, 93, 140
Cliveden 94
Code of Canon Law 232
Collins, Rodney 97
communism 13, 29, 234, 303
competitiveness 5, 11, 25–6, 29, 281
Congregation for the Doctrine of
  the Faith Ratzinger 226
Connolly, Billy 179
Conservative Party, Scotland 276
consorts 102
Constantine, Emperor 59

Constantinople
  Bishop of 218
  Haghia Sophia 216
contraception 71, 105
Cook, Margaret 2
Cook, Robin 46, 159, 289
Cooper, Lady Diana 116
Coote, General Sir Eyre, MP 147–8
Coptic Christians 213
Cornwell, John 231
create or destroy 122–38
creative arts and architecture 304
creature comforts 249
Crimea, empire of Catherine the
  Great 200
Croatia, anti–Semitic atrocities 234
Cromwell, Elizabeth 120
Cromwell, Oliver 53, 55–61, 131,
  140, 204, 278, 285
  blood sports 291
  Civil War 208
  depression 257
  fondness for children 292
  henchmen 294
  impatience 281
  intimate life 120
  mental crisis 255–6
  militant 226
  military celibate 114, 118–19
  military service 48, 55–8
  misogyny 292
  mood swings 58–9, 287
  untidy and unkempt 288
Cromwellian England 225
Crosby, Bing 83
Crusades 213–17, 220–1, 227, 238
Cuba 163, 280–2
Curley, James 79
Currier, Guy 74
Curtin, John (Prime Minister of
  Australia) 250
Czechoslovakia 137, 164, 167

Dahomey, King 34–5
Daily Telegraph 49
Daitch, Phyllis 91
Dalhousie, Lord 185
Damasus I, Pope 59, 219
Danube basis 65
Daoist beliefs 239
Darwin, Charles 23, 29–30, 180,
    220–1
  Origin of Species 226
  power and privilege 89
  power for reproductive ends 44,
    71
  power–for–sex rules 81, 103
  prediction 121
  principles 36, 71
  rules 176
  success story 72
  theory about motivation 201
  theory of evolution 270–1
Darwinism 30, 102–3, 268
Davies, Ron 150
Dawkins, Richard
  Climbing Mount Improbable 66,
    272
  The Selfish Gene 24, 270–1, 273,
    293, 306–8
Day of Judgement 211
de Chardin, Teihard 246
de Gaulle, Charles 181, 278–9
de Pompadour, Madame 33
de Torquemada, Tomas 224
death 206–7, 209
decision–makers 14
deference and disempowered 157–80
Delors, Jacques 192
Deng Xiaoping 42, 261–2, 277
depression 197, 205, 244, 250,
    255–60, 277
des Rosiers, Janet 77
despots 36–7, 106–8, 121, 209
Deutsche Zukunft 115
Developing World territories,

capitalist–communist battles
    281–2
Devereux, Robert, Earl of Essex
    198–200
Dewar, Donald 6
Diamond, Jared, *The Rise and Fall
    of the Third Chimpanzee* 99,
    157–8
Diana, Princess of Wales 96, 187
dictators 64, 127–8
Dilke, Sir Charles 94
Dinitz, Simcha 189
Disraeli, Benjamin 41–5, 47–8, 94,
    174
  dalliances with married women
    148
  favours 155
  financial risk–taking 292
  first budget speech 280
  freeloading 290–1
  homosexual acts 139
  mental health 256
divine intervention 208
doctor–patient relationships 238
doctors 236–8
Dominic (monk) 221–2
Dominican Inquisitors, *Malleus
    Maleficorum* 225
Donald, David Herbert 278
Donovan, Bill 296
Dostoevsky, Fyodor Mikhailovich,
    The Brothers Karamazov 224
Dreyfus, Alfred 251
Driberg, Tom, MP 149
Drogheda 59
Dubcek, Alexander 164
Dudley, Robert, Earl of Leicester
    198
Dukakis, Michael 255
Dulles, Allen 296
Dulles, John Foster 262, 296
Dunbar, Battle of (1650) 56, 60
Dunblane 107

Dunkirk 76
Durham, Bishop–elect 151
East Timor, Indonesian invasion 274
Ecclestone, Bernie 155, 275
Eden, Anthony 116, 254–5, 264
Edinburgh University Students'
    Union 28
Egypt 31
Eisenhower, Dwight D 138
Elizabeth I, Queen of England
    196–202, 209
Elizabeth II, Queen 197
Elliot, T S 246
England, influence overseas 61
Enron 275
entrepreneurs 4
epidemics of infectious disease 207
Ershad, General Hossain
    Mohammed 183–4
eternal life 212–13
Eugenius IV, Pope 228
eunuchs 35, 194
Europe, royal families 33
euthanasia deaths 234
evolution 16–17, 23, 29–30, 66,
    126, 135–6, 207–8, 270
    psychology 23, 71
exterminations 294
eyes 271–2

Fairbairn, Nicky 95, 291
Falklands War 192, 283
fat cats 3
Fe Ti, Emperor (China) 31
federalism 304
Felix II, Pope 219
Ferdinand and Isabella of Spain 224
figureheads 38
Fiji 34
Final Solution 234–5
First World War 62, 73, 107, 133, 181
No Man's Land 307–8
Fitz, Honey 81

Fitzgerald, Rose 73, 76, 78
Fitzroy, Sir Charles 93
Fleming, Rhonda 81
Flowers, Gennifer 87
folic acid deficienty anaemia 13–15
Formosus, Pope 218–19
France 232
King of 221
Franciscan friars 224
Franco, Francisco 129–34, 169–71,
    242–3
    appeal of war in Africa 140
    Basques and other terrorists 243
    behaviour 146
    doppelgänger 169
    exterminations 294
    exuberant showmanship 208
    fascination with cinema 291
    fixation with hunting, fishing and
        shooting 131–2, 291
    follower of Mussolini and Hitler
        133
    homosexuality 133, 139
    oratory 278
    Parkinson's disease 242–3
    risk–taking behaviour 292
    Spanish Civil War 277
    women 133, 292
Fraser, Antonia 186
Fredegund of Neustria 201
Frederick the Great 147
Frederick II, King (the Great) of
    Prussia 196
    Frederick William, Prince (later
        King Frederick III) of Prussia
        187–8
Freemasons 226
funeral pyres 214–15

Galeazzi-Lisi, Profesor Ricardo
    245–6
Galilei, Galileo 225
Galloway, George 95

Galtieri, Leopolo Fortuno of
    Argentina 192
game-playing 306–7
Gandhi, Indira 183, 190, 201–3,
    201–5, 231, 261, 277, 280
Gandhi, Rajiv 205
Gandhi, Sanjay 202–5
gang rape 137
gay
    genes 143, 151
    men 146–8
    scenes 144
    see also homosexuality
gender bias 10
genes 24, 30, 50, 64, 143, 151, 206,
    267–8, 272
and environment 16
geneticists 28
genome 143
George IV, King of Britain 34
Germany
    Catholic population 233
    Christian Democratic Union
    Party 275
    Church 234
    illegitimacy 137
    murder of defectives 303
    'Night of the Long Knives' 233
    non-Jewish wives 234
Giancana, Sam 79, 82, 287, 291
Gidal, Nachum Tim 102
Giscard d'Estaing, Valery 191, 275
Gladstone, William 41, 46, 94,
    175–6, 256–7, 263
    favours 155
    freeloading 290
    House of Commons speeches 280
    oratory 173–4
    risk-taking behaviour 292
    self-flagellation 156
    swimming 292
Glasgow, prostitution of schoolgirls
    180

GM food 276
Goebbels, Joseph 139
Goering, Reich Marchall Hermann
    249, 253, 287
Gombe, chimpanzees 18
Goodall, Jane 18, 26
Gorbachev, Mikhail 160, 166–7,
    279–80, 284, 287
Gordon, General George 147
Grace, Princess of Monaco 96
Gran Canaria 99
Grantham, Labour Group 190
Grayson, Dr 248
Gregory I, Pope
Gregory VII, Pope 220–1
Gregory IX, Pope 222
Gregory XIII, Pope 230
group identification 168–9
Guevara, Che 25
Gui, Bernard 223
Gulf War 283

H-bomb 264
Hadrian III, Pope 218
haematology 16
Hall, Juanita 86–7
Hamilton, Lady 293
Hamilton, Thomas 107
Hampson, Keith 150
Hampstead Heath 149–50
Hanoverian kings 33
Hansfstaegl, Putzi 101
Harcourt, Sir Hector, MP 149
Hardy, Françoise 96
harems 32, 35, 207–8, 270
Harrow School 178–9
Harvey, Ian 149
Hasina, Sheikh 184
Hattersley, Roy 153
Hatton (suitor of Elizabeth I) 198
Havel, Olga 257, 293
Havel, Vaclav 43, 45–6, 167, 262–3,
    277, 284

alcohol 257
depression 257, 262
smoking 249, 262
unkindness to wife 293
women 91
Hayes, Jerry 149
Heath, Edward 95, 277
hegemony, aura of 168
Henry, Holy Roman Emperor 220
hereditary
monarchs and emperors 38–9
titles and privilege 306
hero-worship 6
Herod 174
Heseltine, Michael 192
Heydrich, Reinhard 234
hierarchies 27–8, 30, 37, 129
Himmler, Heinrich, *Lebensborn*
stud farms 138
Hinduism 211–12
Hinduja money–for–passports affair
155, 275
Hippocratic oath 236–7
Hitler, Adolf 44–5, 63, 127–8, 175,
187–93, 232, 280–1
appeasement 76
army and Slav and Russian
women 137
Aryan youths 177
behaviour 106
Berlin bunker 277, 288
chancellor 63–4
Churchill 64–5
cocaine addiction 253
Darwinism 102–3
demands from his generals 119
dropout years 108, 257
egotism 62
entourage 286–7
euthanasia programme (1939)
106, 234
Eva Braun 100, 140
evil 108

exterminations 294
family 106
fascination with cinema 291
First World War 133
fondness for children 292
genetic theory 104–5
hypnotic powers 172
madness 172
male alliance–making formula
130
Mein Kampf 48, 63, 65, 103, 107,
171
military fixation 105–6
military service 48, 62
mood swings 47–8
moral dimension 107
murderous regime 234
narcissism 279–80
National Socialist activities 233
1930s 191
obsession with hate 107, 128
oratory 171–2, 278
personal appearance 288
philosophy 267
pill-popper 252–3
plans for Berlin 209
propaganda 63
racial purity 138
rage 287
rages 287
Reich 168
Reich Concordat 232–3
risk-taking behaviour 292
SA 204
Second World War 278
seizure of Austria 64
sex life 101–2, 139
Sturm Abteilung 67
table-talk 280
tactics 75
tyrannical agenda 233
unproductively restrained 122
war service 104

war and use of force 181
Weltanschauung 107
women 52, 100–5
zealot 155
Hitler, Alois 106
Hitler, Angela 102
Hitler, Hohann Nepomuk 106
Hitler, Johann Georg (Hiedler) 106
Hofmann, Frau 101
Holland, Napoleon's empire 294
Holocaust 107, 246
Holy Roman Church 224
Homo erectus 124
Homo sapiens 17–18, 27, 97–8
homosexuality 143–5, 147, 150–2
    almost 139–56
    bonding 146
    careers 155
    and male–male bonding 153–4
    speculation 139
Hoover, J Edgar 47, 82, 162, 288,
    303
    drugs 252
    fascination with cinema 291
    FBI 296–8
    fondness for children 292
    oratory 278
    stealth 304
    tribal instincts 295–7, 300, 302
    women 297
Horobin, Sir Ian 149
House of Commons 174
Howe, Geoffrey 192
humans 37
    ambition 41–2
    behaviour 12–13
    brains and intelligence 28
    genetically programmed
    behavious 53
    post-industrial societies 127
    recent history 17
    sex-obsessed animals 21–2
    sociable way of life 158

Humphrey, Hubert 67–8
Hung Siu-Tshuen 172–3
hunters of men 134
hunting 21, 123, 125, 129, 131–2,
    165, 291, 300
Hus, Jan of Bosnia 223
Hussein, Saddam 91, 280, 286–7,
    292, 294
Hussein, Udai 91
Hutschnekcker, Dr Arnold 250
Hyam, Robert, *Empire and
    Sexuality* 144
hydrogen bomb 115

Iceni tribe 184
identical recessive traits sickle cell
    disease 106
ideology 51–2
idolomania 190
immigration 305
immortality 210
immune system 270
important men, youth of consorts
    102
Incas 26, 31–2, 34–5
incest 180
income inequality 3
Independent 177
Index of Prohibited Books 226
India
    British Raj 31, 183, 185
    Congress Party 203–4
    election results in Gujarat and
    Tamil Nadu 204
    Golden Temple at Amritsar 205
    Punjab 205
    Sikh regiments homosexual
    practice 146
Indian Mutiny 185
infants 15
Innocent III, Pope 221, 277, 294
Innocent IV, Pope 222
Innocent VIII, Pope 228

Inquisition 222–7, 232
insects, male genitalia 293
instant results 281
Iran, Shah of 69, 243, 247, 260, 286
Iraq, exterminations 294
Ireland 59, 169
Irvine, Derry 277
Islam 211, 213, 217, 224, 294–5
Israel 34, 189, 213, 258
Italy 232–3, 294
Ivan VI, Tsar 200–1

Jackson, Guida M, *Women Rulers throughout the Ages* 181–2
Jacobson, Dr Max 251–3
Jagas tribe 193
James I, King 54, 61
James VI/I, King 147
Jang Qing 88
Japan, sexual torture 180
Jellicoe, Earl 95
Jena-Auerstady 188
Jenkins, Roy 155
Jerusalem 214, 217
Jesus Christ 213
Jews 110, 213, 215, 224, 232–4
    diaspora 169
    husbands 234
Jiang Zemin 262
Jinga, Queen of Angola 193–4
Jocelyn, Percy (Anglican Bishop of Clogher) 151
John Paul II, Pope 17, 226
John XI, Pope 220
John XII, Pope 219–20
John XXII, Pope 227
Johnson, President L B 111, 283, 287–8
Joseph, Keith 190
Judaism 210
Julius II, Pope 228
Julius III, Pope 230

Kalashnikovs 213
Kamenev, Lev Borisovich 109
Kass, Ludwig 233
Kautsky, Karl 120
Keane, John 91
Keeler, Christine 95
Kelly, Grace 81
Kennedy, clan 39, 43, 67, 77, 88, 122–3, 208, 290–1, 296
Kennedy, Bobby 84, 86, 204, 252, 282, 294
    homosexual acts 84–5, 139
Kennedy, Bobby Junior 85
Kennedy, David 85
Kennedy, Edward 249
Kennedy, Jack *see* Kennedy, President J F
Kennedy, Joe 153–4
Kennedy, Joe Junior 40, 78, 85–6
Kennedy, John Junior 6
Kennedy, Joseph Patrick 72–80, 281, 290, 292, 307
    ambassador to the Court of St James, England 75
    control of family 85, 247
    Hitler 75–6
    I'm for Roosevelt 75
    sexual privileges 76–7, 89
Kennedy, Michael 86
Kennedy, President J F 6, 39–40, 278, 280–1, 283
    Addison's disease 80, 247, 251
    admiring men 45
    Air Force One plane 286
    assassination 296
    Castro 282–3
    Cuban missile crisis 163
    destiny in Dallas 78
    father's control 79–81
    feel–good drugs 251–2
    fondness for children 292
    homosexual acts 83, 139
    libedo 81–4, 89, 93

lovers 45, 81–2
low boredom threshold 281
male-bonding skills 139
meanness 290
medical history 247
military service 48
presidency 78–82, 85
risk-taking behaviour 48, 292
sex appeal 81
sex exploits 288
stinginess 52
verbal abuse 287
water fetish 92, 292
women votes (1960) 113
Kennedy, Robert 276, 290, 292, 296
Kennedy, Rosemary 78–9
Khan, Genghis 31
Khashoggi, Adnan 69
Khomeini, Ayatollah 243
Kim Il Sung 110
King, Martin Luther 40, 91, 296, 302
Kinnock, Neil 153–4
Kinsey Report (1948) 141
Kipling, Rudyard 47
Kissinger, Henry 251, 274, 278, 284
Kitchener, Lord Horatio 49–50, 139
Knights Hospitalers and Templars
    216, 224
Kohl, Helmut 275
Konstantinovna, Nadezhda 120
Kopechne, Mary Joe 67
Koran 211, 222
Korean War 110
Kosovo, Serbs in (1987) 118
Kruschev, Nikita 90–1, 162–3, 276,
    280–3, 287–8
Kubizek (friend of Hitler) 100
Kung San bushmen 134–5
Kyle Browning, Dolly 87

Labour Party, power–pack 159
lady rulers, depression 197, 205
lady-leaders 182

Ladysmith, relief of 51
Lambton, Lord 95
languages 207, 271, 301
Lansing, Robert Secretary of State
    248
Lanskoi, Alexander 197
Last Common Ancestor 17, 123
Lateran Treaty 232
Lawrence of Arabia 147
Lawson, Nigel 192
leaders
    competitive instincts 281
    family relations 292–3
    mainting their position 273
    medical histories 243–4
    oratory 278
    potential 38
    psychotic 137–8
    self–selecting 173
    sexually ascetic 121
    sick 260
    young people 272–3
learning curve 38–52
Lebensraum 99
Leigh, Janet 82
Lenin, Sasha 118, 130
Lenin, Vladimir 46, 108, 118–19,
    159–63, 190, 242, 285
    depression 257
    energetic power 160
    exterminations 294
    family of women 120
    fixation with hunting, fishing and
    shooting 131–2, 165, 291
    fondness for children 292
    Franco comparison 133–4
    homosexuality speculation 139
    impatience 281
    magnetism 130
    male relationships 120, 130
    marriage 120
    military celibate 114
    neurological illness 242

New Economic Plan 278
rages 287
relish for the kill 119, 278
reputation 242
social racist 294
swimming 292
Leo IX, Pope 220
Leo XIII, Pope 231
Lewinsky, Monica 88
Li, Dr Zhisui 238–42, 278
Li Peng 262
Lidice, murder of entire male
   population 234
life preservation 237–8
life–experience 8–9
Lincoln, Abraham 46–7, 255, 278,
   295, 300
Lloyd George, David 44–6, 94, 176,
   289
   Churchill 116
   risk–taking behaviour 292–3
Lloyd George, Margaret 1, 94–5, 289
Lollobrigida, Gina 96
lords of the earth 17
Loren, Sophia 96
Lorenzo the Magnificent 228
Loretto School in Musselburgh 179
Louis XIV, King of France 33
Louis XV, King of France 33–4
Louise, Queen of Prussia 187–9
Ludwig, King of Bavaria 147, 172
Luther, Martin 224
lymph nodes 269–70
lymphocytes 268–9, 301

Maarat an-Numan 214
McCarthy, Senator Joseph 296
   Senate Investigation Committee
   (1955) 84
Macdonald, Sir Hector 148
McDougall, Susan 87
McGovern, Senator George 67–8,
   255

Machiavelli, Prince 66–7, 230
McIntyre, Dr (Admiral) 244–5
Macmillan, Sir Harold 264
McMurray, J 46
Mafia 295–6
Major, John 46, 95, 150, 192, 283
malaria 16, 254
males
   bonding 20, 45, 140–1, 147, 1130
   female orientation 142
   homosexuality 141
man-hunters 135
Mandelson, Peter 7, 113, 152–5,
   277, 292
Mangele, Joseph 13
Mansfield, Jayne 81
Mao Zedong 3, 42–3, 46, 88–9,
   104, 110, 114, 227, 238–42, 245,
   254, 261
   cult status 242
   death 242
   depressions 257
   Emperors of the past 241
   fascination with cinema 291
   Forbidden City swimming–pool
   277, 288, 292
   homosexual acts 139
   lack of cleanliness 288
   love life 196, 240
   military service 48
   reproductive strategy 123
   sex life 239
   sleeping aids 255
   sleeping habits 239–40
   smoking 249
   tribal instincts 300
   war and use of force 181
   water fetish 92
   youth 47
Marcos, Ferdinand (President of the
   Philippines) 69, 260–1
Marozia family 219
marriage 303

Martin V, Pope 218, 228
Maruti car 203
Marx, Karl 13, 120, 236
Marxism–Leninism 109, 241
Mary, Queen of Scots 197
Masjid al-Aqsa 215
Maxim Gorky Institute, Moscow 13
Maxwell, Robert 249, 278–9, 281,
    286–7, 289, 291–2
Lady Ghislaine 291
medicine 236, 238
Meir, Golda 189–90
Mellow, David 95
men
    ailing and failing 7
    leadership opportunities 182
    sexual monopolies 196
    sport–lovomg 140
    working lives 304
Mendel, Gregor 143, 270–1
mental illness 78–9, 255
Mexican Inquisitors 227
Middle East
    exterminations 294
    War (1973) 251
military celibates 97–121, 139, 182,
    194, 216
military leaders, homosexual 147
Milosevic, Mira 117
Milosevic, Slobodan 44, 116–18,
    131, 169–70, 285
    bipolar mood swings 259–60
    military celibate 114
    oratory 278
    war crimes 134
ministers 5, 9
misogyny 292–3
missionary bishops 151
Mississippi 34
Mittal, Lakshmi 275
Mitterand, François 275
MMR vaccine 276
Molyneux, Bishop 151

Mongolian Empire 31
Monopoly 306
Monroe, Marilyn 81
Montgomery, Field Marshall 139
Montrose, Earl of 60–1
mood swings 47–8
Moorish enclaves 224
Morales de Toha, José amd Victoria
    285
morality 53, 209, 267, 299–309
Moran, Lord 4, 116, 176, 244, 247,
    254, 258
Morell, Dr Theodor 252–3
Morgenthau, Henry 296
Mormon sect 211
Morris, Desmond 128–9
Morris, Roger, *Partners in Power*
    87
Morrison, Herbert 152–3
Morton, Desmond 116
Mosques 215
Mountbatten, Lord Louis 116
Mugabe, Robert 277
Mundo Aborigen 99
Munich Illustrated News 102
Murat 32–3
Murdoch, Rupert 281
Muskie, Edmund 67–8
Muslims 32–3, 213–15, 217
Mussolini, Benito 2, 64, 90–1,
    127–9, 232, 257, 279–81, 287,
    290
    Bohemian image 288
    homosexuality speculation 139
    invasion of Albania 23
    Lateran Treaty 232
    political opportunism 285
    risk–taking behaviour 292
Mussolini, Rachele 90
Mwanga, King 156
My Lai 112
mystics 226

Naples 136, 294
Napoleon *see* Bonaparte, Napoleon
narcissism 279–80, 303
Native Americans 98
nature versus nurture 12, 15–16, 268
Navarra (personal attendant to
   Mussoli) 90
Nazi Germany 13, 62–3, 101,
   104–5, 156, 307
Neanderthals (*Homo
   neanderthalensis*) 97–8
Nehru, Jawaharlal 39, 183
Nelson, Frances 1
Nelson, Lord Horatio 42, 44, 129,
   140, 284
   melacholy 255
   military celibate 114
   narcissism 279–80
   risk-taking behaviour 292–3
neo-Darwinism 30
Nero 32
New England, Puritan colonies 225
New Guinea tribes 156
News of the World 151, 281
Nicholas III, Pope 227
Nirvana 212
Nixon, Julie 259
Nixon, Pat 112–14
Nixon, President Richard 44, 66–7,
   111–14, 233, 274, 283, 297
   anti–democratic activities 69
   depressions 258–9
   election (1960) 79
   enemy–lists 67–8
   homosexuality speculation 139
   impotence 113
   instability 250–1
   Mad Monk 133
   megalomania 69–70
   military celibate 114
   plans for his family 294
   relationships with men
   113–14297

swimming 292
   women 112–13, 292
nomadic troupes 125–6
Norris, Steven 95
Northern Ireland 213, 294
Nureyev, Rudolf 84
nursing homes, abuse of elderly 179

Ochterlony, Sir David 93
Octavia 187
Odainat, King 194
offspring 143
Oius X, Pope 231–2
Omdurman, Darvish army 50
ominid ancestors, social life 21
'One of Us' 191–2
Operation Mongoose 282
Orlov, Gregory 196–7
Orthodox Christians 213
Orwell, George, *1984*; 66
Otto, King 219
Ottoman Empire 32–3, 35
Oxford University Union 64

Pacelli, Cardinal Eugenio 75, 232–3
   see also Pius XII, Pope
Pacón (Franco Salgado–Araujo,
   Francisco) 132
paedophilia 179
pair-bonding 21–2, 124–5
Pakistan 203
Palestine 189
Palmerston, Lord 93, 173
Papal States 232
papal succession 218
paranoia 244, 292
Parris, Matthew 141, 148, 150
   Great Parliamentary Scandals
   93–4, 149
partners, preferences 145
party politics 28
Pasqualina, Mother 245
Pathé News 74

pathological depression 260
Paul II, Pope 228
Paul III, Pope 230
Pavelic, Ante 234
Pen Parade 3, 36
personal physicians 244–5
Peruvian Inquisitors 227
Petacci, Claretta 90, 290
Peter the Great, Tsar of Russia 34, 176, 196
Petrovich, Paul, Grand Duke of Russia 201
The Phallic pyramid 25–37
pharmaceutical industry 237
Philippe, King of France 224
Piltdown Man 97
Pinochet, Augusto 131, 134, 169–70, 180, 285, 292, 294
  military celibate 114, 117
  Slobodan Milosevic 116–17
Pinochet, Lucia 117, 285
Pius I, Pope 230
Pius II, Pope 228–9
Pius III, Pope 228
Pius IV, Pope 226, 230
Pius IX, Pope 231, 261, 292
Pius XII, Pope 234–5, 245–6, 276, 292–3
Plekhanov, Georgi 120
Poland 65, 119–20, 200, 234
polical affiliations 14
politicians 8–9, 36, 46–8
Pompidou, President 247–8
Popes, 20th century 231
population density 36–7, 126
Portillo, Michael 150
Post, Jerrold and Robert S Robins, When Illness Strikes the Leader 273
post-industrial man 129–30
Potemkin, Lieutenant General Gregory 197
Powell, Enough 148

power 4–7, 10, 34, 89, 249, 265, 304
  of speech 125, 173
Prasutagus, King 184
prehistoric man 31
Prendiville, Kran, Care 177–8
Proctor, Harvey 149
Profumo, John, scandal 83, 95
Prohibition (1919) 73–4
Protestant sects 224–5
Prussia, rulers 187–8, 200
psychology 168, 222–3
Pym, Francis 192
Pym, John 56

Qin Shi Huangdi, Emperor 3, 10
Qing, Jiang 241–2
Question Time debates 306

Rahman, Sheikh Mujibur 184
Raleigh, Sir Walter 198
Rani of Jhansi 185
rape 180, 216
Raubal, Geli 102–3, 111
Rauchning, Hermann 102
Reagan, President Ronald 208, 248, 265, 276, 291
Rebozo, Bebe 113–14, 233, 297
Reich Concordat 232–3
Reiter, Mimi 103
religions 14, 17, 27–8, 53, 160, 205–6, 209–10, 236
  antipathies 232
  orders 303
  child abuse 178
Renaissance 227–8
renal disease 260–1
rent-boy network 147
reproductive profligacy 34
reputations 302
residential homes 177–8
respect and compliance 9
Rhineland, Jewish groups 215

Rhodes, Cecil 139
Richard the Lionheart 147, 215
Ridley, Matt 127, 144, 291–2
Genome 17–18
risk-taking behaviour 48, 149, 156,
    208, 292
Roberts, Alderman 190
Roberts, Margaret *see* Thatcher,
    Margaret
Robinson, Mary 304–5
Röhm, Ernst 152
Roman, Jews 234
Roman Catholic Church 27–8, 72,
    177, 211, 221, 223, 227, 231, 295
    celibacy 150
    Inquisition 232
    Northern Ireland 213
Romania 65
Romanovs 33, 119
Rome 31–2, 34
    Fascists 2466
    homosexual emperors 147
Rometsch, Ellen 83
Roosevelt, Eleanor 258, 296
Roosevelt, Jimmy 75–6
Roosevelt, President Franklin D
    74–6, 78, 115–16, 244–5, 247, 279
    depression 258
    FBI 297
    homosexuality speculation 139
    Yalta Conference 245
Rosselli, John 82
Rousseau, J J 46
royalty 33, 59, 306
rulers 5, 186, 188, 201–2, 277
Rump Parliament 58
Russia *see* USSR
Russian–Prussian pact 187, 200
Russo, J 77
Rykov, Aleksei Ivanovitch 109

St Peter 219, 228
Saladin 215, 217

Saltykov, Sergei 196
Same-sex bonding 146, 153–4
Samoa 34–5
Samuel (Old Testament prophet) 5
Sandwich, Lord 94
Sarfatti, Margherita 90
Saudi Arabia
    Civil War (1975) 250
    families 71
Saul, King of Israel (200BC) 172
savannah, hunting males 22–3
Scargill, Arthur 192
Scotland, royalist supporters 59
Scott, Norman 148
Second World War 105, 116, 146,
    303–4, 278
    sexual appetites of the rank and
    file 136
secrecy 246–7
seed, reverting to 274–98
self-absorption 52
self-belief 276
self-confidence 43
self-destruction 156
self-selection 38
Semiramis of Assyria 194
Serbia 259
Sergius III, Pope 219–20
sex 30–1, 34, 71, 142, 144–5, 156,
    180, 300, 303
    favours 44–5
    hallucinations 136
    love, nearness to social bonding
        141
    strategies 20, 25
    torture 180
    tourism industry 144
Sforza, Catherine 201
Shastri, Lal Bahadour 183
Sicily, capture of 136
sickle cell disease 16, 143
Sikhism 212
Sinatra, Frank 82

Siraj-ud-Daula 92
Sixtus IV, Pope 228
Skinner, Colonel James 93
slavery 179
small eye genes 272
Smith, John 47
smoking 249
society, behaviour 126
socio-sexual lifestyles 127–8
soldier-monks *see* military celibates
soldiers, sex drive on active duty
    135–6
South Africa 156, 225
South America 227
    Indians 268
South Korea, jumbo jet shot down
    (1983) 166
South Pacific 301
Southeast Asian countries,
    sex–tourism industry 144
Soviet Union
    communist societies 303
    history of 20th century 159
    leaders 29
    see also USSR
Spain
    Caudillo 133
    Civil War 169
    conquistadores 25, 98
    Inquissitors 224
    Islamic menace 224
    kings 33
    La Sima de los Huesos (The Pit
    of Bones) 99–100
    Napoleon's empire 294
Spartan buddy system 146
speech, power of 125, 173
speech-making 176–7
Speer, Albert 101, 209, 253, 280–1
spin-doctors 5–7
sporting activities 27
Stalin, Joseph 108–11, 115, 120,
    129–30, 176, 192, 257, 261, 286

career 242
exterminations 294
fascination with cinema 291
feasts 249
Jewish groups 110
married life 110–11
memory 163
purges 161–2, 276, 278
regime 222–5
religious leader 161
scorched-earth policy 281
sexual indulgences 110–11
successor 209
Stalingrad re-named 163
Stambolic, Ivan 118
Stephen VI, Pope 218–19
Stephen VII, Pope 219
Stevenson, Adlai 296
Stevenson, Frances 94, 289
Stockwood, Bishop of 152
Stone Age 98, 124
Strasser, Gregor 102
Strasser, Otto 102
Sturm Abteilung (SA) 62–3
successors 209
Suez Affair 255
sugar plantations 179
Suleyman the Magnificent 32
Sullivan, William Cornelius 296
Sun Yat Sen 45–6
supremacy, origin of 12–24
swagger and scrimmage 53–70
Swanson, Gloria 46, 74, 76
Swaziland, king of 71
swimming 292
    pools 82–3, 89–90, 277, 288, 292
Switzerland, Napoleon's empire 294
Symonds, John 178–9

Talleyrand, Charles Maurice de 188
Tamara, Queen of Georgia 195
Taoism 156
Tasmanians 99

Tatchell, Peter, 'Outrage' lobby
group 152
territory 129
terrorism, campaign against 168
Thackeray, William Makepeace 178
Thatcher, Margaret 7, 9, 43, 47,
164, 189–93, 290
Falklands War 192, 283
problems with son 201–2
tribal instincts 295, 300
Thatcher, Mark 201–2
Thebes Sacred Legion 146
Theodosia, Express 218
Thieu, President of South Vietnam
111
Thorpe, Jeremy 148
Tiberius 32
Tierra del Fuego 98, 129
The Times 47
Tkach, Dr Walter 251
Tolson, Clyde A 297
Tomsky, Mikhail 109
totalitarian regimes 29
Toulouse 221, 223
Toynbee, Polly 178
Travell, Janet 247
Trevor-Roper, Hugh 107
tribalism 294–7, 300, 302
Trotsky, Count Leo Nikolayevich
109, 120, 159–60, 242
Truman, President 296
Turkey, sexual torture 180
Tuscany, Napoleon's empire 294
Twells, Bishop 151
twins 13–15, 142, 273
tyranny 167–8
Tyrone, Earl of 199

Ugly Rumours 43
UK *see* Britain
Umar, Caliph 213
United Nations War Crimes
Tribunal 259–60

United States
army 136–7
Constitution 264–5
Constitution (22nd Amendment)
111
Urban II, Pope 215, 219–20
USSR
alliance with Prussia 187, 200
brainshing 267
communism 13
glasnost 167
Military Army Council 110
non-Russian republicans 109–10
Red Army 119–29, 137
Revolution (October 1917) 119,
130–1, 159–60, 296
rulers 188
Stalin's empire 167
war with Denmark 200

Vasil-chikov, Alexander 197
Vatican 231, 234, 246
Council 226, 231
Vaughan, Reverend Dr Charles
178–9
venereal disease 136, 247
Versailles, Treaty of 64
Victoria, Queen 185, 197
Victorian
homosexuality 156
prostitution 180
Vienna Summit (1961) 282
Vietnam Task Force 283
Vietnam War 9, 111–12, 274
Vigilius 218
Volkogonov, Dmitri 161
von Arnim, Elizabeth 95
Von Hindenberg, Field Marshall 63

Wagner, Frau 101
Wall Street crash 74, 77–8
Wallace, George (Governor of
Alabama) 68

war, hatred of 20
Ward, Stephen 95
Warsaw Ghetto 234
Watergate 68–9
wealth 4
Wedgewood, Josiah 75
Weimar 188
Wellesley, Richard Marquis 93
Wells, H G 95
West Africa, indigenous people 268
West, Rebecca 95
Western-style democracies 274
Westphalia, Napoleon's empire 294
White House 82–3, 112
Whitehall mandarins 190
Whitewater scandal 87, 186
Wilkes, John 94
Williams, George 23–4
Williams, Shirley 152–3
Wilmot, Sir John Eardley 93
Wilson, Charles *see* Moran, Lord
Wilson, President Woodrow 248
Wilton, Bishop 151
Windsor, Duke and Duchess of 52
women 1
  conflicts 181
  emancipation 2, 52

feared 225
honorary men 188–9, 192
leaders 10, 158, 181
rulers 186, 201–2
sex 144, 180, 303
voices 190–1
warriors 193
working lives 304
Wu Hou 201

Xian, China, terracotta warriors 2–3

Y chromosomes 145
Yeltsin, Boris 167, 259, 279–80,
  284–5, 287
  alcohol 250, 284
Yufeng, Zhang 242
Yugoslavia 65

Zavadovskii, Peter 197
Zenobia, Queen of Palmyra 194–5
Zhisui Li, Dr 89
Zia, Begum Khaleda 183–4
Zia ul-Haq, General Mohammed 182
Zinoviev, Grigori Yvseyevich 109
Zionist movement 189
Zoastrians 213